WHITE TRASH

WHITE TRASH

The Eugenic Family Studies
1877–1919

edited and with an introduction by
NICOLE HAHN RAFTER

Northeastern University Press
Boston

Northeastern University Press

Library of Congress Cataloging-in-Publication Data

White Trash

   Bibliography: p.
    1. Eugenics—United States—Collected works.
I. Rafter, Nicole Hahn, 1939–
HQ755.5.U5W52 1988   306.8′5′0973   87–34996
ISBN 1–55553–030–3 (alk. paper)

Designed by David Ford

This book was composed in ITC Bookman by The
Anthoensen Press, Portland, Maine. It was printed
and bound by The Maple-Vail Press Co., York,
Pennsylvania. The paper is Sebago Antique, an
acid-free sheet.

MANUFACTURED IN THE UNITED STATES OF AMERICA

92 91 90 89 88   5 4 3 2 1

FOR ELIZABETH WILSON FISCHER

CONTENTS

PREFACE

This volume brings together a series of historically influential but virtually inaccessible texts. More importantly, the collection provides an opportunity to identify a social science genre and analyze it as a distinctive form of discourse. The introduction renders this type of analysis by discussing the genre's characteristics, ideological assumptions, and methodological strategies. In the introduction I also investigate historical circumstances that fostered the genre and note factors in its production and dissemination that helped make the family studies' message persuasive to a powerful segment of the decision-making public for some fifty years. Indeed, the ideology of the family studies remains potent today.

The introduction reflects my interest in both the history of science and the social construction of knowledge. This analysis of the family studies forms part of the current exploration of the relation between science and society, and of the relation of both to ideology. In recent decades this type of investigation has been stimulated, in particular, by the work of de Beauvoir (1974), Foucault (e.g., 1977) and Kuhn (1970); but its origins go back at least as far as Marx and Engels's observation in *The German Ideology* that "life is not determined by consciousness, but consciousness by life" (1970:47). Thus my analysis is part of an effort to break away from essentialist thinking about "truth" in science and to examine, instead, ways in which knowledge is created, received, and used.

The family studies collected here are reproduced in their entirety except for the photographs and captions that appeared in the originals of the works by Blackmar (1897), Kite (1913), Sessions (1918), and Rogers and Merrill (1919). Deletion of the illustrations was necessary because of their very poor quality, but it involves some loss. The photographs provide vivid images of "degenerates" and their "habitations," and the accompanying comments often reveal the authors' expectation that mental defect will be expressed through physical stigmata. The first photograph in Sessions's *Feeble-Minded in a Rural County of Ohio,* one of the best examples, is a full-length portrait of an elderly man in rough work clothes, leaning on a stick and holding an ax across one shoulder. Its caption reads:

> Hank Hickory, known as "young Hank," or "sore-eyed Hank," member of a defective clan discovered in the county surveyed. "Young Hank" is thought to be about 70 years old and is partially blind as a result of trachoma. He has never done any work except to make a few baskets and has lived a wandering,

makeshift life. He married his first cousin and so far as known had seven children of whom three, all defective, are now living. The number of his grandchildren and great-grandchildren is increasing every year. He, himself, is so feeble-minded that he cannot count his own children, nor can he name them without being prompted.

Several years ago Stephen Jay Gould discovered that photographs in Goddard's study *The Kallikak Family* had been doctored: "all the photos of noninstitutionalized kakos were phonied by inserting heavy dark lines to give eyes and mouths their diabolical appearance" (1981:171). A number of photos omitted here also seem to have been touched up, suggesting that the authors had toward photography the same complicated attitude that they had toward data collected in the field: both reflected reality, but both could be improved through a bit of manipulation.

References to the illustrations are also deleted from the texts. I have corrected minor misspellings and mispunctuations when these were obviously unintentional. Other errors remain as in the originals. In my introduction and prefaces when I refer to pages in the family studies, I use the page numbers of this edition.

For permission to reprint I am grateful to the Cold Spring Harbor Laboratory (Danielson and Davenport 1912; Finlayson 1916), Ohio Department of Human Services (Kostir 1916; Sessions 1918), and University of Chicago Press (Davenport 1907).

In the process of compiling this collection I have run up a number of debts. I wish to thank, in particular, Wini Breines, Robert S. Hahn, John H. Laub, Alexandra D. Todd, and Nancy Waring for their thoughtful comments on an earlier version of the introduction.

INTRODUCTION

Overview of the Collection

This is a collection of family studies—investigations of purportedly degenerate clans—produced in the late nineteenth and early twentieth centuries. Combining genealogical techniques with those of a primitive social science, these studies identified tribes whose inferior heredity was considered the source of alcoholism, crime, feeble-mindedness, harlotry, hyperactivity, laziness, loquacity, poverty, and a host of other ills. The eugenic implications seemed obvious: if those afflicted with "bad germ plasm" could be prevented from "breeding," society would be cleansed of social problems.

Mythic in message, mildly salacious in detail, and Progressive in promise, the family studies attracted an enthusiastic audience among welfare workers and the general public. They also influenced social policy. For instance, their apparent proof of the inheritance of feeble-mindedness fueled the turn-of-the-century movement to expand vastly the network of institutions for the mentally retarded (Tyor and Bell 1984). The family studies, moreover, seemed to validate the popular criminological theory of "defective delinquency," according to which crime is caused by feeble-mindedness and the feeble-minded are inherently criminal. Acceptance of defective delinquency theory led to establishment of institutions where criminalistic "morons" could be held on completely indefinite sentences—up to life (Hahn 1978, 1980). The family studies also influenced poor relief policy. Most importantly, they helped persuade the reading public of the validity of eugenics.

The eugenics movement started in England in the 1860s when Francis Galton, a cousin of Charles Darwin, formulated the movement's principles and, simultaneously, began to develop the family-study method (Galton 1914 [1869]). In this country the Eugenics Record Office, founded at Cold Spring Harbor, Long Island, in 1910 became the major center for research on "cacogenic"[1] (bad-gened) families. Funded by Mrs. E. H. Harriman, widow of a railroad magnate, and headed by Charles B. Davenport, America's leading eugenicist, the ERO was established to collect data on and investigate the laws of human heredity. One of its early bulletins, *How to Make a Eugenical Family Study*, outlined some of the organization's beliefs: "Eugenics has to do with the racial, inheritable, qualities of a population. The peculiar importance of such qualities ... is that they inevitably pass through the generations ... and that ... in time

---

[1] According to Estabrook and Davenport (1912:1), the term "cacogenics" was coined by Dr. E. E. Southard in 1912. Galton himself had coined "eugenics."

they tend to disseminate throughout the whole population" (1913:3). These qualities, the bulletin continued, include "physical, mental and moral hereditary traits." The ERO used these guidelines to do trait studies of a variety of families (it encouraged the public to send in genealogical information for free analysis). But because of its funding by wealthy benefactors such as Mrs. Harriman, the ERO was able to train eugenics "field workers" to investigate cacogenic families in particular, and to publish the results of this research. In one way or another the ERO was responsible for the production of seven, or nearly half, of the family studies.

Although the family studies generated by the ERO and other sources shared basic ideological and methodological assumptions, they also differed considerably among themselves. Research typically began with living representatives of a group that appeared to be characterized by a set of unsavory traits. From there the authors worked back in time, using public records, memories of neighbors, and recollections of family members themselves to show that similar disabilities had characterized the group's ancestors—and thus must be hereditary. The researchers came from various backgrounds—biology, the ministry, sociology, even business—but most were middle class (frequently lower middle class) and Anglo-Saxon in origin and, as the genre evolved, their professional stakes in eugenics increased. Their studies had diverse publication histories: one first appeared as part of a report to the New York State legislature; several in *The Survey*, a popular public policy magazine; two in the *American Journal of Sociology*; two in expensive editions underwritten by John D. Rockefeller, Jr.; yet others as research bulletins. Some were brief and story-like in format; others were scholarly works replete with charts and detailed data descriptions. While several of the family studies became enormously popular, reaching wide audiences, others could have had but few readers. Cumulatively, however, they created a powerful myth about the somatic nature of social problems.

The eugenics movement generated a large body of literature on topics ranging from alcoholism to zoology, but in terms of ideological impact, the family studies genre was its most influential product. The family studies gave the movement its central, confirmational image: that of the degenerate hillbilly family, dwelling in filthy shacks and spawning endless generations of paupers, criminals, and imbeciles. For the interpretation and control of social problems, the genre created a new, sociological paradigm, a master symbol that supported an ideology of power justified by biology. "The eugenic theory of society," writes Donald MacKenzie in one of the most provocative recent analyses of the movement, "is a way of reading the structure of social classes onto nature" (1981:18). The family studies helped fix that reading in the public imagination.

I have located fifteen family studies[2] published in the United States,[3] some mere articles, others book-length works. Only the two most popular, both books, are in print: Richard L. Dugdale's *"The Jukes": A Study in Crime, Pauperism, Disease and Heredity* (1877)[4] and Henry H. Goddard's *The Kallikak Family: A Study in the Heredity of Feeble-Mindedness* (1912).[5] The shorter family studies that appeared in journals and pamphlet form are today difficult—in some cases, nearly impossible—to find.

Because of the physical impossibility of including all fifteen family studies in one volume, this collection excludes six—the two that are in print and four others that exist in book form (see the list of family studies, below).[6] It includes the nine remaining family studies along with an 1877 elaboration of *"The Jukes"* by Dugdale himself and a preliminary version of *The Kallikak Family* by its researcher, Elizabeth Kite. These last two pieces are virtually unknown. The collection has also been designed to include all family studies authored or coauthored by women. As I explain below, research on cacogenic families provided an entrée to social science for female field workers. The types of tasks they performed and their professional relationships with male leaders of the eugenics movement illustrate broader developments in the history of science and throw light on the way in which the family studies were produced.

Three observations will help define both the significance of the family studies and my approach to them. First, they were not merely a type of bad

[2] I define a family study as an article or book that focused on a specific defective family or tribe, thus excluding reports that dealt explicitly with large numbers of families. As I explain in the section on methodology, however, even those studies that purported to concentrate on a single clan in fact covered numerous families.

[3] Gertrude Davenport's study of the Zeros was based on a study published in German, which she cites (1907:68) as having appeared in 1905. However, Estabrook and Davenport (1912:1) cite it as 1908. On the same page they refer to a "family described by Poellmann" characterized "by prostitutes and procurers"; apparently this one, too, was published in Europe.

[4] Putnam's issued a new edition in 1910: Robert [sic] L. Dugdale, *The Jukes: A Study in Crime, Pauperism, Disease, and Heredity,* with introduction by Franklin H. Giddings; Arno reprinted the 1910 version in 1970.

[5] Reprinted in 1913, 1914, 1916, 1919, 1922, 1923, 1927, 1931, and 1973, *The Kallikak Family* has proved the most popular of all the family studies. I suggest some reasons for its popularity in my prefaces to Davenport's "Hereditary Crime" and Kite's "Two Brothers."

[6] Three of these four books are relatively accessible: Winship's *Jukes-Edwards* (1900), A. H. Estabrook's *The Jukes in 1915* (1915), and Estabrook and McDougle's *Mongrel Virginians: The Win Tribe* (1926). The fourth, Estabrook and Davenport's *The Nam Family* (1912) was published by the ERO in the same oversize volume as *The Hill Folk;* I decided to reprint one representative from this volume, choosing *The Hill Folk* because it was coauthored by a woman. (For reasons noted below, the role played by women in production of the family studies was significant.)

science. While they were clearly methodological disasters, it is less easy to fault them for distorting methods and conclusions with an overlay of ideology. Indeed, today it is becoming difficult to hold that any science is "pure." As Kaye (1986:5) remarks:

> The influence of philosophical presuppositions, social position, cultural context, and other "extrascientific" elements is not confined to motivating the fateful transition from facts to values; nor can they simply be denounced as sources of scientific error. As philosophers of science and sociologists of knowledge have begun to argue, every scientific investigation . . . is also "an exegesis of our fundamental beliefs in the light of which we approach it" . . . and through which we attain scientific knowledge.

Or, as Jane Flax has put it:

> Perhaps "reality" can have "a" structure only from the falsely universalizing perspective of the master. That is, only to the extent that one person or group can dominate the whole, can "reality" appear to be governed by one set of rules or be constituted by one privileged set of social relations [as quoted in Harding 1986:26–27].

I am not arguing that all scientific knowledge can be reduced to mere perception, but rather that the family studies were far from alone—and may, rather, have been typical—in failing to recognize that apparent objectivity can mask scientists' preconceptions (see Gould 1981, Harding 1986,

---

* Indicates a study reprinted in this volume.

[7] Although Oscar C. McCulloch's name is spelled "M'Culloch" in the original of this article, all other sources (including biographies [n.a. 1892 and McCulloch 1911]) use the former spelling, as I do here.

and Smith 1974 for further arguments along these lines). From the standpoint of the sociology of knowledge, what is of interest is the interrelationship between science and belief systems—an interrelationship that is unusually explicit in the family studies but hardly unique to them.

Second, the theses and themes of the family studies were not merely turn-of-the-century aberrations. We find similar propositions about inheritance and/or bad families in contemporary criminology, psychology, and sociobiology (Eysenck 1973; Herrnstein 1973; Hirschi 1983; Wilson 1975; Wilson and Herrnstein 1985). Kaye (1986) argues that sociobiological theories become popular for their capacity to comfort groups that have deep-seated needs for reassurance. Writing of the current "scientific mythologies" of Jacques Monod and E. O. Wilson, Kaye holds that these "dramatic and often anthropomorphized representations of how the world works . . . arouse our emotions, validate our hopes, answer our most troubling questions, and lend both cosmic and scientific sanction to a new order of living" (1986:5; also see Rosenberg 1974:232–35). The family studies seem to have provided similar solace to their authors and readers although, as I argue below, their sociobiology also furthered specific professional interests. At any rate, even though eugenics itself lost credibility in the 1920s and 1930s, its ideology of natural hierarchy and heritability of social traits remains healthy today.

Finally, contrary to the traditional view, the family studies were not merely propaganda for the social Darwinist doctrine of survival of the fittest. Hofstadter's classic interpretation of eugenics (including the family studies) as an aspect of social Darwinism, and of social Darwinism as a justification for cutthroat capitalism, has been challenged in recent years. Bannister (1979) argues that the eugenics movement was not social Darwinist in Hofstadter's sense at all, a point which the family studies support. The later authors had little confidence in survival of the fittest; what worried them was survival of the unfit. The family studies did indeed promote social class interests; but, as I explain later, these interests were less those of the laissez-faire conservatives of Hofstadter's view than of the professional middle class—to which the field workers and other authors of the tracts belonged.

The Genre: Characteristics and Development

A belief that social problems are not only biologically based but also biologically linked lies at the heart of the family studies. Each of these works was concerned with not one but a multiplicity of problems and the interrelations among them. The authors conceptualized cacogeneity as a kind of core rot, a degeneration of the germ plasm which might manifest itself in any one of a number of forms. Thus in McCulloch's "Tribe of Ishmael" we learn that the Ishmaels were prone to licentiousness, criminality, pauperism, polygamy, premature death, and "wandering blood" (vagabondage); and the author was surprised that "strangely enough, they are not intemperate" (1888:51). To be sure, in the later studies families are identified with particular traits. Charles Davenport observes in his introduction to *The Dack Family* that "the present study . . . illustrates again the fact that the aberrant behavior of each family group is stamped with its peculiar characteristics. . . . In the Dacks we have a group of hyperkinetics . . ."(Finlayson 1916:214). Yet Davenport goes on to note that "their reactions . . . are restlessness, quarrelsomeness, loquacity, abuse, pugnacity, intermittent outbursts of violent temper and sex offense." Similarly, Sessions's *The Feeble-Minded in a Rural County of Ohio,* by definition focused on a central problem, is also concerned with alcoholism, blindness, criminality, epilepsy, insanity, sex offending, syphilis, and the propensity to wander. That even "specialized" families bore a multitude of stigmata did not disturb their chroniclers; each new defect merely confirmed the underlying assumption that inferiority had many facets (also see Rosenberg 1974).

Three other assumptions also typify the family studies. According to the first, if a trait shows up in more than one generation, it is inherited. Thus Dugdale, observing promiscuity among mothers and daughters, concludes that "harlotry may become a hereditary characteristic" (1877a:24). Second, the authors assume that in the causation of social problems, personal defects are far more important than social or environmental factors. Blackmar reports of the Smoky Pilgrims that "there is no drainage connection with either habitation, and no water supply. But of water the occupants apparently have little need" (1897:60); his innuendo blames the impoverished for their condition. Of a Dack who disappeared many years ago we learn that "he lost practically all of his property through poor management and alcoholic excesses" (Finlayson 1916:234–35). And Rogers and Merrill (1919), like many of the other authors, were oblivious to the possibility that environmental factors such as maternal malnutrition and childhood brain damage might cause mental retardation (cf. Stevens 1915 and Sarason and Doris 1969).

Lastly, the authors assume that the distribution of social power can be explained in hereditarian terms. The poor are destitute, the criminal wicked, and the feeble-minded retarded owing to unfortunate heredity; conversely, members of the middle class are thrifty, law-abiding, and intellectually superior thanks to genetic virtue. After the early twentieth-century rediscovery of Mendel's laws of inheritance, the authors used this model to map social worth. In their works heritable unit characteristics became codes for social hierarchy. Genetic and social worth coincided exactly, in perfect fit.

This equation of genetic and social value encouraged a dichotomous world view: the family studies divide the world into "us" (the writers and readers of the works) and "them" (cacogenic families). This bifurcation, which I analyze later as a rhetorical device, helped demonstrate that "they" were "social sores" who, if not subjected to the eugenic cure, would infect the body social.

In view of the tendency of Progressives in general, and eugenicists in particular, to romanticize rural values, it is astonishing to realize that the dominant theme of the family studies is the degeneracy of country life. Dugdale established this theme in the first family study by telling us that "the ancestral breeding-spot" of the Jukes "nestles among the forest-covered margin of five lakes, so rocky as to be at some parts inaccessible. . . . Most of the ancestors were squatters upon the soil, [and] lived in log or stone houses" (1877a:13). Blackmar devotes his introduction to "The Smoky Pilgrims" to establishing that "social degradation" is at least as characteristic of rural as of urban areas—that "the country has its own social evils and social residuum." The Zeros lived in Zand, "an isolated village in a Swiss valley," the Pineys in the Pine Barrens of New Jersey, the Sam Sixties "in the river hills of Ohio," the Dacks "in or near small mining towns" of west-central Pennsylvania, the Yaks and Chads in a Minnesota ravine called Hog Hollow.

To some extent this emphasis on rural degradation was a by-product of the authors' genealogical method: they traced the families' progenitors back to revolutionary war days or earlier, when farm life was common; and it was easier to track generations of rural than urban families through local records and long-term residents. However, the rural degradation theme is remarkable given that much of the literature on proto-Progressive and Progressive reform movements attributes these to participants' longing for a simpler, rural, more "American" past (Connelly 1980; Gusfield 1963; Hofstadter 1955a; Ludmerer 1972; Pickens 1968; Platt 1977; Rosen 1982; Schlossman 1977; Sproat 1968). As I argue later, the authors' scorn for country life—at times even horror of what they portrayed as its uncontrolled bestiality and squalor—may be explained by their membership in an emerging class of professionals involved in the business of social control.

Another, less insistent, theme concerns the inferiority of foreigners and dark-skinned people. McCulloch traces the Ishmaels' afflictions to a liaison between a diseased man and "a half-breed woman." The Smoky Pilgrims were so named by "the people of the town" because of their "dusky color and their smoky and begrimed[8] appearance"; some had a "sickly yellow color, on account of the negro blood in [their] veins." The original Hickory married "an Indian squaw" and Suse, one of Kite's Pineys, had "black hair, sparkling black eyes, finely shaped oval face, and dark gypsy coloring."[9] A Dack "frequently deserted her husband to live with other men, some of whom have been foreigners" (Finlayson, 1916:241) and Beck, a Dweller in the Vale of Siddem, "was a mulatto. Her father was 'Nigger Ned' who used to hang around the ravine. . . . Her children show their negro heritage. The oldest boy is an imbecile with very vicious tendencies. He will steal whenever the opportunity offers . . ." (Rogers and Merrill 1919:368). Most racist of all was *Mongrel Virginians*, a study of the dire consequences of miscegenation among Indians, blacks, and whites (Estabrook and McDougle 1926). The family studies were written during decades when assumptions about native white superiority were both widespread and unselfconsciously expressed. Their authors "read" interracial and foreigner "matings" much as they "read" consanguineous marriages, drunkenness, and criminality—as another sorry expression of degenerating germ plasm.

As the genre evolved, four lines of development were particularly important: gradual rejection of the possibility that environmental factors might contribute to social problems; introduction of concepts from the rapidly developing field of genetics; increasing hostility toward "the feeble-minded"; and ever stronger endorsement of eugenic solutions.

The family studies moved from a mixture of hereditarian and environmental explanations in the earliest example, Dugdale's *"The Jukes,"* to reliance on purely biologistic explanations.[10] Dugdale struggled to iden-

---

[8] Blackmar's "begrimed" was a necessity because in fact seven of the ten family members were white. The three Smoky Pilgrims who were black were offspring of "A——," who had "married a colored man." The others had to be "smoky" from dirt.

[9] Despite her apparent nativism, Kite urges us not to confuse the Pineys with "the thriving Jew colonies . . . [or] the Italian communities. . . . Whatever resemblance there is, is indeed superficial, such as: large families, often unsanitary and crowded conditions of living, small and incommodious dwellings" (1913:172). The Pineys, she assures us, were even worse. Sessions, too, exempted foreigners and blacks. "Neither the negro race nor recent immigration could be blamed for the large number of defectives in the county, but rather the deterioration of the native stock or else the perpetuation of the mental defects of the old stock" (1918:276). That these two authors resisted the temptation to blame foreigners and people of color underscores the strength of their hostility to the white rural poor.

[10] This change was encouraged by the acceptance in the early twentieth century of August Weismann's theory that human germ plasm is not affected by environmentally induced changes in the body. Acceptance of Weismann's theory required rejection of the neo-Lamarckian theory of inheritance of acquired characteristics to which Dugdale ("Environment tends to produce habits which may become hereditary" [1877a:57]) and other early family studies authors subscribed. It also seemed to require giving up all hope of improving the species through environmental reform.

tify the separate and interactive effects of heredity and environment,[11] a struggle that later authors often overlooked when discussing his work. In the selection reprinted here he calls strict hereditarians (including, he implies, Galton himself) "extremists" (1877b:35–36). Like Dugdale, Blackmar too was cautious about hereditarian conclusions; in "The Smoky Pilgrims" (1897) he pulls back at the last moment to endorse environmental solutions. *The Hill Folk* (1912) is less wary: it considers the possibility of environmental influences only to discount them. The next year Kite allowed that the Pineys might be susceptible to environmental improvements, but she clearly didn't believe her own caveats (see Kite 1913:171, Moron Family Tree). The studies that followed seldom bothered to include such caveats. This progression from mixed hereditarian-environmental to purely biologistic explanations went hand in hand with another: a movement from cautious conclusions to dogmatism. In *"The Jukes"* Dugdale warns that his conclusions "are purely tentative" and acknowledges the "great defectiveness" inherent in his methods (1877a:7). In contrast, the last study reprinted here assures us "That feeble-mindedness is hereditary is no longer open to question" (Rogers and Merrill 1919:345).

The family studies reflect ways in which thinking about heredity changed over the five decades during which they were produced. Those written before 1912 showed little interest in the processes by which degeneration was transmitted. Rather, their authors were fascinated by degeneration itself, portraying it as an affliction that could express itself through various symptoms. An alcoholic parent might have a feeble-minded daughter and a criminalistic grandson. Each negative trait was interpreted as a sign of the family's degenerative tendency and evidence that the tendency was hereditary (Hahn 1980). But after Mendel's laws of inheritance were rediscovered and applied to humans in the early twentieth century, the authors became more interested in the mechanisms of heredity. (For an example of how some eugenicists used Mendel's laws, see the discussion of feeble-mindedness as a recessive trait by Rogers and Merrill [1919:345–46].) The later studies try to isolate specific strains of degeneration and demonstrate their inevitable transmission as Mendelian dominants or recessives—although, as we have seen, the need to illustrate "specialization" by unit traits did not stop the researchers from hunting for a variety of disabilities. Later still, some of the family studies

[11] Carlson has argued that "neither Dugdale nor his Jukes study was hereditarian" at all (1980:535), while others—including nearly all subsequent family study authors—have read Dugdale as a strict hereditarian. The Dugdale selection reprinted here and earlier versions of *"The Jukes"* show that both Carlson and the opposite camp were mistaken. Yet the misinterpretations are understandable; it is difficult to decipher what Dugdale says about the independent and interactive effects of social and biological factors.

veered away from the rigid, single-gene model of Mendelianism. Rogers and Merrill offer the standard analysis of "the modus operandi of ... inheritance" but go on to criticize this model as simplistic:

> The small number of offspring in the human family and the consequent limitation of the various possible combinations that might occur, makes it very difficult to apply this law of Mendel's, which is a law of averages, to the human family at all. And then, too, it seems improbable that so complicated a thing as general intelligence can be considered a unit character [1919:346].

But even Rogers and Merrill find it difficult to give up the simple Mendelianist model. In a footnote (1919:364) they discuss two baffling cases in which indisputably normal children have been produced by feeble-minded parents. They conclude that "the reputed father may not be the real father"— the feeble-minded mother in each case probably having sneaked out to become pregnant by a normal man.

One of the most dramatic developments in the family studies over time lay in their changing attitude toward mental retardation.[12] Dugdale was almost indifferent to the subject: he seems[13] to have located only one "idiot" and one "weak minded" Juke, and he attributed both cases to syphilis (1877a:28–30). Subsequent family studies turned up ever more feeble-mindedness because their authors adopted ever-looser identification criteria. As Rogers and Merrill admit in the latest of the studies reprinted here, "A few years ago we did not recognize the high grade moron as feeble-minded" (1919:346). They and others had relaxed the criteria under pressure to show that disabilities were inherited in Mendelian fashion:

> Obligated to show transmission of specific disabilities, Progressive-era genealogists found feeble-mindedness most suitable to their purposes because it was so easy to attribute. Low intelligence had for some time been associated with low social class; and the intelligence test, introduced in the United States just as the second series of family studies began [1912], was initially so primitive that it actually encouraged use of social class criteria... [Hahn 1980:12; also see Gould 1981: chap. 5; Kamin 1974; Lewontin et al. 1984: chap. 5; and Sarason and Doris 1969, esp. chap. 15].

[12] Terminology for mental retardation changed over the five decades spanned by the studies. Until late in the nineteenth century *idiocy* and *imbecility* were the favored labels, the latter often used to refer to a milder subtype. At the turn of the century, when the criteria for mental retardation were relaxed to include people who earlier would have been considered normal in intelligence, *feeble-mindedness* became the preferred generic term. In 1910 the *moron* category was created to further expand the generic category and label those in whom only experts could detect feeble-mindedness. Later still *mental defect* and *mental deficiency* were adopted as less stigmatic than "feeble-mindedness."

[13] "Seems" because in some passages in *"The Jukes"* he also speaks more generally about "idiocy," as though he had more cases; and indeed there are more mentally defective Jukes in the selection reprinted here.

As the family studies claim hundreds of times over, their authors were able to determine at a glance (or even without one) the mental defectiveness of the rural poor. And thus the authors were able to construct charts showing the inheritance of defect according to Mendel's laws.

Closely linked to the relaxation of criteria for feeble-mindedness was the development of "defective delinquency" theory—the equation of high-grade mental defect with criminality. This development mainly occurred outside the family study literature (see Hahn 1978) but was reflected in it, especially in *Dwellers in the Vale of Siddem*, which is crowded[14] with feeble-minded horse thieves, counterfeiters, and desperados. In line with defective delinquency theory, the authors of this study conclude that "it is not the idiot or, to any great extent, the low grade imbecile, who is dangerous to society . . . [but rather] the high grade feeble-minded" (Rogers and Merrill 1919:346–47). This was a far cry from Dugdale, who associated criminality with not weak-mindedness but vigor (1877a).

Finally, over time the family studies increasingly endorsed a program of "negative" eugenics. Dugdale and his immediate successors believed in "natural" eugenics—that, if left on their own, defective lines tend naturally to "extinction." Thus McCulloch urges social workers to deny relief to tribes like the Ishmaels, and Gertrude Davenport predicts that the Zeros will die out through the natural process of "preventative breeding." In sharp contrast, *The Hill Folk* (1912) warns that paupers and the feeble-minded are multiplying rapidly. Not coincidentally, this is the first family study to endorse negative eugenics—active measures to "control . . . the reproduction of the grossly defective" (Davenport's preface to Danielson and Davenport 1912:85). *The Family of Sam Sixty* is even more explicit: "Society has the right and the duty to save such ever increasing expense from increasing numbers of dependents . . . by *keeping the feeble-minded in custody while they are of child bearing and child be-getting ages*" (Kostir 1916:208; emphases in original).

As indicated by such calls for prophylaxis, and even more so by the studies' overriding concern with the causes and prevention of social problems, these texts were intended as vehicles for reform—"as a weapon to conquer the vice, the crime, the misery which . . . science investigates" (Dugdale 1877b:47). The eugenics movement of which they were a part was closely woven into the fabric of other major reforms of the proto-Progressive and Progressive periods. Conservative though they often seem today, these reforms aimed at cleansing and transforming society.

[14] More accurately, *seems* to be crowded; a close reading shows that in fact relatively few criminals dwelt in the Vale of Siddem.

Eugenics began, as Haller has observed, "as a scientific reform in an age of reform" (1963:5; also see Ludmerer 1972 and Pickens 1968).

The Family Studies and Social Class

Yet this reformist thrust co-existed with another aspect of the family studies, their deeply conservative one-to-one equations of social class with genetic worth. Social class issues are raised by not only the content of the works but also their sponsorship. Wealthy patrons—John D. Rockefeller, Jr., Mrs. E. H. Harriman, the Carnegie Institution of Washington, and Philadelphia philanthropist Samuel S. Fels—were involved in the production and promotion of at least six family studies.[15] But it would be simplistic and imprecise merely to say that the studies furthered upper-class interests. We need to explore *which* upper-class interests were at stake, and why; and how these particular interests led to the targeting of the rural poor.

Many social historians have identified social turmoil as the stimulus for the reforms of the proto-Progressive and Progressive periods. According to this type of analysis, "old" Americans—Protestant, middle-class, Anglo-Saxon—felt enormously threatened by the growing power of plutocrats and corporations, on the one hand and, on the other, by the arrival of "new" Americans—Catholic and Jewish lower-class immigrants from southern and eastern Europe who were crowding into the cities. "Old" Americans began to long for what they believed to have been a simpler, more rural past and to take measures ("reforms") to increase social control over both the misusers of wealth and the alien newcomers (see, for examples, Connelly 1980, Hofstadter 1955a, Gusfield 1963, Rosen 1982).

There is much in the family studies to support this social-turmoil interpretation. Kite's "Two Brothers" (1912), for instance, affirms old-American values by contrasting two branches of one family and tracing the virtuous strain to "sturdy English dissenting stock that had always been sober, industrious and God-fearing." The spermatic anxiety of the later family studies—their fear that the cacogenic were out-multiplying the aristogenic—also lends credence to the social-turmoil thesis. *The*

---

[15] Research for Goddard's *Kallikak Family* (and by implication for Kite's "Two Brothers") was supported by Samuel S. Fels (Goddard 1923: dedication page and p. x). *The Hill Folk* and *The Nam Family* thank John D. Rockefeller and Mrs. E. H. Harriman for assistance, and at the time he co-authored these words Davenport was director of the Carnegie Institution of Washington's Department of Experimental Evolution. The Eugenic Record Office, then funded by Harriman, published *The Dack Family*; the Carnegie Institution published *The Jukes in 1915*. Research for a number of the other family studies was conducted by field workers trained at the ERO with funds from Harriman and Rockefeller; at the time they did the research some worked for institutions, but according to Kevles (1985:55), "The only cost to the institutions was the workers' expenses," with the ERO footing other bills.

Nam Family tells us that the average fecundity of this group was 4.2 children per mother, "much greater than that of the most cultured families of the eastern United States. Consequently, they [the cultured] are falling behind even such a degenerate population as this" (Estabrook and Davenport 1912:74). Furthermore, the social-turmoil hypothesis helps explain the Us-Other ideology that pervades the family studies and their insistence on dramatic increases in social control.

But this standard explanation fails to account for the family studies' preoccupation with the cacogeneity of the rural poor. Why, if reformers were reacting to immigration and the growth of cities, did *none*[16] of the works trace bad immigrant or urban families? Why did they, rather, focus on rural life—the longed-for setting, according to the social-turmoil thesis, of the reformers' nostalgia for a better, more American past?

The answer lies with the fact that these particular reformers were social control professionals for whom increasing eugenic control over the rural poor provided an opportunity to enhance their careers and personal status. To understand why the rural poor provided this opportunity, we must first understand the connection between eugenics and professionalization, a relationship analyzed in depth by Donald MacKenzie (1981). According to MacKenzie, the key to the popularity of eugenics rests in the way it promised to further the interests of an emergent professional middle class.[17] Professionals

> occupy a position that is intermediate between the bourgeoisie and proletariat. They differ from the bourgeoisie (and aristocracy) in that they typically do not own or control substantial quantities of capital (or land). They differ from the proletariat in that their work is defined as mental labour, brain work, and is held to be superior to manual labour. Secondly, recruitment to the professional middle class is generally not automatic, but has to be achieved . . . [1981:27].

One of the most powerful means used by this professional middle class to pursue its interests is "'professionalisation' itself," which gives occupations prestige by implying their work "is based on . . . accredited possession of a body of systematic knowledge . . . while claiming [they] can be relied upon to provide disinterested service to the community" (p. 27). It is this "accredited knowledge," according to MacKenzie, that most distinguishes the professional middle class from both bourgeoisie and proletar-

---

[16] McCulloch's "Tribe of Ishmael" (1888) does not really provide an exception because although the Ishmaels "gypsied" around the margins of cities, they were in no way integrated into urban life.

[17] MacKenzie treats class as a cultural phenomenon, not necessarily equivalent to social class "in the Marxist (or any other) sense" (1981:26); yet there seems to be no reason *not* to consider the American equivalent of his British professional class as a social class in the structural sense.

iat. In the final step of his argument, MacKenzie points out that eugenics "was attractive to many professionals" because

> the core of this view was the idea that social position was (or at least should be) the consequence of individual mental ability. There was a natural hierarchy of talent which could be translated into a social hierarchy of talent which could be translated into a social hierarchy of occupations. At the top were the professions . . . [1981:29].

The only way to enter the "eugenic elite" was "on the professionals' terms: accredited knowledge."

MacKenzie's analysis is persuasive on several grounds. First, the interests behind eugenics were not simply the economic and political interests traditionally associated with social class but also involved the social organization of authority—who was to be considered subordinate and marginal, who could participate in society (through reproduction, for example), and above all, who was to make these determinations (for related discussions, see Gould 1981: chap. 5, and Smith 1978). As the social-turmoil theorists point out, the period in question was one in which rapid social change threatened older power structures based on name, wealth, and tradition. But change also created an opening, an opportunity for a new consolidation of cultural authority on the basis of professional expertise such as that which eugenics seemed both to offer and to sanctify.

Then too, MacKenzie's analysis fits well with the history of the professions in the United States. Psychology, social work, and sociology—new professions in which eugenicists were well represented—were established at the turn of the century, just as eugenics entered its heyday. (Indeed, for a while eugenics itself promised to become something of a profession.[18]) Hofstadter (1955a) holds that professionals of this period—clergy, academics, lawyers—allied themselves with Progressive reforms in reaction to status humiliation by the burgeoning plutocracy. Although the social scientists who rallied to the eugenics flag were less hostile to plutocrats than were the typical professionals of Hofstadter's account, they certainly used this Progressive reform to enhance their professional standing.

Those who stood most to gain from eugenics (and here I am building upon MacKenzie's theory; also see Rosenberg 1974) were professionals

---

[18] Here I am thinking not only of institutional superintendents (such as Edward R. Johnstone and A. C. Rogers) and researchers (such as Charles Davenport and Henry Goddard) whose fame rested on their eugenics work, but also of the over 250 field workers trained in the ERO's summer program; see below and Kevles 1985:56. Mental testers were also heavily involved; and according to Ludmerer (1972:42), in the early twentieth century perhaps half of all American geneticists supported eugenics to some degree.

involved in the new business of social control[19]—welfare workers, eugenic field workers, institutional superintendents, mental testers. Members of these groups were precisely those who contributed most strongly to creation of the American eugenics movement. Their professional domains could be extended by increasing controls over the criminal, feeble-minded, insane, alcoholic, and so on—those whose unit characters (symbolized by C, F, I, A, etc.) march through the genealogical charts of the family studies.[20]

Authors of the family studies were members of the new social control professions. The twelve authors represented in this volume can be divided, in terms of occupation at the time their study was published, into three groups: eugenicists, social welfare workers, and sociologists. The eugenicists category (in which I have classified trained field workers and biologists supported by the Eugenics Record Office) includes eight of the twelve (Danielson, Charles and Gertrude Davenport, Finlayson, Kite, Kostir, Merrill, and Sessions). The social welfare category includes McCulloch, a minister heavily engaged in charity organization work, and Rogers, superintendent of an institution for the feeble-minded. The sociologists were Dugdale (by avocation) and Blackmar (by profession). Of the twelve, only Dugdale can be described as "disinterested" in the sense of having little to gain, professionally; and as we have seen, he was the least eugenical of the lot. Others were explicit about their goal of expanding social control. Mina Sessions noted that she had a card file with entries on almost a thousand confirmed and suspected defectives. "If a system is ever perfected by which the state can exercise control of the feeble-minded at large, or if the time comes when attention is paid to the heredity of applicants for marriage licenses, this index will be invaluable" (1918:274). Of her foray into the Pine Barrens Elizabeth Kite later explained, "Those families who were not potential state cases did not interest me as far as my study

[19] Bannister writes that E. A. Ross's immensely popular *Social Control*, published in 1901, made the term "the common currency of progressive reform." Behind the many different uses of the term

> lay the common assumption that since society was a jungle, more systematic controls were demanded. Supplementing an older humanitarianism, there developed *an ideal of rule by experts in the interest of efficiency.*
>
> During the progressive era this impulse bred a variety of proposed controls, from immigration restriction to new sanctions against nonwhite Americans. However, none was more controversial than the movement to improve the human stock through eugenics legislation [1979:165; emphases added].

[20] Many members of these groups disagreed with eugenics, of course; and in any case, the movement started to lose support in the 1920s. What I am arguing is that members of these groups who *were* strong eugenicists seem to have recognized in the doctrine potential for professional advancement. See Hahn 1978. This was true even of Charles Davenport, who opposed social work and larger institutions for defectives (Rosenberg 1976:95).

was concerned" (as quoted in McPhee 1967:54). Researchers trained at Cold Spring Harbor learned from Davenport himself that their professional mission included increased institutionalization: "Whenever the field worker learns of any defectives who need Institutional care, their names and addresses are obtained" (Davenport et al. 1911:2).

The family studies did more than extend professional horizons. They also *validated* that extension, giving it rationale, scientific authority, an aura of expertise and objectivity, the family-tree technology, and that claim to community service that MacKenzie describes as a hallmark of professionalization. By portraying the cacogenic as insentient subhumans (as well as dangerous), the literature made more palatable the recommendation that a large segment of the population be denied liberty and the right to reproduce. Furthermore, to authors (and readers as well, as I suggest later) the family studies gave the reassurance that they, in particular, ranked high in genetic worth. From this perspective, the family studies constitute a graphic rhetorical gesture, an affirmation of class position and entitlement.

But what attracted the wealthy patrons of the family studies literature? Significantly, Fels, Harriman, Rockefeller, and the directors of the Carnegie Institution were philanthropists, not business people; theirs were fortunes achieved, not in the making. They may indeed have had class-based stakes in reducing crime and disease, increasing social efficiency, and bringing the poor under closer surveillance; but probably more important was the opportunity offered, through sponsorship of scientific research, to disassociate themselves from rapacious plutocrats, affiliate with the eugenics elite, and participate in production of "accredited knowledge." Through the socially responsible act of patronage they demonstrated the worthiness that eugenicists insisted was the main criterion for membership in the top echelon of the social hierarchy.

It is not hard to see why the family study researchers scoured the ranks of the poor for their degenerates: the poor either were most likely to present the traits that the researchers sought or (as I argued earlier) were most easy to label with those traits. But why rurals? The answer lies with the fact that the new class of professional social controllers had not yet established ways of monitoring rural areas. As Danielson and Davenport observe, "while the feebleminded of our cities are promptly recognized and cared for by segregating, those of rural communities are for the most part allowed to reproduce their traits unhindered" (1912:107). The cities had police and social workers, juvenile courts and settlement houses, to regulate the poor; but rural areas had, at best, a county poorhouse (an institution that the family studies attack as totally inadequate to its task).[21] In *The Feeble-Minded in a Rural County of Ohio* (Sessions 1918) and other studies we can see members of the new class for the first time introducing regulatory mechanisms into rural areas. Several conclude with calls for drastic increases in control over the rural poor. Thus the countryside seemed fertile territory to social controllers ambitious to identify new "clients."

There were other reasons as well for the new professionals to beat rustic bushes. Unlike the urban poor, few of the rural poor were members of the industrial workforce, which had its own methods for watching and disciplining laborers (Foucault 1977; Gutman 1977). Moreover, although poor, the country folk of the family studies were independent; hence the authors' extraordinary indignation over the means (berry picking, scavenging, itinerant farm work) by which members of the bad families supported themselves. *These* poor were self-reliant, often indifferent to the charity and outright hostile to the values which some of the new professionals made a career of dispensing.[22] Finally, the authors were alarmed by the indifference of the rural poor to material possessions. As Blackmar advised, "These people must be taught not only to earn money but to spend it properly" (1897:65). In the late family studies disinterest in accumulation is a sure sign of feeble-mindedness.

Thus complex professional concerns merged with nervousness about the rapid changes America was undergoing to mobilize support for the social class ideology of eugenics and focus some of its advocates on the genetic menace seemingly posed by the rural poor. That the class interests involved were not only material but also profoundly personal is demonstrated by the zealousness, the self-righteousness, of many family studies authors. Like other eugenicists, they were not just promoting a new set of public policies but engaged in an almost religious crusade for class preservation and aggrandizement.

"Results That Can Be Secured in No Other Way": Methodology of the Family Studies

The model of heredity on which Mendelian eugenics depended, and the mental testing techniques used to validate that model, have been heavily

---

[21] Although grammar schools—another monitoring institution—also existed in the country, they too were heavily criticized by the family studies: some rural children did not attend at all, while others attended erratically and did not finish.

[22] The family studies do, of course, complain about the costs of relief to the rural poor; but they also complain about country people's resistance to changing their self-sufficient ways, to allowing their children to be institutionalized, and to adopting field workers' attitudes toward poverty and education.

criticized since the early twentieth century (Bronner 1914; Gould 1981: chap. 5; Haller 1963; Heron 1914; Kamin 1974; Kevles 1985; Lewontin et al. 1984; Ludmerer 1972; Pearson 1914; Sarason and Doris 1969; Stevens 1915; Wallin 1916a, 1916b, 1916c). Rather than repeat these now familiar criticisms, I use this section to identify methodological problems characteristic of the family studies per se and to demonstrate that the genre depended on these problems for its very existence. Had they been solved or avoided, the family studies could not have survived as a distinct mode of analysis.

The Unit of Analysis: Fiddling with "Families" One of these problems lay in the definition of "family"—a term whose definition varied from study to study according to the conclusion the authors wished to reach. To be sure, defining a "family" is no simple matter. Who should be included in a family tree? Should there be a single sire at the top (or root), as in a chart of, say, the descendants of George Washington? If we include Martha, should she have a tree of her own showing *her* ancestors? Assuming less interest in family itself than in inheritance of a trait, such as the tooth decay said to have afflicted George Washington, how can we follow this trait through the generations? How are we to determine if an illegitimate and unrecorded liaison at some point along the way contributed to or retarded his (or his descendants') dental problems? Is the condition of Martha Washington's teeth relevant? Similar difficulties confronted those who traced the transmission of degeneration.

The solution devised by Dugdale and his followers was to use "family" as an umbrella term for a number of family units *and* those who married (or mated) into them. In *"The Jukes"* Dugdale freely admits that "there are forty-two family names included in the lineage which, for convenience of treatment, require to be reduced to a generic appellation" (1877a:7). Dugdale traces this family to patriarch Max—but a close reading reveals that Max was not a Juke at all; rather, "the Jukes" consisted of six sisters and their offspring. Moreover, "the probability is they were not all full sisters; that some, if not all of them, were illegitimate. The family name, in two cases, is obscure, which accords with the supposition that at least two of the women were half-sisters to the other four . . ." (1877a:14). We find similar fancy footwork in the definition of family in McCulloch's "Tribe of Ishmael," which began with investigation of 250 families, selected 30 as "typical," and applied to these 30 the Ishmael label (1888:50).

Whereas Dugdale had the integrity to use quotes when he referred to "the Jukes" and McCulloch to explain his definition of "tribe," later family studies seem deliberately to have obscured the relationships (or lack thereof) among those they presented as families. The first page of *The Hill Folk* refers to the "two family trees" of Neil Rasp and an Englishman, Nuke, stating that the aim of the work is to show "how much crime, misery and expense may result from the union of . . . defective individuals." In fact, *The Hill Folk* covers at least nine families (1912:104), and it is simply not true that "practically all of them could be traced back to one of the two original sources" (p. 85); the fifth family (diagrammed on p. 100), for example, lived "a hundred miles away" in another state and was connected with the Nukes by only one marriage. The first page further misleads by claiming that "all these families were connected by marriage, some of them by consanguineous marriages"; the link between the Rasps and Nukes, for instance, did not occur until the third generation, with one marriage (between a granddaughter of the original Nuke and a grandson of Neil Rasp).

A family tree can serve a variety of purposes. If the goal is to study heredity, it is reasonable to expect the tree to include only blood relatives—and not adoptees (Danielson and Davenport 1912:145), "consorts" who produce no children (Finlayson 1916), step-great-grandmothers (Sessions 1918:262), or unrelated inhabitants of the area (Rogers and Merrill 1919:376). If, moreover, the goal is radical reduction of freedom—to "prevent the propagation of inevitable dependents" (Danielson and Davenport 1912:128)—we might expect the unit of analysis to be defined with some precision.

Finally, if the goal is to illustrate laws of inheritance—and many of the studies claim their families are "typical"—we might expect sensitivity to selection bias, a problem Galton identified before the first study was written (1914 [1869]). Yet Blackmar decides to ignore a second-generation Smoky Pilgrim and her family on the ground that they "live respectable and industrious lives . . . and consequently are not to be included in this discussion" (1897:60). Gertrude Davenport similarly limits her sample: "from them descended one of the two good branches of the Zeros, a branch so upright that it no longer enters into this story" (1907:69). Many of the family studies originated with an inmate of an institution, fanning out to investigate the "heredity" of family members still at large. If we are interested in a trait we are certain is rare, there is reason to focus on a small group of trait carriers. But if our interest is in a trait the distribution of which is unknown (and the identification of which will lead to "permanent custodial care"), there is no justification for basing conclusions on highly selected "families."

Gathering Evidence in the Field From first to last the family studies drew on similar data sources: public records; interviews with physicians, schoolteachers and sheriffs; conversations with neighbors and family members themselves. More forthright than his followers about problems inherent in such sources, Dugdale pointed to "the migration of families, the difficulty of determining the paternity of illegitimates, . . . and the necessity of depending upon tradition for facts concerning earlier generations" as drawbacks of his methods (1877a:7)—a list to which we might add the biases of official records, the problems of missing data, memory error, and the unreliability of hearsay.

There was, however, a significant change over time in data collection procedures: starting with "Two Brothers" (Kite 1912b), information was gathered by field workers trained to make rapid assessments of the intelligence of subjects living and dead.[23] Some—most notably Elizabeth S. Kite—were trained by Henry H. Goddard at the Vineland, New Jersey, Training School for the feeble-minded; but far more important in the training of field workers was the summer school run by the Eugenics Record Office at Cold Spring Harbor, New York, from 1910 to 1924. Designed to provide instruction "in human heredity and other eugenical factors" and to teach "the principles and practice of making first-hand human pedigree-studies" ("Alumni Roster" 1919:21), the ERO course was taught by two giants in the U.S. eugenics movement, Charles Davenport and Harry Laughlin. They trained more than 250 field workers, including family studies authors Arthur H. Estabrook (*The Nam Family, The Jukes in 1915,* and *Mongrel Virginians*); Estabrook's classmate in the 1910 session, Florence Danielson (*The Hill Folk*); Anna Wendt Finlayson (*The Dack Family*); Mina Sessions (*The Feeble-Minded in a Rural County of Ohio*); and Mary Storer Kostir (*The Family of Sam Sixty*). Moreover, the ERO funded the research and publication of some family studies produced by field workers.[24]

Earlier we saw that the American eugenics movement drew much of its energy from members of emerging professions, especially those involved in social control. A roster of students who attended the ERO summer school from 1910 through 1918 supports this claim. Most ERO students were indeed members of "helping" or regulatory professions: school and college teachers; superintendents of institutions for the blind, prisoners, and wayward children; physicians; employees of child welfare agencies and state boards of charities; social workers; mental testers ("Alumni Roster" 1919). To these students, clearly, training in eugenics appeared a means of professional advancement.

[23] The use of field workers was anticipated by Blackmar's use of two sociology students to assist with the research for "The Smoky Pilgrims" (1897:64).

[24] See note 15.

The roster also shows that the overwhelming majority of alumni of the 1910–1918 summer classes were women.[25] Sandra Harding points out that the turn of the century was a time when women gained increasing access to higher education, including science instruction, and found increasing opportunities for employment in scientific fields; yet it was also a period in which, through bureaucratization and "professionalization," the sciences developed gender divisions of labor. Thus, "women could hold auxiliary and subservient positions in the scientific fields where men predominated" (1986:62). The eugenics movement formed part of this process, providing new opportunities for women in science while assigning them to "women's" work.

Eugenics field investigation was women's work in several senses. First, it involved intuition and an eye for detail, abilities with which women were thought to be particularly well endowed. Describing how the eugenics researcher develops "a sense of what a feeble-minded person is so that he can tell one afar off," Goddard observed that "the people who are best at this work, and who I believe should do this work, are women. Women seem to have closer observation than men" (as quoted in Gould 1981:165). Second, women (perhaps because less intimidating) were better able to elicit personal information from strangers. In "Method and Aim of Field Work" Kite discusses her techniques of winning the confidence of those who are to be questioned. "Dropping in on a hot day and asking for a glass of milk or water, at once rouses friendly interest," and "even the defective" will respond (1912a:85–86). Third, in serving as assistants to men such as Goddard and Davenport, field workers elaborated the traditional gender division of labor (see Smith 1977, esp. p. 71, for the way this division plays out in sociology).

Charles Davenport was particularly open to working with well-trained female assistants. He met his future wife, Gertrude Crotty, when she enrolled in his graduate zoology course at Radcliffe and, although a biologist in her own right, Gertrude served as Charles's assistant manager at the ERO for many years. Charles Davenport supported women's struggle for equality—so long as it did not lower birthrates among the "fit" (Pickens 1968:58). His liberal attitudes made him a leader in the process described by Harding, simultaneously advancing and segregating women in science.

Field workers performed a variety of tasks. Often affiliated with an institution, they investigated the heredity of inmates by interviewing "near and distant relatives as well as neighbors, employers, teachers, physi-

[25] Using names as a guide to gender, I identified only twenty-six men out of a total of 176 in the roster. Five names were ambiguous, the rest those of women.

cians," and so on (Goddard 1923:13–14). They analyzed "each person in the pedigree in respect to his mental and moral traits from a brief acquaintance and from a comparison of the descriptions of others" (Danielson and Davenport 1912:87; also see Kite 1912a).[26] They did social work, bringing families news of institutionalized relatives; public relations work, informing "relatives, physicians and others" of the work of their institution, thus establishing "a friendly feeling toward" it; and advance work, scouting out candidates for institutionalization (Davenport et al. 1911:1–2). And, of course, some wrote family studies.

The field workers' methods did indeed produce (in Charles Davenport's words) "results that can be secured in no other way" (introduction to Finlayson 1916:212). Trained by prestigious scientists, paid by the ERO or a public agency to flush out the defective, field workers had little incentive to doubt their own sophistication or entertain alternative hypotheses. Asking questions "in the field" about criminality, feeble-mindedness, and other disabilities, they naturally began to receive persuasive answers.

Constructing the Evidence The researchers began by assuming that which they then set out to prove. In "The Smoky Pilgrims" we learn of "B——" that "his physical characteristics show persistent deterioration and constant evolution downward" (Blackmar 1897:61). Among the Hill Folk "cousin marriages are frequent. In fact, even where no known relationship exists between the contracting parties, it is probable that they are from the same strains" (Danielson and Davenport 1912:99). Sam Sixty came to Mary Kostir's attention when he was imprisoned for incest; "Such criminality seemed to point to inferiority of stock" (1916:186). The authoritative Elizabeth Kite informs us that "a glance sufficed to establish his mentality, which was low" (in Goddard 1923:78). Among the Dwellers in the Vale of Siddem, "The prevalence of sexual laxity . . . is a foregone conclusion" (Rogers and Merrill 1919:361). Seeking confirmation, not evidence, the field investigators easily found it.

That hard evidence was not their first priority may explain the authors' apparent lack of concern about errors and internal contradictions. Although McCulloch has told us that some Ishmael "descendants are now . . . prosperous, well-regarded citizens," he laments that "I know of but one who has escaped, and is to-day an honorable man" (1888:50,

[26] Kite's "The 'Pineys' " (1913) gives detailed descriptions of administration of Binet tests "in the field"—and vivid evidence of the tests' biases. Those tested seem to have been intimidated by Kite's hectoring manner and offended by her tone of superiority. One Piney refused to talk—which Kite interpreted as stupidity (p. 179).

54).[27] Old Horror had thirteen children, according to Kite (1912b:76); the number falls to ten in Goddard's study of the same family, published simultaneously (1923 [1912]:19). "A comparatively industrious man, ... dull and unintelligent, but brighter than his wife" (Danielson and Davenport 1912:145) is elsewhere labeled feeble-minded (Chart B). Happy Hickories who "sought shelter in the Infirmary as soon as some unfavorable condition arose" were by definition feeble-minded—even when the "unfavorable condition" was a shooting accident (Sessions 1918:259).

Nor do terminological vagueness and circular definition seem to have caused much embarrassment. How does one qualify as "an alcoholic"? Does a single childhood "fit" make an epileptic? What are the criteria for "below par" and "low-grade family"? How can a "moron" like Hannah Ann raise eleven children, keep them and herself "fairly clean" in a "little two-room shack," go out to work three days a week, and make "a pile of patchwork quilts" (Kite 1913:176)—quilts that might be of some value today?

The authors habitually conflate value judgments with evidence. Old man Nead "alternated excessive religious fervor with long sprees," and another Hill person "was a miserable character, drunken and shiftless" (Danielson and Davenport 1912:129, 158). A Dack wife is described as a "passive, easily dispirited woman" (Finlayson 1916:220). (Given that her husband was "a poor manager, excitable, occasionally intoxicated" and that three of her nine children had been institutionalized, her dispiritedness could have been seen as understandable.) Another Dack woman "became absurdly jealous" (1916:221), while a Happy Hickory was "childishly curious about unimportant things" (Sessions 1918:284). In like manner *predictions* qualify as evidence: to determine the IQ of children, Sessions determined whether they "will always need some wiser hand to guide them" (1916:267); and the Chads "have left a trail of ... degenerates who will patronize our county jails, poor houses and houses of prostitution for several generations" (Rogers and Merrill 1919:358).

Persuasion: Techniques in the Misuse of Evidence Some forms of evidentiary distortion are so common in the family studies as to constitute distinctive techniques. One is *conjecture,* a technique that emerged

---

[27] Davenport, in *Heredity in Relation to Eugenics,* seems to have deliberately misquoted McCulloch in order to make the evidence against the Ishmaels even more damning. McCulloch had written of the family, "Strangely enough, they are not intemperate" (1888:51); Davenport changed this to "'Strangely enough, they are not intemperate to excess'" (1911:235). Davenport also excised the final, exculpatory phrase about medical school in quoting (1911:235) McCulloch's "Another son in the third generation had a penitentiary record, and died of delirium tremens and went to the medical college" (1888:51).

as early as *"The Jukes."* Having tried, unsuccessfully, to trace the "idiot girl tainted with constitutional syphilis" (a description that masks its own guesswork), Dugdale concludes "she is probably dead"—and uses the conjecture as evidence for the vitiation of the hereditarily pauperized (1877a:29). Blackmar, anxious to prove the promiscuity of Smoky Pilgrims, informs us that "A——"'s youngest child "bears the name of her mother's husband, although probably she is illegitimate" (1897:63). In the hands of Elizabeth Kite conjecture becomes outright invention: she can quote remarks made in the mid-nineteenth century and deduce that a listener was "simple-minded" (1912b:77).

Another of these techniques is *unsubstantiated generalization.* The Hill Folk account for "about [*sic!*] 600 years of heavy drinking and 300 years of medium drinking. . . . [O]ur small rural community [*sic;* at least nine families, widely scattered] has consumed, in the last two or three generations, at least 32,000 gallons of whiskey" (Danielson and Davenport 1912:106). Kate Dack "had one period of mental disturbance at the age of about thirty" (Finlayson 1916:219)—thus qualifying as an example of hereditary lack of emotional control. Fishing for evidence of defective delinquency theory, Rogers and Merrill devote a chapter to criminalistic "Little Tommy," even though he "has not been seen around the hollow for a number of years" (1919:370); all residents of the hollow, they imply, are similarly prone to crime.

The *slur* constitutes the most frequent type of evidentiary distortion. Pearl Sixty's husband is a "paramour," and Pearl seems vaguely responsible for the fact that "no one seems to know where [she] is at present" (Kostir 1916:195). Tessie Dack's "history and general reaction are not suggestive of an imbecile" (Finlayson 1916:225). Nearly all the family studies' evidence for "consanguinity" consists of innuendo. Jim Yak's family, for example, although presented as a shocking case of intermarriage, does not provide one clear union of blood relations: "The man 'marries his deceased wife's sister' . . . ; the daughter consoles her mother's discarded second husband; and other daughters marry men of the same name or remotely connected"—not difficult since the authors have dubbed so many people "Yaks" (Rogers and Merrill 1919:358).

The Objects of Objectification The root of many of the methodological and evidentiary problems discussed above lay in the family studies' relentless objectification of their subjects—their insistence on turning people into things. That members of the bad families may have had their own points of view on the conditions and activities described in these works seems not to have occurred to the authors. Consider Thomas Haines's judgment of a fifteen-year-old incest victim in his introduction to *The Family of Sam Sixty:* upon questioning, "she proved herself markedly lacking in capacity to react intelligently" to "her short comings and the bestiality of her father" (Kostir 1916:187); but why should the girl have confided in this stranger (who was, not incidentally, intent on proving her mentally inferior)? The Dacks are frequently accused of paranoia with no inquiry into possible reasons for fearfulness. Finlayson detected congenital defects in children who failed "to see any absurdity in such a statement as 'A young woman cut into eighteen pieces, was found yesterday; people think that she killed herself'" (1916:228). Yet there might have been other reasons for the children's failure to find the statement absurd. Perhaps they were horrified by the description. Perhaps they were embarrassed at Finlayson's talking this way. Perhaps they thought the woman had been dismembered after she committed suicide.[28]

By denying their subjects an independent point of view, the authors denied them authority over their own lives. The "defectives" lost their voice, as the authors assumed the ability to speak for (or, rather, against) them. MacKenzie observes that "the eugenists' typical view of human nature" reduced "the person ... [to] potentially measurable abilities and personality traits," an attitude he analyzes as part of a more general tendency to reification, "the treatment of people and social processes as if they were things. ... Human capacities [such as intelligence] become commodities" (1981:34; also see Gould 1981). Writing more generally of the false "ethic of objectivity" by which sociologists separate "the knower from what he[29] knows," Dorothy Smith warns that

> We may not rewrite the other's world or impose upon it a conceptual framework which extracts from it what fits with ours. Our conceptual procedures should be capable of explicating and analyzing the properties of their experienced world. ... Their reality, their varieties of experience must be an unconditional datum [1974:12].

Had our authors been able to understand such warnings, however, they could not have produced the family studies. Their work depended on objectification.

Because the authors so earnestly presented their findings as objective,

---

[28] It is not hard to guess how the authors would have classified the mentality of two elderly American Eskimos, fathered by North Pole discoverers Matthew Henson and Robert Peary and brought to the United States in 1987. According to a newspaper account, as the two men sat in the cockpit and pretended to steer, they called out dogsled commands to the airplane; and passing tall buildings on the drive from New Jersey to Boston, they yelled "igloo, igloo, igloo" (*Boston Globe* June 1, 1987, 17–18).

[29] A pronoun Smith uses deliberately.

and because in many cases their goal was to deny others liberty, it is not unreasonable to task them with methodological errors and manipulations of evidence. But to criticize their techniques is, ultimately, to take their claims to expertise too seriously and to ignore the fact that—despite the authors' intentions—their works were less successful as science than as myth.

The Hieroglyphic World: Language and Myth in the Family Studies

In this section I shift from analyzing the family studies as science to treating them as literature. My aim is to show how these texts created their ideologically charged mythology. I use "ideology" in what Harding calls "the strong sense of the term: in contrast to merely value-laden false beliefs that have no social power, these beliefs structure the policies and practices of social institutions" (1986:136). I am interested in how the details of the texts are organized by ideology (Smith 1983) and regenerate that ideology. The title of the section derives from Edith Wharton's *Age of Innocence*: "They all lived in a kind of hieroglyphic world, where the real thing was never said or done or even thought, but only represented by a set of arbitrary signs..." (1970 [1920]:45). I try to show how the family study authors turned "the real thing"—the subjects they studied—into a set of signs. By carefully selecting descriptions, using bumpkin pseudonyms, and sending covert signals to readers, the authors constructed a symbolic world.

Animal and insect imagery pervades the family studies. The cacogenic "mate" and "migrate," "nesting" with their "broods" in caves and "hotbeds where human maggots are spawned." Like beasts, naked Hill boys run "about in summer like little wild animals" at the edge of a wood, and a Hill wife looks "more like an animal than a woman." Residing in "low hollows," the Pineys hide "by day...amid the dunes of the seashore." A "monkey-like instinct to steal and hide" typifies the Dacks, some of whom live in "a hornet's nest." The Hickories "eat berries...and turtles and ground hogs"; the Dwellers in the Vale, "known to the surrounding country folk variously as 'timber rats' and 'bark eaters,'" form "nests of social incompetents." Most powerful of all is McCulloch's extended metaphor of the "pauper ganglion of several hundreds" that has attached itself to society as the Sacculina parasite attaches itself to the hermit crab, "suck[ing] the living tissues." Not only do these images suggest danger; they also imply that the cacogenic would hardly notice if they were treated as less than human.

Other images further degrade. Smoky Pilgrims childishly decorate their shanties with "bits of bright-colored papers." Ben (Old Bear) Yak and his wife "would sit day in and day out in their barren shack, shuffling the same grimy old deck and dealing the cards on an upturned dry goods box." "The 'Pineys'" opens with multiple references to descent and despoliation. "Originally covered with a splendid growth of pines," the area has been reduced to "a scrubby growth." The Pineys "fell quickly," their industries are "steadily on the decline." In contrast to "our rising generation," Pineys "penetrate deeper into the woods."

The haunts of the cacogenic become outer manifestations of their inner decay. Many are located in forests, long associated in imaginative literature with mystery, danger, and the illicit. "Hidden deep in the mountain thicket," Old Horror's "crude hut" is the place where his daughters receive men, "leaving behind them a long train of descendants." Pineys, too, go to the woods to indulge in "sensual enjoyment." As if drawn by a magnet, Hickories prefer to live in the township "with the steepest hills and the most inaccessible ridges. The Hickory shanties are as a usual thing tucked away under the protection of a hill in some remote spot." *Dwellers in the Vale of Siddem*, like "The 'Pineys,'" opens with an originally wild but beautiful countryside that has been morally despoiled by its inhabitants. "The caves[30] of the region have taken on a sinister aspect; the dark little ravines have grown forbidding; the shadowy forks leading from the river valley seem menacing; the region has acquired an unsavory fame in all the surrounding country" (Rogers and Merrill 1919:348). The inhabitants, "whether they live in the secluded fastnesses of the ravine or move to the city . . . are still persistent dwellers in the Vale of Siddem," which thus becomes a metaphor for their condition.

Circumspect descriptions of sexual depravity further charge the atmosphere. "Debauchery," "fornication," "harlotry," "impudicity," "lust"—such terms appear frequently in *"The Jukes."* In "The Smoky Pilgrims" farm boys pass the hours "telling obscene stories, in which . . . the use of vile language is habitual." "Plunged into the relaxed atmosphere of [army] camp life," the young soldier of "Two Brothers" "succumbed to excesses unknown in the annals of his family. . . . There were plenty of off-duty times when the fires of patriotism burned lower than the other fires within him." Piney progenitors include land pirates "of utter depravity whose 'lawlessness, cruelty and lust made them a terror to the entire country.'" In Siddem "Danny . . . works around for the farmers in the neighborhood of the ravine, his labor bought with the promise of 'a nice woman for Danny.'" With passages of this sort, the authors simultaneously alarmed

---

[30] The most symbolic of these caves, a rendezvous for outlaws, has a wide mouth and secret exit.

and titillated readers, and perhaps also gave them a satisfying sense of sophistication.

The names of the cacogenic, like their habitations, signify devolution. Tam, Rasp, Nute, Bill Hemp, Jake Rat, Maggie Rust—these crude pseudonyms onomatopoetically reflect character. Many infantilize (Hanner Ann, Joe Boy, Lizzer Anne, Young Hank) or otherwise demean (Crazy Jane, Rotten Jimmy, Muskrat Charlie, Woodchuck Sam). We are given nicknames rather than the surnames we would find in formal genealogies. The Sixties tribe is so called in honor of its progenitor's IQ score, the Hickories because their sire did no work other than "make baskets of hickory splits" (also, no doubt, because of the echo of "hicks"). The evocative "'jukes' means 'to roost.' It refers to the habit of fowls to have no home, no nest, no coop, preferring to fly into the trees and roost away from the places where they belong. The word has also come to mean people who are too indolent and lazy to stand up or sit up, but sprawl out anywhere" (Winship 1900:9).

The aural and visual images of the family studies coalesce around two poles, dividing the world into the two camps of good and bad denoted by "Kallikaks." "They" are drunken, feeble-minded, lawless, squalid, and bestial; "we" are abstemious, intelligent, law-abiding, industrious, and sexually restrained. This stratagem of defining oneself by disparaging others was hardly unique to the family studies; de Beauvoir holds that "the category of the *Other* is as primordial as consciousness itself" (1974:xix). But more was going on here than self-definition. The negative labels of the family studies also served as ammunition in the struggle, described earlier, over allocation of authority in society. The studies themselves were propaganda for a particular (middle-class, professional) view of how society should be organized, part of a bid for ideological control (see Smith 1978, esp. p. 283, and Harding, 1986:119–20).

The family studies employ a variety of rhetorical devices to compel their audience to take a side in this struggle. One is the assumption of a secret understanding between author and reader; author speaks directly to reader over the heads (as it were) of the cacogenic, much as adults speak in codes in the presence of children. In "The Smoky Pilgrims," for example, Blackmar informs us that "'M——C——' . . . is very communicative, although the information gained by the questioner is quite likely to prove an estimate of what she does not know" (1897:63). *We* can understand that; "M——C——" cannot. In the same passage Blackmar writes, "'M——C——' believes in religion (!)," using the exclamation point to signal to us. At one point "The 'Pineys'" unites author and reader in a "superior" understanding of legal matters: Bertha and her husband "'didn't get on' together so went back to the 'squire' who married them and got a separation in writing which they thought legal" (deleted caption in Kite 1913). Sarcasm and irony are sometimes used to cement the secret understanding, as in "Annie Glade married a typical scion of the Chad family" (Rogers and Merrill 1919:365).

The more skillful authors manipulate point of view to encourage readers to adopt their assumptions. "In a sparsely settled portion of L———, Kansas, dwells, or stays, a family for more than twenty years well known to the benevolent people of the town" (Blackmar 1897:59). This line forces us to adopt the author's distinction between "dwells" and "stays" and to align ourselves with "benevolent people." Benevolence here is equated with not just knowledge but a type of superior knowingness. "They are known as people seeking odd jobs of work" (Blackmar 1897:60): we readers are again classed with those who "know." ("They look for work" would have conveyed a quite different meaning.) Like Blackmar, Rogers and Merrill oblige us to regard the cacogenic through their eyes:

> Making your precarious way down the steep sides of the ravine, expecting momentarily to meet destruction around the next turn in the road, you find yourself shortly in the very heart of the hollow. The few widely scattered shacks evince few signs of life. Occasionally a ragged child stands staring to watch you pass and sometimes a slattern woman watches you listlessly from the doorway . . . [1919:362–63].

Near the beginning of "The 'Pineys'" Kite tells us that the land is inhabited by "a group of human beings so distinct in morals and manners as to excite curiosity and wonder in the mind of any outsider brought into contact with them. They are known as the . . . 'Pine Rats' and are recognized as a distinct people by the normal . . ." (1913:165). We have our cues.

The appeal of the family studies lay partly in their structure as quasi-fictional accounts. Although the narratives are often combined awkwardly with scientific data displays, as a group the works present a kind of melodrama, replete with danger, sex, and salvation. As in melodrama, the villain is very bad, the victim innocent, the solutions clear. The cacogenic imperil the good people of society—authors, readers, "our" class[31]—who can be saved by heroic eugenics. By endorsing eugenics we can also become heroes. Drama is provided by this cast; by the master plot according to which, generations ago, a sire moved into the territory and started breeding; and by the mysterious, threatening settings.

The family studies also appealed as a myth of the origins of social problems. Like other myths, they masquerade as historical while incorporat-

---

[31] Sometimes the victims include the children of degenerates, shown to be in need of protection from themselves and their families. Without "our" help these children will remain dirty, ill, vulnerable to incest, etc.; but we can save them.

ing a deliberate vagueness about the remote past, in this case the time when a half-human ancestor lumbered into a primitive land and began sowing spermatic destruction. It is a myth that invents a menace, the half-witted, Grendel-like stranger who likes to live in hollow logs and decrepit shanties—a White Trash myth, to be sure, but with the dimension of danger. Much social science literature analyzes social problems; this genre creates one.

Neither as melodrama nor as myth do the family studies permit the "cacogenic" themselves any role other than symbol. The stories of the subjects are obliterated by the stories in which they are made characters. Dorothy Smith makes a useful distinction between primary narrative, in which those who experience an event tell their own tale, and ideological narrative, which depends not on the experiencer's sequence but rather on "the reader's . . . grasp of the appropriate interpretive schema of the . . . discourse" (1983:328). To help us "grasp the appropriate schema," the second type of narrative provides "assembly instructions," guides to interpretation. In the ideological narratives of the family studies, these assembly instructions are the secret comments directed by authors to worthy readers, the manipulations of point of view which bar us from the primary narratives, and above all the constant pressure of Us-Other bifurcation. We can read critically—guessing at the primary narratives—only by refusing to cooperate with the interpretation intended by the text (Smith 1983:344).

The family studies, then, were far more than bad science and self-serving doctrine. They were crafted documents that, through a process of accretion, fabricated a mythology.

Some dismiss eugenics as a pseudo-scientific fad. However, the movement and its concepts were, as Farrall holds (1979:111) "much too complex and significant to allow [such] simplistic historical judgments to go unchallenged." Eugenics had enormous impact on the direction taken by the newly developing disciplines and professions of criminology and criminal justice, psychology and psychometry, sociology and social work, and statistics. Through legislation it shaped social policy governing crime control, education, liquor consumption, marriage and birth control, mental retardation, poor relief, and sterilization—all topics with which the family studies deal. In fact, as I have argued, the movement would have been much less successful had it not had the family studies to provide its central image of the cacogenic clan, both symbol and embodiment of the theory that social problems are somatic in origin.

Instead of dismissing the family studies as the fantasies of a handful of crackpots, we should recognize that they explored issues of fundamental and enduring concern: the relationship between humans and nature, biology and society, heredity and environment, and the meaning of evolution. Moreover, they enable us to explore yet another relationship, that of science to society (Farrall 1979). This particular type of scientific investigation began with Richard Dugdale's powerful vision of the Jukes family—itself, as we have seen, a social construction. The literature was able to develop from that point in part because it attracted wealthy patrons who supported the research and its publication, in part because it appealed professionally and personally to specialists (and would-be specialists) in social control. As they elaborated their characteristic methodologies and means of signification, the family studies authors created a distinctive genre that both illustrated and advocated a particular relationship between science and society.

As a flood of recent articles and books attests, we are today witnessing a booming interest in the history of eugenics, investigations spurred by the resurgence of sociobiology and debate over the heritability of intelligence. Current discussions of such issues as an alleged "birth dearth" of genetically healthy individuals and of the alleged role of biological factors in criminal behavior gain special urgency from the fact that they occur in the context of sophisticated technologies for genetic engineering. But as the family studies demonstrate, neither the issues nor proposals for genetic solutions are new. We do not have to accept the dogma of the family studies to agree on their historical—and contemporary—significance.

1

RICHARD L. DUGDALE

Hereditary Pauperism as Illustrated in the "Juke" Family*

Preface

Dugdale began his research on the Juke family in 1874 when, as a member of the executive committee of the Prison Association of New York, he was appointed a subcommittee of one to inspect the state's jails. The first version of *"The Jukes"* appeared in the 1874 annual report (published in 1875) of the Prison Association to the state legislature. Somewhat revised, it was published in book form by Putnam's in 1877. By the time Dugdale presented the paper reprinted here, the Putnam's version was in its third printing and Dugdale was famous among reformers in the United States and Europe.

Before Dugdale conducted his jail survey, Elisha Harris, corresponding secretary of the Prison Association, gave him a form to be filled out for each prisoner, including questions on heredity, education, intelligence, income, and "the probable fate of the person questioned" (Dugdale 1875:129). With this questionnaire in hand Dugdale interviewed prisoners in thirteen jails, including one in Ulster County,[1] where he "found six persons, under four family names, who turned out to be blood relations in some degree" (1877a:9).[2] Thus began his work on *"The Jukes."* Soon afterward Dugdale took the momentous step of modifying Harris's questionnaire to add "the element of time" (1877a:11).

In the speech reprinted here Dugdale uses Jukes data to determine whether pauperism is hereditary. His method is to compare four families, those of:

1. Hans, oldest legitimate son of Ada Juke, and his wife, a Juke first cousin. Their descendants manifested numerous defects, including pauperism. Dugdale concludes that this family is an example of hereditary pauperism produced by disease, the syphilis Hans had acquired before marriage.
2. Yope, a full brother of Hans, who also married a Juke first cousin. This is an example of a family free of pauperism. As Yope was "equal" to

* Originally published in Conference of Boards of Public Charities, *Proceedings 1877:* 81–95.

[1] In eastern New York, not the Finger Lakes district as some have supposed from the description of lakes in *"The Jukes."*

[2] Much as Dugdale's inspiration came from finding a number of people with the same surname in a jail, so had Galton's inspiration for *Hereditary Genius*, the 1869 work that started eugenics, come from "his own observations of contemporaries while an undergraduate at Cambridge, where the same surnames appeared perennially on the honors lists" (Bannister 1979:168).

Hans in all respects except for having "no syphilis coursing through his veins," Dugdale decides that disease was indeed the culprit in Hans's case.

3. Getty, half-sister to Hans and Yope (her mother, too, was Ada Juke), married to a "mulatto [who] was lazy, licentious, and stricken with syphilis." Their children were catastrophes; many had to apply for outdoor relief or poor-house care. Dugdale concludes that this family, like the first, is an example of hereditary pauperism, but in this case he attributes pauperism less to disease than to the "cross of repugnant races."

4. A thievish son of Max, who married Effie Juke (sister to Ada). The posterity of one of their daughters "forms one of the most unbroken lines of almshouse and out-door pauperism in the 'Juke' stock." Yet there is no evidence here of inherited disease. Rather, this is an example of environmentally induced pauperism—pauperism precipitated by the poor conditions of Ulster County and its "lax and lavish . . . poor-laws."

Because "the Jukes" became part of the working vocabulary of social reformers in this country and abroad, many biographical dictionaries include entries on Dugdale. Nearly all are based, however, on the memorial of his friend and colleague Edward M. Shepard (1884). Dugdale was born in Paris in 1840 or 1841; he spent his early years in London and, after 1851, in the United States. Beset by ill-health from childhood, he studied drawing, sculpture, and photography, thus honing the artistic skills later demonstrated in "The Jukes." His family seems to have had only moderate means: Dugdale's father was a businessman; after the father's death the two sisters with whom Dugdale spent his adult years in Greenwich Village ran a linen shop; and Dugdale himself was obliged to enter business. According to his own account, he decided on business as a means of supporting his growing interest in social science, which he discovered while attending night classes at New York's Cooper Union:

> At twenty-three, I clearly saw that, even did I possess the most perfect technical training to enable me to analyse the complex questions involved, there was no institution or patron to defray the expenses of a continuous, calm, independent, and unconventional critical study of social phenomena. . . . I met this dilemma by entering the career of merchant and manufacturer, because this combined the opportunity for study of a distinct class of social phenomena and the promise of earning the means for future freedom of investigation. After ten years of this double work, I broke down in health . . . [as quoted in Shepard 1884:4].

The actual story of this decade may have been less heroic, however. According to his friend and publisher George H. Putnam, "Dugdale . . . had inherited a small competency that saved him from giving daily hours to business work" (as quoted in Estabrook 1916:vi). Estabrook reports that Dugdale paid for most of the Jukes investigation himself and at death left a small endowment for social research.

A frail, self-effacing bachelor, Dugdale devoted his adult years to social research and reform. In addition to "The Jukes," he produced Further Stud-

ies of Criminals (the two were published together in the 1877 volume) and sociological articles for the *Atlantic, North American Review,* and *Westminster Review.* His work for the prestigious Prison Association brought him into contact with leading New York State reformers, as did his later efforts for the New York Association for the Advancement of Science and the Arts, New York Social Science Society, New York Sociology Club, New York Liberal Club, and numerous other volunteer groups. Dugdale died on July 23, 1883, of the heart disease that had long afflicted him.

T HE JUKES" IS a pseudonym which was given to a numerous family living in Ulster County, N.Y., who came under the observation of the reader of this paper while making an official examination of the county jails in 1874, in behalf of the Prison Association of New York.

An account of these "Jukes" was embodied in a report and transmitted to the legislature, in which was reviewed the harlotry, illegitimacy, crime, pauperism, disease, and general social condition of the stock. In a revised form, it has since been reprinted, and created sufficient public interest to procure me the honor of an invitation to read the present paper on "Hereditary Pauperism, as illustrated in 'The Juke' Family"; which restricts me to the consideration of only one of the subjects set forth in the Prison Association Report.

When stated in abstract terms, the question I am called upon to treat involves an examination into the correlation which exists between physical, biological, and social phenomena. In discussing it, I am constrained by the terms of the inquiry to notice the difference of effects produced by causes which are constant, as compared to causes which are variable; to note the significance of effects which are constant, as compared to those which are mutable; and to bring adequate proof that a given effect is the result of a cause ascribed, or a given cause the necessary antecedent of an effect noted.

The first observation of hereditary transmission is as old as antiquity, and was purely empirical. It consisted in the recognition of resemblances between the features of parent and child, and occasionally eccentric traits. But when the physicians directed the inquiry in its relation to disease, and the breeders of cattle applied ascertained rules to produce or perpetuate a given quality in a given animal, so as to make it the characteristic of a stock, the study was conducted with a degree of zeal and exactness which established, beyond dispute, that heredity also transmits chronic constitutional affections, insanity, idiocy, disease, longevity, temperament, instinct, and passion.

But the doctrine of heredity has been pushed still further by those extremists who believe it is the preponderating factor in psychology, until it is claimed that genius, special intellectual aptitude, and recondite moral qualities are, of necessity, transmitted to posterity. It is here, more especially, that these extremists are met by those who claim that adaptation to environment by variation of characteristics is just as true as permanence of types, is quite as necessary to the preservation of life through countless ages, enters as much in the formation of human character, and accounts for certain phenomena more satisfactorily than does the doctrine of heredity. They urge that a knowledge of effects by no means necessarily leads to a knowledge of causes, and that for this reason the advocates of hereditary transmission endeavor to fortify their position by adducing doubtful analogies as a justification of their conclusions, if not as a form of proof. For instance, to say that because instinct in animals is transmitted, therefore subtle moral qualities are equally transmissible in human beings, is one of these unsound analogies; because there is a great difference in the effect of an invariable cause which persists unchanged for ages, and of a variable cause that fluctuates in intensity with successive generations. Instinct in the animal is a mode of action which has been fixed by the unchangeableness of the environment through countless generations, until the faculty has become an "eternal memory" which stimulates the automatic acts; while the human being, having the power to alter his environment, has produced such a variety of changes in that portion of it which relates to his social relations, that no fixedness of moral character could be established which would correspond to the automacy of instinct as found in the insect or the bird. Consequently, the human being is forced to have recourse to training to maintain in the child the kind of moral capacity found in the parent, which otherwise would reappear by pure entailment.

Believing that both heredity and variation are true, and that the issue between those who magnify either side relates to the limits of each, and the precedence in order of importance of the one over the other at alternate points, it seemed to me fortunate that I should find in the "Jukes" so many intermarriages within the degrees of first and second cousins that they approximate to what breeders call "breeding in and in," laying, so to speak, alongside of cases of crossing into other stocks, so that the results of homogeneous and heterogeneous causes could be contrasted, and community of parentage submitted to the test of diversity of environment.

I therefore grouped all the obtainable facts in the lineage according to the order of their occurrence, constructing genealogical charts, so as to make the facts comparable generation to generation, condition to condition, sequence with sequence. Thus were brought into relief the constant features that might be hereditary, and, perchance, the cause of this constancy; thus was noted the effect of environment, whether it could produce variation in the posterity, and of what kind and degree. I thus excluded artificial arrangement, accepting what came as it came, because this seemed to be the surest way to exclude preconceptions.

Sometime between 1740 and 1770, six sisters were born, who are the mothers of "the Jukes," from whom have sprung five generations of children, and to which is to be added another generation,—the father of the husbands of two of the Juke women,—so that our study covers seven generations of people.

To distinguish those persons who are directly descended from the blood of these five women from that of the persons they married, the former will be spoken of as "Juke blood" and the latter as "the X blood." In this way we can facilitate the study of heredity. Inasmuch as we have no knowledge of the posterity of one of the sisters, we will call the other five by names which begin with the first five letters of the alphabet,—"Ada," "Bell," "Clara," "Delia," "Effie." "Max" shall be the name given to the father of the two husbands who married respectively Effie and Delia Juke.

There have been tabulated, of the "Juke" and "X" stocks, 709 persons living and dead, 540 of them direct descendants of the "Juke" sisters, and 169 of the X blood. Besides these, about 125 more lives have been partially searched up, but have not been included in the tabulations, or arranged in the genealogical charts. In looking over these charts, upon which the entire present study is based, you will find lines of descent which are distinctively industrious, distinctively criminal, or distinctively pauperized. It is not claimed that because there is continuity of characteristics from generation to generation, therefore the features are hereditary, but it is one essential element in such proof the validity of which is to be established as respects pauperism.

With the Jukes crime preponderates in branches that spring from bastard stock, who have married into X; it favors the male lines of descent, and it is thirty times more frequent than in the community at large. Further, the criminal, as compared to the pauper, is more vigorous; "for very much of crime is the misdirection of faculty, and is amenable to discipline, while very much of pauperism is due to the absence of vital power, . . . which causes from generation to generation the successive extinction of capacity till death supervenes."*

* "The Jukes," 3d ed., p. 50. New York, G. P. Putnam's Sons.

If we follow the intermarried branches, we find a preponderance of girls and of pauperism, which latter prevails to a degree ranging from four to nine times more than for the State, as by the returns of the State Board of Charities for 1871.

The impudicity of "the Juke" women is twenty-nine times greater than that of the average of women, and, as a result, one fourth of the children are illegitimate, not a few of them being born during the imprisonment of the husband. It is further noticeable, that the families which contain criminal or pauper brothers are those in which occur prostitution among the sisters. Where the brothers are reputable and honest laborers, so, in the main, are the sisters chaste; and this relationship between brothers and sisters is so marked that we may affirm of "the Jukes" that prostitution in the woman is the analogue of crime and pauperism in the man.†

We have remarked that the law of heredity is much more firmly established in the domain of physiological and pathological conditions than it is as respects the transmission of intellectual and moral aptitudes. In proportion as we approach features which are moulded by education, they are less transmissible, and more completely governed by the laws of variation, which are largely referable to environment. For this reason, in estimating the significance of persistent social conditions, it is more safe to follow physiological traits as indices of heredity; and where these are found to be necessarily connected with moral, intellectual, or social phenomena, we shall have a firm foundation for asserting that hereditary entailment is the proximate cause of such phenomena.

If we compare the proportion of pauperism among the "Jukes" who are diseased to that among those who are healthy, we shall find that fifty-six out of a hundred of the diseased come under public charge, and only seventeen out of a hundred from among those who are healthy. From the computation of the diseased are excluded children who have died even of hereditary maladies, because such children have no significance as causes of pauperism; they are only effects and exemplars of it.

Out of these eighty-five cases of disease, only two are of tubercular consumption, although this county shows a larger proportionate death-rate from this cause than from any other. If we look at syphilis, however, we shall find forty-two cases of primary and twenty-five of constitutional, making sixty-seven out of eighty-five diseased persons, or seventy-nine per cent.—almost four-fifths. But although, by actual count, nearly eleven per cent. of the "Jukes" are blighted with this disease, I am informed by

† Id., p. 25.

some of the town physicians who have officially attended the poor for a number of years, that from twenty-five to thirty per cent. of the stock is thus tainted.

Significant as are these figures, they are weak as compared to the lesson which they teach, when we follow the ravages of this class of disorders from generation to generation, and see the harvest of death, of blight, and of suffering they leave in their course.

Now, we proceed, by citing instances, to determine how far disease has necessary relation to hereditary pauperism—if the continuity of the one depends upon the persistence of the other.

During the war of 1812, the oldest legitimate son of Ada Juke, whom we shall call Hans, became, at about twenty-five years of age, a volunteer in a regiment partly raised in Ulster, partly in Schoharie County. Following the regiment was a woman so notorious in her time, that she has left a traditional reputation of infamy in both counties which survives to this day. From her Hans contracted malignant syphilis. He was licentious in youth, and in after-life, indolent to a degree that he had to be driven in the harvest-field to get a day's work out of him. At forty-five, and again at fifty-two, he was in the poorhouse. When he died is not certain, but he probably did not survive his fifty-fifth year. This man married a "Juke" first cousin, and had eight legitimate children, seven of them girls, upon whom he entailed his disease, which, combined with the effects of the consanguinity of the parentage, seems to have produced marked social effects.

The youngest daughter by this marriage was a congenital idiot, and drifted into the poorhouse with her father. She stayed there eight years, and, though the records make no statement of her subsequent fate, she probably died there at sixteen years of age. The relation between a fixed pathological condition—syphilis—and a casual social one—pauperism—as seen in the father, becomes a correlation in the case of the daughter. We thus authenticate absolute hereditary pauperism, for syphilis is a cause of idiocy. The disease which pauperized the parent, and no doubt cut short his life, is entailed upon the daughter in a form so conspicuously blighting, that the statement of the case is also the proof that such pauperism is only the social aspect of physical degeneration; and, as it runs two generations before death cuts off the career, it is hereditary. As we have established heredity at this point, let us see if there are not indications of its presence elsewhere in the lineage.

The eldest daughter of Hans is weak-minded and blind, married to a man who is also weak-minded and blind, and she transmits, in the form of premature death, to six out of her eight children, the syphilis she has inherited in the form of imbecility and blindness; the vitality of her two surviving daughters being impaired. A boy, aged five, died in the poor-house; one of the surviving daughters received out-door relief; and the other, at seventeen, was sent for vagrancy to the poorhouse, where a bas-tard child was probably born. This daughter is smitten with syphilis, and has two illegitimate girls, whose fate I could not learn. Here inherited disease precedes, pauperism follows; only a generation is skipped, and that generation is itself gravitating to the poorhouse. I said a generation is skipped, but I forget, this third daughter of Ada's is a prostitute, which in the woman is the analogue of pauperism in the man. Then we have pauperism in that generation also; the only question to determine is, whether the licentiousness is hereditary. As a fact, we find it in every generation—the mother of the stock, Ada Juke; the son Hans; the granddaughter and her husband; the great-granddaughters, who are both punished for "vagrancy," which in these over-nice times is the offi-cial euphonism for prostitution; and the example survives for the great-great-granddaughters, unless they succumb to death. The sexual passion approaches to an instinct; it is more persistent in its entailment than is the sense of sight. In other words, it is organic, and therefore transmitted by inheritance more certainly than the pigment of the negro's skin. Chas-tity, on the other hand, calls for the exercise of will to keep the passion in subjection, and as the "Jukes" have put forth this kind of power very sparingly, chastity has not had the chance to become organized. Laziness is conspicuous in four generations, the fifth being too young to have de-veloped it. The environment of example runs parallel to and constantly attends the continuity of the social habits, and is contributive to their per-petuation. With licentiousness hereditary and wasting the energies, with such a disease entailed and slowly consuming the life, it is not too much to say that the slothful habits are due to an undervitalized condition, which is only deferred death; while at other points disease smites with a stronger hand, and makes a fool or makes an infant corpse, leaving the surviving progeny weak and crippled, capable only of bringing forth a pos-terity of dependents to recruit the procession of woe on its way to extinction.

The third daughter of Hans married a man who died of consumption in the poorhouse after being supported by the town for three years. Two of the four children of this cross between constitutional syphilis in the mother and consumption in the father died young, a surviving daughter becoming a prostitute. The mother then married her "Juke" cousin, who also died of consumption. There is reason to suspect constitutional syph-ilis in his case, for he had a sister so affected, and both himself and

brother were impotent, and consequently had no issue. Then she cohabited with a man who afterwards deserted her, by whom she had three illegitimate children, two of whom died in infancy or youth. The surviving
daughter grew up a prostitute, with acquired syphilis, and has twice attempted suicide. She has had two love-babes; and, although herself white,
one of these was a mulatto girl, who was born in the poorhouse, and died
of syphilis before her first year. Here again transmitted disease or
weakness mows down a portion of the children by premature death; those
who survive being weak and falling back upon public charity, in most
cases with the disease that vitiates their blood renewed by licentious
courses begun by the great-grandmother, Ada, continued unabated
through the subsequent generations, and carrying with them at every
step pauperism or its alternative—extinction.

Of the fourth daughter of Hans, I have no further information than that
she was a harlot before marriage, that she inherited constitutional syphilis, which seems to mark the track of its progress by the death of two
young children out of three.

The fifth daughter was a prostitute, living in her sister's brothels, with
acquired syphilis in addition to the constitutional form. She died at thirty-
nine, leaving three daughters, two of whom are harlots, the youngest child
being born in the poorhouse and adopted by people of fortune. Here we
have premature death, partly owing to inherited disease, producing
almshouse pauperism for the child, who is rescued by strangers. But for
this interposition, she might have grown up in the poorhouse, become the
mother of some pauper's idiotic bastard child, and so helped to make the
present example of hereditary pauperism more conspicuous.

The sixth daughter is also a prostitute, who was married to her "Juke"
cousin, but repudiated her marriage with him; she has three boys and
three girls, all illegitimate. Her boys are lazy and stupid, one of them almost imbecile, who will grow up into a pauper, for his intelligence is low
and his temperament stolid and sluggish.

In reviewing the lineage of Hans, we find a continuity in the licentiousness which is almost unbroken; all his daughters except two being prostitutes, one of these latter being debarred from this fate by her idiocy and
youth. Indeed, it is hereditary. In the next place, we find increasing under-
vitalization as we descend from generation to generation. Ada Juke was
healthy and strong, living to seventy years. Her son Hans died earlier,
probably fifty-five; he was weighted down with syphilis. Out of eight of his
children, one dies prematurely at sixteen, the others showing marks of
weakened constitution by blindness, imbecility, and choosing the prosti-

tute's career in preference to work; while of the grandchildren, over one-third, or thirteen out of thirty-eight, die either in infancy or childhood, the remainder being less vitalized than their parents.

If we could only get another case to contrast with this one, in which the sum of the ancestral traits are equal, but divested of the feature of disease and differing in fate, the case of Hans would then indeed be a lesson. Well, we have just such a contrast in Yope, the younger brother of Hans. There is community of paternity, being children of the same father and mother; there is equal consanguinity in marriage, both wedding "Juke" first cousins. These women were of good repute, and lived beyond their threescore years and ten. But Hans had the advantage over Yope of winning a wife whose mother, Clara Juke, was chaste; while Yope got a wife whose mother, Bell Juke, was a prostitute, having had four illegitimate children, three of them black. Both brothers fought in the same regiment and drew pensions; both were farm-laborers. Thus far the conditions of both sets of children are equal. But Yope had no syphilis coursing through his veins, and his children and grandchildren are free from inherited contamination. Neither is there prostitution in his posterity, nor almshouse. The out-door relief of his stock aggregates only four years in three generations. He acquired fourteen acres of land, and his eldest son five acres more. Out of twenty-six persons, in four generations, there are only five deaths (counting Yope, who was seventy-eight when he died), and one daughter who committed suicide at forty-four, being insane. Health, self-support, self-respect, longevity, flourish where disease is not, therefore pauperism and prostitution fail.

But these two examples do not prove your case? It is by accident that they are juxtaposed. Then it would be fortunate if we could find another instance to lay beside these two, with identity of origin, with pathological conditions similar to either, with social results equivalent.

Well, Ada Juke's fourth child, the sister of Hans, is this opportune example. We will call her Getty. She was a harlot, who married a mulatto of the X blood. Here we have a cross between two races who do not assimilate. This mulatto was lazy, licentious, and stricken with syphilis. I have been unable to learn at what age the disease was contracted, nor can I get positive proof that he entailed it upon his children, but I am told it is probable. This, however, is certain, every one of his children was licentious, two acquired syphilis, and their children died early. Every one of this sister's children received either out-door relief or resorted to the poorhouse; eight out of nineteen grandchildren have received public charity, and some of the rest, when old enough, will yet receive it, for they are licentious, lazy, and given to prostitution or stricken with syphilis. Out of twenty descendants who married or cohabited, six were barren; out of thirty-one descendants, five are known to have syphilis and probably twelve, which would be forty per cent.; and nine have died between the ages of infancy and thirty-seven, or nearly one-third. In addition to the disease, licentiousness, and sloth of the stock of Hans, we have in Getty's issue, a quadroon and octoroon progeny, who as a race are less robust than either of the pure races. The case of Hans is a well-established instance of the degeneration of disease, carrying with it pauperism because of undervitalization. That of the sister, less clearly marked as hereditary pauperism resulting from entailed disease, is an equally clear case of undervitalization caused by a cross of repugnant races, and inheritable for that reason. Of the same stock, lying between the two, and as if for the purposes of contrast, is Yope, in whom neither disease or race admixture deteriorates the posterity, and therefore absence of pauperism and its analogue prostitution.

I now turn to another branch, that of Effie. I have said that Max was born somewhere about the year 1720. He was irregular in his habits, had illegitimate children, and became blind in his old age, the blindness reappearing in his posterity even to the fifth generation. One of his sons, who was a thief, married Effie Juke, the sister of Ada. They had at least four children, but the posterity of only one daughter has been traced to the fifth generation, and it forms one of the most unbroken lines of almshouse and out-door pauperism in the "Juke" stock.

This daughter was a basket-maker, lazy, and has been in the poorhouse and received out-door relief. She married her cousin, of X blood, who was licentious and lazy. He died in the poorhouse at eighty-one. Seven children were their issue, four boys and three girls, every one of whom has been in the poorhouse or received out-door relief, and every boy imprisonment.

Unfortunately, with the exception of the eldest son Fritz, I have little account of these children and their posterity besides that of official records, which do not state what are their diseases or general habits. Fritz was sixty-four in 1874, a finely formed man, erect as an arrow, with a springing step and able-bodied. Nevertheless he has received eighteen years of out-door relief since he was thirty, he has been in the poorhouse, and has served a five years' sentence in state prison. For many years he has been a good church member, and accepts its charity with becoming meekness. His oldest son is illegitimate. By his first wife, who was a "Juke" second cousin, a quadroon, and syphilitic, he had another son, who died in hospital during the war. He has had five more children by his second wife, who is also his "Juke" second cousin afflicted with the same disease in the form of blindness. Of these seven children, five have been upon the town. I have seen Fritz, his eldest illegitimate son, and his youngest boy, inopportunely meet in the parlor of the poormaster, soliciting relief. The father was by far the most of a man of the three. The eldest son was also finely proportioned, but looked more infirm than his father, for he contracted syphilis at thirteen, and limps to this day with a foot which was then deformed by it. The youngest son was more intelligent and less apathetic; he was twenty-three in 1874, and at eighteen years of age had already received public charity.

In this line, I can find no evidence of inherited disease passing from generation to generation. The blindness of Max seems to have been entailed along the other lines of descent and not this one. The only characteristics that are constant are idleness and licentiousness. I cannot, therefore, affirm that the pauperism of this branch is from entailed disease. I cannot affirm that there is weakness in two of these men; they are conspicuously able-bodied. What, then, is the cause of the continuity of the pauper condition? It seems to me to be explainable only by the nature of the environment, geographical, industrial, and social. Briefly, to sum up this environment, I find Ulster County with inferior natural resources of soil, peopled with a poor population burdened by a heavy population of poor. Her laborers receive low wages because they possess little skill, and these wages are made less by the closing up in winter of many callings, while a high rate of local taxation decreases the purchasing power of their income. Add to these, a lax and lavish administration of the poor-laws, which invites dependence, and we have a number of concurring causes which produce a relative retardation of local prosperity that prevents the county from keeping abreast of other sections.

What is the process of social adaptation that has been proceeding for years in this population, and what are its causes and effects? The abundance of flagging-stone and veins of lime and cement rock, which is a rare mineral; the limitation of farming by the stubbornness of the soil; the abundance of timber and tan-bark in its mountains; the existence of a canal that transports coal to tide-water, determine what industries are most lucrative. These are quarrying, cement burning, hay farming, teaming, tanning, canalling, and lumbering; which occupations are mainly of the grade of common labor. They call for muscle-workers, who, because they are muscle-workers, do not organize intellectual functions, and therefore do not transmit them. The population that aspires to skilled or professional work must seek it abroad, and they immigrate. The rude laborers who are needed remain and multiply, and so a preponderance of that grade of population accumulates. The per capita wealth of the county is thus reduced by a double process,—the scattering of the enterprising members of the population; the concentration of those who have neither the disposition, the habit, or the power of saving. Upon this groundwork, in addition to it and at further removes, the closing of industries in winter produces other important social phenomena. It tends to stimulate licentiousness, because of idle time, for occupation is necessary to maintain chastity. It favors laziness as a mere habit, aside from the apathy of disease. The curtailment of wages causes want, which necessitates public charity. This latter soon enters as an element in politics, and becomes an instrument deliberately used to favor pauperism, charity being now thrust on some who otherwise would never ask. The habit of relying on public help in winter is soon claimed as a prescriptive right by the recipients because they vote the proper ticket, and then we have a machine which feeds the evils it was designed to cure.

So far, geographical and climatic causes produce a gradual social growth and organization which shape the fate and fix the status of the community in the industrial field, establish its economic grade, and partially determine its burden of taxation. This social growth seems to act as a "natural selection" of certain stocks which give local individuality to the county. It now remains to see in what other ways the process of social growth specially affects the "Jukes."

The uncommon licentiousness of the "Juke" stock excludes them from social recognition. The prudent housewife declines to harbor their boys as farm-help or their girls in domestic service, for fear of seeing her own children contaminated. Public opinion excludes some of the "Juke" children from the common schools. When they reach the marriageable age, the reputable will not take them "for better for worse," because they see no other alternative than worse. Thus "Juke" blood mingles with the blood of Juke, because it is derived from restricted stocks of Dutch extraction, unadmixed with foreign element, which causes such a breeding in and in that at last the fifth generation of Ada Juke brings forth a child who concentrates the blood of Ada once, Bell twice, and Clara thrice,—six times aggregating the "Juke" consanguinity. Another child in the sixth generation combines the bloods of Bell, Delia, and Effie once, and Clara twice, besides an intermarriage in the X blood, giving a cumulation of seven in the consanguinity; and in another child are commingled the bloods of Ada, Bell, and Clara once, and Effie twice, besides the X blood twice, an aggregate of eight. But these figures are below the truth, for some of the early intermarriages into X have been missed. Had they been fixed, we might, by the addition of a single generation, have a breeding in and in that would be marked by sixteen, or perhaps a higher number, in the consanguinity of the last generation. Here we have a remarkable unity of derivation in the stock, and where it is most close, there pauperism is most fixed. But the point I wish to emphasize is, that this consanguineous heredity is largely determined by social compulsion, exercised by the reputable spurning the stock. This social ostracism vents its contempt by employing the family name of the "Jukes" generically as a term of reproach.

What, then, can we affirm of the ascendancy of the geographical, industrial, and social environment just described? First, it masses a population of a homogeneous grade. Secondly, it compels consanguineous unions within restricted stocks of this selected population. These favor the cumulation and permanence of weakness, stolidity, or passion, and thus control and confirm the hereditary traits of the "Jukes." Thirdly, the hereditary traits thus compelled have produced a special home environment of example which has contributed to fix the heredity acquired. Lastly, society itself has an organic life with features of continuity in the form of customs. Lavish public charity becoming such a custom, it is manifest that certain families receiving help generation after generation will display a persistence of dependence identical in form to that produced by hereditary pauperism from physical degeneration, but entirely different in nature, and as easy to suppress as true hereditary pauperism is difficult to control.

In the lineage of Hans Juke, behold a consanguineous marriage compelled by social environment, coupled with a constitutional disease that produces pauperism and makes it hereditary. In the case of his sister, another instance of entailed pauperism rising from a cross of races, probably combined with disease; and in the next generation intermarriages caused by social thraldom and fastening the acquired traits. In the case of Yope Juke, we see the same social dominance compelling consanguineous union, but no disease transmitted, no race admixture, and in the next generation a cross of bloods in X. Here hereditary pauperism finds no place. Lastly, in the case of Fritz, we have an instance of induced pauperism stretching over several generations, because the organization of society keeps up a vicious mode of administering relief, and we have a case simulating hereditary pauperism, but only illustrating bad government.

In conclusion, let me say that several branches of the "Jukes" have moved away and settled in other States. They have thus left the organized environment peculiar to Ulster County, and lived for several generations transplanted on another soil. The marriages have been in other stocks, and the posterity relieved of the effects of breeding in and in. What changes have ensued would help settle which factor is most potent in forming human character, heredity or environment; and if both contribute, to what degree, and in what form; for we could make a comparison between those who have lived under continuous conditions in the old home and those who now live under altered circumstances in the new. I had hoped to make this addition, believing it better to have a complete study of one family than the partial observation of ten thousand promiscuous individuals; but the study stands still; for how long it will continue to do so, I know not.

What I have herein related, what I have elsewhere written, is purely tentative. The subject has great attractions: as science, because it links phenomena to phenomena, and reveals their laws; as philanthropy, because the knowledge of these laws may be used as a weapon to conquer the vice, the crime, the misery which the science investigates.

2

OSCAR C. MCCULLOCH

The Tribe of Ishmael: A Study in Social Degradation*

Preface

Inspired by Dugdale, the Reverend Oscar McCulloch began tracking members of the Ishmael tribe in 1877, the year *"The Jukes"* appeared in book form. Like Dugdale's "Hereditary Pauperism," with which he may also have been familiar, McCulloch's study traces pauperism through multiple generations. Its grisly central metaphor compares the pauper class to an aquatic parasite which, though a "free swimmer" in youth, reverts to lower form and leads a life of dependency "until there is left a shapeless mass, with only the stomach and organs of reproduction left." This direct projection of a popular understanding of evolution onto society qualifies McCulloch's report as the most purely social Darwinist of all the family studies.

McCulloch selects two families to illustrate how his adopted state of Indiana became encumbered by such throwbacks. The first, engendered by one John and a half-breed woman, came to Indiana about 1840 and produced innumerable examples of criminality, disease, intermarriage, laziness, licentiousness, mental weakness, pauperism, premature death, and vagabondage. The second, the Owenses, descended upon Indiana about 1850 with similar results, including a most peculiar son in the third generation who "had a penitentiary record, and died of delirium tremens and went to the medical college" (p. 51). These two are typical of 30 families, on whom McCulloch has a total of 1,692 histories; and the 30 are typical of 250 families, numbering "over five thousand, interwoven by descent and marriage. They underrun society like devil-grass. Pick up one, and the whole five thousand would be drawn up" (p. 52). By the end of his report McCulloch is speaking less of a group of families than of the poor in general, beggars and swill-gatherers who collectively leave no fewer than six stillborn children in the sinks of Indianapolis each week.

For "perpetuation of this misery" McCulloch blames misguided charity. "Public relief . . . is chargeable in a large degree," along with the "so-called charitable people who give to begging children and women with baskets." He knows from personal experience that charity is not the answer. "I have tried again and again to lift them, but they sink back." Not alms but "counsel, time, and patience," he concludes somewhat vaguely, will "rescue such as these" (p. 54).

Biographical information on McCulloch appears in the memoir that prefaces *The Open Door*, a collection of his sermons and prayers (n.a., 1892) and

* Originally published in Conference of Charities and Correction, *Proceedings 1888:* 154–59.

in Ruth McCulloch's history of the Indianapolis Plymouth Church (1911). Born in 1843 at Fremont, Ohio, McCulloch left school at the age of fifteen to become a clerk in his father's drugstore. Later he worked out of Chicago as a traveling salesman for a wholesale drug distributor. Drawn by more spiritual concerns, at the age of twenty-four McCulloch enrolled at the Chicago Theological Seminary, thereafter moving to Sheboygan, Wisconsin, for his first pastorate. In 1877 he moved again, to Indianapolis, where over the rest of his life he developed the faltering Plymouth Church into a center of religious, educational, and charitable activity.

Indeed—the message of "The Tribe of Ishmael" notwithstanding—charity work was one of McCulloch's major interests. The lower floor of the church he helped his congregation build housed offices of the Indianapolis Benevolent Society, of which he was president from 1879 to 1891, and of the local Charity Organization Society, which he helped organize in 1880. Under his guidance these societies coordinated the distribution of relief, an effort that inevitably led to the recording and investigation of "every case of need" (McCulloch 1911:97)—and to accumulation of data for his family study. In 1891 McCulloch served as president and host of the annual meeting of the National Conference of Charities and Correction. He traveled to Europe to recover from that exertion but cut the trip short, returned to Indianapolis to preach a final sermon, and died in December of 1891.

THE STUDIES OF Ray Lankaster into "Degeneration" are not only interesting to the student of physical science, but suggestive to the student of social science.

He takes a minute organism which is found attached to the body of the hermit crab. It has a kidney-bean-shaped body, with a bunch of rootlike processes through which it sucks the living tissues of the crab. It is known as the Sacculina. It is a crustacean which has left the free, independent life common to its family, and is living as a parasite, or pauper. The young have the Nauplius form belonging to all crustacea: it is a free swimmer. But very soon after birth a change comes over it. It attaches itself to the crab, loses the characteristics of the higher class, and becomes degraded in form and function. An irresistible hereditary tendency seizes upon it, and it succumbs. A hereditary tendency I say, because some remote ancestor left its independent, self-helpful life, and began a parasitic, or pauper, life. Not using its organs for self-help, they one by one have disappeared,—legs and other members,—until there is left a shapeless mass, with only the stomach and organs of reproduction left. This tendency to parasitism was transmitted to its descendants, until there is set up an irresistible hereditary tendency; and the Sacculina stands in nature as a type of degradation through parasitism, or pauperism.

I propose to trace the history of similar degradation in man. It is no pleasant study, but it may be relied upon as fact. It is no isolated case. In all probability, similar study would show similar results in any of our States. It resembles the study of Dr. Dugdale into the Jukes, and was suggested by that. It extends, however, over a larger field, comprising over two hundred and fifty known families, thirty of which have been taken out as typical cases, and diagramed here.* The name, "the tribe of Ishmael," is given because that is the name of the central, the oldest, and the most widely ramified family.

In the late fall of 1877, I visited a case of extreme destitution. There were gathered in one room, without fire, an old blind woman, a man, his wife and one child, his sister and two children. A half-bed was all the furnishing. No chair, table, or cooking utensils. I provided for their immediate wants, and then looked into the records of the township trustee. I found that I had touched a family known as the Ishmaels, which had a pauper history of several generations, and so intermarried with others as to form a pauper ganglion of several hundreds. At the Conference at Cleveland, I reported this case. The investigations have since been extended. Year by year the record has grown. Historical data of two hundred and fifty families have been gathered, and on the accompanying diagram thirty families are traced. This diagram is prepared by Mrs. Kate F. Parker, registrar of the Charity Organization Society, and Mr. Frank Wright, detailed by the county commissioners to assist in the prosecution of this investigation. The number of families here studied is thirty. Of these, only two are known before 1840. They are found here at that time.

The central family—that which gives its name to the tribe of Ishmael—first appears in Indianapolis about 1840. The original family stem, of which we have scant records as far back as 1790, is then in Kentucky, having come from Maryland, through Pennsylvania. Ben Ishmael had eight children,—five sons and three daughters. Some of the descendants are now living in Kentucky, and are prosperous, well-regarded citizens. One son named John married a half-breed woman, and came into Marion County, Indiana, about 1840. He was diseased, and could go no further. He had seven children, of whom two were left in Kentucky, one is lost sight of, and one remained unmarried. The remaining three sons married three sisters from a pauper family named Smith. These had children, of whom fourteen lived; and thirteen raised families, having sixty children, of whom thirty are now living in the fifth generation.

Since 1840, this family has had a pauper record. They have been in the almshouse, the House of Refuge, the Woman's Reformatory, the penitentiaries, and have received continuous aid from the township. They are in-

* The original of the text included no diagrams.—Ed.

termarried with the other members of this group, as you may see by the marriage lines, and with two hundred and fifty other families. In this family history are murders, a large number of illegitimacies and of prostitutes. They are generally diseased. The children die young. They live by petty stealing, begging, ash-gathering. In summer they "gypsy," or travel in wagons east or west. We hear of them in Illinois about Decatur, and in Ohio about Columbus. In the fall they return. They have been known to live in hollow trees on the river-bottoms or in empty houses. Strangely enough, they are not intemperate.

In this sketch, three things will be evident: First, the wandering blood from the half-breed mother, in the second generation the poison and the passion that probably came with her. Second, the licentiousness which characterizes all the men and women, and the diseased and physically weakened condition. From this result mental weakness, general incapacity, and unfitness for hard work. And, third, this condition is met by the benevolent public with almost unlimited public and private aid, thus encouraging them in this idle, wandering life, and in the propagation of similarly disposed children.

A second typical case is that of the Owens family, also from Kentucky. There were originally four children, of whom two have been traced, William and Brook. William had three children, who raised pauper families. Brook had a son John, who was a Presbyterian minister. He raised a family of fourteen illegitimate children. Ten of these came to Indiana, and their pauper record begins about 1850. Of the ten, three raised illegitimate families in the fourth generation; and, of these, two daughters and a son have illegitimate children in the fifth generation.

Returning to William, we have a pauper succession of three families. One son of the third generation died in the penitentiary; his two sons have been in the penitentiary; a daughter was a prostitute, with an illegitimate child. Another son in the third generation had a penitentiary record, and died of delirium tremens and went to the medical college. There have been several murders; a continuous pauper and criminal record. An illegitimate, half-breed Canadian woman enters this family. There is much prostitution, but little intemperance.

I take these two cases as typical. I could have taken any other one of the thirty; or, indeed, I could have worked out a diagram of two hundred and fifty families as minutely as these.

Returning now to the record, let me call your attention to the following: We start at some unknown date with thirty families. These came mostly from Kentucky, Tennessee, and North Carolina. Of the first generation,—of sixty individuals,—we know certainly of only three. In the second generation, we have the history of eighty-four. In the third generation, we have the history of two hundred and seventy-five. In the fourth generation,—1840–1860,—we have the history of six hundred and twenty-two. In the fifth generation,—1860–1880,—we have the history of six hundred and fifty-one. In the sixth generation,—1880–1890,—we have the history of fifty-seven. Here is a total of 1,692 individuals. Before the fourth generation,—from 1840 to 1860,—we have but scant records. Our more complete data begin with the fourth generation, and the following are valuable. We know of one hundred and twenty-one prostitutes. The criminal record is very large,—petty thieving, larcenies, chiefly. There have been a number of murders. The records of the city hospital show that—taking out surgical cases, acute general diseases, and cases outside the city—seventy-five per cent. of the cases treated are from this class. The number of illegitimacies is very great. The Board of Health reports that an estimate of still-born children found in sinks, etc., would be not less than six per week. Deaths are frequent, and chiefly among children. The suffering of the children must be great. The people have no occupation. They gather swill or ashes; the women beg, and send the children around to beg; they make their eyes sore with vitriol. In my own experience, I have seen three generations of beggars among them. I have not time here to go into details, some loathsome, all pitiful. I was with a great-grandmother on her death-bed. She had been taken sick on the annual gypsying; deserted at a little town because sick; shipped into the city; sent to the county asylum; at last brought to the miserable home to die. One evening I was called to marry a couple. I found them in one small room, with two beds. In all, eleven people lived in it. The bride was dressing, the groom washing. Another member of the family filled a coal-oil lamp while burning. The groom offered to haul ashes for the fee. I made a present to the bride. Soon after, I asked one of the family how they were getting on. "Oh, Elisha don't live with her any more." "Why?" "Her other husband came back, and she went to him. That made Elisha mad, and he left her." Elisha died in the pest-house. A mother and two girls, present that night, were killed by the cars.

All these are grim facts; but they are facts, and can be verified. More: they are but thirty families out of a possible two hundred and fifty. The individuals already traced are over five thousand, interwoven by descent and marriage. They underrun society like devil-grass. Pick up one, and the whole five thousand would be drawn up. Over seven thousand pages of history are now on file in the Charity Organization Society.

A few deductions from these data are offered for your consideration. First, this is a study into social degeneration, or degradation, which is similar to that sketched by Dr. Lankaster. As in the lower orders, so in society we have parasitism, or social degradation. There is reason to believe that some of this comes from the old convict stock which England threw into this country in the seventeenth century. We find the wandering tendency so marked in the case of the "Cracker" and the "Pike" here. "Movin' on." There is scarcely a day that the wagons are not to be seen on our streets; cur dogs; tow-headed children. They camp outside the city, and then beg. Two families, as I write, have come by, moving from north to south, and from east to west. "Hunting work"; and yet we can give work to a thousand men on our gas-trenches.

Next, note the general unchastity that characterizes this class. The prostitution and illegitimacy are large, the tendency shows itself in incests, and relations lower than the animals go. This is due to a depravation of nature, to crowded conditions, to absence of decencies and cleanliness. It is an animal reversion, which can be paralleled in lower animals. This physical depravity is followed by physical weakness. Out of this come the frequent deaths, the still-born children, and the general incapacity to endure hard work or bad climate. They cannot work hard, and break down early. They then appear in the county asylum, the city hospital, and the township trustee's office.

Third, note the force of heredity. Each child tends to the same life, reverts when taken out.

And, lastly, note the influence of the great factor, public relief. Since 1840, relief has been given to them. At that time, we find that "old E. Huggins" applied to have his wife Barthenia sent to the poorhouse. A premium was then paid for idleness and wandering. The amount paid by the township for public relief varies, rising as high as $90,000 in 1876, sinking in 1878 to $7,000, and ranging with the different trustees from $7,000 to $22,000 per year. Of this amount, fully three-fourths have gone to this class. Public relief, then, is chargeable in a large degree with the perpetuation of this stock. The township trustee is practically unlimited in his powers. He can give as much as he sees fit. As the office is a political one, about the time of nomination and election the amounts increase largely. The political bosses favor this, and use it,—now in the interest of the Republican, now of the Democratic party. It thus becomes a corruption fund of the worst kind.

What the township trustee fails to do, private benevolence supplements. The so-called charitable people who give to begging children and women with baskets have a vast sin to answer for. It is from them that this pauper element gets its consent to exist. Charity—falsely so called—covers a multitude of sins, and sends the pauper out with the benediction,

"Be fruitful and multiply." Such charity has made this element, has brought children to the birth, and insured them a life of misery, cold, hunger, sickness. So-called charity joins public relief in producing still-born children, raising prostitutes, and educating criminals.

Some persons think it hard that we say to the public, Give no relief to men or boys asking for food, to women begging, to children with baskets, ill-clad, wasted, and wan. "I can't resist the appeal of a child," they say.

Do you know what this means? It means the perpetuation of this misery. It means condemning to a life of hunger and want and exposure these children. It means the education of the street, the after life of vice and crime. Two little boys sell flowers at the doors of church and theatre. They ring bells at night, asking to get warm. Seemingly kind people give them money. They are children of parents who could, if they would, earn enough to support them in comfort. Your kindness keeps them out in the cold. Your own children are warm in bed. They ought to be, but your cruel kindness forces them out in the street. So you are to be made a party to this? You remember the story of Hugo's, "The Man who Laughs,"—the boy deformed for the sake of the profit it would be? So with these children. They are kept in a life of pain, shut in to misery by the alms of cruel-kind people. And this is why our Charity Organization Society ask you not to give alms, but to give counsel, time, and patience to rescue such as these.

Do any of these get out of the festering mass? Of this whole number, I know of but one who has escaped, and is to-day an honorable man. I have tried again and again to lift them, but they sink back. They are a decaying stock; they cannot longer live self-dependent. The children reappear with the old basket. The girl begins the life of prostitution, and is soon seen with her own illegitimate child. The young of the Sacculina at first have the Nauplius form common to their order. Then the force of inherited parasitism compels them to fasten themselves to the hermit crab. The free-swimming legs and the disused organs disappear. So we have the same in the pauper. Self-help disappears. All the organs and powers that belong to the free life disappear, and there are left only the tendency to parasitism and the debasement of the reproductive tendency. These are not tramps, as we know tramps, nor poor, but paupers.

What can we do? First, we must close up official out-door relief. Second, we must check private and indiscriminate benevolence, or charity, falsely so called. Third, we must get hold of the children.

3

FRANK W. BLACKMAR
The Smoky Pilgrims*

Preface

Frank Blackmar regarded his study as a contribution to the Juke–Ishmael tradition, claiming that the Smoky Pilgrim "family, or tribe, though much smaller, resembles" the other two (p. 59). Like Dugdale's "Hereditary Pauperism" and McCulloch's "Tribe of Ishmael," this study focuses on "pauper characteristics"; and like his two predecessors, Blackmar had direct contact with living family members. In this case, however, such contact was the author's sole source of information.

Compared to the Jukes and Ishmaels, the Smoky Pilgrims were a small family indeed. Blackmar describes it as "now numbering ten persons," hinting that he has knowledge of others, but gives information only on the current clan. The discussion is organized around the family's two "habitations," perhaps to give an impression of different family strains. In fact, the Smoky Pilgrims consisted of three generations of one family so tightly knit as to "pass daily to and fro" between the two homes. Blackmar blames the small size of his sample and his "meager records" on the family itself: "Only those who have had dealings with this class of people know how difficult it has been to ascertain this much truth" (p. 64).

Blackmar's lengthy introduction establishes two themes. The first, with a kind of inverted patriotism, holds that large eastern cities have no monopoly on "social corruption." A resident of Lawrence, Kansas, which evidently was the setting for this study, the author argued that rural areas of "the great West" have their "own social evils." Conditions in the West actually encourage development of "the tramp family" because the strongest desert the country for the city, leaving behind "a social residuum" that cannot compete in the struggle for existence.

Blackmar's second theme concerns the need to intensify social control in rural areas, where isolation, monotony, and lack of supervision encourage "pauper and criminal characteristics [to] develop quite rapidly." More stringent restrictions, especially on loutish country boys who are "permitted to run at large," will raise the level of morality. Reading "The Smoky Pilgrims," one gets the decided impression that its professorial author had at some point been humiliated by rough youths of the region to which he was, clearly, very much attached. Blackmar demands, in an argument unintegrated with the genealogical part of his study, that such boys be brought under much tighter discipline.

Despite its hereditarian overtones, "The Smoky Pilgrims" concludes by advocating environmental solutions, specifically extensive institutionali-

* Originally published in *American Journal of Sociology* 2 (January 1897): 485–500.

zation. "The adults should be sent to the county poor farm and there be forced to earn a living. . . . The older children should be sent to the reform school," irrespective of whether they have committed specific offenses (pp. 64–65). Very young children should be placed in foster homes— even little"M——," whose family has gone to great trouble to keep her in school. In Blackmar's view, placement "in a good home" is the only hope for turning"M——"into a respectable woman (p. 63). Unlike later family study authors who recommend institutionalization as a means to prevent reproduction, Blackmar favors it for its power to encourage self-restraint and teach Smoky Pilgrims higher ideals.

Born in Pennsylvania in 1854, Blackmar came from the modest, Anglo-Saxon background typical of family studies authors. His father, a farmer, had immigrated from Scotland; his mother's family, of Huguenot ancestry, had come to America in the eighteenth century. The youngest of ten children, Frank became a highly successful academic, teaching college-level mathematics, history, politics, and sociology. He received degrees from the Pennsylvania normal school at Edinboro (1874), California's University of the Pacific (1881), and Johns Hopkins (Ph.D., 1889), after which he went to the University of Kansas as professor of history and sociology. He served as dean of the graduate school at the University of Kansas from 1896 to 1922 and as president of the Kansas Conference of Social Work from 1900 to 1902. Blackmar published many articles and books on economics, education, and sociology before he died in 1931.

IT IS A POPULAR belief that large cities are the great centers of social corruption and the special causes of social degeneration, while rural districts and country towns are quite free from immoral influences. It is held that the tendency of social life in a large city is downward, and that of country life is upward. No doubt that the congregation of a large population in a city has a tendency to develop in a geometrical ratio certain criminal and pauper conditions which are in marked contrast to those of sparsely settled districts, where life moves less rapidly and overcrowding is less apparent. Yet the country has its own social evils and social residuum; for while an abundance of fresh air and sunshine may be in themselves redeeming features of social improvement, it takes something more than these to make a healthy social atmosphere. The limits of industry are as certain in the country as in the city, and if more seek labor than are able to find it there is a clear case of economic over-crowding. While this over-crowding is less marked, a man without a place in the world is as much crowded out when the broad fields are before him as in the large city, amidst the rush of hurrying industry. While the country has some advantages over the city in respect to the condition of the poor and unfortunate, it may appear after all that social degeneration in the country, if not quite in proportion to the decline in large cities, according to the population, moves with accelerating ratio.

In support of this suggestion it must be understood that the country has been constantly supplying the city with much of its best material, and thus building up the city population at its own expense. The population that joins the march to the city is upon the whole of superior character, while the vicious that go are comparatively few. The popular notion that all rogues go to London is not to be followed by the supposition that the country is the chief source of supply for city criminality and pauperism. The thorough investigation of Mr. Charles Booth, in London, shows that the country population is quite free from criminal conditions and characteristics for the first generation, and that it is only in the second generation, under the influences of bad economic and social conditions in which the fierce struggle for existence occurs, that social deterioration is noticeable.

In the peopling of the great West this struggle for existence, and, indeed, for place and position, has always been observable among the poorly equipped for life. There have marched, side by side, in the conquest of the West, the strongest, most energetic, and the best, along with the vicious, idle, and weak; in fact, with the worst of the race. The movement of populations always carries with it a social residuum. The constant shifting of population and of conditions tends to increase and make permanent this helpless class. While the pulsating life of the city may feel more quickly the evil results of a sudden economic change, the country is not free from its evil influences. As a rule the food supply is not lacking in the country, and seldom it is that people suffer from hunger; but the weakening conditions are there. Many suffer from under-vitalization and lack of proper sanitation. The weakening tendency of isolation and monotony is as evident as are the effects of urban over-crowding.

If the city has its paupers and criminals, the country has its tramps and vagabonds. The tramp has become a perpetual hanger-on of town and country life. As a rule he likes the city environs best, but he can be found everywhere. The tramp family is of comparatively recent development. Everywhere in the West may be seen the covered wagon drawn by poor horses and conveying from place to place a family group that lives chiefly by begging and by what it can pick up along the way. This is a different species from the family of movers that travels from place to place with a definite purpose; although the former class may be said to have come from the latter. They are a product of the method of settlement of the West. Moving on and on, with ever repeated failures, they are finally outclassed in the race for land, and lose place in the ranks of self-support.

The towns and villages of the country all have their pauper families, which demand the constant care of the benevolently disposed to keep them supplied with food and clothing. Here, as in the city, indiscriminate charity and the lack of proper administration of local government tend to increase the pauper conditions. Hence it is easy for a pauper family to fasten itself upon a rural community, without hope of doing better, and with no other intention than to be fed and cared for by their neighbors. These pauper and semi-pauper families are found in every village, and, their life being largely without restraint, pauper and criminal characteristics develop quite rapidly. Just as typhoid and malarial fevers prevail to a greater extent in small towns than in large cities, on account of the difference in the care exercised for sanitary and health measures, so under the loosely constructed governments of western villages pauperism tends to flourish. This lack of positive preventive measures or checks in the loose government of a small town has its results in the growth of immorality among the boys, if they are permitted to run at large. Thousands of children having the freedom of the street grow up in idleness and viciousness. This could be readily remedied, and in some cases is, by proper restrictions, in the place of reliance upon the safety of a small town.

The farm is always considered the ideal place to rear a family. Perhaps the ideal farm is the best place for a family to be reared, but here, as elsewhere, we find the good mingled with the evil. The farm life has its dangers as well as the city. The isolated life, bad economic conditions, and the morbid states that arise therefrom bring about insanity and immorality. The farm hands are, many of them, substantial boys from neighboring families. But many of them form a group of irregular workers of a vile nature. The lack of variety in life, the little time to be devoted to books and papers, and the destruction of all taste for the same bring the mind to a low status. Their spare time on the farm and when out of employment is spent in telling obscene stories, in which perpetual lying is necessary to keep up a variety in the conversation, and the use of vile language is habitual. All this tends to weakness of mind and the decline of bodily vigor and health. The youth who is so unfortunate as to listen to all this, and to be associated with such characters, is in danger of having his imagination polluted and his standard of life degraded. The crowd that gathers at the corner grocery may be of a different type from the city hoodlum, and less dangerous in some ways, but as a type of social degeneration it is little above imbecility itself. Its weakness and wickedness are evident. With ideals of life destroyed or of a very low grade, with the imagination polluted, with nothing elevating or moral for consideration, social degeneration may proceed as rapidly in the small town as in a large city where the ceaseless activity of life at least sharpens the wits of individuals and keeps them from stagnation. When boys come under these evil influences in the country their minds are vitiated by the contact, and their whole lives become modified thereby. These evidences show that the country has its dangers as well as the city.

Further consideration of these conditions is reserved for another paper. The present article is concerned with a single family group, that of a pauper family which has fastened itself upon a small town. The family, or tribe, though much smaller, resembles somewhat that of "The Jukes" or the "Tribe of Ishmael." It may be an extreme case, but is similar to a group of families found in nearly every town and village. It is characterized and classified as the family of decided pauper characteristics and weak criminal tendencies. It gives the same lessons in social degeneration which are enforced by the larger families alluded to above. It has been thought best to follow in detail the life and character of this group, rather than to attempt wider generalization of the subject of rural pauperism and criminality.

HABITATIONS.

In a sparsely settled portion of L———, Kansas, dwells, or stays, a family for more than twenty years well known to the benevolent people of the town. The house is made of loose boards and scraps of tin and sheet iron rudely patched together. In summer it is a hot and uncomfortable shed, in winter a cold and dreary hut. The main room or living room, 14 x 16, contains a meager supply of scanty furniture and soiled and even filthy bedding. A small shed or "lean-to" attached to this room serves as kitchen, storeroom and chicken house. One small window allows the light to show the scanty furniture of the room and to exhibit its untidy appearance. The walls of the room are decorated with cheap pictures and bits of bright-colored papers. Among the larger pictures is that of Abraham Lincoln, which makes one pause for reflection, as his benign countenance beams upon the observer in these unpleasant surroundings. This small house is, or rather was until the number was increased as stated below, the home of seven individuals. For the use of the land on which the house stands they pay a nominal rental of twenty-five cents per month.

Another habitation used by a branch of the family is situated on P——— street. It is a board house of a single room 12 x 14, which is the home of three persons. This single room serves as living room, sleeping and cooking room, and for the entertainment of guests. The same scanty and cheap furniture is here as in the other habitation, and squalor and filth abound. The evidences of poverty and wretchedness characterize the surroundings. The rental paid for this habitation is $1.25 per month. It protects from the heat of summer and the cold of winter somewhat better than does habitation No. 1, but otherwise it has much the same appearance in the interior. The difference in rent is an economic problem not completely solved. There is no drainage connection with either habitation, and no water supply. But of water the occupants apparently have little need. Between these two homes the various members of the two families pass daily to and fro.

FAMILY GROUPS.

To the family, now numbering but ten persons, living in these two habitations the name "Smoky Pilgrims" has been given; chiefly on account of their dusky color and their smoky and begrimed appearance. Possibly the sickly yellow color, on account of the Negro blood in the veins of part of the family, may have suggested the name. By this name they are known to the people of the town. They represent a family or tribal group with loose habits of family association. They are known as people seeking odd jobs of work, with an air of fear lest possibly they may find them; as petty thieves, beggars, in part as prostitutes, and in general as shiftless, helpless, and beyond hope of reform. The mother of the tribe, who is of German or Dutch descent, was born in Ohio. When about sixteen years of age she married and with her husband lived on a small farm near Columbus. Four children were born to them. Unfortunately when the youngest child was a small boy the husband and father died, leaving the mother to struggle against fate in a world of burdens. The home was sold to pay funeral expenses and the mother, perhaps unwisely, started "west" with her children, having in all about $100 in cash as a representative of all her worldly possessions. By some means they reached the town of L——, where they have since remained, being absent at times for short intervals only. Here they have never been able to improve their economic condition and have gradually descended in the social scale.

The family is divided into three groups. The oldest girl married a colored man and lives with her husband and several children in the country on a farm. They live respectable and industrious lives so far as is known, and consequently are not to be included in this discussion. In habitation No. 1 live, with the mother of the tribe, her second daughter and four children, and her only son. In habitation No. 2 live the third daughter and her two children. These families visit back and forth every day and are very sociable. Indeed, sociability is one of the chief characteristics of the entire tribe. They are much of the time on the street, and show to a great extent an aimless, easy-go-lucky life, irregular of food, sleep, and shelter.

PERSONAL CHARACTERISTICS.

The mother of the tribe, whom we will call "T——," has industrious habits and still retains industrious notions. She still has an idea of giving something in return for what she receives. Since coming to L—— she has worked at odd jobs, principally washing, housekeeping, and cleaning. At one time she was called to care for a sick woman who subsequently died. After the death "T——" took charge of the home and cared for the husband of the deceased and subsequently married him. He was shiftless and improvident, and finally died and was buried at the expense of the county. At another time "T——" found a home for a time at the county poor farm, but preferring her present mode of existence she left the home prepared for the needy. At present she is just recovering from protracted sickness, and is too weak for any work. It is pitiable to think of a person confined to a bed of sickness for months in such a rude hovel, but it is the life she prefers rather than the one which a county provides for her. Were the other members of the tribe as much inclined to industry as this one, there might be some hope of bringing them back into the ranks of industrial society. "T——" deplores her present condition and considers her life a chain of misfortunes.

In habitation No. 1 is "B——," the only man of the tribe, an easy-going, good-natured fellow, whose intellect seems to have been weakened by under-vitalization, laziness, idleness, and bad personal habits. While a strong intellect would not engage in the mode of life which he leads, the mode itself would weaken and degrade the strongest intellect. His eyes are weak, suspicious, and tell-tale. If he were to commit a crime or break the law it would be difficult for him to conceal it. He walks with a weak, shambling, doubtful gait. His very demeanor says that he has not a place in the world. His physical characteristics show persistent deterioration and a constant evolution downwards. He works but a trifle, steals a little, begs a little; but as none of these occupations are pursued with any vigor or determination, he does comparatively little harm to the community. He might work a little if he could be induced to try, but the person who employed him would probably have a bad bargain. With poor physical structure, weakened mental condition, laziness, and shiftlessness becoming a disease, what chance is there for any reform in such a person? About all that can be said is that some day he will die and be buried and not be missed by the body of toilers.

The eldest daughter, "A——," is between thirty-six and forty years of age. Like "B——" she shows marked weakness of character, with low order of physical structure, decidedly weak mentality, and lack of energy of any kind. She constitutes an organization of low order due rather to habits of life and social environment than to natal characteristics. Her face is ugly and repulsive, and her whole demeanor shows under-vitalization and degeneration on account of her mode of life. Some years ago she married a colored man named "B——," who subsequently died. She has four children, one white and three colored, each one having a different father. The oldest was born a long time before her marriage. The woman works a little, does considerable foraging and tramps the street much of the time, but is considered a harmless creature so far as social order is concerned. With her, as with all of the remainder, sexual relations are irregular.

"N——," the oldest son of "A——," is about eighteen years of age, and has a fair degree of physical strength. He is not much at home but remains most of the time in the portion of the town known as "the bad lands." Several times he has been apprehended for stealing. More recently he has done a little work. He has intellect enough and sufficient physical endurance to become a criminal if his mode of life is not changed. "N——" is supposed to be always "finding work."

"S——," the second child, is also a colored boy, about fourteen years of age. He is inclined to stupidity, but shows extreme good nature and is perfectly contented with a happy-go-lucky life. When questioned he shows a disposition to do something if he had a chance. But with a real test he is inclined to succumb to the influences of his home life. He has attended school but little and is now out "doin' nothin'," as he says. His schooling has been so irregular as to be of little service to him. Begging and idling in the streets is his occupation most of the time. His cousin goes with him to act as spokesman for the twain. They indulge in light pilfering and foraging, and have been before the police court for stealing.

The third child, "G——," is white and shows a degree of intelligence superior to the rest. With proper training he would make a bright, intelligent, and industrious boy. His eyes show lack of mental and moral strength, but not so great as to preclude the possibility of improvement. His father is the husband of "T——"'s sister. "G——," with the others, has been arrested for stealing small household utensils. With care he would make a good citizen, yet he has traits which if developed would make of him a dangerous criminal. At present he shows more of a disposition to attend school than formerly.

The fourth child, "M——," is a colored girl about seven or eight years of age. A bright appearing child, but dull in school and at everything requiring any direct mental effort. She, of all the children, bears the name of her mother's husband, although probably she is illegitimate. Special care has been taken to keep her in school, as she is the pet of the household. Day after day "B——" accompanies her to school and appears at the corner to await her return at the close of the session. If placed in a good home doubtless "M——" would make a respectable, self-supporting woman. There seems to be little hope for her unless something of this kind is done to remove her from the gypsy-like life of her family.

In the habitation No. 2 lives "M—— C——," the third daughter, aged about thirty-five, and her son "D——" and daughter "S——." The husband died about six years ago. "M—— C——" is a hard-featured woman given to dissipation. She shows a vigorous mental condition and is very talkative. She knows how to use her tongue in a manner frightful to the modest and the timid. She does a little work,—chiefly washing,—but obtains her chief support from an immoral life. It is quite remarkable how these people do bits of washing for others but seem never to practice it for themselves, for their clothing and personal appearance would seem to indicate that washing is one of the lost arts. "M—— C——" believes in religion(!) and at times attends the Free Methodist church. She is very communicative, although the information gained by the questioner is quite likely to prove an estimate of what she does not know. She shows a capacity for almost everything and is capable of being a much worse woman than she is. Drunkenness, disturbance of the peace, and prostitution are her known offenses against social order.

Of her two children "S——" is the elder and about twenty years of age. As a law-breaker she is the worst of the members of the tribe. She has been in jail several times for stealing and disturbing the peace. But her arrest is not thought desirable, as it only entails extra expense upon the city and accomplishes nothing, since fines are seldom paid. She spends most of her time upon the streets except when entertaining guests at home. Her features are regular, and if she kept herself tidy she would not be a bad-looking woman. But her career is downward, and it is only a matter of time when her life will end in destruction. Wretchedness and misery will be her future, while she is a menace to the town because of her evil deeds.*

The second child, "D——," is bright and interesting. Usually talkative and cheerful, at times he shows a morose disposition and tendency to quarrel with his companions. He is perfectly fearless and is the chief beg-

---

* Since these data were collected "S——" met a sudden death in T——. She had been on a drunken carousal and was taken suddenly ill and died. This broke up habitation No. 2 and increased the inmates of habitation No. 1 to nine.

gar of the lot. It appears quite impossible for him to tell the truth except by accident; it is his custom to tell what he thinks will please his listeners. There is a possibility of making a respectable man out of "D——" by proper training. He attends school quite regularly and makes a little progress, and on Sunday he attends a mission school at the courthouse. He nearly always appears to be perfectly happy, without a care in the world. If this happy disposition could be properly combined with his ability, possibly he would grow into a self-supporting man. He has within him more of the elements of self-support than the others. If these are rightly directed and applied, his character would yield to better influences.

Such are the meager records of this strange and irregular family. Only those who have had dealings with this class of people know how difficult it has been to ascertain this much truth. Only by approaches in every conceivable way, by different persons, and by carefully sifting the information and comparing notes, could anything definite be ascertained.† The lie is the only means of defense of weak people of this class, and they use it freely. After reviewing their chief traits the reader will readily characterize them as belonging to the pauper and weak criminal class. Not essentially vicious in their fundamental character, they have reached their present status in consequence of bad economic conditions. Once thrown into the struggle for existence on a low plane, they have adapted their lives to a standard which has developed pauper and criminal tendencies.

But why has this family been permitted to live in this manner? Primarily because they have been placed, on account of misfortune, and on account of conditions and characteristics, in a helpless condition. That they have been permitted to live in this condition in one of the most respectable, substantial, and moral towns of the land gives evidence of a lack of earnest effort or else of an exercise of misguided efforts on the part of citizens. In this particular case the facts show that both of these causes have been prominent. Much has been done by the good people of L—— to relieve the distress of the members of the tribe, and much has been done unconsciously to help them onward in the road to ruin.

It will appear evident that no reform of any permanent character can obtain in this tribe without a change in their present mode of habitation. The home must be improved or entirely broken up. It is impossible to reorganize a group of this kind so long as they live in dirty hovels and lead a semi-gypsy life. The adults should be sent to the county poor farm and there be forced to earn a living. Unfortunately this is not easy, on account of the loose methods of administration of county almshouses, and from

† Mr. Alonzo Bell and Miss Belle Spencer, students of sociology, have rendered valuable assistance in this investigation.

lack of compulsory acts to force unwilling inmates to remain. The older children should be sent to the reform school. This statement is met with two difficulties. The first, that a person can be committed to the Kansas reform school only upon sentence by the judge of a competent court on some specific charge. This is a difficult thing to obtain. Secondly, at present the reform school of Kansas is overcrowded, and if a person were committed he would be obliged to remain in a county jail until there was room for him. This would be worse than the present mode of existence, for our county jails are at present the most prolific breeders of crime in the land.‡

It is seen at once that families of this class, although not considered particularly dangerous to a community, are the most difficult to deal with, because they have no place in the social life, and it is very difficult to make a place for them. Their influence can be bad in a general way only. However, with the concerted action of citizens much could be done to relieve the situation. In fact, since this investigation began there are some marks of improvement in the children of this group. They have attended school more regularly and seem inclined to be free from thieving. But let it be repeated, better home influences, which means a breaking up of the family group, steady enforced employment until the habits of life are changed and become fixed, are indispensable means of permanent improvement. The difficulty of the task appears when we consider that these people must be taught not only to earn money but to spend it properly; they must be taught to change their ideals of life as well as their practices. The arts of civilization must begin from the foundation. The warp and the woof of the whole fabric must be constructed. Their desires for a better life are not sufficiently persistent to make a foundation for individual and social reform. How difficult the task to create new desires in the minds of people of this nature! Considered in themselves, from the standpoint of individual improvement, they seem scarcely worth saving. But from social considerations it is necessary to save such people, that society may be perpetuated. The principle of social evolution is to make the strong stronger that the purposes of social life may be conserved, but to do this the weak must be cared for or they will eventually destroy or counteract the efforts of the strong. We need social sanitation, which is the ultimate aim of the study of social pathology.

‡ Persons seeking the causes of increased criminality would do well to investigate the condition of the county jails.

4

GERTRUDE C. DAVENPORT
Hereditary Crime*

Preface

In "Hereditary Crime," the only family study of a European tribe to be published in the U.S., Gertrude Davenport summarizes a report published several years earlier[1] in German by Jörger, director of a Swiss insane asylum. Like Dugdale at the Ulster County jail, Jörger embarked on his research after noticing that many of the institution's inmates were related. He identified 310 members of the family, covering nine generations. To protect its "good" branches, Jörger renamed his clan the *Zeros* and their isolated Swiss village *Zand*. Unlike the other inhabitants of Zand, "the Zeros drank, wandered aimlessly from home, persisted in no occupation, and almost always married foreign women" (pp. 68–69).

Davenport discarded Jörger's title, "The Zero Family," in favor of "Hereditary Crime," thus presenting her report as a parallel to Dugdale's "Hereditary Pauperism." She conceives of the habitual criminal as a special breed of human, analogous to the racehorse as a special breed of horse ("They can no more help committing crime than the race horse can help going" [p. 70]). The title notwithstanding, the main defect of the Zeros was not crime but vagabondage. Their degenerative tendency also manifested itself in drunkenness, early death, illegitimacy, insanity, weak-mindedness, and such physical stigmata as crossed eyes, dwarfism, halting gait, pustules, and rickets, all said to be hereditary in origin.

In "Hereditary Crime" we find an early treatment of a concept that structures several family studies: the idea that mothers are more responsible than fathers in generating bad offspring. The family studies convey this notion by showing good and bad "lines" with the same father but different mothers. Good branches are produced by chaste, docile, and healthy mothers, whereas the bad branches proceed from women who are promiscuous or illegitimate or, as in this study, foreigners and "tainted with insanity." This theme appears in embryonic form in several passages of *"The Jukes."* Blackmar missed an opportunity to develop it in "The Smoky Pilgrims" by excluding a respectable branch from his study; he did not recognize the potential in comparing good with bad. Winship built *Jukes-Edwards* (1900) around a contrast of virtuous and worthless families, but as Goddard later observed (1923:52), Winship's comparison could prove little about heredity since "the two families were utterly independent, of different ancestral stock, reared in different communities." Not until Kite's "Two Brothers" and Goddard's *The Kallikaks* was the concept of maternal culpability completely developed. Both works focus on a single sire who heads two lines, one

---

* Originally published in *American Journal of Sociology* 13 (November 1907): 402–09.

[1] See Introduction, note 3.

growing out of a marriage to a monogamous wife, the other from liaison with a loose woman.

Although Davenport does not articulate the mother-blaming theme as fully as did Kite and Goddard, she carries it forward by tracing the Zeros' troubles to the union of Andreas Zero, a miller born in 1639, with Ida Olga Lauter, a blood relative and carrier of insanity. Their son Peter married a healthy, moral woman, thereby founding one of the family's two good branches. Their other son, Ernst, married twice: first a Lauter relative, thus starting "the vagabond and criminal branch"; second a better wife, giving rise to the other good branch. Men in the bad branch compounded its problems by constantly marrying foreign vagabonds. Thus the bad seed was planted by insane Ida Lauter and brought to flower by other evil women.

Davenport is of two minds about whether environmental factors contributed to the Zeros' downfall. She records Dr. Jörger's opinion on the influence of alcohol ("his whole account of them sounds like one vile tale of rum"). On the whole, however, Davenport is inclined to regard the Zeros as "outside the pale of beneficent environment." Yet, though more hereditarian than her forerunners, she does not go so far as to recommend the negative eugenics endorsed by later authors. Instead, Davenport expects nature to eliminate the Zeros, whose "physical weakness is becoming more pronounced with each generation and [whose] infant mortality is great" (p. 73).

Gertrude Davenport, née Crotty, was born in 1866 in Colorado—in a prairie schooner, according to several obituaries. Having received her B.S. from the University of Kansas in 1889, she enrolled in the Society for Collegiate Instruction of Women (now Radcliffe College) for five years of graduate work in zoology. There she produced *The Primitive Streak and Notochordal Canal in Cheloria* (1896) and met Charles B. Davenport, her zoology instructor and later her husband. After Charles became director of the Station for Experimental Evolution at Cold Spring Harbor, Long Island, in 1904, the Davenports bought land nearby and settled down. Gertrude helped Charles manage the station and, later, the affiliated Eugenics Record Office; edited his manuscripts (Davenport 1911:vi); taught courses; and published extensively, collaborating with her husband in research on the heredity of skin pigment, hair form, and eye color in humans and conducting her own research on sea-anemones and local flora. The couple's *Introduction to Zoology* (1900), a secondary school text, went through numerous editions. Kevles (1985:51) portrays Gertrude Davenport as an ambitious, strong-willed, and money-conscious woman. Long outliving her husband, she died in a nursing home in 1945 at the age of eighty.

MAGNIFICENT ARE THE scope and effectiveness of our organizations of charity, church, and state, for the repression of crime. They can cope, however, only with crimes that are the product of unfit environment by diminishing temptations or by strengthening the individual's inhibitions. But even if they should succeed in eradicating all such crimes there would still remain those committed by habitual criminals—criminals who are bred as race horses are bred, namely, by the process of assortive mating. Such are outside the pale of beneficent environment. They can no more help committing crime than race horses can help going. Precise information about these criminal breeds is hard to get; so much the more valuable, therefore, are the remarkable results obtained by Dr. Jörger, director of the Insane Asylum of Waldhaus-Chur in Switzerland.* Dr. Jörger noticed that the inmates of his institution very frequently bore the same family name. He marveled at this fact, the more so because it was the name of one of the most sturdy, sane, and respected families in the neighborhood. He was therefore led to make inquiry concerning the coincidence. His investigation showed indeed a blood relationship between the inmates of his institution and the respected family; but the respected family never furnished a single patient to his asylum. He found that the respected family descended in two lines, each of which maintained its integrity. Unfortunately there was a third line, the one that furnished not only all the inmates of that name to his institution but inmates to other kinds of state institutions. His full investigation disclosed such depths of degradation in the bad branch of the family that he has been constrained, out of consideration and respect for the good branches, to assume in his account of his researches a fictitious name for the family and for their dwelling-place. He has assumed these names, however, according to a code in order that the true names may be made known at some future time. The family, including both the good and the bad branches, he has called the Zero family and their dwelling-place Zand.

Zand is an isolated village in a Swiss valley. It consists of 700–800 inhabitants only. The ancestry of each and every family he has been able to trace back to the seventeenth century. The isolation of this village has preserved in its inhabitants' racial peculiarities in all their purity. The people of Zand are a branch of the German Walser colony. They are an industrious, economical, earnest, cautious, moral, and temperate people. Into many of their houses alcohol does not find its way year in and year out. They are either of medium height or tall of stature, and walk with the long stride of the mountaineer. Lack of pasture in season or the failure of other resources sometimes forces them out of the valley, but when affairs prosper with them their strong love of home brings them back again. They almost invariably marry women of their own valley and end an industrious life there—all of them except the Zeros. The Zeros drank, wandered

* Jörger, "Die Familie Zero," *Archiv für Rassen- und Gesellschafts-Biologie,* July–August, 1905.

aimlessly from home, persisted in no occupation, and almost always married foreign women. They usually returned home only when accompanied by police escort.

Dr. Jörger finds in the archives of the town that a Peter Zero was the chief magistrate in 1551, and later that a Eugene Zero held the same office. In 1727 a Carl Eugene Zero was baptized with rich and noble people as god-parents; hence he concludes that the family is one long native to Zand and one formerly held in high esteem there. Also he has been able to establish the fact that all the Zeros now living in Zand are descended from an Andreas Zero, a miller, born in 1639. Andreas married Ida Olga Lauter. This woman not only was a blood relative of her husband but her blood was tainted with insanity. She bore two sons, Peter and Ernst. Peter married Sina Frohmam, a woman from a healthy, moral, and sturdy family, and from them descended one of the two good branches of the Zeros, a branch so upright that it no longer enters into this story. The second son, Ernst, married twice. His first wife was a blood relative, a Lauter from the same family as his mother. Their son, Paul Alexius, was the founder of the vagabond and criminal branch. Ernst's second wife, Christina Scholler, bore a son Paul. Paul was an officeholder in Zand and married Ida Frohamt a relative of the Sina Froham from whom the first good branch descended. This marriage gave origin to the second good branch of the family, a branch that has no further connection with this narrative.

Paul A., the son of the first wife, was not only the product of two generations of blood relatives but of marriage for two generations with blood contaminated by insanity. Paul's character was one not without suspicion before his own marriage. But his physique was good, for he lived to be 106 years old. It seems probable that he was an itinerant kettle-mender. At any rate his wanderings led him to the Valle Fontana in Italy—a place long noted for its kettle-menders and venders, a people so notoriously disliked that an old decree of Zand forbade them to enter its boundaries. Paul married a woman of this place. No record of his wife's name can be found, and he himself died away from home. This marriage with a woman of wandering and vicious disposition is, according to the opinion of Dr. Jörger, the cause of the permanent downfall of this branch of the Zeros. The Lauter blood, despite its kinship with the Zeros and its insanity, he believes, cannot alone be responsible for the complete and lasting degradation of this branch, for the two good branches descended from the first union with it. These good branches numbered only one degenerate in all their lines of descent. This one will soon enter into our story. However much or little the Lauter blood may have contributed to the decline, the

---

† This name is spelled both Frohman and Froham in the original text.—Ed.

marriage of Paul Alexius with the Italian kettle-mender and of their son Paul Jos with a German vagabond settled the fate of this line. Paul Jos, born in 1722, was the only child of the Italian marriage. He led a vagabond life very similar to that of his father. His vagabond wife was from the Marcus family, a German family that has remained in vagabondage until today. This Olga Marcus gave birth to seven children, but so persistently did the parents wander that each child was born in a different place. The oldest was a girl; the remaining six were boys. These seven children were the parents of seven lines of degenerate Zeros. The rest of this story is an account of their children, grandchildren, great-grandchildren, and of a few great-great-grandchildren. Dr. Jörger has named them in succession Prima Zero to Sesto Zero.

Prima Zero, the daughter, married one of her Zero relatives of the first good strain. The man was well educated for his time and place, and during his early life was a teacher. He had degenerated, however, even before his marriage, into a confirmed drunkard and a consequent idler. He soon deserted his wife, who died early. Fortunately she had given birth to only two children, a son and a daughter. The daughter, with better instincts, voluntarily ran away from her father after the mother's death and was brought up in Swabia. She was a respectable woman, never married, and spent her entire life as a servant. Her only brother had different instincts. He grew up in the care of some of his vagabond relatives and could scarcely write his own name. He followed various occupations such as kettle-mending and basket-weaving. He was displeasing in appearance, weak-minded, and with very rudimentary moral conceptions. His wife was illiterate, vagabond, bold, and disreputable. Of their 8 children, 6 were vagabonds, 4 criminals (1 a murderer), 2 were drunkards, and 6 unlawful parents. These 8 children had borne 28 offspring up to 1903. Of these 10 were illegitimate, 6 vagabonds, 10 either weak-minded or idiotic, and 2 drunkards. Seven died in infancy or early childhood, and so were spared a worse fate. The 2 known great-grandchildren are illegitimate. One died the year of its birth. So much for the descendants of the daughter Prima Zero.

Secondo Zero, her oldest brother, married three times. His third wife was an Italian from the Valle Fontana. She bore him no children. On the whole, however, he chose better wives than was the custom of his kindred. His first wife bore one son; his second two, idiotic sons. All three were vagabonds. The eldest and youngest bore children, 8 each. Of these 16 children 4 were vagabonds, 1 was a drunkard, 2 were unlawful parents, 2 criminals, and 7 were mentally abnormal. The 17 great grandchildren number 2 unlawful parents, 1 criminal, 2 illegitimate, and 2 mentally abnormal. One of the five great-great-grandchildren is illegitimate.

Terzo Zero, the second brother, was the father of 7 children; 6 of them were vagabonds, 2 drunkards, 1 an unlawful parent, and 1 weak-minded. There were 12 grandchildren, 5 of whom were weak-minded, 2 drunkards, and 1 an unlawful parent. There are several dead great-grandchildren, 4 only are living, 2 of these are half-witted.

Quarto Zero, the third brother, married an Italian from Valle Fontana, who bore him 4 sons. Three of them were vagabonds and 1 was a drunkard. Of the 12 grandchildren, 4 were criminals, 5 unlawful parents, 2 drunkards, and 1 was weak-minded. There are 17 known great-grandchildren of whom 7 are illegitimate, 3 criminals, and 1 is an unlawful parent. All the known great-great-grandchildren, 4 in number, are illegitimate.

Quinto Zero, the fourth brother, was the parent of 2 vagabond sons who gave him 6 legitimate and 1 illegitimate grandchildren. Of these 4 were vagabonds, 1 was a drunkard and 1 an unlawful parent. Two of his 3 great-grandchildren are vagabonds.

Sesto Zero, the fifth brother, married twice and had 4 children, of whom 2 were idiotic and 2 vagabonds, 2 criminals, and 2 unlawful parents. The record of his grandchildren is no better, for 2 of them were illegitimate, 4 unlawful parents, 4 idiots, 6 vagabonds, and 2 criminals. There are 42 known great-grandchildren, 9 of whom are illegitimate and 7 idiotic. Twelve died in very early infancy. Of 13 neither the date of birth nor the fate are known to the investigator.

Settimo Zero, the sixth and youngest brother, was a drunkard. He is the father of 5 children, of whom 4 are vagabonds, 2 idiots, 2 unlawful parents, 1 is a murderer, and 1 a drunkard. These bore in all 16 offspring: of these grandchildren 2 are illegitimate, 8 vagabonds, 5 weak-minded, 5 unlawful parents, and 3 criminals. There are 22 great-grandchildren, 13 of whom are illegitimate, 6 weak-minded, 2 others not ordinarily bright, and 11 of them have already died.

In the foregoing categories it will be seen that the individual frequently appears in two or more classes. In all Dr. Jörger has investigated the characteristics of 310 persons, of whom 190 are still living. On account of the high percentage of illegitimacy many relationships have doubtless escaped his inquiry. Notwithstanding all difficulties he has been able to trace the genealogy of the family for nine generations. Many individuals of the last three generations are personally known to him.

External signs of degeneracy were early observable in the Zeros. They had a halting gait in contrast to the long stride of the other people of Zand. Their stature diminished until now very many of them are conspicuously dwarfed. For a very long time the people of Zand have recognized that these Zeros are different from themselves and that they are an element to be avoided. Strabismus and pustules on the face are a family characteristic of the Zeros. Indeed the frequency of cross-eyes was only rivaled by that of rickets. The Zeros, both from lack of desire and parental encouragement, attended neither school nor church unless compelled by village authority. Nor were they mentally capable of much accomplishment. Many of them, however, had considerable mechanical skill, a gift which permitted them to lead their itinerant life.

In the days when police interference was light they wandered over the country singly or in bands, like gipsies. Not infrequently, indeed, they associated with gipsies. Their language, however, is of German origin and shows that they are not of gipsy descent. They have in addition many words peculiar to themselves. They were wont to drive about in old wagons followed by numerous dogs. Indeed their advent in a neighborhood was a warning to the inhabitants to shut up in safe inclosures as quickly as possible all valued dogs. For want of sufficient draught animals the women and children were often forced to carry heavy burdens. The men ostensibly practiced such professions as crockery- and kettle-mending, rag- and bone-picking, basket-weaving, house-cleaning, etc. In reality they worked little and smoked much, while the women sold wares and begged. Indeed vending was, for the most part, only an excuse for begging, and clever beggars they were. They knew the inclinations and whereabouts of all the industrious inhabitants as well as the location of all their possessions. Thieving was just as common with them as begging. Parental responsibility was light with the Zeros and consequently infant mortality was high. Thus of 300, 74 died in early childhood. Illegitimacy was great. Parental irresponsibility, idiocy, and poverty have made this family for one hundred years a burden to the almshouse of Zand.

The real extent of drunkenness and crime in this family history cannot be accurately told. In the earlier days, especially when police control was lighter, much thieving went unrecorded and unpunished. The categories of their thefts are so numerous that many kinds must needs escape observation under any circumstances. They stole milk from the cows in the fields, vegetables from the gardens, poultry and dogs from the barnyards. On their vending expeditions they found opportunity to steal all kinds of wearing-apparel and articles of personal adornment as well as of the household. They were a highly superstitious people with a large supply of signs and omens, but, strange to say, they had little awe of the church.

Robbing of alms-boxes, which in earlier days were placed outside of churches or on posts by the wayside, was a most common practice with them. The bolder of them robbed tailor shops, markets, monasteries, and even the altars of churches. A few of the more clever have been counterfeiters. Murder, the most desperate of their crimes, seems to be incited either by jealousy over women or by illegitimacy.

In discussing the various environmental causes that have contributed their share to the maintenance of such a state of vagabondage, immorality and criminality as exists among the Zeros, Dr. Jörger states that he considers alcoholism the most important. It plays so great a rôle in the fate of the Zeros that, he says, his whole account of them sounds like one vile tale of rum.

One great effort was made to break up the life habits of the Zeros and if possible save Zand from this burden. In 1861 an energetic Capuchin priest came to Zand. Under his influence most of the children of all the poor families in Zand were taken from their own parents and divided among the respectable and industrious inhabitants to be reared and educated. The experiment brought good results with most of the children that were not Zeros. All the Zero children either ran away or were enticed away by their worthless kinsmen. It is clear, therefore, that the Zeros cannot be reclaimed by favorable environment. It is a matter of selective breeding, or better still of preventative breeding. Nature is already at work by the latter and more effective method. Physical weakness is becoming more pronounced with each generation and infant mortality is great.

5

ELIZABETH S. KITE
Two Brothers*

Preface

This is an early version of the all-time best-seller among family studies, Henry H. Goddard's *The Kallikak Family*, published the same year. Goddard freely acknowledged his debt to his research assistant, publicly in the preface to his book (1923:xi) and privately in his inscription on her personal copy:

> To Elizabeth S. Kite—without whose indefatigable labor the material in this book would never have been brought to light; and without whose skill and excellent judgment would not have been worth publishing, even when collected [n.a. 1954:201].

At the time, Kite was a field worker at the Vineland, N.J., Training School for Backward and Feeble-minded Children, which Goddard, its research director, and Edward R. Johnstone, its superintendent, had built into one of the country's foremost centers for eugenic investigation. Though overshadowed by the two men, Kite also contributed significantly to both the reputation of the institution and the menace-of-the-feeble-minded doctrine that it promulgated. More than a field worker, she also authored two popularizing family studies (this one and "The 'Pineys'" [1913]) and translated into English major French works on mental testing.

"Two Brothers" enables us to sort out the contributions of Kite and Goddard, respectively, to the final *Kallikaks* study. The genealogical information in the book version is pure Kite (indeed, she was sole author of its chapter 4, "Further Facts about the Family"), but Goddard added the framework of Mendelian eugenics. His version contains charts that map the march of feeble-mindedness through the generations as a Mendelian recessive. (In contrast, Kite relies on the older explanatory concept of "degenerate tendency" [p. 76].) Moreover, whereas Kite's conclusion is garbled, almost strangled,[1] Goddard formulates policy recommendations, endorsing eugenic segregation of the feeble-minded in institutions such as Vineland and, more tentatively, surgical sterilization. And in Goddard's version the family is given the Kallikak (from the Greek for "good" and "bad") surname that so brilliantly summarizes the fundamental message about heredity.

The first family study fully to realize the potential of the bad-mother theme

---

* Originally published in *The Survey* 27(22) (May 2, 1912): 1861–64.

[1] Goddard may have given Kite permission to publish her version on condition that she not scoop him scientifically. On the other hand, the conclusion of "The 'Pineys'" is also far from clear, suggesting that she was far less able than Goddard to articulate eugenic doctrine.

(see the preface to "Hereditary Crime"),[2] "Two Brothers" presents a sire who fathered two lines, one healthy, the other degenerate. The (half-) brothers of the title, though unknown to one another, were both sons of a revolutionary war soldier. The older, Old Horror, was illegitimate, the product of a lustful encounter between the soldier and a wayward girl, in a tavern in 1776. Three years later the young man married a Quaker woman of sound family; Kite selects their eldest son to serve as the fraternal foil to Old Horror.

In an extended comparison that may have been inspired by Winship's (1900) contrast of the Juke family with that of Jonathan Edwards, Kite unveils the consequences of the soldier's two unions. The lawful marriage produced "a clear normal line of intelligent citizens," including doctors, lawyers, ministers, and bankers. The illegitimate union gave rise to at least 143 almshouse cases, brothel keepers, criminals, and feeble-minded persons—including the Vineland inmate with whom her field work began. "Whence," asks Kite, "this astonishing difference ... ?" answering that it "must be found in the women who became the mothers of the respective lines" (p. 78). Blame for engendering degeneracy is thus made to fall heavily on the mother while the father, by and large, is exempted.

A lengthy defense of her research techniques published later the same year (Kite 1912a) indicates that from the moment of publication "Two Brothers" drew heavy fire for its free-and-easy attributions of feeble-mindedness, especially to those long dead. Kite's narrative skill (the flip side, as it were, of her mental testing techniques) has received less attention. Taking the dry facts of genealogy, she develops them here into a series of vignettes embellished with authenticating details and quotations. She also handles imagery thematically. Descriptions of the good branch are marked by spaciousness and light: "broad acres," "lordly river," "lifting ... energies to an ever broadening outlook," "entered our large cities," "pioneers in the West," "summer." Descriptions of the bad branch, on the other hand, are full of images of darkness, enclosure, descent: "low huts falling apart," "uncleared ground," "habitual filth," "waterlogged humanity that settles at the bottom," "crude hut deep in the mountain thicket." These imagistic polarities reinforce the underlying contrast of good and bad.

Born in Philadelphia in 1864, Elizabeth Sarah Kite attended Westtown Boarding School before traveling extensively in Europe, where she acquired fluency in French and her interest in history. She was trained as a field worker at Vineland, working there from 1912 to 1918 and simultaneously helping the prestigious Committee on Provision for the Feebleminded lobby for more extensive institutionalization (Haller 1963). This was, moreover, the period in which she translated key works on mental testing by Binet and Simon (1916a, 1916b, 1916c). Kite returned to Vineland in 1927 to work for a year with its new director of research, Edgar A. Doll (see Doll 1928 for the results). Although she did not produce "Two Brothers" until she was nearly fifty, it was but the first of many publications, the majority of which dealt with

---

[2] For an analysis of the process by which hereditarians arrived at the conclusion that mothers were more responsible than fathers for the "quality" of offspring, see Rosenberg 1974; for a fascinating example, contemporaneous with "Two Brothers," of where such thinking could lead, see Neff 1910.

French–American and Catholic history. Kite was active in Catholic set-tlement work and archivist for the American Catholic Historical Society of Philadelphia. In 1933 she became the first laywoman to receive an honorary doctorate from Villanova University and was also recognized by the French government with the Chevalier de la Légion d'Honneur (n.a. 1954:202). Kite died in 1954 at the age of 89.

DURING THE EARLY days of the last century, two half brothers having had the same father but different mothers began their respective careers in one of our older states. Nothing could have been more widely divergent than the social standing, the mental endowment, the material possessions of the two brothers, who none the less in physical feature bore a striking resemblance to each other.

One of them, the inheritor of the homestead farm, whose broad acres overlooked a lordly river, was a man respected by all who knew him, intel-ligent, well married, with children who in themselves or in their descend-ants would cast nothing but honor upon the family name. The other, feeble-minded and morally repulsive, lived on a mountain-side in a hut built of rock fragments so loosely put together that more than once the roof slid from the walls. For a quarter of a century this hut existed as a hotbed of vice, the resort of the debauched youth of the neighborhood, and from its walls has come a race of degenerates which, out of a total of four hundred and eighty descendants, numbers in almshouse cases, in keepers of houses of prostitution, in inmates of reformatories and institu-tions for the feeble-minded, in criminals of various sorts and in feeble-minded not under state protection, 143 souls!

And yet the progenitor of this social evil gave in early manhood hopes of something better. The freshness of youth hid the degenerate tendency that was soon to assert itself. He married a young woman of decent family and the two together saved a few dollars with which they bought an acre and a half of uncleared ground. Here they built their hut and here began to appear, in quick succession, the offspring of the pair, who almost as quickly were bound out among the neighboring farms. Twice, during the next few years, the couple added to their initial plot of ground, for the county records show that once a half-acre was purchased for five dollars, and again two-thirds of an acre for eight dollars. From this date no gleam of ambition illumes the dark way the couple were going, and it was not long before the wife, poorly nourished, overworked, and scantily clad, suc-cumbed to the inevitable, dying with the thirteenth child.

Left to himself the husband lived on, much as he had lived before—avoiding work perhaps a little more effectively, drinking perhaps a little

heavier. His wife's family had moved to Cincinnati, where they had prospered, and during her life-time offered to pay the price of transportation if
the couple would join them, but this along with other inducements had
been set aside by the husband, who had neither the mind nor the will to
grasp the opportunity offered him. As time went on, the grosser elements
of his nature gained ascendancy, which, added to habitual filth, made
him a most repulsive person, so that he merited the name bestowed upon
him of the "Old Horror." At election time he was a well-known figure. Then
he would appear dressed in a suit of cast-off clothes given him for the occasion, very conscious of the ephemeral importance which his power as a
citizen gave him. It was well known that his vote was the possession of
any one who would give him a drink, and there was no lack of men ready
to make the bargain. But with all this, his utter inoffensiveness, coupled
with a genuinely kind heart, characteristic of the family, won for him a
sort of protecting pity in the vicinity. Many an old farmer would allow him
to sit on the porch and draw off, unnoticed, measure after measure of
cider from the barrel which was always in evidence. When the old fellow
had taken so much that he lost his balance and rolled off, the farmer
would chuckle—"Well, well, I do declare! Them steps of mine does need
fixin'!"—at which the simple-minded neighbor would gather himself together, really believing the steps had caused his fall!

After the death of their mother, three of this man's daughters subsequently known as "Old Mol," "Old Jane," and "Old Kate," came back to
their father and either settled near or lived with him. It was then that the
crude hut, hidden deep in the mountain thicket, became known in the
neighborhood. Memories of the scandals that now and then leaked out,
involving the names of sons of prominent citizens, are still in the minds of
many living persons, although the perpetrators of the deeds have long
since passed to their reward, leaving behind them a long train of descendants, many of whom now may be found among such water-logged humanity as settles at the bottom of our big cities, or remain in their native hills
and continue to carry on the work of their progenitors.

How different the story of the other half-brother! In his case there is a
clear normal line of intelligent citizens, who in their varied activities have
constantly tended to increase the preserving force of our commonwealth,
lifting its energies to an ever broadening outlook.

The same is true of his five full-blood brothers and sisters who attained
manhood and womanhood. Among their three hundred and fifty descendants are many who have entered our large cities, where they are to be
found as doctors, lawyers, ministers, merchants, pharmacists, bankers,
manufacturers, teachers; still others have become pioneers in the West,

while those who have remained in the country are land-owners, farmers, blacksmiths, undertakers, store-keepers and mill owners, always capable and industrious, abreast of the problems of life, which they meet with the intelligence of normal citizens.

But whence, it may well be asked, this astonishing difference in the characters of these two branches, springing, on the paternal side, from the same source?

Reason will at once decide that this difference must be found in the women who became the mothers of the respective lines, and in the subtle subjective forces that brought about and accompanied each mating.

Fortunately, church and family records, local tradition, our nation's history even, can aid in finding an answer to the question, Who and what were these two women? And under what circumstances did each enter into the life of her husband?

The early records of the province where these events took place tell us that in 1774 "a simultaneous blaze of indignation from North to South, broke out at the tidings of arbitrary acts of the British Government perpetrated against the port of Boston. Measures were at once taken for organizing the various counties into a combination of the friends of liberty who should insure promptitude and unity of action throughout the province." On Sunday, September 23, 1775, at precisely four o'clock, the news of the Battle of Lexington "carried by express riders reached the chambers of the New York Committee of Safety and thence the stirring news spread on to Princeton and Philadelphia, spreading like wild-fire over all the neighboring counties. Meetings were called and resolutions adopted for regulating the militia of the colony."

By spring of the following year, companies had been organized and stationed at the various strategic points. To one of these on the "King's Highway"connecting two important trade centers came in April, 1776, a youth not yet twenty-one, who had lost his father five years before. He had been reared by his mother with four "spinster sisters" on a farm of some two hundred acres, situated about five miles away, that had come to them in direct line, part of an original purchase made in 1734 by their paternal great-grandfather. This ancestor was of sturdy English dissenting stock that had always been sober, industrious, and God-fearing. The young soldier inherited these qualities, but having been so early deprived of father's care, and so suddenly plunged into the relaxed atmosphere of camp life, succumbed to excesses unknown in the annals of his family. Ready he was to answer his country's call and to fight when the time came, but in the various monthly tours which he served there were plenty of off-duty times when the fires of patriotism burned lower than the other fires within him. Even to-day the remains of numerous old taverns scattered along the road, still called the "King's Highway," attest the ancestral thirst which called them into being. That our young friend frequently found means to quench his own thirst is not to be doubted, and it is equally certain that among the wayward girls who frequented these taverns was one, a native in the locality, who attracted the soldier, now in the full swing of re-action from the restraint of his well-ordered home. This girl it was who became the mother of him who subsequently built his hut on the mountain-side scarcely two miles distant. She, in accordance with an instinct that has been followed by her descendants for generations, gave to the child the full name of its father, thus making his identity known.

Of this girl, history has nothing and tradition very little to tell. That she attained an advanced age is learned from her great-granddaughter, who remembers that her mother "lived with the old woman after she had become completely imbecile and that she often told of how difficult it was to care for her." She lived in a log cabin back in the woods, and at one period, late in life, had passed as the wife of an old soldier, who belonged to a good family, but was of striking peculiarity. At his death she failed to receive his pension, since it could not be proved that she was his lawful wife. She died about 1842. Of her name or ancestry no trace can be found to-day. Her son, who seems to have been her only child, did not live long with his mother, but was bound out with a well-to-do farmer of the vicinity. There is no evidence that the father ever at any time recognized either the mother or her child, although he could not have remained ignorant of the latter's existence nor of the name which the lad bore. The shifting fortunes of a soldier's life did not permit him to remain long in one locality and he probably was changed long before the child was born.

When we next find him, it is on the eve of battle when an accidental wound in the right arm disabled him for further service. He then returned to the home farm, and during a summer of subdued activity fell in love with a young Quakeress of the vicinity. The girl found his suit acceptable, but her shrewd father was not so easily moved. At first he objected to the union, for the young man was too much handicapped by lack of worldly possessions, by his sisters, still minors, and by his disabled condition. In reply to the objection of the old man, the young suitor is recorded as saying, "Never mind, I'll own more land than thee ever did, before I die"—a promise which he made good. The paternal objection must have been shortly overruled, for the church records give the date of his marriage with the Quakeress as January, 1779. No uncertainty shrouds the ancestry of this woman whom he made his wife. She came of a respected Eng-

lish family, which, however, having imbibed principles too broadly democratic to be tolerated in that country, had been compelled to seek shelter
in the New World. Here it had quickly taken root and through thrift and
industry had acquired material possessions which placed it in the front
provincial ranks. Its best possession, however, was that uncompromising
rectitude which forms the backbone of our nation and which invariably
has made for intelligence and ability in its offspring.

The eldest son of this union was the respected farmer referred to in the
beginning of this article. In the family Bible is a carefully preserved record
of the five daughters and two sons born of this union, but no mention is
made of the older son, born of the other union, whose name, had the
whole truth been told, would have headed the list of his father's children.
Of this illegitimate son, no family Bible ever held the record, and his existence would certainly have been allowed to pass unnoticed, had it not
chanced that his great-great-grand-daughter was placed in a home for
feeble-minded, where she was long studied and watched before an attempt was made to unravel the thread of her past history. When once undertaken, it was traced back to the mountain hut, where it might have
rested, had it not been found that the degenerate man bore the full name
of the Revolutionary hero, married as the records show in 1779. Persistent search revealed the fact that several persons still living had always
known of the blood relationship of the two brothers, whose lives were in
such striking contrast to one another, and that they retained a vivid impression of the strange doings and disorderly ways of these wild people of
the woods. For it will surprise no one to learn that the degenerate family
has always been a complex problem, inheriting and preserving from its
normal ancestor strong and attractive personal characteristics along
with the low mental and moral endowment from the subnormal side, thus
from its complexity impressing itself deeply upon the community. This
strange mixture shows itself even to the sixth generation.

As the above recorded facts were being dug from records it began to
seem a singular coincidence that these two brothers, here singled out for
comparison, should have been born so near the time of the promulgation
of that basic principle of our democracy that "All men are created
equal"—and both of them, in a way, the direct outcome of those forces
that made its establishment possible. It was as if to epitomize in them and
in their descendants the necessity for drafting such a social context for
this great doctrine as will make it, with each generation, more nearly true.

6

FLORENCE H. DANIELSON AND CHARLES B. DAVENPORT

The Hill Folk:
Report on a Rural Community of Hereditary Defectives*

Preface

The Hill Folk reveals considerable tension between its authors' regard for scientific procedures on the one hand and dedication to eugenics on the other. Unable to resolve this tension, Florence H. Danielson and Charles B. Davenport produced a family study in which evidence and conclusions fail to mesh. *The Hill Folk* is marked, moreover, by a problem that Augusta Bronner identified several years later in a review of Davenport's *The Feebly-Inhibited*: it is "exceedingly elaborate. Perhaps in this very fact lies the reason for its lack of conviction; it is almost too elaborate to bear the super-structure placed on it" (1916:311).[1]

The Hill Folk was the first product of the Eugenic Record Office's long-range plan for stimulating research. Trained under Davenport as a field worker at the ERO's summer school, Danielson remained affiliated with the organization, which sent her to study the heredity of inmates at the Monson, Massachusetts, state hospital for the epileptic and feeble-minded. Working with Monson superintendent Dr. Everett Flood, Danielson located a promising community, collected data, and then worked up the findings in collaboration with Davenport, the ERO's director. The interpretations show the influence of his recently published *Heredity in Relation to Eugenics* (1911).

The study focuses on three principal family groups, descendants of Neil Rasp (chart A, p. 161), Nuke (an unrelated Englishman, chart B, p. 162), and Nute Rasp (brother of Neil, chart C, p. 163). Together with at least six other "families," these constitute the Hill Folk—even though some lived at a considerable distance from "the Hill."

The following comments summarize sections of the study that are somewhat obscure.

The "General Survey of the Strains" (Part 3) attempts to show, first, that cacogeneity has a snowball effect: the progeny of two mentally defective individuals "show an accumulation and multiplication of bad traits" (p. 92). Second, it tries to demonstrate that "certain traits follow certain lines of descent, so that after one generation, related families may each have a different

---

* Originally published as Memoir no. 1, Eugenics Record Office, Cold Spring Harbor, N.Y., August 1912.

[1] Estabrook and Davenport's *The Nam Family*, published in the same volume as *The Hill Folk*, suffers from similar problems.

characteristic" (p. 92). Thus, while Neil Rasp's descendants are characterized by feeble-mindedness and alcoholism, those of Nuke exhibit "shiftlessness and a stolid dullness." Finally, in this section the authors acknowledge that "the outer circle on each chart [current generation] contains a comparatively large number of individuals designated as normal," but they explain this embarrassing fact by noting that "these children have not yet displayed all their potentialities" (p. 92).

In "Inheritance" (Part 4) the authors struggle with a dilemma: their data indicate that feeble-mindedness "does not fit the Mendelian expectation very closely"—the predicted ratios did not pan out (unnumbered table, p. 93)—yet they desperately want it to. They resolve the matter by deciding they must refine their analysis of feeble-mindedness. There must be different *types* of feeble-mindedness: "We may find one case . . . wherein the individual is cruel, and keen in the pursuit of mischief, but unable to learn, and another case in which he is kind and learns quite readily, but is shiftless and devoid of judgment" (p. 95). These sub-varieties of feeble-mindedness may obey Mendel's laws, as illustrated, hypothetically, in the tables and figure on pages 96 and 97. The paragraph that concludes this section is almost painful to read. In it Danielson and Davenport hold that feeble-mindedness is not a biological but a "legal or sociological term," yet they go on to argue that its sub-varieties are inherited as unit characters.

In view of the claim that "all" of the Hill families "were connected by marriage, some of them by consanguineous marriages" (p. 85), we might expect the fifth section, "Marriage Selection," to give supporting data. However (as noted in the introduction to this volume), evidence for intermarriage and consanguinity among the Hill Folk is in fact sparse[2]—which may explain why this section focuses instead on proving "endogamy, or in-marriage, among the mentally deficient." By equating the mentally deficient with the "class of semi-paupers" (p. 98), the authors do indeed succeed in showing that the rural poor gravitate toward one another. That "like will consort with like even in exogamy, or out-marriage," is proved by case B III 9 who, though he "migrated a hundred miles eastward," married into yet another defective family, with the sad results shown in figure 3. The conclusion, left implicit here, is that defectives should not be allowed to marry at all.

Part 6, "The Financial Burden," attempts to demonstrate the enormous cost of allowing defectives to propagate. Danielson and Davenport begin by showing that the Hill Folk consume a substantial and growing proportion of local relief funds.[3] Next they show the costs of criminality—over the preceding thirty years "sixteen persons from The Hill families have been sent to

[2] The thumbnail sketches given in the Appendix do report many cases of marriage between relatives; but these examples are often given twice, and in any case the relationships often were not close. For instance, the Description of Chart A reports that in Line A, IV 1 "married her father's own cousin, III 47"; later, under line E, we are told that III 47 "married the daughter (IV 1) of his cousin." Thus the evidence for consanguinity is less persuasive than it may at first appear.

[3] As we do not know what proportion of all the poor in the area were Hill Folk, it is impossible to judge whether the family actually extracted more than its "share." However, this objection might have seemed irrelevant to Davenport, who objected to poor relief in principle.

prison for serious crimes" (p. 102)[4]—and of maintaining state wards. The "Comparison with the Jukes" illustrates, again, the tension between evidence and presupposition that characterizes this family study. The Jukes turn out to have been worse than the Hill Folk on nearly all counts: more bastards, more prostitution, more state aid, more crime, and a longer cumulative sentence length. The Massachusetts clan scored below its New York counterparts mainly on measures that Dugdale ignored—alcoholism, indolence, lack of ambition, school progress, and feeble-mindedness. Although the results of this elaborate comparison point to no clear conclusion, Danielson and Davenport hypothesize (p. 106) that the tribal differences they have detected are "probably due to initial difference in . . . heredity."

As they reckon up the costs of the Hill Folk, the authors' argument grows particularly strained. The total of nearly $500,000 (over sixty years) includes money spent for drink, labor lost owing to drink (640 years for hard drinking, 280 for medium), and one life "sacrificed by murder" at $1,700. The section concludes with the "conservative estimate that all such *rural* centers of 'degeneration' together are costing the commonwealth half a million dollars *each year*" (p. 106; emphases in original), money that could be saved by preventing reproduction.

The "Survey of the Present School Children," (Part 7) asks whether the apparently normal fifty percent of current Hill children "will be able to keep up to the same standard" in adulthood. The answer, we learn, "depends largely on the comparative weight of hereditary and environmental influences," leading to "Heredity and Environment" (Part 8). Danielson and Davenport address the nature-nurture issue by investigating whether the children of defectives improve when removed from their homes. They find that some do, some do not; and that even children who are raised in wretched environments occasionally do well. Faced with this evidence, which contradicts their assumptions about the power of heredity, the authors turn to the family tree (figure 4) of defective parents who produced a crop of nearly uniformly defective offspring. These children, if institutionalized, would cost $48,000 over their lifetimes, a figure Danielson and Davenport compare to the mere $16,380 it would have cost to place "Jim and his second wife . . . in custodial care at sixteen years of age . . . for forty-five years" (pp. 127–28).

Unlike Florence H. Danielson, on whom there is little personal information,[5] Charles Benedict Davenport has received considerable biographical attention (e.g., Haller 1963; Kevles 1985; Rosenberg 1976). The dominant figure in the American eugenics movement, Davenport was also, as we have seen, the driving force behind many of the family studies. Like other family

---

[4] If we subtract the 4 instances of lewdness, 1 of perjury, 1 of concubinage, 1 of habitual drunkenness, 1 assault that was evidently minor (sentence of 2 months), and 1 offense that did not result in conviction at all, we are left with just 7 cases that might be deemed "serious." Moreover (and to carry these objections to the verge of silliness), as we do not know the total number of Hill Folk of crime-committing age over the preceding thirty years or have comparative figures on other groups, it is difficult to determine whether their serious-crime rate was high or low.

[5] Danielson held a master's degree at the time she coauthored *The Hill Folk*. After completing the family study she helped Davenport with research on heredity of skin color. According to "Alumni Roster" (1919:21), by 1918 Danielson had become Mrs. Joseph S. Davis and was living in London, assisting "Dr. Davis in his office work with Shipping Mission."

study authors, he was middle class, American-born, well educated, and a professional. At his father's insistence, Davenport first studied engineering; later he pursued his own interests at Harvard, from which he received a doctorate in zoology in 1892. After teaching at Harvard and the University of Chicago, Davenport entered the most important phase of his career when, in 1904, he became director of the newly established Station for Experimental Evolution at Cold Spring Harbor, Long Island, a position he held till retirement thirty years later. After 1910 he also headed the Eugenics Record Office at Cold Spring Harbor. Although *The Hill Folk* and other eugenic works raise questions about his scientific precision, Davenport made significant contributions to genetics and biometry. Kevles speculates (1985:49–54) that Davenport's eugenic beliefs were fostered by such personal characteristics as ambition, conservativism, defensiveness, and rigidity.

PREFACE

This memoir is the first of a projected series which is intended to embody some of the more extended researches of the Eugenics Record Office, especially such as, on account of extensive pedigree charts, require a page of large size. Against the inconvenience of the quarto size has to be balanced the very practical necessity of a large surface to show relationships in a great network.

The present memoir is a study of a rural community of a sort familiar to sociologists in the work of Dugdale and of McCulloch in this country. The work began in connection with studies on the pedigree of some inmates of the Monson State Hospital, at Palmer, Mass. Miss Danielson was assigned by the Eugenics Record Office to work at that institution under the direction of its Superintendent, Dr. Everett Flood. Dr. Flood gave Miss Danielson every facility for prosecuting this inquiry, and took the broad stand that it is quite as desirable to make an extensive study of all the connections of an epileptic subject as to make numerous brief pedigrees of a much larger number of inmates. This memoir is the product of such an extended inquiry. The thanks of the Record Office, and, I am sure, of all students of human heredity and of sociologists, are gratefully offered to Dr. Flood, as well as to the trustees of the Hospital, of whom it may not be invidious particularly to mention Dr. W. N. Bullard, chairman of the Board.

The primary value of this memoir is, it must be confessed, to the sociologist rather than to the student of inheritance of human traits. Our field work of the first year has hardly risen to the point of analysis required for a study of heredity. This work will take much more time and will come later. But the sociological importance is clear. We are dealing with a rural community such as can be found in nearly if not quite every county in the older states of the union, in which nearly all of the people belong to the vague class of the "feebleminded"—the incapable. The individuals vary much in capacity, a result which follows from the complexity of their germ plasm. Some have capacities that can be developed under proper conditions, but for many more even the best of environmental conditions can do little. They must remain a drag on our civilization; a condition for which not they, but society, is responsible. It is to be hoped that a presentation of the facts will hasten the so much desired control by society of the reproduction of the grossly defective.

All of the field work on which the report is based, the preparation of the charts, and the writing of the major portion of the text, including all of the tabular matter and the Appendix are the work of Miss Danielson. Grateful acknowledgment is made of the financial assistance of Mr. John D. Rockefeller in the publication of this report. The expense of the study was borne in part by the Monson State Hospital and in part by Mrs. E. H. Harriman.

C. B. Davenport.

I. INTRODUCTION

THE FOLLOWING REPORT is the result of an investigation of two family trees in a small Massachusetts town. It aims to show how much crime, misery and expense may result from the union of two defective individuals—how a large number of the present court frequenters, paupers and town nuisances are connected by a significant network of relationship. It includes a discussion of the undesirable traits in the light of the Mendelian analysis. It presents some observations concerning the relation of heredity and environment, based on their effects upon the children. While it is not an exhaustive study of all the ramifications of even these two families and their consorts, it may be sufficient to throw some light on the vexed question of the prevention of feebleminded, degenerate individuals, as a humane and economical state policy.

In the fall of 1910 a field worker from the Eugenics Record Office was placed in the employ of a state institution to study the inheritance of certain traits. One of the cases which was investigated led to a community where feeblemindedness, immorality, and alcoholism were rife. An investigation of the group of families which showed these traits followed. It brought to light the fact that all these families were connected by marriage, some of them by consanguineous marriages, and that practically all of them could be traced back to one of two original sources. The economic and educational influences in this rural district have not been abnormal, but from the nucleus of these two families has developed a shiftless, weakminded element which is notorious in the county.

The town in question lies in a fertile river valley among the New England hills. It is on the direct railway line between two prosperous cities. East and west of it are more hilly, less productive towns. Its present population is about 2,000. Most of the people are industrious, intelligent farmers. A lime kiln and a marble quarry are the only industries of importance. In summer the population is nearly doubled by city boarders.

Into one corner of this attractive town there came, about 1800, a shiftless basket maker. He was possibly of French origin, but migrated more directly from the western hill region. About the same time an Englishman, also from the western hills, bought a small farm in the least fertile part of the town. The progeny of these two men, old Neil Rasp,* and the Englishman, Nuke, have sifted through the town and beyond it. Everywhere they have made desolate, alcoholic homes which have furnished State wards for over fifty years, and have required town aid for a longer time.

Enough of the families still live in the original neighborhood so that, although they occupy tenant houses of respectable farmers, for they own no land now, the district of "The Hill" is spoken of slurringly. Where the children have scattered to neighboring towns, they do not remain long enough to secure a residence and are consequently referred back to the original town when they require outside aid. As the younger generations have grown up, they have, almost without exception, married into American families of the same low mental grade, so that "The Hill" people are linked by their consorts to a similar degenerate family a hundred miles away.

The attitude of the townspeople is that of exasperated neighbors. They have lived beside these troublesome paupers for so long that they are too disgusted with them, and too accustomed to the situation, to realize the necessity for aggressive work upon it. A few of them realize that hard cider is a large factor in the cause of their neighbors' poverty, but more of them, apparently ignoring the fact, keep it on tap free or sell it. This poor class of people are left largely to themselves until they need town aid, or some member becomes so drunk that he disturbs the peace, or some girl becomes pregnant and has to be taken to an institution. About once every eight or ten years, a state agent is informed of the conditions, and four or five children are removed from the families. Then the father and mother

---

* The few names which are used in the description of this community are fictitious. The local setting and the families and all the other details actually exist, but for obvious reasons imaginary names are in every case substituted for the real ones.

find that their financial problems are relieved for the time and settle down to raise another family.

A few of the men and some of the women have soldier's or widow's pensions and state aid, but most of them work, when they do work, as wood choppers or farm laborers. Most of their wages go for hard cider or, if handed to the wives, are spent in other equally foolish ways. They move frequently from one shanty or tumbled down house to another. So long as food and a small amount of clothing are furnished by some means, they live in bovine contentment.

From the biological standpoint, it is interesting to note that mental defect manifests itself in one branch of the pedigree by one trait and in another branch by quite a different one. Thus, in one line alcoholism is universal among the men; their male cousins in another line are fairly temperate, plodding workers, but the women are immoral. Another branch shows all the men to be criminal along sexual lines, while a cousin who married into a more industrious family has descendants who are a little more respectable. These people have not been subjected to the social influences of a city or even of a large town, so that the traits which they show have been less modified by a powerful social environment than those of urban dwellers.

Even under these conditions, a study of their germ-plasm is full of complexities. One can readily conceive of the difficulties of analyzing an individual's characteristics and placing him concisely in a certain class, even after a prolonged acquaintance. The problem that a field worker meets is to analyze each person in the pedigree in respect to his mental and moral traits from a brief acquaintance and from a comparison of the descriptions of others. After all the evidence from personal visits, interviews with relatives, physicians, town officials, and reliable neighbors, and facts from court and town records have been collected, it is, even then, difficult to represent these characteristics exactly by the standard symbols which are used for the biological study of inherited traits. The distinction between an ignorant person who has normal mental ability and a high grade feebleminded one who has not, is often as impossible to make as that between medium and low grade feeblemindedness. The term normal, therefore, as it is used in these descriptions is often applied to a person on the borderline, so that only a few of the "normals" are clear cut, ordinary persons, but most of them fall into that category from a lack of sure evidence of any striking censurable defect. So in this report, hard and fast lines are not drawn, but the symbols which most closely represent the character are placed on the chart and the description supplies more detailed information.

II. EXPLANATION OF CHARTS

The scheme which has been adopted to represent the descent from the common ancestors in this pedigree is that of a wheel. The lines which diverge from the center to the first circle indicate the children of the original couple. The decendants of this second generation in turn form the second circle, and the lines which indicate their descent diverge from the line of union between their parents. Considering the common ancestor as the first generation, the generations are numbered with Roman numerals. The individuals in each generation are numbered by Arabic figures, independently of other generations and are referred to in the descriptions by the generation number and their consecutive number in that generation, as I 2 or III 16. When an individual appears twice on the chart through a cousin marriage, he is always designated by the number which indicates his descent.

A key of the symbols and letters accompanies each chart, but a word of explanation in regard to the use of F and Sx is due. A distinction has been made, in the grades of feeblemindedness, between high and low. The former term, represented by the F in a white square or circle, refers to those persons who support themselves in a meager way, but who lack ambition, self-control, common sense and the ordinary mental and moral capacity for differentiating right and wrong; the latter, represented by the solid black square or circle with the F in white, refers to those who are not capable of self-support, and who are a special menace to the community from their lack of all mental and moral stamina.

The other symbol which may require explanation is Sx, which refers to a lack of self-control that takes the form of illicit relations with the opposite sex. This is used to indicate a distinct trait rather than the mere breach of social law. It refers to those persons in whom the sex impulse and self-control are not balanced, but in whom the former is relatively stronger; in such persons, then, the sex impulse works unhindered. Not all persons who have made illegitimate unions are marked Sx on the charts, but only those where this trait seems, from the history of the case, to be the direct cause of the illegitimacy.

The same general scheme has been used on each of the three charts. The first one represents the Rasp family, which is connected by marriage to the Nuke family, which in turn is plotted on Chart B. Chart C represents the descendants of a branch of the Rasp family, viz., a brother of the original Neil Rasp, I 1, on Chart A. It also includes a family which is closely connected by marriages with both the preceding pedigrees.

III. GENERAL SURVEY OF THE STRAINS STUDIED AND THEIR TRAITS

A brief survey of the charts will be sufficient to show the trend of the characteristics of each group of descendants from the original ancestors. On Chart A, the larger of the two principal families originated from a very alcoholic, shiftless man and his feebleminded wife. All of their five children were feebleminded to a greater or less extent and produced offspring who vary widely in their characteristics of feeblemindedness.

The children and grandchildren of II 1 are shiftless and deficient in a general way, and in some instances have uncontrolled sexual instincts. The daughter, II 1, married a man who was her inferior in mental ability and five of their six children were feebleminded; the sixth died at nineteen years of age. One son, who married an immoral woman and had a family of eleven children, was imprisoned for incest with his daughter, and two of his children show uncontrolled sexual desires. All of them are feebleminded and some of his grandchildren are also. One daughter, III 7, had only one child by an alcoholic man, and this child was not particularly defective. Another daughter, III 9, kept a house of ill-fame. She had three children, one of whom is very shiftless and feebleminded, another one has migraine, but appears fairly intelligent, and the third one has not been located. The last son, II 11, married his own cousin and had three children, viz., an imbecile daughter and two sons, one alcoholic, and one epileptic.

The descendants from the most feebleminded daughter in the second generation, II 4, are characterized by abnormal sex instincts, some feeblemindedness, and, where a better stock has been introduced through outmarriage, by some normal traits. This daughter married an extremely alcoholic man and four of her seven children are criminal, three of them having committed serious crimes against sex. One daughter, III 12, married her own cousin; she also had a mulatto child, and finally two illegitimate children by another cousin. Another daughter is immoral and still another is a pronounced neurasthenic. Some of the grandchildren also show feeblemindedness and uncontrolled sexual instincts, while others who have descended from a union of this stock with a normal strain, seem to be normal or only neurotic.

The offspring of the only son, II 6, are extremely alcoholic, more alcoholic than any other branch of the pedigree. They are also shiftless and consequently very poor. They exhibit a high grade of feeblemindedness and some normal traits. This son was married twice. Both of the alcoholic sons by his first wife have large families of ten and eleven children. Most of these children are feebleminded, and some of them have been removed from home on the grounds of neglect. The second wife was a high-grade feebleminded woman with a cleft palate. Six of their eight children are feebleminded, one of them is a cretin, and another has a cleft palate. Two girls are fairly normal, one married a normal man and has normal children; the other married a feebleminded man with a hare-lip and has some normal and some feebleminded children.

The descendants from the third daughter, II 8, who married into a normal strain, show a very high grade of feeblemindedness. One son committed rape. There were four sons but only two of them have families of any size; and one of these married a cousin. Many of the third generation are borderline cases of feeblemindedness.

The offspring of the fourth daughter, II 10, who also married into a normal family, show some normal traits and also high-grade feeblemindedness and a little alcoholism. Three of the eight children who grew to maturity are normal. One of the feebleminded sons, III 47, was imprisoned for attempted rape, and afterwards married his cousin by whom he had five feebleminded children. This family is the lowest grade mentally, of any of the third generation, though several others are high-grade feebleminded families.

The second family, whose pedigree is plotted on Chart B, is not characterized by much alcoholism, but rather by shiftlessness and a stolid dullness. There are both high and low grades of feeblemindedness, epilepsy, and some normal traits. The original ancestors were probably a little more energetic than the originators of the above pedigree, for they owned a small farm. The father was not very intelligent, however, and the mother very neurotic. All of their eleven children of whom anything is known were feebleminded or neurotic; five of them married and had families.

The descendants of II 1 are the most defective branch of this pedigree and form a third of the individuals on this chart. II 1 married a feebleminded man by whom she had seven defective children and one who is of average intelligence. The latter had no children but her six feebleminded brothers and sisters who married produced twenty-nine children for the next generation. Four of these were comparatively normal, two died in infancy, and the remaining twenty-three vary in intelligence from the grade of a moron to an epileptic imbecile. The fraternity to which this imbecile belongs (children of III 14 and 15) is noteworthy on account of its number of epileptics and dependents. Four of the thirteen children have had epilepsy and ten have been taken away from the parents because they were neglected. The one child, III 3, of II 1 and 2 who did not marry, is extremely feebleminded and has been in prison for arson. His sister, III 11 [*sic*], is the individual who married into the family plotted on Chart A and appears there as the wife of III 1 and the mother of a large defective family.

Children of II 9 and her alcoholic husband show alcoholism, epilepsy, and some normal traits. Six of her children died in infancy. The two who have epilepsy are able to support themselves. This is the most respectable fraternity on this chart.

Nothing is known of the illegitimate children of II 12, but four of her five legitimate children by a feebleminded, choreic man lived to maturity and are typical high grade feebleminded persons,—shiftless, easily influenced, dull and alcoholic. One son married, and had two hydrocephalic twins who died; and one daughter has ten children all but one of whom are high-grade feebleminded individuals. Those of school age are very backward in their studies. The one daughter who is superior to her brothers and sisters married, and has a daughter who has married a respectable man and has a good home.

The descendants from II 17, who married an eccentric man, show insanity, eccentricity, and feeblemindedness in the few cases of which data were obtainable. One son murdered his uncle and has been sent to the Hospital for Criminally Insane. The feebleminded son, III 61, has eight children, most of whom show signs of mental deficiency.

The high-grade feebleminded daughter, II 19, had but one illegitimate and one legitimate child. The former is epileptic, but has no children. The husband of II 19 is also epileptic. Their one son, however, has had no attacks of epilepsy, but is a feebleminded neurasthenic. He has married a feebleminded woman and has three deficient children.

On Chart C, I 1 is the brother of the originator of Chart A, while the other half of the wheel is made up of a family into which many of the previous families have married. The traits which are most prominent here are alcoholism, laziness, and some feeblemindedness. As a whole, the families on Chart C are a little more intelligent than those on the other two charts.

From the one son of the alcoholic ancestor, I 1, there were six feebleminded or alcoholic children, one fairly normal son, and one daughter who died in infancy. Four persons in the next generation are very feebleminded, IV 1, IV 11, IV 15, IV 38. The others are high-grade or normal. Two sons, III 7 and III 9, have large families of ten and twelve children. Two older members of one fraternity have shown an inability to control sexual desires. The school children from both of these families lack attention and mental energy.

The children of I 3 and 4 were extremely shiftless. Two of them were very alcoholic. II 3, one of these, married a woman who became insane late in life. They had eight children, one of whom is insane, three alcoholic, one shiftless and feebleminded, one normal, and the other two are unknown. The normal girl married her own cousin and has an alcoholic son and an imbecile daughter.

The daughter, II 8, who married a high-grade feebleminded man had two normal and two alcoholic children.

From II 12, a feebleminded, shiftless man, has sprung an indolent group of feebleminded persons, with the one exception of a daughter who has moved to a distant town and who seems to be normal. The second generation from II 12, the school children, are lazy and unable to progress in their studies.

The conclusion of this brief survey, then, must be that the second and third generations from a union of mentally defective individuals show an accumulation and multiplication of bad traits, even though a few normal persons also appear from such unions. It is also evident that certain traits tend to follow certain lines of descent, so that after one generation, related families may each have a different characteristic trait. The outer circle on each chart contains a comparatively large number of individuals designated as normal. These are the undeveloped children who will be a constantly changing factor for several years. So the increase in the number of so called normals in the growing generation cannot be taken offhand for evidence that the old stock is improving. The fact that these children have not yet displayed all their potentialities is one that must be considered.

IV. INHERITANCE

In view of the difficulties already pointed out in analyzing individuals accurately, the study of the inheritance of their traits can be only suggestive. It may show tendencies where it cannot afford clean-cut laws. Let us assume for the moment that feeblemindedness is a unit, and acts as a simple recessive to normality. Here we are confronted by the difficulty that in "feeblemindedness" as the term is commonly used, several degrees are recognized. We have recognized two such degrees and called them "high-grade feeblemindedness," and "low-grade feeble-mindedness." This gives us three grades in an unanalytical series; viz., normality, high-grade feeblemindedness, low-grade feeblemindedness. Let us test the hypothesis that feeblemindedness of any grade is "recessive" to normality; and that in like manner low-grade feeblemindedness is recessive to high-grade feeblemindedness and normality.

To aid in this test we may compare the proportion of defectives arising from each of the six theoretical matings. In the first hypothesis, according to the formulae of these matings "N" stands for normality and "n" for the absence of normality (or high-grade and low-grade feeblemindedness massed together). Now the six matings are:

Mating.	Percent of Defectives.		Mating.	Percent of Defectives.	
	Expected.	Found.		Expected.	Found.
1. NN × NN	0	0	4. Nn × Nn	25%	33.2%
2. NN × Nn	0	0	5. Nn × nn	50%	53.6%
3. NN × nn	0	37.5%	6. nn × nn	100%	77.3%

Two letters are used to represent the constitution of the germ cells of each parent, because these germ cells may be of two kinds as well as all alike. Opposite each mating is given the percentage of offspring, who, on typical "Mendelian" expectation should be "defective" in high or low degree, and also the actual percentage found. The results are plotted in Fig. 1 in a graphic form for a comparative study. These numbers are in agreement in matings 1 and 2 only; deviate widely in mating 3, and for the other matings run fairly close. In respect to mating 1, the accord with expectation is largely without significance, because just the absence of defectives from two normal parents is the main criterion for classifying in mating 1. In mating 6, the case of nulliplex by nulliplex,—hypothetically a pure recessive strain,—77.3 per cent. of the children are defective where 100 per cent. is expected. This large majority on the side where all of the offspring were expected indicates that the tendency of nulliplex by nulliplex is to reproduce itself. The 22.7 per cent. discrepancy requires some further explanation. It is evident that the hypothesis which includes all mental defects in one category does not fit the Mendelian expectation very closely.

A more careful analysis of some of the matings in case 6 may throw some light on the reasons for this misfit. The children who are classed as normal in the cases of IV 4 and 5, IV 33 and consort, III 27 and consort, III 39 and consort, III 46 and consort, on Chart A, and IV 27 and 28 on Chart B, are still so young and undeveloped that their traits now exhibited are not a reliable index of their true potentialities, but, apart from age, the results indicate that we are not dealing with a simple Mendelian phenomenon, simply because we are not making a study of one trait at a time. Take, for instance, the cases of those adults of feebleminded parentage, who are plainly much superior to their parents and to their defective brothers and sisters. Families of III 28 and 29, II 6 and 7 on Chart A, and II 1 and 2, III 14 and 15 and II 12 and 13 on Chart B show such variations.

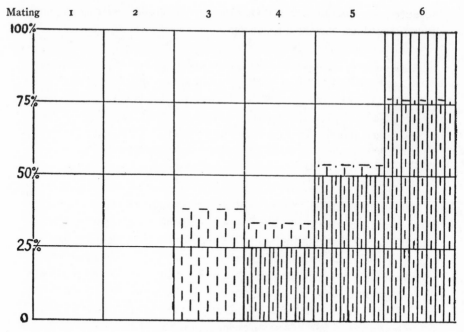

Figure 1.

In the family of III 28 and 29 on Chart A, IV 76 is a daughter about seventeen years old. Her filthy home shows the shiftless, untidy habits of both parents. The father is rough and boisterous and often ugly; his wife is more quiet. In contrast to her parents and her home, this girl is neat about her person, comparatively quiet in her manners, and responds intelligently in general conversation. She had to leave school on account of severe heart trouble, but was interested enough in her lessons to attempt to study at home. Conditions in the home, however, prevented her from accomplishing much and she soon gave up the attempt. Two children who died, IV 75 and 77, are reported to have been very like her, while all the rest of the family are more or less feebleminded. In the offspring of II 6 and 7, both of whom were decidedly deficient mentally, there are two practically normal girls. One of them, III 34, is a borderline case, but the other is more definitely normal. She has a comfortable home which she keeps fairly neat. Her conversation on her husband's business, on school matters and on her children disclosed the ideals and ambitions of a woman of ordinary intelligence. In the same fraternity are alcoholism, feeblemindedness, and cretinism.

One daughter of II 1 and 2 on Chart B presents a decided contrast to her parents and her numerous feebleminded brothers and sisters. None of the latter have risen above the grade of shiftless, unintelligent laborers and loafers, such as their parents were. She was associated with them in childhood and later was engaged in domestic service or a similar employment. She married a normal, industrious man who was able to furnish her with a good home. She is comparatively energetic, ambitious and neat. As a member of a local church, she mingles in its society and shows the ability and intelligence of an ordinary person. In her brother's family, III 14 and 15, there are two daughters in a fraternity of thirteen, who are capable of maintaining the usual standards of life. These girls were removed from home when eight and ten years old respectively. Their youth was spent in domestic service. Now, one of them is somewhat shiftless in her housekeeping, but aside from this carelessness she shows no marked defects. She responds to the interests and duties of her station in life as well as the average woman. Her sister is more careful of her home and has taken care of an elderly invalid, besides her own family. Doubtless an improved environment has played a part in the success of these two sisters, but others in the same fraternity who had had similar advantages (see IV 37 and IV 39) have been unable to react to them, and still exhibit evidences of feeblemindedness, such as untrustworthiness, poor judgment and immoral tendencies.

These facts raise the question whether an analysis on the basis of high and low grades of feeblemindedness is not too broad. We may find one case of feeblemindedness wherein the individual is cruel, and keen in the pursuit of mischief, but unable to learn, and another case in which he is kind and learns quite readily, but is shiftless and devoid of judgment and the ability to apply his knowledge. Such instances seem to indicate that these different traits which characterize the types of feeblemindedness may furnish a truer basis for a theory of inheritance. One combination of certain traits presents one sort of feeblemindedness, and another combination another sort. Working on this hypothesis, the possibility of obtaining from two parents whose defects are due to different traits (or the lack of them) a child who may be superior to either parent as a member of society, is to be expected. For instance, if such traits follow the Mendelian principle, a man who is industrious but apathetic and unable to connect cause and effect (i. e., lacks good judgment) so that he cannot compete in business, married to a shiftless woman who is keen and shrewd, even to a vice, may have offspring in which the father's industry and the mother's mental ability are combined so that they may be superior to either parent. For if the feeblemindedness of the father's type and that of the mother's type are gametically independent and each recessive to the normal condition, they may produce normal children according to the following formula.

Trait.	Gametic Description of Father.	Gametic Description of Mother.	Gametic Description of Offspring.	Somatic Description of Offspring.
Judgment (J)	jj	JJ	all Jj	All persons have good judgment.
Industry (I)	II	ii	all Ii	All are industrious.

The make-up of the father's germ cells (gametes) in respect to judgment is nulliplex, and is expressed by jj, while the gametic make-up of the mother in respect to the same trait may be duplex, since she exhibits the dominant conditions, and is expressed by JJ. In respect to industry, the father's gametic make-up may be II and the mother's ii. The children of this union, in respect to the first trait, would all appear normal and gametically would be Jj, or simplex, for that type of feeblemindedness. In a similar manner all the children would be normal in respect to industry, but gametically they would be simplex Ii.

Again, using the same union as an illustration, if the father in addition to his nulliplex condition for judgment were also simplex in regard to industry, one half of the children would be nulliplex for the latter trait, as is shown by the following formula.

Trait.	Gametic Description of Father.	Gametic Description of Mother.	Gametic Description of Offspring.	Somatic Description of Offspring.
Judgment	jj	JJ	100% Jj	All persons have good judgment.
Industry	Ii	ii	50% Ii 50% ii	50% are industrious but 50% are shiftless.

In a similar manner, it can be shown that if the mother were also simplex in regard to judgment, one half of the children would exhibit that type of feeblemindedness. In fact it is probable that a person who shows one type of feeblemindedness is simplex, rather than duplex, in respect to other types. For the unwritten but powerful social law which prevents one

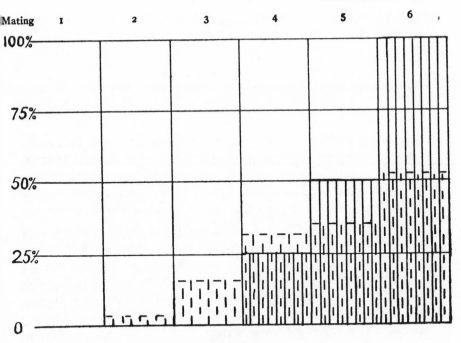

Figure 2.

stratum of society from marrying into another forces one type of feeble-mindedness to mate with another. In a few generations, then, the off-spring may be feebleminded in several different ways, we may get many defective children and a few normal ones. The large percentage of defec-tive children from the mating of defectives with defectives points to such an accumulation of undesirable traits, rather than any dispersion of them. The further study, therefore, of both abnormal and normal charac-teristics should proceed on the basis of the elementary trait or "unit character."

Again, when we test the hypothesis that low-grade feeblemindedness is recessive to high-grade feeblemindedness, we fail even more strikingly to fulfill expectation in matings 5 and 6. High-grade feeblemindedness in this case is massed with normality and included under the symbol "N," while "n" refers only to low-grade feeblemindedness. The graphic form of the correlation between the expected and observed results is plotted in Fig. 2.

The reason for this more striking failure to meet expectation is that, having defined our recessive or defective class even more strictly, a still larger proportion of offspring show no such defectiveness, just because the parents again do not lack similar traits.

Matings.	Percent of Defectives.		Matings.	Percent of Defectives.	
	Expected.	Found.		Expected.	Found.
1. NN × NN	0	0	4. Nn × Nn	25%	30.7%
2. NN × Nn	0	2.7%	5. Nn × nn	50%	33.7%
3. NN × nn	0	14.3%	6. nn × nn	100%	52.6%

The analysis of the data, then, gives statistical support to the conclusion abundantly justified from numerous other considerations, that feeblemindedness is no elementary trait, but is a legal or sociological, rather than a biological term. Feeblemindedness is due to the absence, now of one set of traits, now of quite a different set. Only when both parents lack one or more of the same traits do the children all lack the traits. So, if the traits lacking in both parents are socially important the children all lack socially important traits, i. e., are feebleminded. If, on the other hand, the two parents lack different socially significant traits, so that each parent brings into the combination the traits that the other lacks, all of the children may be without serious lack and all pass for "normal." However, inasmuch as many of the traits of such "normals" are derived from one side of the house only (are simplex), they may, on mating persons of like origin with themselves, produce obviously defective offspring.

V. MARRIAGE SELECTION

The large majority of the matings which are represented in this report are of defectives with defectives. A few of those who have drifted into a different part of the country have married persons of a higher degree of intelligence, but the most of such wanderers have, even in a new location, found mates who were about their equal in intelligence and ambition.

In a rural district which supports such a class of semi-paupers as has been described, the social advantages which come to them are meagre and narrow. After a long day's work on the farm or in the kitchen, the farm laborer and kitchen girl find their recreation in an evening of gossip, for they know everyone in the neighborhood. They may live near enough to their homes to go there at night. If such is the case, one dirty kitchen may hold half a dozen men and the women of the house. They smoke and drink cider and pass rude jests together and in the end sometimes fight. Away from home, they are ostracized by the other social classes. They occasionally have a dance which will bring together many of the same class from neighboring towns.

Under these circumstances it is not surprising that early marriages are the rule. After the legal age is passed, school work is dropped and, for a girl, the servant's life often begins, unless she is married at once. At any rate she anticipates marriage and works with that as a goal, not to escape work, but to gain a certain independence and that end of all effort, "to be married." Nor is it surprising that cousin marriages are frequent. In fact, even where no known relationship exists between the contracting parties, it is probable that they are from the same strains.

The early marriage is usually followed by a large family of children. Some die in infancy in nearly every home, but most of them survive a trying babyhood and develop fairly robust physical constitutions. They are born into the same narrow circle that their parents were, and unless some powerful factor changes the routine, they are apt to follow the same path until past middle age. For, except where tuberculosis has ravaged, disease has spared these people.

So it is that the meagre social life, the customs of their parents, the natural ostracism of the higher classes, and the individual's preference for a congenial mate induce endogamy, or in-marriage, among the mentally deficient.

It has been maintained that the dispersion of such communities of feebleminded persons would stimulate out-marriage and that this would increase the chance of marriage with different and perhaps better blood and thus diminish the frequency of appearance of defects in the next generation. The instances of the two daughters, II 8 and 10 on Chart A, who married comparatively normal men supports [sic] this view. Their progeny are, as a whole, a better class of citizens than the progeny of their sisters who mated with feebleminded men. Nevertheless, the fifty percent of the offspring who were feebleminded or criminal, even in these cases, constitute a menace which should be considered.

Another case still more to the point is that of III 19 on Chart A. He was from a criminal, alcoholic family and possessed both of these traits. He migrated to another state and married a woman who had more intelligence than either of the normal husbands of II 8 or 10. Only one of their children shows the criminal tendencies of the father, though the two youngest are neurotic, and backward in school. After the mother found out the real character of her husband and his family, she left him. While such repression of defective traits in the progeny by marriage into normal strains is beneficial to the community, it involves a great sacrifice on the part of the normal consort. However, the consort is only one; the progeny many.

The more frequent result of the migration of a feebleminded individual is his marriage into *another defective strain* in a different part of the country. The change in locality usually means that two different kinds of feeblemindedness are united instead of two similar types. The pedigree of the consort of III 9 on Chart B illustrates this point. Here is a union of stolid, shiftless feeblemindedness with a type of mental defect close to insanity. Let us examine this case in detail. III 9 on Chart B was a farm laborer who migrated a hundred miles eastward. He located in a rural community and married a girl whose family had lived in this place for several generations. Her family's pedigree is given below in Fig. 3 and its history is the following.

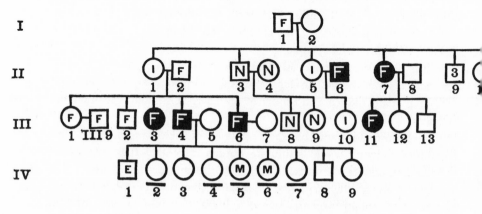

Figure 3.

The grandfather was always pointed out as a simple-minded man, harmless and inefficient. Nothing is known of his wife. They had eight children; one of whom is normal, three are mentally affected and the conditions of four are unknown.

The mother of the wife in question was known as a "crazy fool." Early in life she appeared merely feebleminded, but symptoms of insanity developed later. She now has a strong religious mania. She married a man who lacked judgment and ambition. He was easily imposed upon. He lived with her until they had five children, then, unable to endure his wife's mental condition, he left home. All of their children are feebleminded.

III 1 is the high-grade feebleminded girl who married III 9 on Chart B. III 2 was a son who worked out as a farm laborer. He was feebleminded and naturally the butt of his companions. When twenty years old, he was killed by eating poisoned melons by mistake. III 3 is a daughter who died at sixteen years of age and was defective mentally and physically. III 4 is a son now about fifty, who works for a farmer. He is a typical feebleminded man. He lives in a tenant house with one son. His wife, who is described as a fairly respectable woman, left him and took the two youngest children with her. They had nine children in all, five of whom are in institutions.

The oldest son (IV 1) who lives with his father has typical epileptic attacks; he does a little work as a farm laborer. The second child (IV 2) has been taken to the State Industrial School for Girls. The third one (IV 3) has begun the usual occupation for such girls,—housework in a farmer's family, though she is but fifteen. She is about normal mentally. Finally, there are four girls in the County Home for Children. Two of them have severe attacks of migraine, and none of them are strong children.

The last son married and left that part of the country. He was not normal, whether feebleminded or insane could not be determined.

The one son of the second generation who has become a good citizen is a bright, respected man, and keeps a small country store. He has married and has two bright children. His sister (II 5), known as "crazy Maud," married a feebleminded man and they had one child who became insane. Her sister's (II 7) mental defect was characterized by "foolishness." She was probably more feebleminded than insane. She married a man of whom nothing is known and had three children. One of these children is feebleminded like her mother. Finally, there were in this fraternity three brothers and one sister of whom nothing is known.

This pedigree is not cited as a rare example of a consort's defective family tree, but as a typical case. We must conclude, then, that the social laws and natural preference of the individual are so powerful that like will consort with like even in exogamy, or out-marriage. Consequently the benign results of exogamy to the next generation are realized only to a limited degree. The extent of the improvement in the characteristic defective traits will depend on the normal traits of the consort, or on the different type of feeblemindedness which he exhibits.

VI. THE FINANCIAL BURDEN ENTAILED BY CRIMINALS AND DEPENDENTS

A. Pauperism and Crime

Looking at the relation of The Hill families to society on the financial side, we see the three chief ways in which they have been an expense to the public are through town relief, court and prison charges, and their maintenance as the State wards. The town of about 2,000 inhabitants in which the original ancestors settled has had to bear most of the burden of the petty bills for relief. The poor records of this one town have been used to get an estimate of the cost of these families to the town, and these records run back only to war time. From 1863–64 to the present time, some families of The Hill have had partial or entire public support. The proportion of the town's poor bill which went to those families was not obtainable for the earlier years. Fairly accurate figures for the two decades, however, may give an idea of how the expense of aiding them has increased during the last thirty years.

Decade.	Total Aid to Paupers.	Aid to The Hill Families.	Percent of Total to The Hill Families.
1879–89 excluding 1888	$15,964	$1,483	9.3%
1901–1910	$27,045	$7,873	29.1%

In the accompanying table, the expenses for ten years from 1879 to 1889 inclusive have been used, except the report of the year 1888 which was not available. The names of families aided were omitted in the intervening years 1889–1900, but from 1901–1910 more detailed reports were published. In the first decade, 9.3 percent of the town's bill for paupers was paid for The Hill families. In the second decade, 29.1 percent of the total bill was paid for the same families or their descendants. During the thirty years covered by these decades, the total aid given to paupers increased 69.4 percent, but that given to The Hill families increased 430 percent. It is probable that more than 9.3 percent of the $15,964 expended from 1879–89 went to these people, for in some instances the names of those aided were not recorded. This possibility, however, would only slightly lessen the enormous proportion of 430 percent increase. Besides the usual bills for rent, provisions, fuel, and medical attendance, the last decade contains the item of partial support of three children in the State School for Feebleminded. The births, minus the deaths, during this same period caused an increase of about 59 percent in the number of individuals connected with The Hill families. This means, then, that for 59 percent increase in numbers, their expense to the public has increased 430 percent.

Turning to the court and prison records for the last thirty years, we find that at least sixteen persons from The Hill families have been sentenced to prison for serious crimes during that time (see Table I). A majority of these crimes were against sex, and the sentences varied from ten years to two months, or were indeterminate. Only four of these criminals are still in institutions, five are dead and the rest have served their terms and been discharged.

Table I. Cost of Crime

Person.	Crime.	Sentence.	Court Costs.	Penal Institution.	Total.
Chart A, III 1	incest.	9 years.	$236.89	$1423.54	$ 1660.43
" IV 1	lewdness.	2 years.	39.20	294.00	333.20
" IV 9	lewdness.	died after 2 years.	40.00	294.00	334.00
" III 12	perjury.	1 year.	25.00	216.44	241.44
" IV 31	lewdness.	2 years.	20.00	236.80	256.80
" III 18	assault with at-tempt to rape.	10 years.	304.86	1449.50	1754.36
" III 22	concubinage.	5 years.	147.66	767.40	915.06
" III 42	adultery.	5 years.	75.73	869.81	945.54
" III 47	burglary with at-tempt to rape.	6 years.	113.87	805.70	919.57
" III 36	assault.	1910—indeter-minate.	28.03	24.34	52.37
Chart B, III 3	arson.	5 years.	122.80	624.00	746.80
Chart B, III 54	assault and murder.	1899—indeter-minate.	384.38	1873.30	2257.68
Chart C, IV 38	lewdness.	1910—indeter-minate.	29.55	154.00	183.55
" III 24	assault.	2 months.	11.30	55.74	67.04
" III 46	habitual drunk-ard.	1910—indeter-minate.	25.44	18.75	44.19
" III 1	rape.	case filed, not sentenced.	51.40	—	51.40
					$10,763.43

The cost of these sixteen persons to the County and State through the courts and institutions has been at least $10,763.43. The accompanying table presents a slight analysis of the cost, and gives the crimes and sentences. The arrests for drunkenness and disorder have not been included. They are very frequent and the cases are usually disposed of by a fine or thirty days' imprisonment. About a third of the business of the district court comes from these families.

The third large item of expense which falls upon the public, through the State treasury, is the maintenance of the wards which have been taken from their homes. Table II gives the list of those who have become State charges from 1888 to September, 1911. Of the thirty-five, twenty-one are still under the control of the State as institutional cases or because they are under twenty-one years. The expenses of commitment, board, clothing, school tuition and officers' salaries is difficult to compute, but as accurately as can be estimated, these children, during the last twenty-three years, have cost the State $45,888.57. This means that for nine families about $2,000 each year has been expended to maintain children whose parents were unfit to care for them. One other expense to the State has been the care of the insane man III 15 on Chart C. His commitment and care in two different institutions since 1902 has been $1,831.32.

Table II. Cost of Maintenance of State Wards

Person.	Age when Committed.	Cost of Commitment.	Maintenance by State Board and Institutions.	Total.
Chart A, IV 14	12		$1,404.00	$ 1,430.30
Chart A, IV 16	6	$26.30	10.00	10.00
Chart A, IV 15	4		2,184.00	2,184.00
Chart A, IV 18	16	15.00	910.00	925.00
Chart A, IV 29	34	10.00	436.43	446.43
Chart A, V 31	4		384.00	409.00
Chart A, V 28	11½	25.00	384.00	384.00
Chart A, V 29	2		1,284.00	1,284.00
Chart A, IV 60	11			
Chart A, IV 61	8	25.00	5,091.84	5,116.84
Chart A, IV 62	5			
Chart A, IV 63	3			
Chart A, IV 104	10		18.00	77.67
Chart A, IV 105	4	59.67	18.00	18.00
Chart A, IV 106	3		18.00	18.00
Chart A, IV 112	6	49.77	756.00	805.77
Chart A, IV 115	1		756.00	756.00
Chart A, IV 117	11		1,224.00	1,259.00
Chart A, IV 119	8	35.00	1,656.00	1,656.00
Chart A, IV 121	7		2,010.00	2,010.00
Chart A, IV 118	9		1,692.00	1,692.00
Chart A, IV 138	10		1,140.00	1,180.05
Chart A, IV 139	8	40.05	1,200.00	1,200.00
Chart A, IV 140	7		1,140.00	1,140.00
Chart A, IV 141	4		1,178.00	1,178.00
Chart B, IV 28	12	26.51	1,404.00	1,430.51
Chart B, IV 29	10	6.20	1,560.00	1,566.20
Chart B, IV 31	8	19.70	2,028.00	2,047.70
Chart B, IV 33	5	19.10	4,108.00	4,127.10
Chart B, IV 35	4		2,652.00	2,652.00
Chart B, IV 36	10	25.00	2,818.00	2,843.00
Chart B, IV 37	8	15.00	1,404.00	1,419.00
Chart B, IV 38	6	15.00	1,716.00	1,731.00
Chart B, IV 39	4	15.00	2,213.50	2,228.50
Chart B, IV 41	9	12.00	651.50	663.50
			Grand total	$45,888.57

The financial burden, then, which The Hill people entail is constantly increasing, and that far beyond the proportion of their increase in numbers. This burden rests especially upon the town in which they live. The 400 percent increase in the financial aid which they have required in the last decade presents this fact in a startling manner. The large percentage of the crimes which were against sex indicate that the influence which such persons exert in a community is of far more importance than the 10,700 odd dollars spent in punishing the criminals after the influence has been established. The money expended on the State wards is well spent where even half of them are trained for useful citizenship, but the imposition upon society of an equal number of undesirable citizens calls for a policy of prevention which will work hand in hand with the present one of partial alleviation.

B. Comparison with the Jukes

A comparison of the results of this study with that of Dugdale on the Jukes will be profitable. The total number of individuals studied here is about the same: 737 persons as contrasted with 709 persons given in Dugdale's Summary. Of this number, in our study there are in generation I, 13; in gen. II, 68; in gen. III, 191; in gen. IV, 360 and in gen. V, 105.

Of the 737 persons represented in our charts 18 are known to be illegitimate, or 2.4%. This is in rather striking contrast to the Jukes where of 709 persons 91 are given as illegitimate, or 12.8%. There is other evidence of a greater regard in our community for legal marriage and, on the whole, considerably more sex-control.

Our community comprises 180 described persons of marriageable age. Of these, 152 are married (including 82 females) and 28 are not married. As compared with the Jukes our community has relatively twice as many unmarried persons. Of the married women, 14 had bastard children before marriage and 6 have had bastard children since marriage; or, together, 20 out of 82 married females, or 24%. In the Jukes there were 37 who had bastards out of 118 or 31%. In our community there are recorded 8 prostitutes, all married women, or 10% of the married women. Among the Jukes there were 128 prostitutes to 229 women of marriageable age. This form of sex-offense is, consequently, much less common in the Massachusetts community. Indeed, promiscuity, without any commercial aspect, is quite as common as prostitution here.

In our community charitable relief of all sorts, including almshouse, out-door relief, State wardship and out-farming, was given to 65 persons, of whom 37 were State wards. This is about 8.8% of all. Among the Jukes

204 out of 709 or 29% were recipients of aid. But Civil War pensions have contributed at this later date to the support of a larger proportion of persons than at the time the Jukes were studied. Our community comprises 136 "feebleminded" or about 48% of all. There are also 10 epileptics. Of the marriages 20 were between cousins, or about one fourth of all.

Criminal tendencies are clearly shown in 24 persons, 3.3%; and 16 have been convicted of crime, or 2.2%; and their total sentence is 37.5 years. In the Jukes there were 76 persons sentenced out of 709 or about 11% and the total sentence was for 110 years. Crime is much less rife in the Massachusetts community. It is, on the other hand, characterized by much alcoholism. If we recognize three grades in the use of liquor; viz., heavy, medium and light drinkers, and estimate the number of years during which they have used liquor, then it appears that there have been about 600 years of heavy drinking and 300 years of medium drinking. If the heavy drinker averages one pint of whisky per day and the medium drinker one third as much, then our small rural community has consumed, in the last two or three generations, at least 32,000 gallons of whisky at, say, $2.00 per gallon, costing altogether, $64,000.

In general, this Massachusetts community differs from that of the Jukes in having a larger proportion of indolent, unambitious persons, unable to progress at school, and probably a larger proportion of alcoholics; but, on the other hand, a smaller proportion of criminals and of sex offenders. They are, on the whole, less *active* as offenders. And this difference is probably due to an initial difference in their heredity constitution.

We may now attempt to give, following Dugdale, an estimate of the expense to the State of this one obscure community. [See list on next page.] The most of this loss has been incurred during the last sixty years, just because little is known about the community earlier than that time. Not until the third generation, born 1840 to 1860, do we begin to get a fairly complete view of the community. During the period of the past sixty years the cost to the State of this rural community of whose very existence the State is only beginning to take cognizance, has been half a million dollars. And there are probably a score or more of such communities within the borders of the State, some of them much more expensive than this community. It is probably a conservative estimate that all such *rural* centers of "degeneration" together are costing the commonwealth half a million dollars *each year*. These rural communities, just because relatively unrecognized by the State, and neglected, are, at the present time, of proportionately little direct cost to the State; but they are a rapidly increasing expense and the longer they are neglected the greater will be the eventual reckoning. While the feebleminded of our cities are promptly recognized and cared for by segregating, those of the rural communities are for the most part allowed to reproduce their traits unhindered and to create and send forth the broods of prostitutes, thieves, and drunkards that flock into our cities.

Number of adult paupers	20	
Cost of charitable relief		$ 15,000
Number of state wards	35	
Cost at $1,300 per year		45,800
Number of criminals and offenders	24	
Years of imprisonment	37.5	
Cost of maintenance and court costs		10,760
Number of persons guilty of habitual thieving	10	
Cost of depredations,		
at $100 per year for 10 years, each		10,000
Number of lives sacrificed by murder	1	
Value, at $1,700		1,700
Number of prostitutes	8	
Cost to the state and people, at Dugdale's estimate		170,000
Cost of property destroyed, arson, brawls, etc.		7,000
Money spent for drink		64,000
Number of years of		
labor lost during 640 years of hard drinking	320	
Ditto, during 280 years of medium drinking	28	
Loss, at $500 per year		174,000
Total Cost		$498,260

VII. SURVEY OF THE PRESENT SCHOOL CHILDREN

Most of the previous discussion has been in regard to the first four generations,—those individuals who are old enough to have their traits fully developed and their habits firmly established. There is, however, a comparatively large number of children between the ages of six and sixteen years, who are growing up to form the fifth generation of The Hill people. A brief study of the school record of seventy-five of these children as outlined in Table III may give one an idea of the prospect for the next generation.

The school record of seven of them is not known. The others have been divided into two classes, those who are up to grade and those who are

Table III. School Children From Sixteen to Six Years of Age

Person.	Age, September, 1911.	Parents.	Up to Grade.	Below Grade.	Grade Unknown.
Chart A, V 4	15	F—Industrious but feebleminded man; good workman; not alcoholic. M—Feebleminded; shiftless; epileptic till 16.		Nervous, hysterical and dull; epileptic till 12 years.	
Chart A, V 5	13	F—Industrious but feebleminded man; good workman; not alcoholic. M—Feebleminded; shiftless; epileptic till 16.		Nervous; slow to learn; dislikes school.	
Chart A, V 6	10	F—Industrious but feebleminded man; good workman; not alcoholic. M—Feebleminded; shiftless; epileptic till 16.	Slow, but not unusually dull.		
Chart A, V 7	8	F—Industrious but feebleminded man; good workman; not alcoholic. M—Feebleminded; shiftless; epileptic till 16.	Normal.		
Chart A, V 17	14	F—High-grade feebleminded; shiftless. M—From a low family; feebleminded; and immoral.		Slow; takes two years in a grade.	
Chart A, V 18	12	F—High-grade feebleminded; shiftless. M—From a low family; feebleminded; and immoral.		Inattentive and irresponsible; takes two years in a grade.	

Table III.—*Continued*

Person.	Age, September, 1911.	Parents.	Up to Grade.	Below Grade.	Grade Unknown.
Chart A, V 19	10	F—High-grade feebleminded; shiftless. M—From a low family; feebleminded; and immoral.		Inattentive and irresponsible; takes two years in a grade.	
Chart A, V 19 [sic]	8	F—High-grade feebleminded; shiftless. M—From a low family; feebleminded; and immoral.			1
Chart A, V 21	10	F—Son of marriage of feebleminded cousins; very alcoholic. M—Normal.	In fourth grade, does only fair work, slow to grasp new ideas.		
Chart A, V 22	9	F—Son of marriage of feebleminded cousins; very alcoholic. M—Normal.	Is in third grade; is a bright child.		
Chart A, V 25	7			First grade; is incapable of doing the work which other children do.	
Chart A, IV 47	14	F—Alcoholic; feebleminded; criminal tendencies. M—Normal.	Nervous; is defective in articulation; does fair work.		
Chart A, IV 64	11	F—Feebleminded; very alcoholic; unable to control sexual instincts; married his cousin.		In first grade for several years; seems impossible for her to learn.	
Chart A, IV 65	8	F—Feebleminded; very alcoholic; unable to control sexual instincts; married his cousin.	Is in second grade, and precocious in some lines.		

Table III.—*Continued*

Person.	Age, September, 1911.	Parents.	Up to Grade.	Below Grade.	Grade Unknown.
Chart A, V 38	9	F—Alcoholic; wanderer.			2
Chart A, V 39	7	M—High-grade feebleminded woman.			
Chart A, V 41	9	F—Very high-grade feebleminded; comparatively industrious. M—Migrainous; immoral tendencies; high-grade feebleminded woman.		Backward in school.	
Chart A, V 42	7	F—Very high grade feebleminded; comparatively industrious. M—Migranous; immoral tendencies; high-grade feebleminded woman.	Normal.		
Chart A, IV 78	12	F—Very alcoholic, shiftless, feebleminded. M—High-grade feebleminded woman.		Is about a year behind grade; not well, subject to fainting spells; is profane.	
Chart A, IV 79	9	F—Very alcoholic, shiftless, feebleminded. M—High-grade feebleminded woman.		Is in first grade; backward in book learning but grasps practical things quickly; untruthful and profane.	
Chart A, IV 104	10	F—Feebleminded; alcoholic; shiftless. M—Feebleminded and deaf.		Is in first grade; no power of attention.	

Table III.—*Continued*

Person.	Age, September, 1911.	Parents.	Up to Grade.	Below Grade.	Grade Unknown.
Chart A, IV 114	7	F—Alcoholic; shiftless. M—Tubercular; probably a high-grade feeble-minded woman.	Normal in school; has had epileptic fits.		
Chart A, IV 129	10	F—Neurotic; moderate drinker; average intelligence. M—Migrainous; average intelligence.			Valvular heart trouble.
Chart A, IV 132	11	F—High-grade feeble-minded man. M—Shiftless; high-grade feeble-minded woman with immoral tendencies.		Is in third grade in school; interested in his work, but unable to grasp ideas.	
Chart A, IV 134	9	F—High-grade feeble-minded man. M—Shiftless; high-grade feeble-minded woman with immoral tendencies.		Is in first grade; does only fair work.	
Chart A, IV 135	7	F—High-grade feeble-minded man. M—Shiftless; high-grade feeble-minded woman with immoral tendencies.		Not in school; tests a year backward by Binet.	
Chart A, V 48	10	F—Unknown. M—Immoral; average intelligence.	Normal.		
Chart A, V 50	8	F—Unknown. M—Immoral; average intelligence.	Up to grade; has one limb congenitally shorter than the other.		

Table III.—*Continued*

Person.	Age, September, 1911.	Parents.	Up to Grade.	Below Grade.	Grade Unknown.
Chart A, IV 154	11	F—Alcoholic; high-grade feeble-minded; poor physique. M—High-grade feebleminded; untruthful.	Normal.		
Chart A, IV 155	9	F—Alcoholic; high-grade feeble-minded; poor physique. M—High-grade feebleminded; un-truthful.	Normal.		
Chart A, IV 156	15	F—Migrainous. M—Migrainous; subject to fainting spells.		Anemic; subject to migraine; left school; poor student.	
Chart A, IV 157	13	F—Migrainous. M—Migrainous; subject to fainting spells.	Normal.		
Chart A, IV 158	11	F—Migrainous. M—Migrainous; subject to fainting spells.	Normal.		
Chart A, IV 159	9	F—Migrainous. M—Migrainous; subject to fainting spells.	Normal.		
Chart A, IV 171	14	F—Normal. M—Feebleminded; immoral tenden-cies.	Normal.		
Chart A, IV 172	7	F—Normal. M—Feebleminded; immoral tenden-cies.		Mischievous and quarrelsome; a poor student.	
Chart B, V 1	9	F—Normal. M—Very high-grade feebleminded.	Normal.		
Chart B, V 2	7	F—Normal. M—Very high-grade feebleminded.			

Table III.—*Continued*

Person.	Age, September, 1911.	Parents.	Up to Grade.	Below Grade.	Grade Unknown.
Chart B, IV 8	16	F—High-grade feebleminded, industrious. M—Feebleminded; shiftless.		Is in first grade; very feebleminded.	
Chart B, V 12	9	F—Unknown. M—High-grade feebleminded.	Normal.		
Chart B, V 13	6	F—Unknown. M—High-grade feebleminded.	Normal.		
Chart B, V 18	9	F—High-grade feebleminded. M—High-grade feebleminded.	Normal.		
Chart B, V 19	8	F—High-grade feebleminded. M—High-grade feebleminded.	Normal.		
Chart B, V 23	7	F—Normal. M—Normal; daughter of feebleminded parents.	Normal in school work but a delicate child.		
Chart B, V 25	8	F—Neurotic. M—Normal daughter of feebleminded parents.	Normal in school work; is cross-eyed.		
Chart B, IV 43	8	F—Feebleminded; shiftless. M—Imbecile.		Talks indistinctly; progresses slowly in school.	
Chart B, IV 61	12	F—High-grade feebleminded; shiftless. M—High-grade feebleminded.		Backward in school; unable to learn.	
Chart B, IV 62	10	F—High-grade feebleminded; shiftless. M—High-grade feebleminded.		Feebleminded; can not count above five.	

Table III.—*Continued*

Person.	Age, September, 1911.	Parents.	Up to Grade.	Below Grade.	Grade Unknown.
Chart B, IV 64	8	F—High-grade feebleminded; shiftless. M—High-grade feebleminded.		Very slow in school.	
Chart B, V 33	15	F—Unknown. M—High-grade feebleminded.			1
Chart B, V 34	11	F—Unknown. M—High-grade feebleminded.	Is in fourth grade; does good work.		
Chart B, IV 89	15	F—High-grade feebleminded. M—Unknown; tubercular.		Is in sixth grade; is slow and unable to grasp ideas.	
Chart B, IV 90	12	F—High-grade feebleminded. M—Unknown; tubercular.		Is in fifth grade, but not as bright as other children.	
Chart C, IV 1	10	F—Alcoholic; feebleminded; deaf and criminal tendencies. M—Feebleminded.		Very backward and troublesome in school; the butt of the other children.	
Chart C, IV 2	14	F—Alcoholic. M—Normal.		Is neurotic, dislikes school; is inclined to truancy.	
Chart C, IV 13	13	F—Apparently normal. M—High-grade feebleminded; migrainous.	Seventh grade; does fair work.		
Chart C, IV 14	12	F—Apparently normal. M—High-grade feebleminded; migrainous.		Is in sixth grade; slow to learn.	
Chart C, IV 15	7	F—Apparently normal. M—High-grade feebleminded; migrainous.		Has been in first grade two years; cannot count to ten.	

Table III.—*Continued*

Person.	Age, September, 1911.	Parents.	Up to Grade.	Below Grade.	Grade Unknown.
Chart C, IV 25	14	F—High-grade feebleminded. M—Migrainous; fair intelligence.		Is quiet and well behaved in school but requires two years in each grade.	
Chart C, IV 26	12	F—High-grade feebleminded. M—Migrainous; fair intelligence.		Is quiet and well behaved in school but requires two years in each grade.	
Chart C, IV 27	10	F—High-grade feebleminded. M—Migrainous; fair intelligence.		Is quiet and well behaved in school but requires two years in each grade.	
Chart C, IV 28	7	F—High-grade feebleminded. M—Migrainous; fair intelligence.		Is quiet and well behaved in school but requires two years in each grade.	
Chart C, IV 47	13	F—Alcoholic; feebleminded. M—High-grade feebleminded; shiftless.		Is nervous and deficient in school work.	
Chart C, IV 48	8	F—Alcoholic; feebleminded. M—High-grade feebleminded; shiftless.	Does fair work.		
Chart C, IV 57	12	F—High-grade feebleminded; shiftless. M—Shiftless.		Is in third grade; an indifferent student.	
Chart C, IV 58	11	F—High-grade feebleminded; shiftless. M—Shiftless.		Has not been able to do second grade work.	

Table III.—*Continued*

Person.	Age, September, 1911.	Parents.	Up to Grade.	Below Grade.	Grade Unknown.
Chart C, IV 59	9	F—High-grade feebleminded; shiftless.	Are in first grade.		
Chart C, IV 60	twins.	M—Shiftless.			
Chart C, IV 61	7		Normal; in first grade.		
Chart C, IV 73					2
Chart C, IV 74					
Chart C, IV 66	13	F—High-grade feebleminded; shiftless. M—High-grade feebleminded.		Is in third grade; stupid and lazy.	
Chart C, IV 68	13	F—High-grade feebleminded; deaf; shiftless. M—Tubercular; probably feebleminded.		Is in third grade; tries to learn but has not the mental ability to grasp his work.	
Chart C, IV 69	10	F—High-grade feebleminded; deaf; shiftless. M—Tubercular; probably feebleminded.		Slow and deficient.	
Chart C, IV 70	8	F—High-grade feebleminded; deaf; shiftless. M—Tubercular; probably feebleminded.		Slow and deficient.	

below the grade they should be in. Brief descriptions of the mental traits which they have exhibited in school serve as an index of the characteristics which are developing. Glancing down the list of thirty-eight children who are below grade, two causes for their backwardness stand out most prominently. Either they are unable to fix their attention upon one thing long enough to grasp it, or else they require so much more time to comprehend ideas upon which they have concentrated, that they progress only half as fast as the average child. They are frequently irregular in attendance so that they even lose the stimulus of regular systematic work.

All of these children attend rural schools where no special provision is made for the backward child. Because the schools are so small, this class of children not only constitute a drain upon the teacher's time and resources, but retard the progress of the entire class in which they are studying. Occasionally they develop mischievous qualities, but usually they are quiet, stupid laggards. They will leave school as soon as the law will allow and go to form the lower strata in the industrial world as they have in the academic. Five of these thirty-eight have one parent who is approximately normal.

Thirty children from similar families have kept up to their grade. Most of them do as well as children of ordinary parentage, though only eleven of them have one or both parents who are not feebleminded. A few of them are the slow ones in their classes.

This brief survey, then, indicates that before adolescence half of the children from The Hill families show evidences of their mental handicap. The detrimental influence which such children may exert upon the rural schools which they attend is an important matter for consideration. How many of the other half, who have held their own with children of average parentage, up to adolescence, will be able to keep up to the same standard from sixteen to twenty-five is an open question. Its solution depends largely upon the comparative weight of hereditary and environmental influences during that period.

VIII. HEREDITY AND ENVIRONMENT

Some of the children who were taken from home in childhood or early youth have improved over others of their fraternity who were left in a poor environment, and some have not. A comparative study of the varying results of good and poor environment upon individuals from the same germ-plasm increases the evidence of the power of individual potentialities.

Table IV has been compiled to show the two factors, heredity and environment, and the result of their combined action. The age of the individual at the time when the change in his environment occurred, and at the present time also, is given as another important factor. In view of the careful investigations of the State Board of Charity which precede the placing out of its wards, it is assumed that their new environment is conducive to normal development. Where details of the new home are known, they are inserted. The data on the present condition of the wards have been obtained from personal interviews with the individuals and from the records of the State Board of Charity. It is admitted that some of the data are unsatisfactory. The reports concerning the younger

Table IV. Relation of Heredity and Environment Upon Thirty State Wards

Person.	Age When Taken.	Age, September, 1911.	Parents.	Environment.	Result to September, 1911.
Chart A, IV 14	12	32	F—A feebleminded man, imprisoned for incest. M—A feebleminded woman who had two illegitimate children while her husband was in prison.	Placed on a farm; a good home; foster parents interested in him; they employ him since the state discharged him.	Was unable to progress in school. A good workman under supervision. Unable to care for his own money. Married a feebleminded girl and has two children.
Chart A, IV 15	4	24	F—A feebleminded man, imprisoned for incest. M—A feebleminded woman who had two illegitimate children while her husband was in prison.	Placed in several homes but none were permanent, chiefly on account of the boy's disposition.	Was untruthful and stubborn; inclined to petty thefts. In school was a fair, but disorderly scholar. Ran away from his last home.
Chart A, IV 16	6		F—A feebleminded man, imprisoned for incest. M—A feebleminded woman who had two illegitimate children while her husband was in prison.		Died at six years.
Chart A, V 28	11½	14	F—Feebleminded and very alcoholic. M—The illegitimate daughter of feebleminded cousins; also feebleminded.	Placed in a good home.	Is well and strong.
Chart A, V 29	2	10	F—Feebleminded and very alcoholic M—The illegitimate daughter of feebleminded cousins; also feebleminded.	Placed in a good home.	Does good work in school.

Table IV.—*Continued.*

Person.	Age When Taken.	Age, September, 1911.	Parents.	Environment.	Result to September, 1911.
Chart A, V 31	4	6	F—Feebleminded and very alcoholic. M—The illegitimate daughter of feebleminded cousins; also feebleminded.	Placed in a good home.	Is in good health; is a bright boy.
Chart A, IV 60	11	19	F—Feebleminded and very alcoholic; the illegitimate father of the mother above. M—Imbecile; daughter of cousin marriage; had the same mother as the above woman.	Placed out at service.	Neurotic, a good house maid; engaged to be married.
Chart A, IV 61	8	16	F—Feebleminded and very alcoholic; the illegitimate father of the mother of IV 33. M—Imbecile; daughter of cousin marriage; had the same mother as the mother of IV 33.		A good workman; forgetful, not strong minded.
Chart A, IV 62	5	13	F—Feebleminded and very alcoholic; the illegitimate father of the mother of IV 33. M—Imbecile; daughter of cousin marriage; had the same mother as the mother of IV 33.	Placed in a home with her younger brother.	Is a slight girl, untruthful and unkind to her younger brother.

Table IV.—*Continued.*

Person.	Age When Taken.	Age, September, 1911.	Parents.	Environment.	Result to September, 1911.
Chart A, IV 63	3	11	F—Feebleminded and very alcoholic; the illegitimate father of the mother of IV 33. M—Imbecile; daughter of cousin marriage; had the same mother as the mother of IV 33.	Placed in a home with the above sister.	Is dull and unattractive; quick tempered, and laughs without provocation.
Chart A, IV 112	6	11	F—Alcoholic and shiftless. M—Tubercular; probably feebleminded.	Placed in a good home.	Is amiable, quiet and well behaved; not bright for his age.
Chart A, IV 115	1	4	F—Alcoholic and shiftless. M—Tubercular; probably feebleminded.	Boarded out.	Attractive looking, large for his age and very healthy.
Chart A, IV 117	11	32	F—Neurotic; cousin to his wife's mother. M—Migrainous.		Had a satisfactory record till discharged by State Board. Is at work as a farm laborer.
Chart A, IV 118	9	31	F—Neurotic; cousin to his wife's mother. M—Migrainous.		Very slow to learn when young, but gradually improved; large for her age, is married.
Chart A, IV 119	8	30	F—Neurotic; cousin to his wife's mother. M—Migrainous.	Placed in a good home and attended school till seventeen.	Good and kindhearted, but slow to learn; now married.
Chart A, IV 121	7	29	F—Neurotic; cousin to his wife's mother. M—Migrainous.		Was inclined to steal and seldom told the truth; gave birth to an illegitimate child when sixteen. Discharged by the State Board.

Table IV.—*Continued.*

Person.	Age When Taken.	Age, September, 1911.	Parents.	Environment.	Result to September, 1911.
Chart A, IV 138	10	17	F—High-grade feebleminded; imprisoned for rape before his marriage to his cousin's daughter. M—Feebleminded; had chorea; imprisoned for lewdness.		In good physical condition. Has a difficult disposition; unbalanced mentally; untidy in his person.
Chart A, IV 139	8	15	F—High-grade feebleminded; imprisoned for rape before his marriage to his cousin's daughter. M—Feebleminded; had chorea; imprisoned for lewdness.		Was placed in State School for Feebleminded when fourteen.
Chart A, IV 140	7	14	F—High-grade feebleminded; imprisoned for rape before his marriage to his cousin's daughter. M—Feebleminded; had chorea; imprisoned for lewdness.	At board in a private family.	Has a disagreeable disposition; is given to use of profanity. Has poor mental ability; is in sixth grade at school.
Chart A, IV 141	4	11	F—High-grade feebleminded; imprisoned for rape before his marriage to his cousin's daughter. M—Feebleminded; had chorea; imprisoned for lewdness.	At board in a private family.	Over grown for his age; admitted to School for Feebleminded at eleven years.

Table IV.—*Continued.*

Person.	Age When Taken.	Age, September, 1911.	Parents.	Environment.	Result to September, 1911.
Chart B, IV 28	12	35	F—Shiftless and feebleminded. M—An imbecile.	Bound out at service.	High-grade feeble-minded but tries to care for her family well; married a feeble-minded man, has four apparently normal children.
Chart B, IV 29	10	33	F—Shiftless and feebleminded. M—An imbecile.	Bound out at service.	Shiftless, but has average intelligence; married an electrician; has one normal child.
Chart B, IV 31	8	31	F—Shiftless and feebleminded. M—An imbecile.	Bound out at service.	Has average intelligence; married and has one normal son.
Chart B, IV 33	5	28	F—Shiftless and feebleminded. M—An imbecile.	Placed on a farm with her brother.	Developed epilepsy at thirteen years; now in State Hospital.
Chart B, IV 35	4	27	F—Shiftless and feebleminded. M—An imbecile.	Placed on a farm with the above sister.	Has migraine; always sickly; of average mentality.
Chart B, IV 36	10	23	F—Shiftless and feebleminded. M—An imbecile.	Placed in a Children's Hospital.	Had epilepsy when removed from home, now in State Hospital.
Chart B, IV 37	8	21	F—Shiftless and feebleminded. M—An imbecile.	Placed out till seventeen, then lived in high-grade feeble-minded aunt's home.	Cannot support himself nor manage his own affairs; has committed petty larceny.
Chart B, IV 38	6	d. 17	F—Shiftless and feebleminded. M—An imbecile.	Placed out on a farm.	Could not talk plainly till ten years old; was not bright. A good workman; sometimes untrustworthy; d. at a State Hospital.

Table IV.—*Continued.*

Person.	Age When Taken.	Age, September, 1911.	Parents.	Environment.	Result to September, 1911.
Chart B, IV 39	4	17	F—Shiftless and feebleminded. M—An imbecile.	Placed in a good home where the woman was interested in her.	Had chorea and recovered. Was slow in school and inclined to truancy; has thievish and immoral tendencies. Now in a State Hospital.
Chart B, IV 41	9	13	F—Shiftless and feebleminded. M—An imbecile.	Placed in a Charitable Home, and placed out several times, but was always returned.	Is not very bright but a trusted boy about the Home.

children naturally emphasize the physical rather than the mental health of the child. In most cases, however, information on the mental and moral traits has been obtained.

Of the thirty state wards who have been away from home long enough to be affected, fourteen, approximately half, are at present, or probably will be, good, average citizens. Of these, seven carry an almost intangible burden of unfortunate heredity which may always be a retarding factor. For instance, a person is a good workman, but forgetful and easily influenced; or a good workman, but always physically handicapped; or a trusty boy, but slow to learn. The remaining seven whose ages vary from thirty-two to four are apparently without a serious handicap. But in three of these cases children from the same family who were younger when removed from home, have not developed desirable traits, like their older brothers and sisters. On the contrary, IV 62, on Chart A, who was five when her environment was changed, is untruthful and unkind to her brother, IV 63, who is dull and quick tempered and shows some evidence of mental deficiency. He was only three when taken from home, while the more successful children, IV 60 and IV 61, were eleven and eight years old. From another family, the three older children, IV 117, 118 and 119, developed satisfactorily while their sister, IV 121, who was but seven when taken to a good environment, was thievish and untruthful and gave birth to an illegitimate child when sixteen. The third contrast is on Chart B between IV 29, IV 31 and IV 35, and IV 37 and IV 39. The first three responded to their improved surroundings and have taken their places in the outside world very acceptably. The other two have not. IV 37 cannot care for his own money, nor support himself and has committed petty larceny. IV 39 has immoral and thievish tendencies and cannot progress at school. Here, IV 35 and IV 39 were both four years old when taken from home. It seems evident that the potentialities of the different members of these fraternities varied widely.

In some instances we can compare with those who were removed to a good environment, the careers of other members of the same family who were brought up in the poor environment of home. One sister in the fraternity where there are two successful and two unsuccessful State wards (Chart A, IV 60, 61, 62 and 63) married a drunkard. She is immoral and a common nuisance. A brother is becoming a confirmed drunkard; a sister eleven years old is decidedly feebleminded, but the three younger children, ranging from eight to four years, do not as yet show any abnormal traits. The children in the fraternity to which IV 117, 118, 119 and 121 belong, who remained at home, are of the same mediocre grade as three of those taken by the State. Apparently none of the children at home have shown the thievish and untrustworthy characteristics such as the State ward IV 121 has evinced. In the fraternity on Chart B which includes IV 28 to 43 there are normal children, epileptics and feebleminded among the ten who were removed from home. Only two, aged eight and ten, remained with the parents. One of these is an epileptic imbecile and the other is shy and somewhat backward at school. On Chart A, IV 112 and 115 also have a brother and a sister who were left at home when their family was broken up. The girl has a fairly good environment at her aunt's home and is apparently normal. Her brother who is epileptic lives with a feebleminded family and does well in his school work. All of the children in this family are so young and there is so little information in regard to the younger State ward, IV 115, that this case is of little value. In these cases, therefore, the children who have been left at home have usually, but not always, been behind their brothers and sisters who had better advantages.

We have been considering only the State wards who showed normal traits, and their fraternities in contrasting environments. Turning now to the families of III 1 and III 47 on Chart A, we have two examples of an entire family of subnormal children. IV 14 and 15 are uncles of the children of III 47. Both IV 14 and 15 were placed out in private homes. IV 14 is a plodding workman with good morals, but low mental ability. IV 15 was evidently more restless and had criminal tendencies. Among the brothers who remained at home, two very similar types occur. IV 5 on Chart A is industrious, dull and spiritless, efficient mentally rather than morally, while his brother, IV 8, was more active but not industrious; he was a sexual offender and has drifted out of the town. The differences in their environment had no appreciable effect on these boys. The one brother of IV 138–141, who is not dependent, has been adopted and has a fairly good home. He learns with difficulty but apparently has a more even disposition than the older children, 138 and 140.

There is one more aspect of the combined influences of heredity and environment to be considered. Occasionally in a fraternity all of whom had lived at home during their youth, one individual will stand out as superior to the others. The unfortunate parentage and environment have not left their mark on such persons, except in minor ways. The most striking instances of this are III 30 on Chart A and III 12 and III 39 on Chart B.

III 30 on Chart A has always lived among her brothers and other feebleminded relatives, and, as may be expected, shows her ignorance and lack of culture, but at the same time she has an interest in the condition of her home and children and in outside affairs, such as the church society, which her brothers and mother do not have. On Chart B, III 12 is the only one of seven married brothers and sisters who has a respectable home. The other homes are dirty and ill-managed. Hers is neat, modest and apparently well conducted. She also is interested in the local church. She was brought up with these shiftless, feebleminded children until the father's premature death scattered the family. She then entered service and the influences of this period of her life are not known. The third person, III 39, on Chart B is one of four children. She was always associated with her family and cared for her feebleminded mother who was addicted to the use of opium, until her death. Her home is comparatively neat and her daughter shows good home training. It is true that these exceptions are not frequent in comparison with the number of children in the same fraternity who do not rise above the level of their parents, but that they do occur is sufficient reason for noting them.

These cases, then, prove that persons belonging to these strains who have been brought up under good influences may turn out well or ill, and that even when placed *early* under the good conditions the result may be highly unsatisfactory. On the other hand, of members of the same fraternity who remained at home under the same poor environment, some turned out relatively well. It is not to be denied that the latter would have done better if their culture had been superior, nor that the "easily influenced" workman would have taken a wrong path if surrounded only by bad influences instead of good. But, on the other hand, it is clear that the capacity of these people for good or evil is born with them and bred in the bone and environment acts as a more or less effective screen or lure, as the case may be.

The five State wards who will always require custodial care (Chart A, IV 139 and 141, and Chart B, IV 33, 36 and 39), as well as the others who promise to be active troublemakers or passive drags, raise the old question of a more effective control of defectives. The appearance of an occasional normal child from very defective strains does not lessen the importance of the question, for the evil influences of the rest of the fraternity greatly overbalance such an exception.

The following history of the progeny of two persons who were plainly unfit for parenthood at sixteen years of age constitutes a powerful argument, especially from the financial point of view, for the policy of segregating positively defective germ-plasm. This family has lived most of the time on The Hill near the Rasp family, but only the parents are at home now as nine of the thirteen children have been taken by the State, three died in infancy, and one, in a Women's Reformatory. The father of IV 9 on Chart A may be called Jim (see Fig. 4). He came from a poor family of whom little is known, except that on his mother's side there was a criminal tendency that was shown by her brother and nephew. Jim had two brothers who were criminals; but he was not intelligent enough to commit a crime. He went to the war and became entitled to a pension. His guardian obtained one for him and for forty years has cared for it so that it might help support the family. Jim increases this income by day labor.

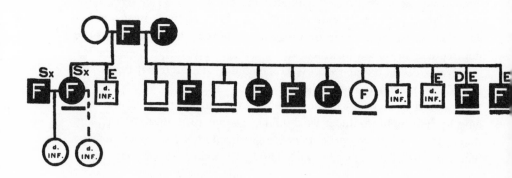

Figure 4.

The sixteen year old girl who became his first wife was from a fairly good family. She had two children, one of whom died in convulsions. At twenty-one she died from starvation and exposure to the cold. Jim soon married a woman who was very defective. She says she is nine years old and has had several children,—she cannot tell how many. The other members of her family are practically normal; and she seemed to be until after an illness at twelve years. The result of Jim's second marriage has been at least eleven children.

When the oldest children were ten, seven, and five years old respectively, the State removed them from home, charging the parents with neglect. They left a year-old baby with the mother. About the same time, the daughter of the first wife who had married IV 8 on Chart A was taken to a Women's Prison, where she died two years after the birth of her illegitimate child.

Ten years later the case of this family was again brought before the State and four more children were taken away on the grounds of neglect. Meanwhile, two of the babies had died, one at two years with typhoid fever, and one at three with convulsions. After another ten years had elapsed, the father inquired why his two remaining boys were not taken away. He complained that they ate too much. Neither of them could talk, one being both deaf and dumb. Both of them had "fits." The home was in the edge of a wood so that the boys ran about in summer like little wild animals. They often wore practically no clothing and were always chewing the stubs of old pipes. The State finally complied with the father's wishes and these two boys were removed.

On tracing the careers of these children, we find that the oldest one was discharged by the State Board when nineteen years old, with nothing unfavorable in his record. The second one was sent to a School for Feebleminded when eight years old. The third one was discharged with a very favorable record. Nothing definite is known of him since his discharge. Of the group of four, three were placed in the School for Feebleminded at twenty, fourteen, and four years respectively. The fourth one is now about fourteen years old. She is not very strong, has not recovered from an operation for adenoids, and does not develop rapidly mentally. The two youngest boys who have been recently removed are in a State Hospital. They can never care for themselves.

If we compare the possible cost of early segregation with the actual cost of this family, we find that if Jim and his second wife had been placed in custodial care at sixteen years of age at three and one half dollars per week, which is the average rate for institutional care, and had been maintained for forty-five years, they would have cost the State $16,380. Allowing the children now in institutions to live until fifty years of age, and computing the past cost for maintenance of the wards already discharged, we find that they will require $47,942, or nearly three times as much. This estimate does not include the frequent town aid which Jim has had, nor the possible expense the discharged wards may entail.

Such cases are not rare. The family of III 14 and 15 on Chart B would show a similar record, and these are only two taken from a limited area. Should the industrious, intelligent citizen continue in each generation to triple or quadruple his taxes for maintaining these defectives, and even then be subject to the increasing social menace of their offspring, or can steps be taken to strike at the root of the trouble and prevent the propagation of inevitable dependents?

SUMMARY

1. The analysis of the method of inheritance of feeblemindedness shows that it cannot be considered a unit character. It is evidently a complex of quantitatively and qualitatively varying factors most of which are negative, and are inherited as though due to the absence of unit characters.
2. The value of out-marriage, or exogamy, as a means of attenuating defective strains is diminished by the action of social barriers and the natural preference of individuals, which induce marriages among like grades of mentality, in a foreign as well as a native locality.
3. The amount of town aid which this one group of defective families requires decennially, has increased 400% in the last thirty years. In the same length of time its criminal bill has been $10,763.43 for sixteen persons; and the bill for its thirty children who were supported by the State during the last twenty-three years is $45,888.57. During the past sixty years this community has, it is estimated, cost the State and the people half a million dollars.
4. Half of the present number of school children from these families who are living at home show evidence of mental deficiency.
5. One half of the State wards from the community in question have reacted favorably in an improved environment and give promise of becoming more or less useful citizens; the other half consist of institutional cases and those which have not reacted to the better environment, but are likely to become troublesome and dangerous citizens.
6. The comparative cost of segregating one feebleminded couple and that of maintaining their offspring shows, in the instance at hand, that the latter policy has been three times more expensive.

IX. APPENDIX

Description of Chart A

I 1.   Old Neil Rasp, the originator of the pedigree shown on Chart A, came with his wife across the low mountains into a fairly good agricultural region about 1800. He was a basket maker by trade and his home was in various shanties in the woods. With the proceeds from his trade, and his hunting and fishing, he eked out a living. He was always very poor, for he drank heavily. His family was helped by neighbors. He is described by old men as a harmless fellow, "rather decent" as far as criminal tendencies are concerned, but very shiftless. Not much could be learned about his mental ability. His alcoholism impressed these old men most when they were boys. He died in 1866 and it was said that he was a hundred and one years old. His wife was a high-grade feebleminded woman who worked out for farmers' wives. She, too, drank but not to such excess as her husband did.

Two brothers of Neil appeared in this region about the time he came, but one of them had no posterity and the other one, Nute, settled in a neighboring town where his decendants form a low-grade strain plotted on Chart C.

Neil had five children, all of whom were defective. They have all had large families of criminal, feebleminded and alcoholic children. Twenty-five of their posterity have been, or are, State wards and others will be soon.

II 1.   One daughter, II 1, was born in 1811. She received no
b. 1811.   early education. She married a shiftless feebleminded fellow, II 2 (b. 1813–d. 1883), who was even less intelligent than herself. She worked out for farmers' wives.

II 4.   Another daughter, II 4, was also feebleminded. She mar-
b. 1815.   ried into a Nead family, which is said to have descended from a Hessian soldier who was left in this region when Burgoyne passed through, and which had always been noted for marauders and drunkards. Old man Nead, II 3, was very alcoholic, and in his later life, he had epileptic fits. He alternated excessive religious fervor with long sprees. II 4 was a tartar and "would have made a fiend of any man." They lived in a rude house and she did washing which gave her the opportunity for innumerable petty thefts. Her boys

show the most criminal tendencies of any in the pedigree.

II 6. The only son of old Neil Rasp was II 6, who was very shiftless and drank heavily. Like his father, he lived in shanties in the woods, and he devoted so much time to hunting woodchucks that he was known as "Woodchuck Sam." He was married twice and his decendants are the most alcoholic branch of the pedigree. At one time his entire family, wife and eight children, were wholly supported by the town, but for the last thirty years they have required only partial support.

II 8. The daughter, II 8, was weak-minded and acquired a very bad reputation, though no definite accounts of her life could be obtained. She married a man (II 9, b. 1830–d. 1885) who was on the list of the town poor but was fairly intelligent. He drank only moderately. Their offspring seem to be improving on the old stock in intelligence and thrift, but their morals are still low.

II 10. The daughter II 10 was "the brightest in the family," though not of average intelligence. She married a normal man and their children are brighter than any of the others in their generation.

Each of these five children will be taken as the founder of a line (Lines A to E). Among their children in the second generation there are seven cousin marriages.

Line A (Offspring of II 1)

Of her six children one, III 6, died at nineteen years, but the rest married.

III 1.
b. 1860.
d. 1900. III 1 worked about for farmers and finally married a very feebleminded woman from the Nuke family whose pedigree is found on Chart B. They had at least eleven children which the town helped them to support. When visited, the wife of III 1 was in the field husking corn. Her uncombed hair, heavy fleshy face and protruding lower lip made her look more like an animal than a woman. She could not tell how many children she had had nor where many of them were. Three of them had been taken by the State as neglected children and she had never heard from them. Her husband was in State Prison for nine years for incest with his daughter. During that time she had two illegitimate children (IV 19

and 20). Of one of them nothing is known. The other one is a farm laborer, a good worker, and has average intelligence.

IV 1.
b. 1874.
d. 1909.

Of her legitimate children, IV 1 was committed to a Women's Reformatory for two years as a result of her father's crime. This was when she was seventeen years old. She later married her father's own cousin, III 47, who had been in prison for burglary with intent to rape. She was able to read but was feebleminded and had chorea. Her children are described in her husband's family, page 142. She died at twenty-five years of age of heart trouble.

IV 3.
b. 1874.
d. 1901.

The twin brother of this girl was feebleminded and worthless. Nothing is known of his wife. Both of their children died in infancy, one at two years of bronchitis, the other at nine days of congenital debility.

IV 5.
b. 1872.

Another brother is a plodding, faithful workman on a farm, with little ambition and low mental ability. He earns good wages which he turns over to his wife. She is a very shiftless and incompetent woman from a feebleminded family. She was subject to epileptic fits until sixteen years old. They live in a farmer's tenant house five or six miles from the railroad. The four children do not like school and do not get on well. They live near the school house, so the teacher sends them home, sometimes, to be cleaned up.

The oldest girl is fifteen. She had epileptic attacks until twelve years old, and is now nervous and dull, and has the heavy stupid expression of an epileptic. One of the boys is nervous and slow to learn and seems deficient mentally. The eight and twelve year old children appear normally bright, but it is a question how long they will develop normally. Three of this fraternity died in infancy; two were twins who lived three weeks and then succumbed to whooping cough.

IV 7.
b. 1878.

IV 7 is a high-grade feebleminded woman, who is possibly syphilitic. She married her father's own cousin, III 46, in whose family her children are described (page 142). Before her marriage she had one illegitimate girl, V 11, who is now about seventeen years old.

Another daughter gives satisfaction in the small boarding house where she is employed, but is very untruthful and persists in making friends of the girls who hang about the railroad station at train time, though her employer, a good, intelligent woman, has tried to dissuade her from it.

IV 8.
b. 1869.

A son was a wild immoral fellow, who married a feeble-minded girl (b. 1872–d. 1897) from a family which has had all its nine children that lived through infancy removed by the State Board of Charity, as neglected children (see page 126). They lost one child. She became pregnant by a town loafer and was taken to a Women's Reformatory. This illegitimate child died there when a year old, and the mother died about two years after her commitment. The husband lived with various women after his wife was taken away and all trace of him has been lost.

Of the three children of this fourth generation who were taken by the State, one was twelve, one six, and one four. The six year old boy, IV 16, died soon after his removal.

IV 14.
b. 1879.

The twelve year old boy was boarded out with a farmer. He was deficient mentally so that he could not progress at school. He was a good workman but lacked judgment and any idea of the value of money. When discharged by the State, he remained in the employ of his foster father who cares for him as a guardian. To everyone's surprise he found a girl who consented to marry him. She is a slattern and comes from a low-grade family. They live in a small unplastered house near the farmer's home. His foster father reminds him when his wood pile needs replenishing and goes to town with him to get his provisions, and his daughter makes clothes for the children. With this supervision he keeps his family fairly comfortable, but otherwise they would be continually in distress. His two children are five and three years old. The oldest one was a bright baby, but is losing her keenness and seems apathetic. In the case of this man, a good environment was not able to overcome the influence of his heredity. Note, too, that there is no restraint to the propagation of a large family here, like the father's own. This family, as soon as, or perhaps before, his old friends are gone will become a public burden and menace.

IV 15.
b. 1887.

The four year old boy was also placed out. He was stubborn and untruthful and committed petty thefts. He was a fairly good but disorderly scholar. He finally ran away with some other boys and no trace of him has been found.

IV 18.
b. 1890.

The youngest child was working in a neighboring state and was placed in the State Industrial School for Girls because her surroundings were conducive to trouble. She could not progress above the second grade in school, and was subject to violent fits of temper which have recently become less frequent.

There were at least two children in this fraternity who died in infancy, one of diphtheria and one of convulsions, and the mother remembered that she had given birth to one still-born child.

III 5.
b. 1844.

We return, now, to the third generation. The oldest brother is a high-grade feebleminded man, shiftless and happy-go-lucky; he cannot read nor write. He married a woman of the same type who inherited a small farm from her father, where they now live in a dirty little house in a pasture. He also has a little money in his own right inherited from his mother. She obtained it from the government through a long law suit after the death of her son II 6, who died in the war. III 5 has no children.

III 7.
b. 1853.
d. 1907.

The second sister has a short history. She was a high-grade feebleminded girl, and married a farm laborer who was very alcoholic. She had but one child (b. 1869) who was migrainous and is subject to "fainting spells." This daughter married her mother's own cousin who is described under III 52, page 143. The mother died in a hospital from an operation.

III 9.

III 9 was an immoral feebleminded woman. She kept a kind of country tavern six or seven miles from town. Of the various men who lived there she was probably married to a drunken, shiftless fellow whose name the children bear. She was shot in a drunken brawl while trying to separate two men who were quarreling about her.

Of her children, IV 22 has migraine and is of fair intelligence. She married her mother's cousin and the family is described under III 41, page 141.

IV 24 is shiftless, dull of comprehension and easily influenced. He works some of the time in a mill; married an immoral French woman from a low family, and lives with her in a very dirty, ill-kept tenement with her four children. The oldest boy is a low-grade imbecile, he can do a little mechanical work in the mill, but is known in the village as the "foolish fellow." The daughter is untidy but was doing the house work when the home was visited. In school both she and her two younger brothers are inattentive and irresponsible, often staying two years in a grade.

Little information could be obtained concerning IV 25, except that he married and had seven or eight children who are scattered in the nearby city, most of them with families of their own.

III 11.
d. 1872.

III 11 was a plodding, dull, drinking fellow who went to war and on his return married his own cousin (III 12, b. 1847–) who is so feebleminded that she has a guardian to care for her pension money. The result of this marriage was a daughter who is a low-grade imbecile (IV 27), but the mother of eleven children; one son who is very alcoholic (IV 28), but the father of seven children; and an epileptic son (IV 29). About four years after his marriage, the father died from pneumonia, contracted, it is claimed, by spending a night in the pig pen when he was so drunk that his wife would not let him into the house. His family were entirely supported by the town for the next six years, costing over $1,300, and then partially supported for two years. By that time the widow had secured a pension which, with State aid and help from the town fund for dependent soldiers, has supported her for the last thirty years. A few years after her husband's death she had an illegitimate colored child, IV 31, and was imprisoned in the Women's Reformatory for a year on the charge of perjury in regard to the child's father. Soon she had two more children, IV 33 and 34, by a cousin, III 27, who later married her imbecile daughter (IV 27). Their family is given under III 27, page 137.

IV 28.
b. 1871.

The alcoholic son married III 21 (the former wife of his mother's cousin) while her husband was in jail. He has often been arrested for drunkenness and disturbing the peace. His home is a typical one for a drunkard. The children were sucking old pipes for playthings. The hard-working wife is ignorant but of average intelligence. There were seven children of whom two died in infancy. The oldest boy is ten; both he and his older sister are slow in school, but not abnormally dull. Two other children are very backward in their school work; the youngest is not of school age.

IV 29.
b. 1872.   The epileptic son is also feebleminded and congenitally lame, probably from clubfoot. He was supported with his mother for years, but has now been placed in a State School for Feebleminded Children.

IV 31.
b. 1877.   The mulatto daughter married and had one child. She left her husband and was living with another man who had served a term in the State Reformatory for theft, when she was sent to the Women's Reformatory for sixteen months for lewd and lascivious conduct. She was then twenty-one years old.

IV 33.
b. 1881.
d. 1907.   One of the illegitimate daughters by her cousin was feebleminded and married a very alcoholic man from a family of the same grade as her own, in the neighboring town. (See Chart C, IV 41.) She had three children, one of whom, a blue baby, died when five days old. She was arrested for adultery once, but no case was proven. Her two year old child was taken by the State at this time. When only twenty-six she died from the kicks and blows of her drunken husband, and the two remaining children became State wards. All three children are well and strong and still (at 14, 10 and 6 years) getting on nicely in school. They have, so far, reacted well to their good environment.

IV 34.
b. 1886.   The remaining illegitimate child is a high-grade feebleminded girl who keeps a comparatively neat cottage near the tiny shack in which her mother lives. She married a decidedly feebleminded man who drinks heavily. They have no children.

Line B

Returning to the second generation, the next in order is II 4. She was the daughter who married into the Hessian family and whose sons are criminal.

III 12.   III 12, who has just been described as the consort of III 11, was one of this family.

III 15.   III 15 is probably feebleminded. She appears of average intelligence, for she is sharp-tongued and voluble. She is immoral and somewhat addicted to the use of alcohol. She has been married twice to drunkards, and has two boys by her first husband and a daughter who is illegitimate. Her second husband drinks so much that he can not conduct his business of caning chairs. One son is a wild fellow who is not married but who cohabits. The other son has married and is a "good fellow," but drinks heavily. The daughter is fairly intelligent, but very ignorant. Her husband, also, is a drunkard and is not strong. They have three small sickly children.

III 18.   III 18 was the black sheep of this rather black family. He could not progress at school and was wild and dissolute. He was finally sentenced to State Prison for ten years for assault with intent to rape. His trial and maintenance in prison cost the State over $1,700.

III 19.   The next brother is a high-grade feebleminded man and a confirmed drunkard. He stabbed his father in a drunken row, wounding him severely. He moved from his native town and married a normal woman who says she would never have married him if she had known his family. She will not live with him now, but hires a few rooms for herself, and her sons help to support her. They have six boys. The oldest son formerly drank, but through church influences has reformed; has married a normal woman and has a good home and two little boys. The second son married an Italian girl and went to the city. IV 44 is a good workman in a factory and helps to support his mother. The fourth son is unmanageable. He is underhanded and wild and has been arrested for petty larceny. The school record of the two youngest boys shows that both of them have neurotic tendencies. One was subject to violent fits of temper, and both had some difficulty in articulation. They were fair scholars.

III 22.
b. 1855?   This son would not progress in school. He was immoral before his marriage to a girl who was working for his mother. They had two children, one of whom, the boy, lives with his mother. The girl died in infancy. This man was sentenced to five years in State Prison for concubinage, about thirteen years ago. Soon after he went to prison his wife married IV 28, her husband's nephew. The former is now at liberty, a shiftless, immoral wanderer.

III 24.   III 24 was employed at housework when a girl and gave satisfaction. She had three children by one man before she was twenty-one and then married him, as she learned that otherwise she could not legally claim anything from him. She is now a confirmed neurasthenic and very hysterical.

At one time she was sent to an institution for treatment for mental trouble. Her husband is a collier and fairly respectable. They have a comfortable home. Their son is not ambitious, but works in a small store, is a "slim stick"; caused the downfall of a girl that was a ward of a charitable institution, and finally married an apparently bright intelligent girl. The older daughter is an imbecile of a low grade, the cause of whose deficiency is given as scarlet fever, but it is probably congenital. The younger daughter has migraine, but nothing definite could be ascertained about her mental ability; she works in a factory.

The youngest daughter of II 4 was a good-natured, fairly industrious girl, who married a barber. They had two boys. The family could not be located.

Line C

II 6.
b. 1830.?
d. 1894.
"Woodchuck Sam" was married twice. Nothing is known of his first wife by whom he had two boys, III 27 and 29. Both of these boys are alcoholic and have large families living in abject poverty. Sam, himself, had town aid almost continually. The oldest entry of such aid dates back to 1864.

III 27.
b. 1850.
One son is the man by whom II 12, his cousin, had two illegitimate children. He then married her imbecile daughter, IV 27 (b. 1869). Immorality and alcoholism are his worst vices, but he has also committed petty thefts. He works as a teamster or woodchopper when he is sober. He has sprees which last two or three weeks. At such times he uses all his money for hard cider and then his wife begs or steals more cider for him. Two of their eleven children are married and four have been taken by the State. When they are not travelling around the country visiting, they live in an old house on the edge of the woods three or four miles from town. There is almost no furniture in it and the broken windows are stuffed with rags. An agent from the State Board of Charity investigated the case recently, preparatory to removing the four youngest children. The family became alarmed and moved to a neighboring State, so that the matter is delayed until their return.

IV 57.
b. 1888.
The oldest daughter married a drunkard and lives in a small hamlet where the stage is the only means of communication with the town several miles away. She is lazy, un-

truthful, and immoral. Her filthy home is often the center of drunken disturbances.

IV 58.
b. 1889.
The second daughter married her own cousin, but died of tuberculosis before she had any children.

IV 59.
b. 1890.
The oldest boy, about twenty-one years old, is following his father's drinking habits. He is a farm laborer.

IV 60.
b. 1892.
Of the four children who were taken by the State, IV 60 is neurotic and not very strong mentally. She earns good wages at service and is engaged to be married.

IV 61.
IV 61 is not strong physically or mentally, and is very forgetful.

IV 62 & 63.
One brother and one sister are together in a home. The girl is not very strong, and is untruthful and unkind to her brother. He is dull, unattractive, quick-tempered and laughs without provocation.

IV 64–67.
The four younger children are underdeveloped and ill-cared for. Their school work is often interrupted when the father is on a spree and the mother takes them visiting. They are shy and apprehensive. IV 64 is feebleminded. At ten years of age she is in the first grade and cannot learn anything. The younger children are under eight and have not developed the traits of their older brothers and sisters.

III 29.
b. 1852.
The next younger brother of III 27 is very alcoholic, and when drunk, extremely cruel to his family. He chops wood in the winter and loafs or works, as it happens, in the summer. His wife is a very high-grade feebleminded woman. Her mother is a hard-working, dull, but respectable woman, who has cared for various illegitimate children of her other daughters. The former home of this family was a tumbled-down house on a stage route six miles from town. It was a rendezvous for all relatives when they were especially down on their luck, but this family has also moved over the line to prevent the State from taking their children. There have been ten of these (IV 69–81), of whom an account follows.

IV 69.
b. 1881.
The oldest girl is a high-grade feebleminded woman. She has been married twice. She left her first husband on the ground of non-support and married a laborer who is a wanderer. They never live long in one place. He has a spree about every month. They have three children (b. 1902,

1904, 1906), the oldest of whom was very backward in learning to walk and talk.

IV 72.
b. 1884.
IV 72 is a slovenly woman who has severe attacks of migraine. She married a somewhat feebleminded laborer, but they have separated. Their dirty home was situated at a cross roads where teamsters often stopped. The woman has a reputation for immorality and one of the three children is a small dark type very different from the others. This one has a hip congenitally undeveloped, but it is improving as she grows older. All of the children are under ten years of age. This mother and children have also left the State to escape a warrant of the State Board for neglected children.

IV 73.
b. 1886.
IV 73 is a woodchopper and a drunkard. He brought his feebleminded wife to his father's already over-crowded house. They fled with the father's family to save their dull anemic baby (b. 1908) from the State Board. One daughter in her teens was found with a broken neck at the foot of an embankment. It is supposed that the father in a drunken rage chased her from the house and off the bank.

IV 76.
b. 1892.
The next daughter is a delicate girl who has a chronic heart trouble and cannot live many years. She is fairly intelligent and keeps herself comparatively clean.

Two boys died; one in infancy from convulsions, and one of appendicitis. The latter was considered the brightest of the family.

IV 78 and 79 are in school but are slow and backward, partly because the family have moved so often. The boy does poorly in the first grade at nine years, but grasps practical things quickly. Both children are untruthful and profane. The youngest children (b. 1903 and 1906) do not attend school.

II 7.
After his first wife died "Woodchuck Sam," II 6, lived about in the woods in shanties with his two little boys, but soon married a feebleminded woman, II 7, from a low family. She has a cleft palate. The result of this marriage was eight children (III 30–40), the youngest of whom is a typical cretin.

III 30.
b. 1869.
The eldest girl is apparently normal. She married a man from a shiftless family. He formerly had a long court record for drunkenness, but through the church he has reformed

and is conducting a paying business. He has a comfortable home and three apparently normal children.

III 31.
b. 1881.
III 31 has a good trade at which he could easily earn four dollars a day, but he does not work regularly and drinks up all his wages when he does work. He married his cousin's daughter, IV 123, who is about the grade of a moron. She has had two children and one miscarriage. The children are underfed and underdeveloped physically and mentally. One of them has fits which the country doctor attributes to malnutrition.

III 32.
III 32 is feebleminded. He is married but does not live with his wife. He returned to his mother's home.

III 34.
III 34 is practically normal mentally. She married the brother of her uncle, II 9. He is a high-grade feebleminded man, and has the physical defect of a hare-lip. They live four miles from town in a lumbering district where he works as teamster. They have seven children living, and lost a baby at three months.

Two boys are normal and one girl's characteristics are not known. IV 89 is feebleminded and has immoral tendencies. She married her mother's cousin III 54 (page 143) and her children are described in his family. Since his death she has lived with her uncle though not married to him. Two of the boys have hare-lips: one of them, 92, is a good workman and is normal mentally; the other, 98 (b. 1888), is decidedly feebleminded and lives at home. IV 95 is the only child who shows the mother's weakness, and has asthma.

III 36.
b. 1878.
III 36 is a shiftless drinking fellow. He married a feebleminded woman who became deaf following scarlet fever. She had the same surname as her husband, but is no near relation. She has been married eleven years and has had nine children and one miscarriage. Four children died in infancy. The family moved continually from place to place and had almost constant town aid. The father worked a little on wood jobs but spent all his wages on hard cider. He was finally brought into court for neglecting his family; but conditions did not improve and when warrants were taken out to remove the children they left the State. On their return three children were committed to the State and the father was sent to the State Reformatory for assaulting an officer. The mother being pregnant, although a menace to

the community, was allowed to take her youngest child and go to her sister's home, an undesirable place, where she is now with that younger child and the new baby.

The oldest girl, of ten years, is like a little animal. She begged the sheriff for tobacco and spat and swore like a trooper. All the children were accustomed to chew old pipes at home. They were dull and anemic.

III 38.   III 38 is a high-grade feebleminded man. He has a cleft palate like his mother. He is less shiftless than his brothers and does not drink to excess.

III 39.   This son is a big, strong, laboring man, but a drunkard. He married a fairly normal woman (Chart C, III 42) who died of tuberculosis at twenty-nine years of age, leaving four little children,—two others had died in infancy. The father is forced by the court to pay for the board of one child who is with his maternal grandmother. This boy, IV 114 (b. 1904), is epileptic. The State took two children, 112 and 115; 112 (b. 1900) is not bright for his age, but is a quiet, well-behaved child, and 115 is normal. An aunt is caring for 113 (b. 1906) who is apparently normal.

III 40.   The youngest girl at twenty-six years of age was three feet tall and weighed sixty pounds. She is a typical cretin.

Line D

II 8.   II 8, who married into a normal family, had four sons. This family has been aided by the town at various times, but is more industrious and less alcoholic than those previously described.

b. 1838.
d. 1908.

III 41.   One son married his cousin's daughter, IV 22, and has had ten children. He is neurotic and drinks moderately, but is of average intelligence. His wife has migraine. They live in a tenant house three miles from town and keep their family fairly comfortable. In his early married life he drank more and did not provide for his family, so that four of his children were taken by the State.

b. 1857.

The boy has returned home and married and works for a farmer in a neighboring town. He is normal.

The three girls were always slow in school but gradually improved. One of them, I 21, was always inclined to steal and seldom told the truth. When sixteen she had an illegitimate child. The other two girls have good moral reputations. The daughter who married her father's cousin has been described under III 31 as a moron.

The other children are practically normal, but their environment is poor. The boys work for farmers. IV 127 has married a shiftless, alcoholic lawyer, and has one child. They live in a tiny village seven miles from town. IV 128 is a nervous girl about sixteen years old. She left school and went away to be married, as her mother supposed, but she returned in a week unmarried.

III 42.
b. 1871.
The only criminal in this branch of the family was imprisoned for rape. He afterwards married and had one daughter.

III 44.
Another brother married a woman from a low miserable family. His whereabouts are unknown.

III 46.
b. 1877.
The fourth brother married his cousin's daughter, IV 7, who already had an illegitimate child. He is a teamster and lives in a prosperous town. He is a high-grade feebleminded man and drinks moderately. He earns good wages but his home is very poor. The children are dirty and ill-cared for. All except the oldest and youngest children are in school and are a little backward. The oldest boy (b. 1896) is a farm laborer, the usual occupation for this type of boy.

Line E

II 10.
d. 1900.
The brightest of old Neil Rasp's daughters married into a family of ordinary working people. Many of them drink but they have fair mental ability. She had eleven children (III 47–61), three of whom died in infancy, four are practically normal and the others are weak mentally or morally.

III 47.
b. 1865.
d. 1904.
One of the sons was a wild fellow. He was arrested for breaking into a house with intent to rape, and was sentenced to State Prison for five years. On his return to his native town, he married the daughter (IV 1) of his cousin. She was a feebleminded girl who had chorea and who had been in a Woman's Prison for two years for lewdness. She had five children, besides the one by her father. The State removed four of these children on the charge of neglect when the oldest was ten years old. The youngest boy was adopted by a friend.

Of these five children IV 138 is in good physical condition, but has a difficult disposition. He seems somewhat unbalanced mentally and is untidy in his person. Two of these wards who were eight and four years old, when removed from home, have been placed in the State School for Feeble-minded Children. IV 140 was seven years old when taken by the State and placed at board in a private family. She has a disagreeable disposition, is given to the use of profane language, and at fourteen years of age is only in the sixth grade at school. The adopted child has a good home but does not progress at school. In these cases, the hereditary tendencies have been such as to lead to a favorable reaction to the good environment.

III 48.
b. 1863.
One of the normal daughters of II 10 married a drunken fellow who has not lived with her for twelve years, but who supports one of the four children, IV 148 (b. 1889). Of these the eldest had one illegitimate child (b. 1901) before her marriage. She seems to be normal. Of the two children by her present husband, the older one has one limb congenitally shorter than the other and is a delicate child; the younger one is normal. IV 147 has spinal trouble so that she is obliged to use crutches. She is married but has no children. The son IV 149 (b. 1892) is normal.

III 50.
III 50 is a good workman but very alcoholic. He is round-shouldered, narrow-chested and in a poor physical condition. His wife is an untruthful feebleminded woman whose first two children were still-born. Their boys are about normal mentally; they progress fairly well at school. The two oldest are like their father, narrow-chested and round-shouldered.

III 52.
Another son has a plain but comfortable home. He does not drink to excess. He suffers from migraine and has a severe cough. He married the daughter (IV 21) of his own cousin who is normal mentally, but ignorant and brazen. She is subject to migraine and to numb spells, when she will talk incoherently. All but one of their eight children are living, and only one of the seven seems to be below the average. She is anemic, has migraine, and is dull mentally.

III 54.
Another brother died in middle life of a cancer. His chief characteristics were his ability as a workman and a stubborn, disagreeable disposition. He was married twice. By his first wife he had seven children, two (IV 165 and 166) of whom are very stubborn; one of them had to leave school for that reason. One daughter (IV 170) is a high-grade fee-

bleminded girl, but the other children are normal. His second wife was the feebleminded daughter (IV 89) of his own cousin, who after his death lived with her uncle. There were two children of this second marriage, IV 171 and 172, one of whom is normal, and the other is not defective, but is mischievous and quarrelsome, always getting into trouble with the other boys.

III 55.   III 55 was accidentally shot. He was the most promising child in the family.

III 60.   The last two daughters were both high-grade feeble-minded women, and both died from blood poisoning as the result of abortion. The first of these (III 60) married into an unintelligent family which was not addicted to the use of alcohol. Three feebleminded boys, a neurotic daughter and three miscarriages were the result of this marriage. The daughter, a nervous, hysterical girl, married her own cousin on her father's side. He is feebleminded and shiftless but manages to make a living from his trade, paint-ing, and his trapping. They have had two children. The older one, who was hydrocephalic and never sat up, died at two years of age. The younger one, now a year old, is normal physically.

III 61.   The second daughter married a man who is very alco-holic, and whose father also was a drunkard. One of his brothers was a respectable man, the other, a typical tough. Of the two sons from this marriage, one is untrustworthy and degenerate, and the other is practically normal.

Description of Chart B

I 1.   The Nuke family which settled in the same corner of the town as the Rasps and intermarried with them, is charac-terized by shiftlessness and feeblemindedness. One line of offspring developed insanity and two other lines have several cases of epilepsy. There is less alcoholism in this pedigree though the environment is the same as that of the Rasp family. There is a tendency in this family to migrate farther back into the country, while some of the Rasp family have sought the towns.

The first individual of whom we know came from a neigh-boring state about 1810. He bought a small farm in the least productive part of the town. He lived here and raised a large family, but the farm has passed out of the family through one son. None of his progeny have acquired any property. This original ancestor was a high-grade feebleminded man. During his last years he was lame from sores on his legs, the nature of which his granddaughter did not know. His wife was never strong. She had migraine and hysteria. Of her fifteen children, eleven became adult, and six had children.

It is the offspring of II 1 which connects this pedigree with the Rasp family by marriage.

II 1.
b. 1825?
d. 1900.

This daughter was decidedly feebleminded. Her first husband, II 2, a comparatively industrious man, was dull and unintelligent, but brighter than his wife. They lived in a miserable home in a tiny hamlet ten miles from the railroad, and three or four from a store. One stormy Christmas night she insisted upon his walking to the store for gifts. Returning, he became exhausted and was frozen to death. His wife and youngest children were taken to the almshouse. The other children were bound out. The mother soon returned to her old home and married a drunken fellow who, earlier in his career, had traded a dog for a baby girl whose vagrant father wanted to get rid of her. She appears again as III 14, the mother of a large family of dependents. II 1 had nine children (III 1–15), one of whom died in infancy.

III 1.
b. 1866.
d. 1910.

III 1 was bound out when a child. She was a high-grade feebleminded woman, but she had more conception of family ties and responsibilities than most of her relatives, for at the time of her death she was caring for her feebleminded brother and nephew, III 3 and IV 37. No definite information could be obtained concerning her husband, except that he was a day laborer. He is probably a high-grade feebleminded man. The oldest of their two children (IV 1, b. 1885), a girl, is a neurasthenic of poor mental ability. The boy (b. 1889) is also mentally defective.

III 3.
b. 1857.

This brother of III 1 has always been very feebleminded. He was placed in the town almshouse at fourteen years and was entirely or partially supported until he was twenty-six, when he was sentenced to five years in State Prison for arson. This crime cost the State over $740. On his release he went to the home of his sister, III 1, where he now lives.

III 5.
b. 1850.
Another brother lives in a small village four miles from the railroad and works in a lumber mill. He is deficient in judgment and reasoning ability but is industrious, and can calculate for his business very accurately. He married a feebleminded woman and has a poor, untidy home. They had four children, one of whom died in infancy.

IV 5.
b. 1884.
The oldest girl married an industrious, normal teamster. Before her marriage she gave satisfaction as a house maid, but her home in a hill settlement ten miles from town is poorly kept and her children are ill-cared for. She seems to be a very high-grade feebleminded woman. Her two oldest children (b. 1902, '04) are bright in school. The third one (b. 1905) is undersized, anemic and abnormally serious. She had one convulsion when three years old.

IV 6.
b. 1890.
The second daughter is very deficient mentally. Her husband is an ordinary farm laborer. She is almost continually on the street of the country village where she lives, and hangs about the Hotel. She has no children but has had one miscarriage.

IV 8.
b. 1894.
IV 8 is a boy of sixteen years who is still in the first grade of school—very feebleminded but strong physically.

III 7.
b. 1864.
Another high-grade feebleminded woman in the third generation married a man who is now apparently insane. This is the only family in the pedigree which lives in the city slums. The father is a janitor or boiler tender,—the children could not give a lucid account of his business. The mother goes out as a midwife. Their home at the top of two flights of dark crooked stairs is typical for a crowded filthy tenement. The father was so excited over my call and became so violent in his talk that the daughter explained that he had spells when he was "out of his head." The three daughters are all mentally deficient. Two of them are married. One has a pair of sickly twins which a clairvoyant is treating by correspondence. The other has a shy, stupid-looking boy. She is very peculiar and rolls her eyes upward in an abnormal manner when she talks. The youngest child is stupid, slow, and very untidy in appearance.

III 9.
b. 1855.
III 9 is a shiftless farmer. He has little mental ability. He migrated to another state and there married a feebleminded woman from a family of feebleminded insane per-

sons whose surname is used in their locality to express simple-mindedness, incompetency and shiftlessness (see page 100). The insane mother-in-law is living with her daughter. None of the eight children (IV 14–26) is of average intelligence.

IV 14.
b. 1882.
The oldest girl is very neurotic; she has hysteria and migraine. She works in a mill in a small town and is self-supporting.

IV 16.
b. 1884.
The oldest son is a high-grade feebleminded boy. He married a woman who has a bad reputation. They have no children of their own, but have adopted a little girl. Neighbors consider the environment very bad for the child. This man has been in the county jail twice for drunkenness.

IV 18.
b. 1887.
One girl lives at her father's home, as she is too feebleminded to keep house for herself. She had one illegitimate child which died before her marriage to a feebleminded man. He has since been in jail for larceny. They have one little boy.

IV 21.
b. 1885.
Another sister who is a very high-grade feebleminded woman, the type of a moron, has married a stationary engineer and lives in a large town. Her home is comparatively neat and her children comfortably clothed. Two of the children have had a few fits from indigestion. They are all under ten and appear normal.

IV 23.
b. 1891.
The youngest girl is simple-minded and sluggish. She has married an apparently normal German who has little ambition. He attended a small college for three years to please his mother, then married secretly and went to work on a tobacco farm.

IV 25.
b. 1893.
One boy is very feebleminded. The father claims that his condition is the result of typhoid fever, but neighbors affirm that he has never been normal mentally.

IV 26.
b. 1896.
The youngest boy though handicapped by his environment and poor mental ability, is interested in school work and wants to study. He is the brightest in the family though "not quite up to the average."

III 2.
b. 1852.
The feebleminded daughter who married into the Rasp family has already been described on page 88 as the wife of III 1 on Chart A.

III 12.
b. 1860?
III 12 is the only normal daughter. She married a normal man and has a neat, comfortable home in a small town. She

attends one of the churches and the minister remarked upon the superiority of her mental ability in comparison with that of her niece, IV 1. She has no children.

III 15.
b. 1853.

The brother who has produced the most defective family in this group is feebleminded and shiftless. He might have steady employment but will not work regularly. He married the girl referred to on page 145. Nothing is known of her mother. Her father was a drunkard who wandered into a backwoods town twelve or fifteen miles from a railroad and wanted to get rid of his baby girl. He succeeded in trading her for a dog. This child was brought up by II 21 and his first wife, a coarse, drinking woman. She developed into a heavy-faced imbecile and married III 15 who is slightly more intelligent. They have had at least thirteen children, ten of whom have been taken from them by State or County officials as neglected children, and four have had epilepsy. They have lived in various rural districts, always at least seven miles from a town. When visited they were living in the woods in a one-roomed, unplastered shack beside a brook which had to be forded. There was barely room to place the broken chair which was taken as the only available seat, as a filthy bed, a rusty stove, and boxes occupied the rest of the floor space. The mother could not remember how many children she had had, but knew that most of them had been taken from her. Two are still at home, IV 42 and 43.

IV 42.
b. 1900.

IV 42 is an epileptic imbecile of ten years. Her epilepsy began when she was a year old. During infancy and early childhood she was not backward, but since then her mind has failed until it is almost entirely gone. Her face is dull and expressionless, and she talks very indistinctly. She has the physical defect of a congenital union of the second and third digits on both hands and feet. The other child at home

IV 43.
b. 1903.

is about eight years old. At eighteen months he had one epileptic attack, but has had none since. In school he is slow to learn and speaks indistinctly.

The five oldest children (IV 28, 29, 31, 33, 35) were removed by the State Board of Charity when the oldest one was twelve. They left a baby a few months old at home. These children turned out as follows.

IV 28.
b. 1875.

IV 28 is a high-grade feebleminded woman who "does as well as she can." She married a laborer who has little ability in any line, mental or physical. They live in a small ill-kept house in the country near a railroad flag station. Their first child died from starvation, as they were having a particularly hard time to get along just then. The other four boys ranging from eight to one years are apparently bright and active. They attend the country school regularly.

IV 29.
b. 1878.

The second daughter is practically normal. She was placed out by the State Board of Charity, and finally married an intelligent electrician who is the father of IV 34 by a former marriage. She has an ill-kept home in a manufacturing town. She is shiftless and ignorant but cannot be considered feebleminded. Her two children were very small at birth. One died in infancy, the other, which weighed three pounds at birth, is a small, delicate child.

IV 33.
b. 1883.

IV 33 was placed out on a farm with her brother, IV 35. She was wayward and hard to control. At thirteen years of age she began to have epileptic attacks and was placed in the State Hospital for Epileptics where she now is. She is weak mentally but is able to help with the housework.

IV 35.
b. 1884.

The brother who was on the same farm has never been strong. He is an industrious machinist, but migrainous, and dizzy attacks often interfere with his work. He has been treated for tuberculosis of the bone. His wife, the daughter of IV 30, is a bright energetic little woman and keeps her home and children neat and clean. Both husband and wife are prominent in the local Salvation Army. They have four normal children and lost one in infancy with spinal meningitis. Though handicapped in many ways by his heredity, he had good inherent qualities which, under a good environment, have enabled this man to become a useful citizen.

IV 36.
b. 1888.

The child who was a baby when the five oldest children were taken by the State, remained with her parents until she was ten years old. She was then removed, and also three younger children who had been brought into the world since the first experience with this couple, but nothing was done to prevent the parents from furnishing more dependents. This girl, IV 36, had developed epilepsy at four years of age, so she was placed in a Children's Hospital for four years and then removed to the State Hospital where her sister IV 33 joined her a little later. She is feebleminded but helps with the housework of the institution.

IV 37.
b. 1890.

Another child who was placed out is now about twenty, but is mentally deficient. He cannot care for money or manage his own affairs. He has been arrested for petty larceny, but is now cared for in the home of his aunt, III 2.

IV 38.
b. 1892.

IV 38 could not talk plainly until he was ten years old. He was fairly bright but sometimes untrustworthy. He was doing well at farm work at seventeen years, when he was taken ill and died at a State Hospital.

IV 39.
b. 1894.

IV 39 was only four years old when taken from home. She, too, had difficulty in talking plainly. Until eight years old, she seemed bright in school, but after that she deteriorated, —became dull and inclined to truancy. She had one attack of St. Vitus dance but recovered, though she is still very nervous. At sixteen she is inclined to petty thieving. She was recently taken to a State Hospital for an operation and is reported to be quite feebleminded with immoral tendencies.

IV 40.

One of the children died about seven years of age in convulsions. His epilepsy began when he was only a few weeks old.

IV 41.
b. 1898.

IV 41 was removed from home by the County officials of a neighboring State into which the family had moved. He was nine years old when he was placed in a charitable institution. He has been to various places to work but has always been returned to the Home in a short time. Though not quick nor bright he is one of the trusted boys of the institution.

This one fraternity has had constant dependents for twenty-three years. During that time they have cost the State and County $20,045, exclusive of outdoor relief furnished by the town. It will probably be only a question of time before the two youngest children will be public charges. Whether that will be soon, so that the few socially useful traits of the lad may have some chance of development, or later after the stage for such development has passed, will be decided by the townspeople who best know their condition.

II 3.
b. 1834.
d. 1910.

To return to the second generation, II 3 was a feebleminded shiftless man who died of old age. He drank moderately and had been arrested for petty larceny, but was usually a harmless, useless citizen. He never married but lived on his father's farm until he became very old. He then gave it to a farmer's wife to pay for her care of him.

II 4. One brother went to war and was killed, and one migrated to New York State.

II 6 & 8. Two older daughters married and had small families which had no progeny. No definite information could be obtained about these families.

II 9. This daughter was sickly and neurotic and was always spoken of as "high-strung." She married a shiftless, alcoholic man and lived near a little village six or seven miles from the railroad. The husband was shot by his nephew, III 54, who was insane. They had twelve children (III 16–32), six of whom died in infancy and one was a still-born child. Of the others, two have had epilepsy, two are normal and one is characterized as the "black sheep."

III 23. III 23 is a good carpenter, has married and lives in a rural community, twelve miles from the railroad. His wife and six year old girl are both normal.

III 25. One daughter is very nervous and hysterical and has had
b. 1874? epileptic attacks. When a child she was bitten by a dog and three years later developed a mania which the doctor called rabies. She recovered from that and a number of years afterwards began to have typical epileptic attacks. They are not very frequent. She is a bright woman and keeps a neat house. She has been married twice, but was divorced from her first husband who was a worthless chap, the brother of II 13. She has no children.

III 27. There is no definite information concerning III 27. He was a wild alcoholic fellow who went to the city.

III 28. The son who has occasional epileptic attacks is a farm
b. 1880. laborer. He is not bright and married a woman of only fair intelligence. They have a comfortable home in the tenement house of his employer. They have two little girls, the older of whom is precociously bright.

III 32. The last daughter in this family is practically normal. She
b. 1872. married a man of whom little is known except that his brother had a very degenerate family. They have one daughter who has a dull heavy face, but is somewhat ambitious, as she is studying typewriting through a correspondence school. III 32 separated from her first husband and has remarried. She has a neat home in a small town.

II 12.
b. 1820.
d. 1906.

Another daughter of the second generation was so feeble-minded that she was considered mildly insane at one time. She lived to be eighty-six years old and in her later life was addicted to the opium habit. She had two illegitimate children before her marriage to a high-grade feebleminded man, who had chorea. Little is known of the illegitimate son,

III 35.

III 35, except that he had two children by one wife, then left her and married again. His father was from a family of ill-

III 37.

repute. The illegitimate daughter married an alcoholic man and, when forty-one years old, committed suicide under the stimulus of domestic troubles, by throwing herself in front of a railroad train. They had six children, all of whom are reported to be so far normal.

III 39.
b. 1860.

The daughter with whom II 12 lived during the last years of her life, is a woman of average intelligence. She married a normal man and has a good home in a manufacturing town. Her daughter is normal, has married an industrious man and has two bright children.

III 41.

The two boys are very alcoholic. III 41 is feebleminded but a good workman, when not intoxicated. He married a distant cousin, a feebleminded girl who is deaf and almost totally blind. They have a poor home which the mother-in-law helps to care for. It is in a hamlet seven or eight miles from the railroad. They had a pair of hydrocephalic twins who died a few hours after birth.

III 44.

The other brother is also feebleminded. He is married and lives near a small town where he works as a laborer. He has no children.

III 45.

A daughter lives in the same hamlet as III 41. Both she and her husband are high-grade feebleminded persons. He has regular sprees, is known for his big stories and has committed petty thefts. Their home is typical for this class of people—a small ill-kept house swarming with dirty children. She has had ten children, and one miscarriage.

IV 52.
b. 1887.

The oldest son is untrustworthy, cruel and quick-tempered. He drinks moderately. He married a girl from a notoriously low family who had one illegitimate son before her marriage. She is fairly bright. Since her marriage she has had three sons, two of whom are twins. The father does not work steadily, but is trying to pay for his house.

IV 53.
b. 1889?

The second son is practically normal. He does not drink and has steady employment. He married a German girl and has two apparently normal children.

Little is known of the next two daughters except that they go out in domestic service. They are wild girls and have acquired a bad reputation. Probably both are high-grade feebleminded girls. None of the younger children do well in school. 61, 62, and 64 are especially dull; and 62 is so feebleminded that at ten years of age he can only count to five. 65 is still a baby at home.

The last daughter is not living. She is reported to have been a high-grade feebleminded woman, but nothing is known of her husband. Of her four children only one is known to be feebleminded, IV 66. IV 66 has three children, one of whom has been the victim of rape. Both IV 69 and 70 married very alcoholic men.

II 14.

One of the fraternity of the second generation went to war and his fellow soldiers called him "foolish" and "crazy." He was married and had one child whose whereabouts and condition are unknown.

II 17.

II 17 was a high-grade feebleminded woman like the rest of the family. Little is known of her husband except that he was "odd." All of her children were considered "odd" and in some of them this oddity amounted to insanity. The children are as follows:

III 52 & 60.

One son and two daughters are married but no definite information about them was obtainable.

III 53.
III 54.

Another son who was mentally unbalanced never married. Another insane brother was committed to an Insane Hospital twice, and discharged. He finally shot his uncle, II 10, and was placed in the State Prison for the criminally insane, where he has been for the last twelve years. He has cost the State through court and institutions $2257.68.

III 56.

III 56 is irritable and nervous. He lives on a farm three or four miles from town. He is supported by his pension money and works very little. His wife is dead and little could be learned of his children. They are all plain, ignorant, labor-

III 57.

ing people. One brother died of tuberculosis. Another is a laboring man who is reported to be normal.

III 61.
b. 1850?

The last son of II 17 is a high-grade feebleminded man. His wife died of tuberculosis leaving a family of eight children. They live on a farm four miles from town. None of the children are very bright. One of the older boys, IV 84, is known to be a high-grade feebleminded fellow. Another, IV 86, did not get on well at school and was finally expelled for misconduct. IV 87 is about seventeen years old and is the housekeeper. She attends the high school but is mentally deficient and cannot do the work, but is allowed to carry a few studies. The two youngest children are backward in school, slow to grasp ideas or to retain them. If they are kept after school to make up lessons the father whips them.

II 19.
b. 1837.

The only living member of the second generation has a fairly neat home in the hamlet where III 41 and 45 live. She is a high-grade feebleminded woman who is very neurotic. Her husband formerly had epileptic fits but has not for several years. He owns five acres where his home is and lives on his pension. II 19 had one illegitimate daughter before her marriage, and one son and a miscarriage after it.

III 64.
b. 1860.

The daughter is feebleminded and has epileptic fits. She is married and lives in the neighborhood of the Rasp family. She has no children.

III 66.
b. 1870.

The son is a feebleminded neurasthenic. He works on wood jobs or other day labor. His wife is a feebleminded slattern from another low-grade family. They have four children (b. 1906 to 1909) none of whom are normal. The oldest one is almost an idiot. He is five years old but does not talk, and none of the younger ones talk yet.

Description of Chart C

The descendants from Neil Rasp's brother referred to on page 88 are plotted on Chart C together with the family into which they and persons on Chart A have married. As a whole, Chart C presents a class of high-grade feebleminded people who are simply shiftless and alcoholic. There is less criminality than on Chart A, but the men are town nuisances, drunken and disorderly.

I 1.

Nute Rasp was alcoholic and shiftless, but evidently more enterprising than Neil. He located about fifteen miles from his brother in a river valley where there were some manufacturing interests and a stone quarry. Nothing is known of his wife.

II 1.

Their son owned a small farm in the hills which may have belonged to old Nute. It is in the most unproductive part of the town. Little is known of him, but his wife still lives on the farm. She is a high-grade feebleminded woman. They had eight children (III 1–14), one of whom died in childhood.

III 1.   One of them, a woodchopper, is very deaf. He drinks heavily and is subject to dizzy spells which sometimes interfere with his work. He has been imprisoned for various petty offenses and once for rape, but no case was proven. His wife is also feebleminded and is from a notoriously low criminal family. She had several fainting spells of short duration. Their home is typical for such a family and is located a short distance from a trolley line. They have one boy who attends the country school near by. He is simple-minded and troublesome in school, the butt of the other children.

III 4.   Another brother, a teamster, married the sister of III 2, his brother's wife. Both husband and wife drank heavily and they soon separated. He then married an apparently normal woman. Their one daughter is neurotic. She dislikes school, and avoids going.

III 7.   The third brother lives five or six miles from the railroad on the outskirts of a small village. His home is poor but comfortable. He is a farm laborer, a good workman, who drinks moderately. His wife is a high-grade defective and has migraine, as did her mother and grandmother. Eight of her children (IV 3–17) are living, two died in infancy, and she had one miscarriage at eight months.

IV 5.
b. 1885.   The oldest girl is quite feebleminded. She was a house maid before her marriage and while so employed had one illegitimate child. She married a laborer from a family that is below par, and has two more children. Her home is a well-built tenement, but very dirty and ill-kept.

IV 8.
b. 1887.   The second daughter is a high-grade feebleminded girl who is subject to hysterical fits. She has had one illegitimate child. Before the child was born she became so violent that she had to be confined in a room from which the furniture had been removed.

IV 9.
b. 1891.   The third girl is considered the brightest in the family. She has married the man who was probably her oldest sister's seducer, and lives in the nearby city.

IV 11.
b. 1889.   The oldest boy is about twenty-two. He had spasms when he was young, and also scarlet fever and Bright's disease.

He is now decidedly feebleminded and alcoholic, and works very little.

IV 13. Of the three youngest children who are in school, IV 13, the thirteen year old boy, is in the seventh grade and does fairly good work.

IV 14. The twelve year old boy is in the sixth grade and finds it hard to learn.

IV 15. The seven year old boy has been in the first grade two years and cannot count to ten. He is small and anemic; his mind wanders and his inattention is very marked.

IV 17. The youngest child, six years old, is reported to have some kind of fits, but no definite information could be obtained.

III 9.
b. 1862. This brother has left out-of-door employment which characterizes the Rasp family, and works in the night shift of a mill. He is dull and slow and a moderate drinker. His wife is brighter, but is subject to severe attacks of migraine. They have a small ill-kept home and a large family. Eleven children (IV 18–33) are living, three died in infancy and one was still-born. The living children are as follows:

The oldest boy works on the night shift with his father and appears normal. The oldest girl was obliged to marry a low alcoholic fellow. She is a high-grade feebleminded woman; they have one child. The next three children work in the mill in the day-time, but none of them are well. One has dyspepsia, and a second one is extremely nervous, while the girl has a bad cough. One boy is nearly fourteen, so he will soon leave school and go to work in the mill; he appears normal, but his eyes are badly crossed. The three youngest children in school are well-behaved and orderly, but all take two years in a grade. Their slow progress seems to be due to a lack of mental ability, rather than to inattention or carelessness.

III 10. One sister of the third generation is a high-grade defective. She was a "wild" girl when young, but finally married an ordinary laborer and lives with her mother on the old farm. Her three children are under school age.

III 12.
b. 1875. III 12 is a high-grade feebleminded woman. She married an alcoholic man who is described with his children under III 24.

III 14. The next sister is very feebleminded and lives in the same rickety house in the woods as III 27 of the Rasp family on

Chart A. She is known to keep a house of ill-repute and increases these earnings by such work as cleaning out hen houses for the farmers. She has to support herself as her husband (III 15) is in the Insane Hospital. He is a brother of III 24, her sister's husband. They have two children, a girl and a boy.

IV 38.
b. 1892.
The girl is very feebleminded. She became pregnant when eighteen years old, probably through her mother's influence. She was taken to the State Hospital and then committed to an Insane Hospital which was the only institution open for this class of women. The boy is working for a farmer some distance from his undesirable home, and is reported to be doing well. Nothing definite could be learned about his mentality.

III 15.
The family to which the insane husband, III 15, belongs is one of three whose names are linked together as a byword for shiftlessness, drunkenness, and general troublesomeness in the town. Most of the members of this family are borderline cases so far as mentality is concerned. They can care for themselves after a fashion, but lack ambition and self-control. Some of the members of the Rasp family (Chart A) married into this group.

I 4.
The most remote ancestor obtainable in this family was very alcoholic. His wife was a high-grade feebleminded woman. They had five children.

II 3.
b. 1830.
One was a notorious drunkard and very shiftless. He married a normal woman who was noted for her witticisms. He did nothing toward the support of his nine children, but his wife worked out by the day at housework. She was frankly glad to send him off to the war hoping he would never return, but he did. She worked very hard to keep her family together even after she was crippled with rheumatism. Her employers speak with admiration of her remarkable devotion to her family, and pass lightly over the fact that she had one illegitimate colored child. She became insane late in life and died in the almshouse.

III 15.
The son, who became insane, has been described above, as the consort of III 14.

III 17.
A second son has moved out of the State. He does not drink, but is very shiftless and rattle-brained. He has been married three times, but nothing is known of his children.

III 18.   A daughter married II 7 who had been her aunt's husband, a well known character for shiftlessness. Little is known of her as she died of tuberculosis some time ago, but her husband is still living with his son, IV 43, supported by his pension and State aid. He is a high-grade feebleminded man, the half brother of II 7 on Chart A, the woman with a cleft palate. He drinks moderately. After III 18 died he married a woman from a degenerate family who is described as a "plain fool," and for a fourth wife he took a widow from another feebleminded family. Of his four children by III 18 one, IV 44, died of diphtheria in childhood. The other three children are as follows:

IV 40.
b. 1872.
d. 1892.   One son was characterized by a winking of the eyes which secured for him the name of "a blinker." He was a devotee of hard cider and was arrested for making it illegally. He finally died of tuberculosis shortly after his marriage to his mother's own cousin, III 42. They had no children.

IV 41.
b. 1876.
d. 1907.   Another son also died of tuberculosis. He was a miserable character, drunken and shiftless. He married IV 33 on Chart A, a feebleminded girl from the Rasp family. Three of their children became State wards and are doing well in their new homes (see page 135).

IV 43.
b. 1878.   The third boy is a misshapen, feebleminded fellow. His deformities are probably due to rickets. He was also subject to epileptic fits in childhood. His home is an unplastered shanty near a prosperous town. He is a day laborer. His wife is a feebleminded girl who comes from a degenerate family on The Hill where the Rasps live. They have one anemic, stupid-looking boy.

III 21.
b. 1868.   This woman has a character and lot in life similar to her mother [sic]. She has fair intelligence, but married a worthless drunken man, her own cousin (see III 28).

III 22 & 23.   Two brothers were very alcoholic and shiftless. One of them fell across a stake on a sled when drunk and choked to death. The other is still living.

III 24.   This high-grade feebleminded man is alcoholic and is afflicted with a nervous twitching of the muscles. He has been imprisoned for assault and drunkenness. Under the influence of a strong personality he reformed for a time, but when that influence was removed, he relapsed into his old habits. He has three children living and lost two in infancy.

The oldest girl is thirteen and is in the eighth grade. She is very nervous and has poor mental ability. She is inclined to petty thieving. The eight year old boy is in the second grade and is doing fairly well.

III 25. Nothing is known of the last legitimate daughter who married and has two children.

III 27. The colored child went astray in some way and was sent to the Women's Reformatory, where she died two years later.

II 6. Number 6 of the second generation is one of the worst drunkards on the chart. He is now dead, probably from delirium tremens.

II 8.
b. 1840.
d. 1864. His sister who was the first wife of II 7 died from a tumor some time ago and little is known of her. She had at least four children (III 28–32), three of whom have become respectable citizens.

The first is an alcoholic man who married his own cousin, III 21, and has two children. Their son is feebleminded and alcoholic, working irregularly as a day laborer. Their daughter is a complete idiot and a great care, but her parents are unwilling to place her in any institution.

III 29. III 29 is industrious and owns a house. He was divorced from his wife who was normal because of his cousin III 43 who was living with them. He did not marry her, however. Nothing is known of the children, whom the mother took.

III 31. This son was formerly very alcoholic, but with the assistance of church influences has reformed and is conducting a good business. He has a comfortable home and married one of the few normal women from the Rasp family (see Chart A, III 30).

III 32. The fourth child married a normal man who holds a responsible town office. She is of average intelligence. Their one child died in infancy.

II 9. One son of the second generation was killed in the war.

II 12.
b. 1839.
d. 1909. Another son was a high-grade feebleminded man, shiftless and untrustworthy. He went to the war and his pension partly supports his widow. He received town aid at different times and she now has occasional outside relief. Before her marriage she had one illegitimate son. One of her seven legitimate children died in infancy. An account of each follows.

III 35.   The oldest son is a fair workman, but somewhat shiftless.
b. 1865.   He is below the average intelligence and drinks moderately. He married a lazy improvident woman who teaches her children to beg. She has nine children. They have frequently had town aid. When the whole family had had scarlet fever, they refused to be fumigated until forced to, and then took some clothes to the woods and hid them. Their oldest daughter is now married. She was "light-fingered" and untrustworthy. All the children are borderline cases of feeblemindedness. A sister twelve years old is in the third grade and another eleven years old is in the first grade.

III 37.   III 37 is of fair intelligence. She was well trained in house
b. 1870.   work, but is careless and shiftless when not watched. She has three children who are reported to be normal.

III 38.   Another daughter, who is a high-grade feebleminded
b. 1873.   woman, married a man of the same stamp from a branch of the Nuke family which is not included on Chart B. They live in a shiftless manner in a two-roomed unplastered house. They have two children. The oldest boy, a boy of thirteen, is in the third grade at school; is stupid and lazy. The girl, five years old, is just beginning school.

III 41.   A sister who died of tuberculosis was probably the same
b. 1875.   high-grade defective. She married a brother of III 39, who is
d. 1911.   very deaf and is lazy and unintelligent. He is a day laborer. After his wife's death, he took his five children to his father's home which was already overcrowded with shiftless, feebleminded relatives. One son of thirteen is in the third grade. He tries to learn but is mentally incapable of grasping his school work like a normal child. The sons of ten and eight years are still in the first grade. They are slow and dull.

III 42.   This woman who married her cousin, IV 40, has been re-
b. 1877.   ferred to before. After he died of tuberculosis, she married
d. 1907.   one of the Rasp family, III 39 on Chart A. Their four children are described on page 141.

III 43.   III 43 is apparently normal. She has married an industri-
b. 1869.   ous workman and lives in a small town some distance from her old home. She has at least two children.

III 45.   The youngest son is a teamster and is very alcoholic. He
b. 1880?   has been sent to the State Reformatory for repeated drunkenness. He married an Italian girl but soon left her.

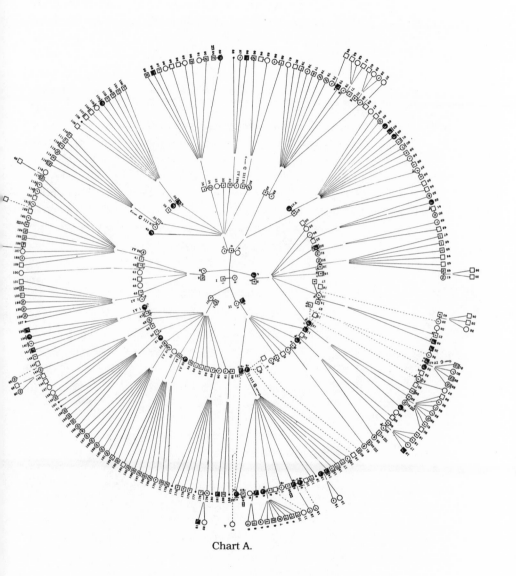

Chart A.

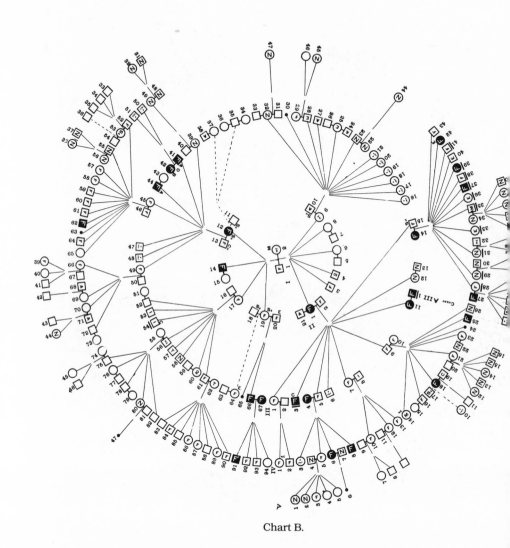

Chart B.

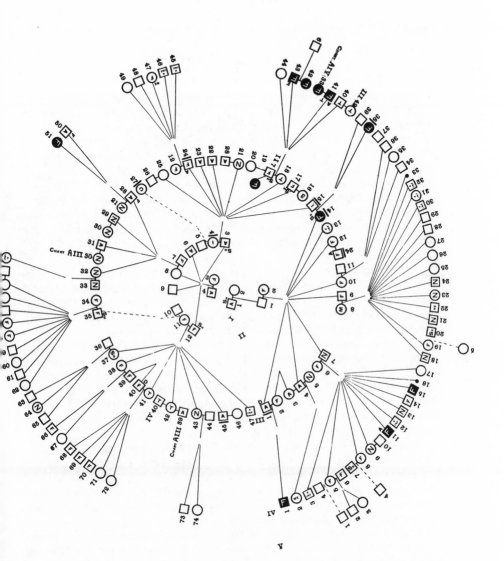

Chart C.

7

ELIZABETH S. KITE
The "Pineys"*

Preface

Kite introduces this family study by weaving together histories of New Jersey's Pine Barrens and the region's inhabitants. Some Piney ancestors were Quakers who, disowned by the Friends for their willingness to fight in the revolutionary war, betook "themselves to the loose lives of the dwellers of the Pines" (p. 166). They were joined by "outcasts from other religious communities" who fled to the Pines to escape punishment for crimes, "land pirates," Hessian soldiers, and impoverished Tories. Kite builds a picture of a desolate, lawless enclave with embattled borders. A "kind of guerrilla warfare" raged on "the edge of the Pines" between its criminalistic inhabitants and their "strictly moral" neighbors, the two groups divided by the latter's "bulwark" of rectitude. Thus Kite creates a topographical counterpart for the "impassable gulf" of morality.

She continues her exposition by presenting two contrasts to the Pineys. "A Yankee and the Cranberry Bogs" pits the entrepreneurial values of the cranberry farmer against those of the lazy "real Piney." "Immigrants, the Latest Comers," contrasts shiftless Pineys with Italian neighbors who work hard, become rich, and maintain the patriarchal family structure.

Kite's paramount concern is sexual immorality. "It is this moral element which entering in makes the human degenerate such a profound menace to social order" (p. 170). Like the woods in Kite's "Two Brothers," the Pines become a place of unrestrained sensuality. Caddie Dink, whose "father . . . would be rather hard to tell," typifies Piney promiscuity: her husband hanged himself because Caddie was "running" with her stepsons, to one of whom she bore illegitimate children.

Although the conclusion of this study, like that of "Two Brothers," is vague, it is certainly eugenic in implication. Kite has presented the Pineys as close to a separate species, "a group of human beings . . . distinct in morals and manners," "recognized as a distinct people by the normal communities." She has even referred to "The Male of the Species." Extinction of such "barnacles upon our civilization" would be no loss at all.

In his more recent description of *The Pine Barrens*, John McPhee tells how Kite spent two years visiting the area from the nearby Vineland Training School. "A fearless young woman," she "wore spotless white dresses as she rode in a horse-drawn wagon through the woods" (1967:48), tracking down relatives of Vineland inmates (see her "Moron Family Tree," p. 171). After publication of her report the governor visited and, on his return to Trenton, recommended "that the Pine Barrens be somehow segregated from the rest

* Originally published in *The Survey* 21(1) (October 4, 1913): 7–13, 38–40.

of New Jersey in the interest of . . . health and safety" (1967:52). McPhee, too, recognizes Piney oddities, but his explanations bear no trace of Kite's hereditarianism.

THE "PINEYS"

—Today morons; yesterday colonial outcasts, "disowned"
Friends, land pirates, Hessians, Tory refugees, revellers from
Joseph Bonaparte's court at Bordentown and other sowers of
wild oats—

B ETWEEN THE coastal plane and the fertile land east of the Delaware River lies 2,000 square miles of almost pure sand. Beginning in Monmouth County it extends southwest through Burlington, Ocean and Atlantic Counties. It was originally covered with a splendid growth of pines, interspersed with iron-producing bog lands. This primeval wealth of New Jersey was long ago exploited, and there was left only a scrubby growth that but slowly replaces the timber of the past, while modern science is turning the low hollows into marvelously productive cranberry bogs.

In the heart of this region scattered in widely separated huts over miles of territory exists today a group of human beings so distinct in morals and manners as to excite curiosity and wonder in the mind of any outsider brought into contact with them. They are known as the "Pineys" or "Pine Rats" and are recognized as a distinct people by the normal communities living on the borders of their forests, although their manner of living arouses neither surprise nor interest, having always been taken quite as a matter of course. In fact the problem is a mixed one, intertwining and extending itself inward and outward from the country to the pines, from the pines to the country so that more than one old family is found to have in some of its branches an infusion of Piney blood. It is this fact which makes the problem not only complex but one of extreme delicacy, and gives it in a way the protection of its surroundings.

Not a few of our "Pine Rat" friends for instance can be traced back directly to where they branch from excellent families, often of sturdy English stock. Others take their rise from religious communities of the North, while a great many are there without any explanation of their existence, their ancestral line soon disappearing in the mists of the past.

The general opinion current regarding the Piney and his class, has been that he is what he is from environment, that surrounded with other conditions and "given a chance" he would come out "all right." That he is a "problem," that his presence tends to lower standards of living among the normal people who come in contact with him, is a universally recognized fact, but until recently it has been confidently hoped that through education and the opening up of the Pines, he would eventually become a normal citizen. Whether or not he is a being capable of such development or whether he has permanently fallen below that possibility, it is not the object of this paper to discuss. Nothing has been determined beyond what he is today and that he resembles several generations of ancestors.

Meager but suggestive have been the results of research into history to find the origins of this degenerate group. Very faint are the traces which the Swedes, the original founders of New Jersey, left behind them. It was the English, and English of sturdy dissenting stock, mostly refugees from neighboring provinces, who with an admixture of French Huguenot exiles, peopled New Jersey. Desire for personal liberty was the dominating note of all the settlements that took root in her soil. Foremost among the sects who sought homes in the newly opened territory were the persecuted followers of George Fox, whose democratic principles, deeply imbued with religious ideals, were so firmly rooted in all that makes for order and civic righteousness as to admirably fit them for expansion in the new world. They were men indeed who had shown themselves willing to die for their principles of equality—but who greatly preferred to live in the cultivation and enjoyment of the peaceful arts of life. For this New Jersey alone of the colonies offered them an alluring outlook. Under the patronage of William Penn, the Society in west New Jersey began a career of democratic expansion that has no parallel in the annals of any other country.

Outcasts of Religion

But there is another side to the picture. In the organization of the Society of Friends, there is but one method of dealing with the persistent sinner. When a member proves incorrigible or when he commits some flagrant misdeed he is dismissed from their ranks. In this way they unconsciously throw upon society at large the responsibility of caring for what they themselves had failed to control.

Particularly in the beginning of its career of material prosperity the society was severe and summary in its dealings with offenders. The early annals of all communities of Friends testify to this fact. In the province of New Jersey, it is certain that "disowned" youths, cast out by the society, did in some cases betake themselves to the loose lives of the dwellers of the Pines.

Outcasts from other religious communities also found shelter there, driven by the laws in force during the early period in east New Jersey. In this province thirteen offences were punishable by death—among them theft, if incorrigible; burglary; rape, subject to the discretion of the court; gross and unnatural licentiousness. For the vice of unchastity, there was imposed a fine of three or five months' imprisonment or ten stripes at the public whipping post if the fine was not paid. A marriage to be legal must be published three times, and must have the consent of the parents, masters or guardians. These laws were intended to uphold the high standard of social order by eliminating the persistent sinner by death, thus ridding not only their own, but all communities of the evil. The vicinity of the Pines, however, offered possibilities of escape with which even these stern laws could not cope.

Only a few years ago, a notorious Piney bearing a perverted Huguenot name died in his cabin in the heart of the Pines at the age of ninety-eight.

Four years before his death, he was found one day returning to his shack after a prolonged absence. Questioned as to where he had been, he said he had gotten "tired o' the gal he had been livin' with"—"too giddy" he said, shaking his head, "too giddy fer me, so I took her down shore an' traded her. Did perty well, too—got this old hoss and this here keg o' rum."

Such conditions are common today in the Pines and many another Piney can be found whose ancestry could be traced back to some off-shoot of a rigid, highly respectable, intelligent family which in other branches, has furnished us some of our best and most valued citizens.

The first historical mention of these outlaws is to be found in the quaint history of New Jersey by Samuel Smith, published in 1720. Speaking of the white and red cedar, he says "the towering retreat of the former have afforded many an asylum for David's men of necessity"—here alluding to First Samuel 22:2, where is recorded "And every one in distress, and every one in debt, and every one that was discontented, gathered themselves unto David."

But during the two centuries that have elapsed since Samuel Smith wrote his history, the Pines of New Jersey have had other settlers besides these "men of necessity." In course of time this valuable timber land was bought up by speculators; first the cedars and later the pines were cut off and shipped from the convenient harbors along the coast. Before the revolution, it had been discovered that the bogs were rich in iron ore, so that a considerable number of furnaces were established at Batsto, Weymouth, Hanover, etc., whose output became the chief native source of the iron supply. Many of the cannons used during the revolution were cast at these furnaces as well as the pots and pans of our ancestors.

Meanwhile the settlers along the river and coast were rapidly developing the agricultural resources of the country and though they had been joined by non-conformists of various sects, the Friends continued to dominate most of the settlements of west New Jersey. As time went on and the great ideas of independence were being developed, the rules of the society in regard to war prevented them from taking active part in the revolution, although many of them were at heart sealed to their adopted country's cause. Their uncompromising attitude in this regard, however, made them seem as a body to favor the Tory side, and many of them suffered at the hands of their warlike fellow countrymen imprisonment, exile, and hardship of every sort.

True, there were notable exceptions to the rule that Friends would not fight. Many a noble youth broke the cherished tie of family and faith and went out a double martyr to his country's call, but such were invariably "dealt with" and where they persisted in their determination, were disowned by the society, which then made a formal protest against this breaking down of their "testimony." Through their stern adherence to peace principles, the Quakers in west New Jersey at the beginning of the revolution, became all unwittingly a kind of protecting bulwark, behind which the most atrocious outlawry was carried on in the Pines. With the coming of Lord Howe to Staten Island in 1776, a partly successful attempt was made to form in New Jersey a military organization of native Tories. Tory troops of between five and six hundred men kept up a kind of guerrilla warfare from the edge of the Pines, spreading havoc and destruction among the neighboring farms.

F. B. Lee, in his history of New Jersey, says: "Associated with these regiments, possessing a semblance of military organization, real or assumed, was a disjointed band of land pirates, known as "Pine robbers." Aided and abetted by the loyalists in New York city whose most active spirit was William Franklin, the deposed governor of New Jersey, these "Pine robbers," among whom were many refugees, raided the tide regions of Monmouth, Ocean, Atlantic, Salem, Gloucester, Camden and Burlington Counties, their depredations being yet vividly remembered in local tradition. These "Pine robbers," most of whom were Jersey men hiding by day in the recesses of the Pines or amid the dunes of the seashore, were said to be men of utter depravity whose "lawlessness, cruelty and lust made them a terror to the entire country." The worst of them were subsequently hunted down and killed, the bodies of some being hung as a warning in conspicuous places.

Hessians and Tories

After the battle of Trenton, certain Hessian soldiers and other deserters from the British army found safety in the seclusion of the Pines, and added still another element to its already mixed population.

After the war was over those Tory families who remained in the state were frowned upon with such uncompromising severity as obliged them to take to the woods for self-protection where, despoiled of their possessions and hardened by the passions which war engendered, they fell quickly into the ways of the other outlaws. Thus political animosity added its uncompromising bitterness to the stern disapproval with which the strictly moral, highly intelligent, virtuous and prosperous Quaker population regarded their neighbors of the Pines. The gulf which separated them became impassable except by illicit means.

Today direct descendants of the finest Quaker stock, living still on the edges of the Pines and who have sought to preserve its folk lore, affirm that many of the Piney names belonged to one time prosperous Tory stock. Some of them found legitimate employment in established industries, for the period after the war saw a great increase in the exploitation of the native wealth of the region. New sawmills were set up; charcoal burners were kept busy over the length and breadth of the Pines, while the iron industry took on a new lease of life.

To carry on these enterprises, skilled workmen as well as laborers were imported. Record and tradition show that from one to two hundred men or even twice that number were employed at the different centers. Some of the landowners, as at Weymouth, built for their men convenient dwellings, grouping them into a village, with a church, store and school house. Others again allowed them to live in more or less crude huts or employed the people living in isolated cabins throughout the Pines. Generally a mansion house stood on a rise of ground overlooking the furnace or saw mill and here the owner lived with his family for a whole or part of the year. Traces of the ancient colonial elegance of these mansion houses can be seen today in the ruins scattered here and there.

Charming Weymouth, sleeping like a lizard in the sun, is the best preserved of these, but the rushing torrent of the great Egg Harbor river where it sweeps its black current madly over the dam amid the ruins of huge walls of solid masonry is all of Weymouth that today shows any signs of life. During the last half century, all these earlier industries of the Pines have been steadily on the decline, for the forests once cut down renewed themselves slowly, while the cost of transportation over the sandy roads together with the lessening supply of bog ore made competition with the developing iron industry of Pennsylvania impossible.

A Yankee and the Cranberry Bogs

It was the Yankee agent of one of the owners of the furnace at Hanover who in 1850, as tradition has it, first conceived the idea of improving the wild cranberry through cultivation. Up to this time, the fruit had been gathered and sold much as the huckleberry is at present. As an old woodchopper of the district put it: "Used to be, cranberries was everybody's—*you* could go or *I* could go or *anybody*." To keep this "anybody," namely the Piney of Brown Mills, from trespassing on the bog adjoining the Hanover Furnace, this shrewd Yankee, while making his first experiments, put up warning signs bidding the natives keep off, which signs they very naturally ignored, since none were able to read. Not discouraged by this failure, the pioneer in cranberry growing hit upon the ghastly expedient of killing a cat, smearing an old coat with its blood and leaving the latter along with scattered fragments of the cat's brain on the path that led from the wilderness to the bog. A terrible time ensued, for it was soon noised about that a man had been murdered. Although they could not find that any one was missing, the Pineys were terribly frightened and thereafter gave the experimenter and his bog a wide margin. From that day to this, there has been a steady development of the cranberry industry which today ranks as one of the most lucrative of the state and forms the chief outlook for speculators of the Pines as well as for the inhabitants who have any desire or ability to work.

But the real Piney has no inclination to labor, submitting to every privation in order to avoid it. Lazy, lustful and cunning, he is a degenerate creature who has learned to provide for himself the bare necessities of life without entering into life's stimulating struggle. Like the degenerate relative of the crab that ages ago gave up a free roving life and, gluing its head to a rock, built a wall of defence around itself, spending the rest of its life kicking food into its mouth and enjoying the functionings of reproduction, the Piney and all the rest of his type have become barnacles upon our civilization, all the higher functions of whose manhood have been atrophied through disuse. This comparison, however, serves only as an illustration and must not be carried too far, for into the degenerate human problem enters an element which has no force where it is a question of mere physical degeneracy. It is this moral element which entering in makes the human degenerate such a profound menace to social order as to demand the careful consideration of those interested in the preservation of the high standards of our commonwealth.

From the beginning of the existence of the Piney type, and especially with the development of industry and prosperity in the Pines, there have been men of leisure, young men of good families, foot-loose men of no

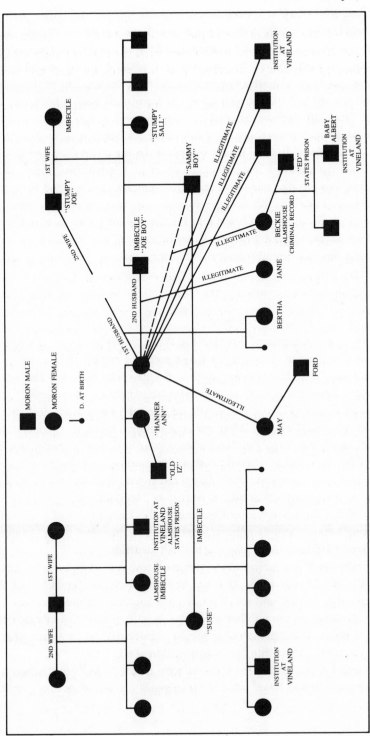

Moron Family Tree.

"Suse," "Old Iz," "Hanner Ann," "Stumpy Joe," and the others are shown in the interlacings of lineage analyzed by Miss Kite.

character, adventurers of every sort, who for shorter or longer periods have delighted in losing themselves in the pleasures of the Pines. There has always been hunting and fishing, the wine of the air, the tonic of the pine breath, and always the unhindered possibilities of sensual enjoyment. Not every one who has come under the fascination of the Pines has succumbed to its illicit pleasures. Far from it, as such a book as Van Dyke's *Days Off* abundantly testifies. But the way is open to those who seek it and many indeed are they that have succumbed as well as they who have deliberately gone for that purpose. In the gay days when Prince Joseph Bonaparte held his miniature court at Bordentown, many were the revels and hunting parties in the Pines which were indulged in by the members of his suite. All these revelers came back, leaving a train of nameless offspring to complicate still further the mixed social problem of the Pines, so that today, in tracing the ancestry of any particular group, one runs up continually against the impossibility of proving exact ancestry.

Immigrants, the Latest Comers

No study of the component forces of the Pines would be complete without mention being made of the thriving Jew colonies established at different points, and of the Italian communities. A superficial observer has often been led to believe that there is much similarity between these people and the native denizens of the Pines, but no one who knew them intimately could ever be so deceived. Whatever resemblance there is, is indeed superficial, such as: large families, often unsanitary and crowded conditions of living, small and incommodious dwellings; but beneath the surface we find on one hand, loose disjointed living, with attendant lack of intelligence, absence of ambition, dearth of ideals of every sort; on the other, solid, compact organized existence; the father head of his home, protecting his wife and daughters, teaching the same attitude to his sons; both parents training their offspring to thrift and industry.

Naturally there are exceptions to this rule, and it is most certainly true, especially in our large cities, that the foreign population tends to lose its characterizing virtues and assume our vices much more quickly than the reverse, leading thus to another problem—not the problem of mental deficiency, but one which though of immense significance to the future of our country scarcely enters into the rural question at all.

To illustrate: one rather exceptional case in the Pines, yet characteristic, is that of "Italian Mike" who eighteen years ago left work in a railroad gang and, burdened by a debt of $40.00 incurred through illness, took up on credit twenty-five acres of woodland in the heart of the Pines and near a small community of typical, thriftless Pineys. Aided only by his faithful wife, "Mike" built a small shack and set to work clearing his land. What he could not sell as timber or cut up into cordwood he converted into charcoal. As soon as he had sufficient land cleared, he set out two thousand strawberry plants. In this small way he began, and during the years which followed he has had the usual round of discouragements, droughts, insect pests, etc., and yet today, besides a considerable bank account and credit good anywhere in the country, he is owner of more than a hundred acres of land, has a comfortable frame house, a large vineyard which is used exclusively for wine which he himself makes for home consumption, to say nothing of a family of eleven fresh, clear-eyed, attractive children who have helped him piece together his competence. In one year he cleared $2,600 on his small fruits which he himself takes to a city thirty-two miles away; his habit being to leave home about 5 o'clock in the afternoon, reaching his destination at 2 o'clock in the morning, his fruit then in perfect condition to command the best price in the market. The next day his oldest son leaves at the same hour and meets his father half way on the road, where they exchange teams, and the next day's market is made in the same way as the preceding one. "Mike" has never had the advantage of schooling for himself nor of much for his children, owing to the lamentable state of affairs in this regard in his section of the Pines, but his alert mind has had time amidst the stress of his active life to acquire the essentials of the three "R's" so that he is by no means an illiterate man.

In striking contrast to "Mike" is a family living on the same road, under the same natural environment, not a quarter of a mile away. Here too, is a family of eleven children, but they live in a ramshackle house for which they pay no rent and the father and mother gain a living by gathering moss in winter and berries in summer. The oldest boy is in the reformatory at Jamesburg, and the oldest daughter, having been committed to the State Home for Girls, had later been put out on probation in a good family. Here she got into trouble with a butcher boy and finally came back to her home a greater problem than she was when she went away.

Questioned as to his neighbors' habits of life, "Mike" showed neither surprise nor interest in what was asked him. Frankly he knew nothing about them at all, and in a few moments his mind came naturally back to home topics which absorb his entire interest. Truly the most convincing proof of a strong progressive mentality.

Down a Sandy Road on the Edge of the Pine Belt

My first introduction to the remarkable community which is the product of outlaw ancestry came one day by way of a sandy road on the edge of the Pine belt. I stopped at a little store to inquire about a certain Harry Reed who was a distant connection of one of the inmates of the Vineland Training School.

"I stopped at Harry's house on my way here," I said, leaning over the counter, "but he wasn't at home. His wife told me that Harry worked for you."

"Yes, Harry does work for me, but that wasn't his wife you saw," said the store-keeper half laughing, half sneering. "Harry has a wife, but she's left him and is living with a man down near Milltown—Bertha there, the woman you saw, just lives with Harry."

"But what about the child I saw?"

"Yes, that's Bertha and Harry's child all right, but they can't get married because Bertha has a husband living. You see," he went on, glad of an attentive listener, "these people in the Pines have ways of their own and I suppose they seem strange to an outsider."

"Are these the 'Pineys' or 'Pine Rats' one hears so much about?"

"Exactly. Some of the better among them dislike the name but most of them do not care. That Bertha you just saw is a case, I can tell you; before she went to live with Harry she lived with Bill Forman over at Gull's Point."

"Bill Forman? Why, he is the uncle of one of our Vineland girls! Do tell me, where is Bill now?"

"State's prison. They got into a fight and Bertha had him locked up. Bill has a wife and children living somewhere—down at Gooseneck, I believe."

Family Tree of a "Piney"

"Who is this Bertha anyway?" I asked, for I had a consuming interest in genealogy.

"Why, her mother was 'Caddie,' 'Caddie Dink' they call her, and her father, but that would be rather hard to tell. Caddie married when she was a young girl an old man 'Stumpy Joe,' who had a lot of boys. Caddie ran with all of them; the old man finally hung himself in the woods—they say, because he couldn't stop her—some say that Caddie and 'Snapper Bill,' another fellow she used to run with, did it—anyway he was found dead, hanging there. Simple old fellow, he hardly had enough sense to hang himself. All Caddie's children are like her, unless it is the youngest May—

she's a pretty little girl that something might come of if she only had a chance."

"Has Caddie many children?"

"Nine or ten. 'Joe boy,' Stumpy's son, is the father of some of them. He stays home with them and when Caddie isn't running with somebody else she comes back to them. He's too lazy to work and when she's away the county has to keep them. Bertha is the oldest child. When she was only sixteen her mother made her marry old Jim Bently who was sixty-eight. Jim had had three wives and eleven children by the last wife—but that didn't stop her running off with Dan Zahmey who left a wife and six children. Bertha and Jim didn't get on, as might have been expected, so they went back to old Squire King who married them, and got a writing of separation. Of course, it isn't legal but they think it is. To come back to Harry that you first asked me about, he's a pretty good fellow to work; he doesn't drink, and what's more, he always pays for what he gets at the store, a matter of seven or eight dollars a week."

The calm tone of acceptance with which these facts were related, astonished me almost as much as the facts themselves. It was soon apparent that they were but an index to the situation in the whole community.

The Manner of the People

Caddie Dink was somewhat exceptional owing to her abounding vitality, but the standards of living were much the same for all. Caddie's youngest sister was married to "Sammy boy," another son of Stumpy. They lived in a shack in the woods on the edge of a cranberry bog and there were five feeble-minded children whose paternal parentage was very uncertain. "Sammy boy" like "Joe boy" was too lazy to work and what his wife did not earn she begged. There were rumors that his shack was a rendezvous for the men and that Sammy drew quite an income from their visits. Suse, his wife, was an energetic, sharp-tongued, shrill-voiced woman, with black hair, sparkling black eyes, finely shaped oval face, and dark gypsy coloring. The freedom of her life gave strength and vigor to her limbs and a rosy coloring to her cheeks. In the woods, on a cold day, with a bit of shawl wrapped about her, the fragment of a scarf on her head, a sack half full of potatoes over her shoulder, she was a wild, almost graceful creature that seemed the genius of the place. Only when togged out in the forlorn cast-offs of civilization could one see how coarse and vulgar she was. One day Suse came into the kitchen of a farm house to warm herself and was left there a minute alone. A few days later she came back and asked to see the mistress of the house.

"I brought back this ladle," she said, drawing something from under her coat. "My conscience wouldn't let me keep it, and I thought," she went on, "perhaps if ye had an old hat you'd give it to me, cause I ain't got nothin' to wear on me head."

The astonished mistress recognized a valued family heirloom in the large silver spoon which Suse held out. The indulgent woman not only readily forgave Suse but gave her the hat besides.

There were several other sisters of Caddie and Suse who were of similar intelligence; one of these was taken into a good family. These people for over ten years labored to make of her a self-directing, virtuous, and respectable young woman. They were finally forced to admit that their efforts had been fruitless, and to let her go her own way. Then there was an imbecile sister who had always been cared for in the county insane asylum, and an imbecile brother who had been sent to the Vineland Training School in the early days. He was a strong and uncontrollable creature who could not be detained in the institution owing to a peculiar violence of disposition, nor were the bars and bolts of the county asylum capable of keeping him safe inside, so for self-protection the community was forced to get him committed to state's prison. After serving his term he was liberated and soon after was killed while walking on the railroad.

Just one out of this notorious family turned out to be a virtuous, self-respecting woman with ideas of loyalty surprising in a person of her mentality. "Old Iz," her simple-minded, kind-hearted, sensual old man, was indeed a trial to her, but she bore up bravely before the world. She raised eleven children in a little two-room shack that stood on the edge of the woods. She was fond of her brood as a mother might be, though she never bothered much with such small matters as shoes and stockings, brushing the hair, and washing the hands and faces of her offspring. She kept herself fairly clean, for she had been brought up in a respectable family, but "with an old man like hers," and having to go out three days a week to work, her eleven children added too much to the already heavy burden. She was far too wise a woman to bother about what she couldn't help, or to attempt to control the uncontrollable. That she would have preferred cleanliness and order had they been easy to attain was attested by a box in the corner in which were laid away in excellent condition a pile of patchwork quilts of her own making. Bed quilts were most satisfactory objects to Hannah Ann; they stayed where they were put and had no perverse habit of rolling in the dirt. Her mentality was equal to caring properly for them—but alas, this was not the case when it was a question of her babies! She did, however, prepare for them food when she was home and at night there was a hole under the roof into which those might crawl who could not find room in the bed.

Moron Types

It would be easy enough to stamp both Hannah Ann and "Old Iz" as mentally deficient, yet there is about the latter in particular a shrewdness, an ability to take care of himself that is characteristic of his class and is very misleading. To give him a precise test would be impossible, and though it is easy to find his children in the schools and to test them along with other boys and girls of the same mental stamp, the result does not enlighten us as the test of an adult Piney would do, so we bided our time.

The opportunity finally came in a round-about way. Caddie Dink had a daughter Beckie, who had married a man named Ed who was much older than she. He had come over at cranberry time and Beckie and he had got to "carryin' on." The squire married the pair after Ed swore that he was not a married man. Of course, Ed had a wife and child living farther up in the Pines, but she didn't count since long ago she had gotten tired of Ed and gone off with another man. But the newly married pair did not live happily; it was only a few weeks after the second child was born that Beckie left him for good, taking the baby with her. Ed, left with the older boy, carried him over to his other woman who agreed to care for the child and he went back to his lonely shack. Soon after this he took a colored man in as lodger. The two got into a fight when drunk and Ed did him up in such shape that he got twelve years in the state prison for attempted murder.

Beckie in the meantime began running the roads and was soon a notorious character. She was finally arrested for criminal neglect of her child and sent to the county house, from which place, aided by a Piney woman who worked there, she ran away within a week of her commitment. Some time afterward she was located in a nearby city, brought back by the constable and sent to jail, thus giving ample opportunity to study and test her mentality.

Beckie is twenty-three; well-formed, robust, healthy looking and bearing no stigma of degeneracy, unless it be a rather flat head, low forehead, and protruding lower jaw. She is fairly clean in her personal habits, is conscious of the value of pretty clothes and likes to look well, also likes what she calls a good time. She can do all sorts of coarse work, and occasionally is willing, but left to herself her idea of housekeeping seems to consist in preparing some sort of food, clearing up the dishes, sweeping the dirt under the stove or just outside the door, after which she sits and rocks herself or walks the streets or the roads smiling at every one.

She can neither sew nor cut out the simplest garment, not even an apron. She has perhaps no stronger characteristic than that of indifference. Fond as she is of dress, when she has no decent clothes, which often happens, she does not mind, but seems to take it as a matter of course. So also with the love of freedom which belongs to her wild, untamed nature. When she was brought back by the constable, her attitude was that of perfect unconcern. I met her at the station.

"Well, Beckie," I said, laughing and shaking a finger at her, "what do you suppose they will do with you now?"

"Send me to jail."

"Well, don't you care?"

"What's the use of caring?"

"Were you ever at school, Beckie?"

"Yes, but I didn't get no learnin'; been awful sorry since."

"Can't you read or write?"

"No."

"Why couldn't you learn?"

"Didn't seem as though there was anything in my head could take it."

Beckie and the Binet Test

When given the precise mental tests it was found she had the mentality of a child of between eight and nine years. She knew the colors, days of the week, almost all the months and the date; she had an excellent memory, could give in immediate repetition seven figures, or sentences of fifteen words, where the thought was within her grasp. She could compare simple objects, as tell how snow and milk are alike, how glass and wood are different, but could define objects only in terms of use; for instance, when asked "What is a table?" She replied, "To eat on." "What is a chair?" "To sit on." "A mouse?" Silence; being unable to think of any use for a mouse she could say nothing. "A spoon?" "To eat with." "A horse?" "To go out ridin' with." (Interesting! Beckie is used to being taken out riding.)

Her judgments, when it was a question of something she could understand, were always good.

"What ought you to do when people give you good advice?"

"Sit down and take it."

"Take what, Beckie?"

"Why, the good advice."

"How did you ever learn so much, Beckie?"

Quickly—"Oh, I know right from wrong, I knew that when I was fifteen, more'n I know now."

"You know but you forget, is that it?"

"Yes, I forget."

"Tell me, Beckie, you people don't think of it as wrong to marry a man when he has another wife?"

"No, we don't think it wrong."

"Tell me, what ought you to do when the house is on fire?"

"Get out what you can."

"When you want to buy something you see at the store?"

"Do what's right and pay for it."

"When another contradicts you no matter what you say?"

"Tell him when you're right you're right," came from Beckie with so much unction that I asked laughing,

"Did Ed contradict you, Beckie?"

"Sure he did!" and her whole expression grew sullen and injured.

Beckie, however, reached the height of her capabilities in answering the following question:

"Why do you judge a person more by their acts than by their words?"

Beckie's experience came to her aid and she instantly caught the sense, and said bitterly: "Why his acts show what he is. You can't believe half he says."

Questions like the following conveyed no idea to her mind and she made no attempt at reply: "Why is it better to persevere in what one has begun than to try something new?"

All her descriptions were extremely crude and unworthy of a child of seven.

"Look at this picture, Beckie, and tell me what you see."

After long pause there was no answer forthcoming.

"Oh, Beckie, you surely see something, tell me what it is!"

Explosively—"All I see is that man a-shavin' the girl's head!"

"Well, that's just what I wanted you to see! Now, what else?"

After a pause, "Only that comb, an' them things," pointing to some bottles on a shelf.

A great stack of pictures was disposed of with the briefest description for each. It seemed an exertion that positively produced pain to hold her attention so long on a subject for which she had no interest. When shown a collection of human figures, in all of which some prominent anatomical feature was lacking, as arms, eye, nose, or mouth, Beckie could see nothing wrong. A Mulatto girl serving a term in jail, who was listening, was much annoyed at this and said with irritation, "Can't ye see that woman ain't got no mouth?" Beckie, still gazing at the picture, protested she could not see.

She was able to make correct change when given two ten-cent pieces in exchange for four imaginary oranges at four cents each. She could not, however, tell how much three two-cent and three one-cent stamps would cost when placed before her, and this not because she could not count, but because she lost her directing idea and forgot what she started to do —a much more significant failure. She could only think of five words in three minutes, even when helped, nor could she understand a rhyme or make a sentence using a given word. She was able to copy a square but after several attempts to copy a diamond was obliged to give it up—she simply could not bring the lines back to the starting point, although encouraged to the utmost.

In giving her the test Beckie was praised for everything she did well and even her failures were covered up by expressions of satisfaction no matter what the answer, or by hastening to give an easier question to which her reply would be correct. By this means she was all the time stimulated and was greatly pleased with herself.

"I ain't so stupid as you'd think," she said.

"Indeed you're not, Beckie" I answered with conviction, and left her supremely satisfied.

The Male of the Species

Another typical case is that of "Ford," a man thirty years old, whose face is still fresh and boyish. When first seen he was taken to be normal. His manners were pleasant and courteous, and, although in working clothes, there was something about him that suggested good blood. It was amazing that a fellow so decent looking should be planning to marry Beckie's youngest sister May, who was following rapidly in Beckie's footsteps. Subsequent acquaintance revealed surprising facts. Although Ford had sworn before a squire that he was a single man and had secured a license and subsequently married May, it was found that he had two other wives living at that date. For several months after this the young man was followed and his past life investigated, and the conviction began to grow that he was not normal, and therefore not responsible for the crimes he had committed. Finally, he was arrested for bigamy and the case was tried. The prosecution could not be continued, however, because in the meantime one wife had died and Ford's marriage with the second wife turned out to be illegal, since, though only eighteen years old when he married her, the wife had a legal husband living whom she had deserted.

The prosecutor in dropping the case said: "Legally, Ford is not guilty, but morally he is, and I wish that I could punish him, for he deserves it."

"Would you punish a child of nine years?" I could not help asking. "Would you send a child of nine to state's prison?"

"Perhaps you are right, perhaps that is the way to look at it," the prosecutor answered.

In jail ample opportunity was afforded to study Ford at leisure. Although his mentality was proven to be on the whole little superior to Beckie's it was of a different type from hers. The chief difference, however, seemed to be in their characters. Instead of indifference at his fate Ford showed a profound interest in what was in store for him.

"Do you think they can punish me?" he kept repeating with pitiful insistence. "I know I done wrong and I'm not sayin' this 'cause I'm in here, but when I get out I'm going to lead a different life. I'm going to join church and me and May's going to live like man an' wife ought to."

There was no possibility of questioning the sincerity of his intentions. But Ford, like all mentally defective persons, and like all children, is open to suggestion and unconsciously takes on the attitude of those with whom he is conversing. For the moment their attitude is his, and without any thought of insincerity, he is capable of changing completely round in an incredibly short space of time. What he lacks is the power to hold a directing idea, which would enable him to follow any chosen course of action; nor has he any conception of right conduct beyond what the impulse or desire of the moment may inspire.

Anxious to draw out his ethical ideas I took occasion to question him about the conduct of some of his friends. His brother George, for instance, has been in three different state's prisons and married a girl with several other husbands who was also a state's prison case. She happens to be a microcephalic, low grade moron whose strikingly small head obtained for her the distinction of having her photograph placed in the rogues gallery of her state. Last winter one of her husbands traded her off to another man who tried to get a license to marry her. Knowing that Ford had been privy to the transaction I questioned him in the following manner:

"What kind of a fellow is Lem Oltman?"

"Lem's all right, I guess; I ain't got nothin' agin' Lem."

"He tried to give Clarissa to Jim Jenks last winter didn't he?"

"Yes, he tried."

"Jim has a wife, hasn't he?"

"He says he has."

"Say Ford, didn't your brother George marry Clarissa once?"

"Yes, an' she's got four other husbands, only one's dead."

"Who are they, Ford?"

"Well, Tom Faust, he's dead, an' Gus Ross, he's livin', and George and Lem."

"She lived once with Bert Ivans, didn't she?"

"Yes, last summer."

"What sort of a fellow is Bert?"

"He's all right only he won't work, an' he swears somethin' awful."

"Tell me, Ford, do you think Clarissa is bright?"

"No, I don't believe she is."

A Nine-Year-Old Man

Given the precise tests, Ford succeeded in attaining the nine-year limit. As compared with Beckie his memory was a little weaker, but his powers of calculation were superior to hers. Like her he could neither read nor write but evidently for a different reason. Ford has never had any schooling, while Beckie had attended school off and on for four years. His descriptions of pictures, far from being crude like hers, were original and interesting. He was not satisfied with describing what he saw but often went back to causes, a distinctly normal trait.

"My, there's trouble here! Guess them boys must a' been doing somethin' or that man 'ud never be a-chasin' 'em so. . . . Guess that fellow must be haulin' flour in them sacks, anyway he's been to the mill."

For the imperfect human specimens, he instantly gave correct diagnoses. His language, however, was poorly developed; he could not make a sentence, using two words given him, nor comprehend a rhyme, nor make comparisons in answer to such questions as: "What is the difference between a butterfly and a fly?"

His definitions were those of a child of seven, he did not know the names of the months of the year, or the date, or even the season. He could not see any absurdity in the statement: "A man painting a house fell off a ladder and broke his neck by the fall. They took him to the hospital and do not think he will get well."

"It's all his own fault," replied Ford, who was in a supersensitive state of personal humiliation. In fact, Ford's consciousness of mistakes is one of his striking characteristics. In this, he shows a judgment superior to Beckie, whose self-satisfaction would prove an effectual barrier to any higher development.

His answers to comprehensive questions were interesting when compared to hers.

"What ought you to do if the house is on fire?"

"Do what you can to put it out."

"When you want to buy something you see at the store?"

"Wait till you can pay for it."

"When another contradicts you no matter what you say?"

"Let them have their own way."

"That's what you do, isn't it, Ford?"

"Yes, I never make trouble."

"How about your brother George?"

"Well George likes a fuss, but then George drinks."

Needless to say, Ford, like Beckie, fell completely under the suggestion test, but, unlike her, he quickly and accurately copied the diamond as well as the square, although he protested that he had never tried to draw anything in all his life.

Ford could not grasp an abstract idea nor hold two ideas together to compare or relate them; all this was particularly significant when taken in conjunction with his life. Kind-hearted and gentle by nature, as well as strictly honest, Ford's crimes had come about through lack of realizing the responsibility of his acts or relating them to one another. Although he proved himself the most atrocious liar, perjuring himself repeatedly, his lies were those of a frightened child and so easy to detect that no intelligent child of nine would have uttered them no matter how malicious he intended to be. Moreover, Ford's lies were usually about things that he could not fully understand, while he showed an equally childish veracity where it was question of simple things which an intelligent adult would keep to himself. His brother George, with about the same mentality, has distinct criminalistic impulses, which make of him a much more serious problem. Opportunity has so far been lacking to make an equally minute and precise examination of him.

The Problem of the Pines

In course of time Vineland Training School hopes to be able to conduct similar studies upon other adult Pineys, but with the material which we have in hand it is possible to point out some things of vital importance; for example, the folly of giving to a man, whose mentality is that of a child of nine years, the right of franchise, thus permitting him to become the prey of men who will buy his vote. Imagine a man living thirty years in the world and not learning to know what month it is, and yet being given a voice in political affairs! Also it is with no small surprise we discover that our laws, which were made to regulate the lives of normal people, do not touch the degenerate problem, for we find that a man cannot be legally punished for bigamy if his wives are of the same type and happen to have extra husbands themselves. Thus it becomes literally true that two wrongs make one right in our commonwealth!

In all the neighboring communities, one is told that conditions in the Pines are better today than they have been in the past. New roads are opening up the country, while delightful winter resorts here and there are giving employment to many and are bringing the Piney in touch with those who do not take his manner of living as a simple matter of course, while the development of the cranberry and chicken industries offers a means of livelihood to those who are willing to work, at the same time that an improved school system, pushed forward by trained workers, is offering the advantages of education to those capable of receiving it. To all this, it may be said that this apparent improvement scarcely touches the real problem at all, for the Piney is known to penetrate deeper into the woods as civilizing influences approach. It is more than a question whether or not he is capable of receiving sufficient education to make of him a desirable citizen, while the lowered moral tone which his presence ensures is a perpetually undermining influence to the work of the schools. Only recently, a prominent lawyer dragged a relative of his by main force out of a cabin in the Pines where he had been living for a few weeks or months perhaps, with a Piney girl, himself drunk most of the time. The lawyer in question, who is in a position to know, asserts that such things are common. It is this phase of the subject, far more than the actual personal problem of the Piney himself, that demands attention. What is true of the Pines is true, with local variations, of all outlying districts, and is also true of certain portions of the slums of our great cities.

Certainly the time has come for us as an enlightened community to set about clearing up these "backdoors of our civilization" and so to save from the worst form of contagion what remains of moral health in our rising generation.

8

MARY STORER KOSTIR
The Family of Sam Sixty*

Preface

This study presents "a problem which the people of Ohio must face" in the form of the family of Sam Sixty, named after Sam's I.Q. ("exactly sixty per cent of the average adult" [p. 187]). Residents of "the river hills of Ohio," the clan consisted of a number of family groups, some related only by marriage. Kostir identifies three "strains," analyzing them through commentaries on a sequence of charts. However, the relationships are more easily grasped in terms of generations:

> *Generation 1:* Born in the late eighteenth century, its members include the families of Sam Sixty's grandparents, John and Polly (Chart II); John's sister Maria (Chart III); John's brother Lafe (Chart IV); and Levy Lanimirc, grandfather of Sam's wife Pearl (Chart VI).
>
> *Generation 2:* Born about 1840, this generation consists of the families of Sam's parents, Abner and Rose (Chart I); Isaac Lanimirc, father of Sam's wife Pearl (Chart V); and Susan Lanimirc, second wife of Isaac and stepmother to Pearl (Chart VII).[1]
>
> *Generations 3, 4, and 5:* The third generation includes Sam and Pearl, the central characters of the story; the fourth, their children; and the fifth, their grandchildren (on whom, however, the genealogist has little information).

Compared to families traced in other studies, Sam and his siblings were a bad lot indeed. Sam was arrested for shooting to kill, non-support, and perjury as well as incest with his four daughters; according to Kostir (p. 191), he had also made "unnatural attempts upon his young sons." Sam's alcoholic brother Jim also had a long record: incest, rape, riot, shooting to kill, and willful destruction of property. Their three sisters were either prostitutes or otherwise "immoral." The impression of criminality is heightened, however, by Kostir's inclusion of negative information on remote, non-blood relatives. She informs us, for example (p. 193), that Pearl's first mate is "said to be a libertine and a thief"; that this man's brother "is said to have 'killed his man'"; and that his nephews "have penitentiary records for burglary and larceny." Introduction of such data enables Kostir to paint a picture far blacker than that she would have produced by limiting herself to Sixties.

Even in terms of contemporary eugenics, Kostir's understanding of the mechanisms of heredity was somewhat regressive. Other eugenicists, as we have seen, had begun to question the earlier view of feeble-mindedness as a

---

* Originally Publication no. 8, Ohio Board of Administration (Press of Ohio State Reformatory), January 1916.

[1] Kostir echoes "Two Brothers" and *The Kallikak Family* by showing two branches of one family, fathered by Isaac with different wives; but unlike her predecessors, she does little to mine the eugenic potential of the contrast.

unit trait, inherited according to the Mendelianist formula. But Kostir adheres to the older view, showing on her charts that feeble-mindedness and other "character defects" are automatically passed from parent to child. *"Feeble-minded parents,"* she concludes, *"have feeble-minded children"* (p. 208; emphases in original).

Like other proponents of defective delinquency theory—the belief that the feeble-minded are inherently criminalistic and that most criminals, by definition, are feeble-minded—Kostir regards the intellect as a kind of harness on the instincts. The feeble-minded cannot control their baser impulses; they must be held in institutions that provide the restraints they lack. Sam is well behaved at the penitentiary, which provides the control he lacks personally; but if he is released, he will quickly revert to crime. "He has not reached, and never can reach, the mental age necessary for adequate self-control" (p. 195). Similarly, Violet, Sam's daughter and partner in incest, should never be released from an institution. Such delinquents "can never attain the usual respect for the laws of morality, because they lack the intelligence which is necessary for this appreciation" (p. 208).

Mary Storer attended the 1913 summer school session in field work at the Eugenics Record Office, where one of her classmates was Mina Sessions, genealogist of the Happy Hickories. She returned to her home state to work for the Ohio Bureau of Juvenile Research under its clinical director, Dr. Thomas H. Haines. In November of 1914 Haines received word that two brothers, Sam and Jim Sixty, had been convicted of incest with Sam's daughters, and that Sam and Violet were still inmates of state institutions. "Such criminality seemed to point to inferiority of stock," Haines recalls in his introductory note (p. 186), "and the father and daughter were given mental examinations." When both failed (at the time, intelligence tests were nearly impossible to pass), Haines assigned his field worker to investigate the family.

Born in Clyde, Ohio, in 1881, Mary Irene Storer received a B.A. from Ohio State University in 1913. In 1915 she married Wancel Jerome Kostir, a zoology instructor (later professor) at Ohio State University. The following year her family study (apparently her only publication) appeared and she received an M.A. degree from the university.[2]

INTRODUCTORY NOTE

In November, 1914, Mr. Starr Cadwallader, then a member of the Ohio Board of Administration, informed the Bureau of Juvenile Research that two brothers, Sam and Jim Sixty, had been committed to the Ohio Penitentiary for incest upon daughters of the former; and that one of these daughters, Violet, had been committed to the Girls' Industrial Home. Jim had been discharged, but Sam was still serving his term. Such criminality seemed to point to inferiority of stock, and the father and daughter were given mental examinations.

[2] I have been unable to find other relevant biographical information. For the personal details mentioned here I thank Thomas J. Reider of the Ohio Historical Society.

The daughter then 14 3/4 years of age tested VIII years, mentally. By the Point Scale, she made 39 points, or forty-seven per cent of the score expected of one of her age. She was an attractive looking girl. She had all the modesty and apparent sensitiveness one would expect of a normal fifteen-year-old, in discussing her short comings and the bestiality of her father. But she proved herself markedly lacking in capacity to react intelligently to these feelings. She had not the capacity to lead a moral life, because she could not anticipate her own feelings, or the feelings and approvals and disapprovals of others.

The father, Sam, proved to be a medium grade moron. His chronological age was 47 1/2 years. By the Point Scale he made a score of fifty-seven points. This is the expected performance of a child of 8 4/5 years, and is exactly sixty percent of the average adult performance in these tests. By the Year Scale he made a score of 8 4/5 years. He was a large brawny man, well qualified physically to support himself and a family. His family of eight, and the crime of which he stands convicted, leave no question as to the physiological maturity of the man. At the same time, his crimes, the intelligence tests, and his general behavior and reactions, all indicate that in self-control and all that constitutes morality, he is a child of less than nine years. On account of this mental immaturity he should never have been allowed to become a father. It would have been a great economy for the community to have prevented his feeble-minded and criminalistic brood, by taking him into custody as a boy and keeping him segregated and at farm work all his life long.

We have called the family Sixty* from the mental endowment of this principal representative, since he has a sixty per cent mental equipment, as measured by the Point Scale. Some of our ancestors were named Smith, Butcher, Cook, Schneider, and Kaufmann, on account of what they did; and others were called Brown, White, and Schwartz, on account of the *colors* of hair, eyes and skin. This family we called Sixty on account of the color of their minds, and the amount of performance this representative can exhibit when his mind is tested.

The data, genealogical, biological and sociological, presented herewith, have been gathered and put together by Mrs. Mary Storer Kostir. She has been most diligent and conscientious in looking up genealogical connections, personal traits and characteristics, and court and institution records. She has been very conservative in her estimation of mental ability. She is familiar with the Binet-Simon Scale, having used it in hundreds of cases. When, therefore, she asserts that an individual is feeble-minded, the possibility that he is not so is very remote indeed.

* In some earlier newspaper notices the family was named Mengold.

Her charts alone show both the prolificness of these feeble-minded stocks and the certainty of transmission of mental defect with criminal tendencies. They present the false economy and great expense of our present temporizing with the problems involved in feeble-mindedness. Her description and summary reenforce these points.

THOMAS H. HAINES, M. D.

January 10, 1916.

THE WRITER UNDERTOOK the task of making an extensive survey of the "Sixty Family," in the spring of 1915. The investigation was pursued, as opportunity permitted, during the spring and summer of 1915.

The Field Worker's report, on file with the Bureau of Juvenile Research, gives the findings in detail. Five generations have been charted, more or less completely. The chart shows 474 individuals, on 261 of whom some data have been secured. Of the 261, sixty are known to have had court records, and fifty-six are known to have been in public institutions, as follows:

Jail	15
Penitentiary	14
Infirmary	9
Children's Home	9
Workhouse	6
Girls' Industrial Home	2
Boys' Industrial School	1
Institution for Feeble-Minded	2

Concerning the personal characteristics of these 261 persons, we have the following record:

Criminalistic (varying degrees)	74
Sexually immoral	77
Feeble-minded	55
Alcoholic	23
Prostitutes	12
Subject to fits (epilepsy?)	4
Insane	3
Wanderers (tramps)	3
Normal intelligence	3

These findings, it must be understood, are very incomplete. Court records, infirmary records, and the like, few of which were kept prior to 1870, were gone over in but three or four counties. Interviews with respectable people, who knew the Sixties more or less vaguely, often disclosed the presence of traits in a given branch, which the investigator was not able to connect with any particular individual. Interviews with certain of the Sixties themselves, who were willing to talk, too often indicated an inability or unwillingness to give exact facts, which made it necessary to weigh every particle of evidence they submitted. Inability of the investigator to locate many members of the family, made it impossible to get information concerning them at first hand. All these conditions, coupled with the limited time in which the study was made, clearly indicate that our report is only a beginning in the study of the traits of these people.

The findings, incomplete as they are, suffice to show that we have in this family a group of notorious law-breakers. Their location, along the Ohio River, has enabled many of them to escape punishment for their crimes and misdemeanors, by means of the simple expedient of slipping across the river from one state to another. Crimes for which certain of the Sixties have been before the courts include burglary, larceny, destruction of property, bootlegging, operating houses of ill-fame, intoxication, riot, perjury, incest, rape, homicide, shooting to kill, and attempting to poison.

The mentality of the group is low. Although in our report, 55 out of 261 are recorded as feeble-minded, it must not be supposed that the 206, not so recorded, are of normal mentality. Only three have been recorded as normal. This leaves 203 concerning the mentality of whom no definite statements can be made. Of these a number are children, too young to show definite defect. Many more are adults, whom the investigator did not see, and concerning whose intelligence no definite data were obtainable. Others are persons long deceased, concerning whom not much is known. Still others are of the class who appear fairly normal, but ignorant. Mental examinations might show many of these to be mentally deficient. In view of the fact that responsible citizens speak of the whole line, of which Sam is a member, as "mentally subnormal" and in view of circumstances pointing to feeble-mindedness in many individuals where no mental diagnosis has been made, it is only reasonable to suppose that many of the Sixties not marked "F" on our charts, are in reality feeble-minded. Where we *have* marked an individual "F," moreover, we have done so only after a careful weighing of all the evidence at hand. In every case, where there has been any doubt as to the existence of definite intelligence defect, we have left the square or circle representing such an individual, blank. In every case marked "F," we have evidence of at least one of the following types: (a) mental examination of the individual; (b) personal interview, without formal examination, in which the intelligence of the individual is gauged by comparison with those whose mentality is known; or (c) the testimony of at least two responsible people, whose judgment has been tested by obtaining their verdict on individuals whose mentality has been determined.

The charts and descriptions which follow will serve to give a fairly definite picture of the Sixties, so far as we have been able to trace them. It is quite conceivable that errors have crept in, particularly with regard to the exact relationship of certain members of this group, one to another. One source of error, which complicates the matter lies in the loose standard of sexual morality which characterizes many of this group. But, while in the matter of relationships some degree of inaccuracy is obviously unavoidable, special efforts have been made to authenticate the data relating to individual traits and histories; and the results here presented are believed to be substantially accurate.

Owing to the abridged and simplified form in which the results of our investigation are here presented, some of the individuals on whom we have data will not be found charted or described in the following pages. Furthermore, facts which would make the group too easily identified have been omitted. There are some among the family and its connections, who are respectable citizens. They would be humiliated by the public exhibition of the shortcomings of their relatives. We wish to avoid every semblance of offense to such persons. At the same time it is our earnest conviction that this family presents, in unescapable form, a problem which the people of Ohio must face.

The problem is presented in seven charts, with their accompanying descriptions. Charts I, II, III and IV deal with blood relatives of Sam Sixty, with whom we started; Charts V and VI deal with blood relatives of Sam's wife, Pearl; while Chart VII deals with relatives of Pearl's half-brothers and half-sisters. From this it may be seen that our study embraces three separate strains; the first two of these converge in the children of Sam and Pearl; while the second and third converge in the half-brothers and half-sisters of Pearl. The branches represented by the several charts, are as follows:

(Strain I)
Chart I	Sam's parents, Abner and Rose, with their descendants
Chart II	Sam's father's parents, John and Polly, and their descendants
Chart III	Marie, sister of John (Chart II), and her descendants (fragmentary)
Chart IV	Lafe, brother to John (Chart II), and his descendants (fragmentary)

(Strain II)
Chart V	Pearl's father, Isaac Lanimirc, and his descendants
Chart VI	Pearl's father's father, Levy Lanimirc, and his descendants (fragmentary)

(Strain III)
Chart VII	Pearl's step-mother, Susan, with her parents, brothers, and sisters (fragmentary)

Chart I

Abner and Rose Sixty spent much of their lives in the river hills of Ohio. Abner was one of a large family, which is represented by Chart II. He was always poor and shiftless; owned no property, and with his family lived in "first one shack, then another." He seems to have been an inoffensive old fellow—at any rate, he left no court record—but was very ignorant, and "not very bright." Said to be of lower mentality than his wife. His wife Rose is still living in a little hut on a steep hillside. She is a vigorous old lady physically, but is unquestionably feeble-minded. Abner and Rose had a large family, none of whom have turned out well. Descriptions of their progeny follow in the order of their birth.

(1) A boy who died as an infant.

(2) Sam, who was committed to the Ohio Penitentiary for incest on his daughter, is a man with the mind of a child of 8 4/5 years. By the Point Scale he scores 60 per cent of the average adult performance. He is alcoholic, a sex pervert of extreme type, and utterly irresponsible. He has been in court at various times for shooting to kill, non-support, and perjury, but his offenses in the sex realm are perhaps his greatest crimes. He is charged with assault upon each of his daughters, dating from their early childhood, and, in addition to this, with unnatural attempts upon his young sons. Some of the testimony regarding his behavior is absolutely unprintable. He never supported his family; and the little shack, where they happened to be living at any given time, was always a place of filth, destitution, vile language and brutal abuse. "It was a common sight to see them trudging across the hills with their few possessions moving from one house to another," neighbors say. Sam is said to have worked very little, and to have spent his money, and all he could get of his wife's and children's earnings, on drink and immoral women.

(3) A boy who died young.

(4) Jim, an alcoholic, who stays with his mother. He is 40 years old and never married. He works on river boats, but never works steadily. He has a quick temper and a long court record, beginning with an assault and battery charge when he was 17. Later charges were, shooting to kill, riot, wilful destruction of property, incest, and rape. He was sentenced to the Ohio Penitentiary for five years, on the last mentioned charges, when he was about thirty years of age. He is charged with the paternity of the illegitimate child of his niece, the second child of his brother Sam. The paternity of that child is a matter of conjecture, but there seems to be no doubt that incestuous relations existed between this man and his niece. After his discharge from the penitentiary, the niece claims he tried to reestablish his relations with her, and hung around the house where she was staying, until she was afraid to go out alone. This man looks brutal and degenerate. His neck is as wide as his head. His right eye is deeper set than his left. His nose and mouth deviate to the right. He is said to be feeble-minded.

(5) A daughter, who was feeble-minded and a prostitute. She had several illegitimate children, "each by a different man." She finally married a feeble-minded tramp. He deserted her soon after, and she was a county charge until her death. She, in company with some of her unsavory relatives, was in the court for riot.

(6) A daughter who is a prostitute. No data on her mentality were obtained. She

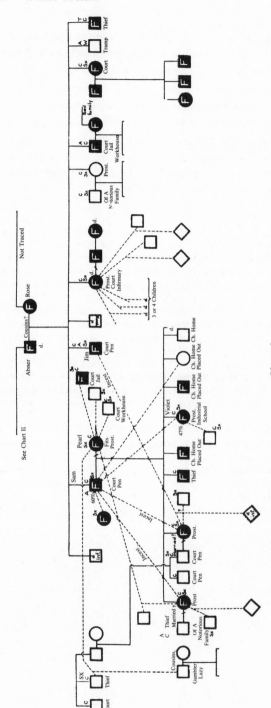

Chart I.

Explanation of the Charts: The squares indicate males and the circles females. A square turned so it rests on one corner indicates that the sex is not known. A horizontal or oblique line joining a square and a circle indicates marriage if a solid line, and illicit sexual relation, if it is a broken line. Perpendicular lines indicate descent. Thus Abner and Rose, of Chart I, were married. Sam, in turn, was married to Pearl, and had illicit relations with another woman and with four of his own daughters. The letter "F" in a square or a circle indicates the person is known to be feeble-minded. Sx. means sexually immoral; C., criminalistic; A., alcoholic; N., normal; W., wanderer or vagrant; T., tubercular; I., insane; and D., deceased.

married a man who has a number of notorious relatives, and who is said to serve as a pander for his wife. They have several children

(7) A son, who is described as a feeble-minded alcoholic, a fighter and a thief. He has been in jail, has served time in the workhouse, and has lived alternately in Ohio and across the river, in order to dodge officers of the law. His wife is a slovenly imbecile, who comes from a very inferior family ("no account imbeciles"), probably all mentally defective. The children of this couple are still small.

(8) A daughter who is said to be immoral and feeble-minded. She married a man of similar mentality, and they have several mentally deficient children. The man was in court for riot.

(9) A son, who is a tramp and an alcoholic. No further data on his mentality.

(10) The youngest son who lives with his mother. He is feeble-minded and tubercular, and said to be a thief, though he has never been in court on this charge. Since Rose, this son, her son (7) and several grand children are living together, and since their income from legitimate channels is practically nothing, the neighbors seem loath to report the boy's thefts.

Sam's wife, Pearl Lanimirc, is said to be of lower mentality than is Sam himself. She too comes of bad stock; (See Charts V and VI). She is said to be slovenly and untidy, and has always borne an unsavory reputation. While yet quite young, she bore an illegitimate child, a boy, who is now married, and who "gambles and does not work much." It is suspected that he steals. The father of this boy was said to be a libertine and a thief. This man too, comes of bad stock. A brother of his was a notorious "bad man" who is said to have "killed his man," and who disappeared, when wanted by the courts for felony; two nephews have penitentiary records for burglary and larceny; one of these is said to have married a daughter of Sam and Pearl.

Pearl and Sam had a large family of children. The older ones have turned out badly, and the younger ones are not particularly promising. The children follow in order of birth:

(1) A daughter who is feeble-minded. Her paternity is doubtful; she may be the daughter of Pearl's cousin. Trained in immorality by her relations with her father, and by the example of her mother, she left home at an early age, went to a nearby town, and began a life of prostitution. Taken from this and placed in a good family, she soon became pregnant, and accused a married man in the neighborhood of being responsible for her condition. The man had always borne a good reputation. It is possible that the accusation was for the purpose of extorting money from him. After this experience, the girl resumed her life of prostitution (during which time her father's mother cared for the illegitimate child), and later is said to have married a man who is described as "tough," an alcoholic, and a thief. This man came of a family quite the equal of the Sixties for anti-social traits. They are said to be somewhat brighter than the Sixties, though not of normal mentality. They are a wild, undisciplined set, who have been represented in almost every kind of correctional and charitable institution available to their locality. Stealing is perhaps their most common crime.

(2) A daughter, who is feeble-minded. She was brought up in immorality, as was her sister. She became the mother of an illegitimate child, who died in

infancy. Its father is variously conjectured as Sam, her father; Jim, her uncle; and a man of the neighborhood, not related, who was implicated, it is said, because he had money. Both Sam and Jim had had relations with the girl, and, upon information supplied by the girl's sister, Jim was sent to the penitentiary on the charge of incest. This Jim has already been described as an alcoholic feeble-minded fellow, who is said to have continued his advances to the girl even after his release from the penitentiary. Later when the girl's father was sent to the penitentiary on a similar charge, the girl, her mother, and her brother and sisters moved to a nearby town, and, as soon as the younger members of the family had been taken to the county children's home, this girl, with her mother, and her sister Violet, became public prostitutes.

The girl is said to have later married a young man who has an extended jail, workhouse, and penitentiary record. Both he and his brother were in the penitentiary for burglary and larceny. This boy's uncle has already been mentioned as the probable father of Pearl's oldest son.

(3) A son, who is feeble-minded and a thief. He has been in court for stealing. He is said to be "like a tramp," and an irresponsible wanderer, if left to himself; but a fair worker under supervision.

(4) A son, "who is not up to average mentally." He was placed in the county children's home when the family broke up, and has since been placed on a farm. He is said to be the most promising of the four children of this family who were in the children's home. He works well under supervision, but is feeble-minded, and needs pretty constant direction.

(5) Violet, Sam's daughter who was seen and examined at the Girls' Industrial Home when she was less than 15 years of age. A slight, modest looking slip of a girl. Her life with her parents was horrible. The home was one of filth and desperate poverty. There was a dearth of clothing and food. The children begged, pilfered and sold junk, to keep soul and body together. The home atmosphere was one of brawling abuse and carnal passions. Their father, the children hated and feared, and fought with all their puny strength. All that is best and noblest was represented to them solely in the person of their mother, a weak-minded slovenly, immoral woman.

From the time she was a little girl, Violet was made the victim of her father's gross and perverted appetites. He often beat his wife and children, and they threatened to inform on him. But he bullied them into silence for a long time.

The girl finally managed to slip away from home, and went to work in a nearby town. After an episode with a worthless man, to whom her mother is said to have entrusted her, the child, then less than 14 years of age, was lured into a life of prostitution by the woman for whom she worked. The matter came to the attention of court authorities, and Violet was sent to the Girls' Industrial Home near Delaware, Ohio, on the charge of being "incorrigible and immoral."

With her mentality that of a child of eight years, it is impossible for this girl to order her life in accordance with the standards of morality in vogue in 20th century civilized society. At the Home, however, she is tractable and well disposed. She said to the writer, "I like it here; it is a better home than I ever had with father." She is a victim of defective heredity and of a depraved environment supplied by her feeble-minded and bestial family.

After a year at the Home, she will probably be sent out to make room for new cases. The sequel may be easily predicted: A life of misery and degradation; of prostitution, debauchery, and disease; and a heritage of defect and degeneracy, passed on to her unhappy offspring. She is a child of good impulses, and under permanent custodial care of the right sort, she would doubtless be content, industrious, and practically self-sustaining. If this girl goes to the depths of degradation and becomes the mother of a feeble-minded brood, as did her parents before her, the fault will lie, not with her, but with those who have it in their power to provide for her care. If they do not provide such care it is because of a short-sighted economy. In that case the blame for the crime and debauchery of this child and her children, will rest upon these false economists.

Of (6), (7) and (8) the remaining living children of Sam and Pearl, there is not much to tell. All shared in the horrible home life just described, and all were taken to the children's home when their father was sent to the penitentiary, and their mother showed herself incapable of caring for them. The first, a boy, said to be mentally deficient, was placed on a farm; the second, a girl, has been placed with a family on trial; and the third is still at the children's home. It is yet too early to predict how these three will eventuate.

No one seems to know where Pearl is at present. After Sam's incarceration, she alternated between public prostitution and temporary living with different men of unsavory reputations. One of her paramours is spoken of as of the "scum of the earth." Another is said to be a member of the notorious family to which her oldest daughter's husband belongs. It was reported that Pearl had married this relative of her daughter's husband.

Sam is still in the penitentiary, where he is said to be an honor prisoner. This shows what controlled environment can do for people of this type. But, it must not be forgotten that his mind is still that of a child; and that as soon as the control is removed, he will slip back into his old ways. He has not reached, and never can reach, the mental age necessary for adequate self-control.

Chart II

John and Polly Sixty were the parents of Abner, who, with his descendants, has been described under Chart I. John and Polly came about 100 years ago from Pennsylvania to southern Ohio, where they secured a grant of land, and brought up a large family. Nothing is known of the mentality of this couple. The nature of their social behavior is also unknown. Our data on their descendants are, for the most part, meagre; but they tend to indicate that Abner's line (Chart I) does not differ greatly from those of his brothers and sisters.

The children of John and Polly were:

(1) A son, who was arrested for burglary, but avoided jail by "skipping out." His present location is not certainly known. This man was twice married, and has several children of whom we know nothing.

(2) A son, who seems to have been a bounty-jumper, in the Union Army. He has several children; we know of five. One of his daughters was sent to the Girls' Industrial Home at Delaware, O., for "leading a vicious and criminal life." This same girl subsequently spent a year at the county infirmary. She is now said to be married, as are two of her sisters, of whom we know nothing. Two brothers died young.

(3) A son, feeble-minded, who is described as brutal and abusive, especially

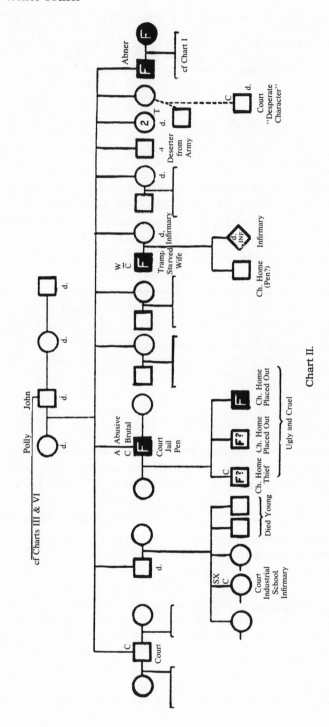

Chart II.

when drunk. He is "willing to cheat his best friends." He has been in court several times on charges of burglary and larceny. He served one penitentiary term, the charge being horse stealing. He has been married twice (possibly three times), and by his first wife, whose death is said to have been hastened by his abuse of her, he had three sons. The children were placed in the children's home. All are said to be ugly and cruel, and to have disagreeable tempers. All, like their father, have speech defects.

The oldest boy was placed in several homes, but failed to make good. Finally he appropriated money belonging to his employer, and left. He was later returned to the children's home and was compelled to repay the man from whom he had stolen. Later, he enlisted in the U. S. Navy, and is thought to have "gotten into trouble there." He is said to be "hardly up to normal, mentally." The second boy was placed in a good home, but as he grew older, he became ugly to his benefactor, and finally left him. He also is "hardly up to normal, mentally." The third boy has been placed with good people. He, too, is ugly and undependable. He is unquestionably feeble-minded.

(4) A daughter, of whom all we know is that she has a speech defect, and is said to be industrious. She is married and has children.

(5) A daughter, married. No data on her or her family.

(6) A daughter (probably feeble-minded) who married a feeble-minded tramp, who is said to have starved her. She died and was buried by the county. She had two children, one of whom was born in the county infirmary. One child died in infancy. The other, a boy, was placed in the children's home. Later he went west, and is said to have been sent to a state penitentiary. The feeble-minded tramp, her husband, later married a niece of this woman. He is also shown on Chart I.

(7) A daughter, now dead, of whose husband and children we know practically nothing.

(8) A son, said to have been a deserter from the Union Army. He died in the south.

(9)–(10) Two girls, said to have died young from tuberculosis.

(11) A daughter (question, whether she belongs in this branch) of whom we know only that she bore an illegitimate son. This son, now dead, was alcoholic, and "a desperate character." He had a court record for stealing.

(12) Abner Sixty. He and his wife Rose are already described as the feeble-minded progenitors of the branch shown in Chart I.

In view of the nature of the data so far obtained in the case of the descendants of John and Polly Sixty, it seems quite conceivable that a further study of the branches barely sketched here might add several to the list of feeble-minded, and probably also to that of the alcoholic, immoral and criminalistic. Whether John and Polly were themselves good citizens, we do not know, but since their progeny, in at least six branches, shows some indications of anti-social behavior, it is possible that, in rearing their family, John and Polly have rendered to society a service of doubtful value.

Chart III

Maria Sixty was a sister of the John Sixty just described as founder of the line shown in Chart II. Maria came to Ohio from Pennsylvania, as did her

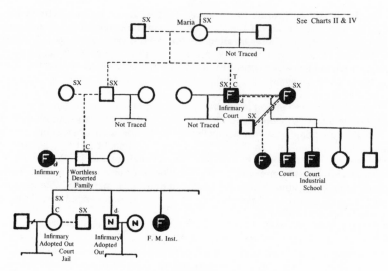

Chart III.

brother. We have no definite data on her mentality, but we know that she became enamored of a man by whom she had two illegitimate sons. She later married, but her subsequent descendants have not been traced. Of the two illegitimate sons, we know the following facts:

(1) This man became the father of an illegitimate son, and later married and had other descendants of whom we know nothing. The illegitimate son turned out to be a worthless fellow, who married a feeble-minded woman, and later deserted her and the children, and is said to have married again. The woman and her children lived for some time at the county infirmary. Two of the children, a girl and a boy, were adopted by a family. The girl later became a servant, with a reputation for immorality. She married a wealthy man, whom she is accused of trying to poison, when she had become enamored of another man. The trial was an extended one, and attracted much attention. This woman's brother grew up to be a respectable man, described as of normal mentality. A younger sister of this man is at present in an institution for feeble-minded.

(2) This man was a familiar character in the county in which he lived. He was feeble-minded. He was somewhat of a vagabond; would leave home for several weeks, "visiting" among relatives and friends. He and one son were in the county infirmary for a time; but the family, though very poor, usually managed to subsist on the old man's pension.

We know nothing of his first marriage, except that he had several children, who are now married and have children. His second marriage, to a young woman not up to the normal mentally, seems to have been forced, as he was in court on a charge of fornication about this time. His second wife, who already had one child (said to be illegitimate), bore him four children. This family seems anything but promising. The two oldest sons were in court for threatening to kill their father. One was not well, so was given a suspended sentence to the Boys' Industrial School. The other was sent to the Industrial School, where he made a perfect record. Both boys are feeble-minded.

There are two younger children, a girl and a boy. The latter appears particularly unpromising. The mother has no control over her children; she is contemplating placing them in a children's home. She is feeble-minded.

From this fragment of the history of Maria's descendants, we get a picture of feeble-mindedness, immorality, and general irresponsibility that is far from reassuring as to the future of the line.

The man marked N on Chart III, together with his wife and oldest child, comprise the only individuals in our whole study who have been described to us as up to normal, mentally. That he should be normal is surprising, in view of the mentality of his immediate antecedents. This man's mother was admittedly feeble-minded, and his putative father was probably so. We regret that we have no data on the habits of the mother, with regard to sexual morality. The circumstances merit further investigation.

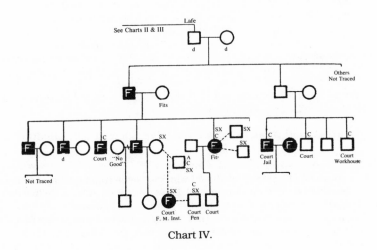

Chart IV.

Chart IV

Lafe Sixty, brother of John Sixty, the progenitor of the branch shown in Chart II, and Maria Sixty, the progenitor of the branch shown in Chart III, came to Ohio from Pennsylvania about one hundred years ago. He settled in eastern Ohio, on a grant of land he secured from the government. Here he brought up his family. Of his children we know only of two sons, Alex and Bert.

Alex, said to be below normal mentally (feeble-minded), was provident enough to keep the farm he inherited from his father. Oil was struck on his farm, and he is now quite well-to-do. He seems to be an inoffensive citizen. At any rate, he has no court record. His wife is subject to fits (epilepsy?) as are several of her relatives. We know of five of Alex's children. They are:

(1) A son, who is married. We know practically nothing of his wife or children. He is said to be feeble-minded.

(2) A son, who is said to have been feeble-minded. He was married. He is now dead.

(3) A son, who is said to be feeble-minded. He has been before the court for assault, and for carrying concealed weapons.

(4) A son who is said to be feeble-minded. He is a day laborer, who can barely write his name. He was twice married. His first wife is described as "no good." They separated, and their boy was taken by the father. His second wife is a woman from a rough family. She had an illegitimate daughter by a man who is described as an alcoholic and immoral, and is said to have a penitentiary record. This woman bore to (4) a daughter who is still small. Her illegitimate daughter is at present in the Institution for Feeble-Minded, at Columbus, Ohio. The girl was committed at the instigation of the juvenile court, after it was discovered that a boarder had been maintaining sexual relations with her since she was 13. The boarder was sent to the Ohio Penitentiary on the charge of rape. It is suspected that (4) also had incestuous relations with this girl, his step-daughter.

(5) A daughter, who is said to be feeble-minded, and like her mother, subject to fits (epilepsy?). She married, and has one boy. She and her husband separated. Since then she has lived with two or more dissolute men. Her son, whom she reported to court for drunkenness and threatening to shoot her, stays with his grandfather, Alex.

Bert married and brought up a family. We know of four children. They are:

(1) A son, who is feeble-minded, and who married a woman of similar mentality. He is said to be wild and irresponsible. He works only fitfully. He has been in court for wilful destruction of property. His children are still small.

(2) A son, on whose mentality we have no data. He, too, was in court for wilful destruction of property. He is said to be "of the same sort as his brother," just mentioned.

(3) A son. We know only his name.

(4) A son. He has been in court for destruction of property, for drunkenness, and for selling liquor to a minor. He bears a hard name in the neighborhood. He has served a term in the workhouse.

Two sons of Bert are said to have stolen money from a man; but the man did not prosecute them, for lack of sufficient evidence. At least one boy besides (1) is below normal, mentally; it is quite possible that all are mentally subnormal.

Among the few descendants of Lafe Sixty on whom we have succeeded in obtaining any data, there appears to be a high percentage of feeble-mindedness. Information concerning the strain is too meagre to warrant more definite conclusions. Enough is known, however, to warrant the assumption that most of the descendants of Lafe, like those of his sister

Maria and his brother John (see Charts I, II, III) could not be classed among our desirable citizens.

From the four charts and descriptions just given, we have a picture of the sort of family from which Sam Sixty came,—Sam, the feeble-minded, irresponsible, sex-pervert now in the penitentiary. Have we the right to expect a better product, given as factors such a strain as this, and such an environment as its members provide for their children? In sending Sam to the penitentiary, we are treating symptoms. This is well, so far as it goes. But it does seem to be the part of wisdom to treat the causes as well, when the causes are so patent. Five, eight, or ten years incarceration are of value in the case of a man like Sam, only in so far as he is restrained from wrong-doing, and is kept from begetting children, during that length of time. Our present "patch upon patch" system of sentence after sentence for the irresponsible feeble-minded offender, commends itself only to the short-sighted. Permanent custodial care for such weak-minded irresponsibles is the only real solution of the problem.

Chart V

Isaac Lanimirc is the father of Pearl Lanimirc, who has been described under Chart I as the wife of Sam Sixty. We have no data on his mentality. He has two families of children. The first family was born him by his wife Ann, a feeble-minded woman, but a hard worker. "She had to split rails, grub, and do heavy work." Her father and at least one brother are said to have been feeble-minded, and her whole family is spoken of as "not bright, poor and shiftless."

Isaac's second family was the fruit of an illegal union with a woman whom he is said to have bought from her husband for a few farming implements. The woman, Susan, is described as feeble-minded, and very immoral. After Isaac's death, she lived with at least three different men. She is reported to have married two of these. If this is true, she was a bigamist. One man who was issued a license to marry her, is subnormal mentally, has been immoral and criminal, and now gives evidence of insanity. He is at present serving his fourth penitentiary sentence. Isaac himself has served a jail sentence for assault. He, Susan, and a daughter, were charged with having shot at a man.

The children of Isaac and Ann were:

(1) Pearl, the feeble-minded prostitute already described (Chart I) as the wife of Sam Sixty.

(2) A son, feeble-minded but "harmless," who had a large family of children by a feeble-minded woman with whom he lived. There is doubt of their having been

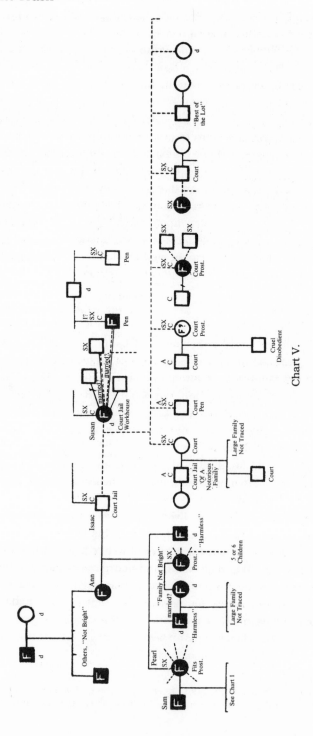

Chart V.

legally married. The woman came of a family described as "not bright; not much to them." Her sister, a feeble-minded woman, had five or six illegitimate children. Both (2) and his wife (?) are dead.

(3) A son, feeble-minded, but harmless, now dead. He worked on a river-boat.

Isaac's children by Susan are:

(1) A daughter, who has been in court for assault to wound. She is said to be immoral. She married a man who is described as alcoholic and criminalistic. He has a jail record, and comes of a very notorious family. His immediate relatives have been in court time after time, but were usually shrewd enough to escape conviction, though some of them drew jail sentences. Their home was known as a place of brawling and debauchery. (1) and her husband have a large family. One child has been in court for stealing.

(2) A son, who is alcoholic, and immoral, and who has served a term in the penitentiary for manslaughter. He shot and killed a man, when both were intoxicated. He is said to have been running with his victim's wife. He had been in another court previously for threatening to murder. Is said to be industrious when sober, but a dangerous man when drunk.

(3) A daughter, who seems hardly up to normal, mentally, though she is neat and tidy in appearance. She is said to be a prostitute, who hands over the money so earned to her worthless husband for drink. Both have been in court for assault; not recently, however. At present, court authorities think fairly well of the woman. She is charged with having kept girls for immoral purposes, but this charge has not been proven. Her son is a cruel, disobedient, unpromising lad, who bids fair to rival his father.

(4) A daughter, who is said to be subnormal, mentally. She is a prostitute. She was divorced by her husband, who is said to be a decent man, and has since lived with at least two other men of doubtful reputation. This woman was in court for keeping an immoral house, and again on a peace warrant. She is said to have been compelled to leave town on account of her obnoxious methods of attracting traffic.

(5) A son, who is said to be the father of an illegitimate son of Sam Sixty's sister (the one, described under Chart I, who married a tramp). He is married and has children. This man, with a number of his relatives, was in court for riot.

(6) A son, who is said to be "the best of the lot" (his family). He married a respectable girl, and has one child. No data on his mentality.

(7) A daughter, who died when a young woman.

It will be noted that Isaac's children by his wife Ann, are feeble-minded and generally incapable; but among his children by Susan, we note more positive traits. Their appearances in court were mainly for crimes of impulse, such as assault, riot, and manslaughter. Adequate data on the mentality of this second family are not at present available. As a whole, they appear brighter than their half-sisters and half-brothers.

It is doubtful whether any of these children are quite up to normal mentally; and in view of his choice of wife and of paramour, one could hardly conceive of their father as a man of normal intelligence.

Chart VI

Levi Lanimirc, father of Isaac (head of line shown in Chart V) and grandfather of Pearl (Sam Sixty's wife), spent most of his life in southern Ohio. His wife was partly negro. Levi had a large family. Our information concerning them is very meagre, except in the case of Isaac (Chart V) and his descendants. The children as described to us, are:

(1) Isaac, see Chart V for description.

(2) A son, who is said to be a respectable man in comfortable circumstances. He became insane from an injury received during the Civil War. He had a large family. One of his sons is said to be thrifty and prosperous, as are his children, in turn. A daughter of (2) is said to have been epileptic. We know nothing of the other children; only the names were given us.

(3) A son, who is described as a heavy drinker and a fighter. He was in court for assault, and for destruction of property, but evidence did not convict him; he has the reputation of being a troublesome person. This son had a large family. Six are said to have died in infancy. A daughter and her husband are described as "not bright but harmless," and the parents of a large family. We know little of (3's) other children.

(4) A son, who was married, and had a large family. He and his wife are dead, we know nothing of the children except their names.

(5) A son, now dead, who married and had a large family.

(6), (7) and (8) Three daughters who died.

(9) A son, who is described as cruel and abusive. He is said to have gone hunting when his first wife lay dying; and to be in the habit of knocking down and choking his present wife. He is said to have been in court for assault to kill or wound. He had several children. A son is alcoholic, and deserted his family. A daughter, now dead, was in court together with a notorious cousin, on a peace warrant.

(10) A son, who is described as "a hard drinker, who has been in several scrapes." He was twice in court for assault and once for carrying concealed weapons. Served time in jail. Twice married. We know of no children.

(11) A son, who has been in court for assault. His wife is described as below normal mentally, and his whole family is spoken of as shiftless. We know practically nothing of his children.

(12) Others not traced.

In this fragmentary account of the children of Levi Lanimirc, we observe a marked tendency to engage in brawls and fights. Whether or not this is indicative of unstable nervous systems, which is shown in more extreme form in the insane son of Levi, our data are insufficient to indicate. This branch would well repay more extended study.

Chart VII

Pearl Lanimirc Sixty's step-mother, Susan (described as common-law wife of Isaac Lanimirc, Chart V), was a woman of such positive anti-social tendencies, that a glimpse into her family history challenges our interest. Her father is said to have been a well-meaning man. He is said to have

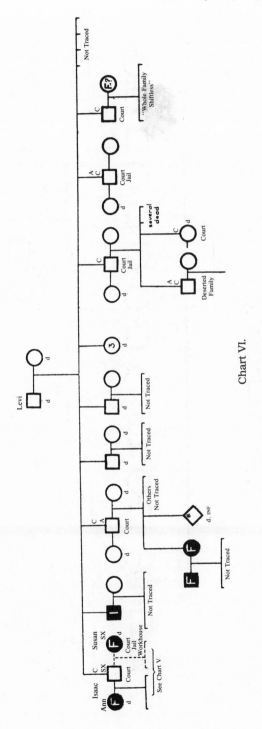

Chart VI.

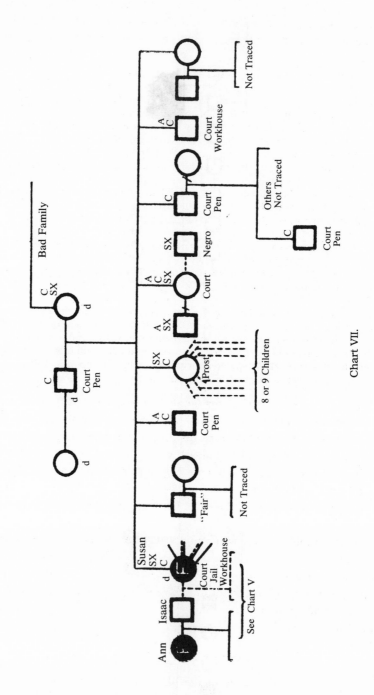

Chart VII.

been sent to the penitentiary for perjury in behalf of a friend. His wife (Susan's mother) was a bad woman, and of a bad family. She is said to have been exceedingly immoral, and to have encouraged immorality in her daughters.

The children of this couple, so far as known are:

(1) Susan, who has already been described under Chart V, as a feeble-minded immoral woman. She served time in jail and in the workhouse, for her misdemeanors, and could probably have been sent to the penitentiary for bigamy.

(2) A son, who is said to be "fair." He is married and has children.

(3) A son, who is alcoholic, and a desperate character. He was in court for house breaking and attempting to kill; and was later sent to the penitentiary for felony (thought to be manslaughter).

(4) A daughter, who is described as "tough," and a prostitute; and is said to be the mother of eight or nine illegitimate children.

(5) A daughter, who is immoral and alcoholic. She married a worthless man of the same sort. Later she left him, and went to live with a negro.

(6) A son, who served a term in the penitentiary for manslaughter. Description in penitentiary records indicates many stigmata of degeneration. This man's son bids fair to outstrip his father in criminality. The son has already served four terms in the penitentiary for burglary and grand larceny. We know nothing of (6's) other children.

(7) A son, who is said to have been a notorious character in times past, but to have settled down somewhat. He has a court and workhouse record, and it is said that he would have been sent to the penitentiary if he could have been apprehended. Guilty of house breaking, threatening to kill, and burglary. (It is suspected that this man served a penitentiary sentence in a neighboring state.)

(8) A daughter, who is married. (Not traced).

Although some members of this family live in Ohio, most of them lived in a neighboring state, and therefore an extended survey of the strain was not undertaken. The fragmentary history of this one branch, however, indicates a high incidence of immorality, alcoholism, and criminality. At least four of the men here charted are habitual criminals; and members of the family are spoken of as "desperadoes and outlaws." There is no question that these people are of a type which it is most dangerous to have at large.

Of their mentality we know nothing, except in the case of Susan, who was feeble-minded. Of their home life we know little, except that the mother was a dissolute woman. An extended study of the strain here represented, together with a careful intensive study of each family and individual of the strain, would be valuable as an exposition of how criminals are bred and reared.

SALIENT POINTS OF THE STUDY

1. In this incomplete study of the offspring of the ancestors of Sam Sixty and Pearl Lanimirc, we have striking evidence of the inheritance

of low mentality. *Feeble-minded parents have feeble-minded children.*

2. In the descendants of Levi Lanimirc, grandfather of Pearl, we find a great amount of lawlessness which seems to proceed from instability, irritability and irascibility of temper. These strains seem to yield less of what is properly designated defect of intelligence. But they have *marked character defects* and these appear consistently and persistently in *successive generations.*

3. These traits combine in the family of Sam Sixty in a most unhappy manner. This mating was a most unfortunate one for society. Both Sam and Pearl found the most unsuitable mates in each other. Of course, being feeble-minded, neither of them had the right to parenthood. Society has the right and the duty to save such ever increasing expense from increasing numbers of dependents, as we see in the children of this pair, by *keeping the feeble-minded in custody while they are of child bearing and child be-getting ages.*

4. In addition to the dependency due to the mental deficiency, the Sixty family exhibits a high incidence of criminality. The crimes are not those requiring ingenuity. There are no embezzlers, forgers, or pick-pockets among them. Theirs are the crimes of lust and passion. They proceed from lack of self-control. And the *feeble-minded*, of the *sixty per cent* variety, can not be expected to have the ordinary amount of self-control. They are *children of nine years' mentality, with all the passion that goes with physical maturity.* Hence the *crimes of the feeble-minded,* which greatly enhance their cost to society.

5. In view of this *dependence of their delinquencies upon their mental deficiencies,* our *present method of handling delinquents appears most short sighted and costly.* Sam and Violet Sixty are in correctional institutions, and both are subject to parole. Violet cannot be legally held where she is, after she becomes of age. The mental endowment of neither can be increased. They are feeble-minded because they have brains incapable of growing up like those of ordinary people. With this handicap, it is impossible to instil into them self-control.

They can never attain the usual respect for the laws of morality, because they lack the intelligence which is necessary for this appreciation. What is true of these two, father and daughter, holds equally of many others of their family. If the community deals intelligently with such people, it will cease to temporize by making efforts at reform, it will recognize the *fundamental deficiency in intelligence* and will *provide permanent custody* for such persons. In custody they will *produce more* and be much *happier,* and at the same time, will *not be producing broods of feeble-minded dependents.*

That the life-long custody of Sam and Pearl Sixty would have been cheaper, to the states concerned, than the crimes and delinquencies of themselves and their children, can not require further demonstration. Such *physically vigorous but mentally feeble persons are a social menace to-day.*

6. Their children threaten to *overwhelm the civilization of the future.*

Our philanthropy, which makes life so easy for them, must also consider our children, and *not burden the future with an incubus of mental deficiency.*

7. For this purpose it is necessary that *courts, social workers, and county and state institutions,* all take their actions, and make their dispositions of cases of dependency and delinquency, with *full knowledge of the mental condition of each subject who comes before them.* Such subjects must be examined by *medical psychologists. Preventive medicine* must come to the aid of courts and schools in this work of saving the social waste which is incurred by the present method of treating the feeble-minded as if they were capable of ordinary self-control, or could be educated to such self-control.

8. Inasmuch as our incomplete study of this group has placed on record forty-seven illicit sexual relationships, and forty-one children known to be illegitimate, *the folly of framing restrictive marriage laws* to remedy conditions here presented, is at once apparent. Many of these people are as irresponsible sexually as are rabbits or guinea pigs. To pass laws to prevent the marriage of such individuals, would serve only to increase illegitimacy. It would not lessen the number of offspring from the least desirable parents.

9. Such genealogical charts as these, with the mental facts and social data which accompany them, are arguments which convince the fairminded that, *some control by society of the increase of the human family is imperative.* They show that *society has the right to take measures to prevent some individuals from becoming parents,* because society pays taxes. It is the public which must support the children of these persons, and must bear the expense of the crimes of the feeble-minded.

9

ANNA WENDT FINLAYSON

The Dack Family:
A Study in Hereditary
Lack of Emotional Control*

Preface

In *The Dack Family* as in *The Hill Folk*, the Eugenics Record Office realized its strategy for promoting eugenic research. Anna Wendt[1] studied at the ERO's third summer school session, thereafter becoming resident field worker at the Warren, Pennsylvania, State Hospital for the insane. Using hospital inmates as her starting point, she followed the threads of their genealogy, writing up her findings in this family study, which was then published by the ERO.

This study shows signs of the decline of feeble-mindedness as an all-encompassing explanation for social ills. By 1916 doubts about the accuracy of eugenicists' mental testing procedures and their simplistic application of the Mendelian model were widespread. At the same time psychiatrists were becoming ascendant over psychometricians as authorities on problematic people. These shifts are reflected in Davenport's introduction, which describes the eugenic field worker as a "field psychiatrist," concerned less with intelligence than "with emotional control—with the affect life" (p. 212). Davenport also scatters "psychiatric" terminology through his introduction: "analysis of the personality," "typical manic-depressive reactions," "the functional psychoses." The shifts are further reflected in the text itself, which states that "feeble-mindedness is not a unit trait, but a complex of many traits" (p. 248) and speaks of "neurotic taint," "manic depressive insanity of the circular type," and "hysterical tendencies."

The tone of *The Dack Family* is defensive. In his introduction Davenport tries to protect his field workers against the charge that they are "not competent because not medically trained" and to justify the eugenicist's use of imprecise terms like "miser" and "spendthrift." Finlayson anticipates charges of bias, assuring us that the study is purely objective, uncontaminated by "preconceived theories" (p. 217). Her work on one line of the family, moreover, was unaffected by knowledge of another: "In some instances the different branches . . . were worked up entirely separately, [so] that the writer

---

* Originally Bulletin no. 15, Eugenics Record Office, Cold Spring Harbor, N.Y., May 1916.

[1] At some point between attending the 1912 summer session at Cold Spring Harbor and publishing her family study in 1916, Anna Wendt became Mrs. Alan D. Finlayson. By 1919 she was living in Burlington, Vermont—two houses down Colchester Avenue, I cannot resist saying, from that in which I have been editing this volume. *The Dack Family* seems to have been her only publication. I have been unable to discover other biographical information.

seldom remembered the details of one branch when looking up the history of another." Her findings, she claims, are completely inductive.

This is a study of an Irish clan, "low white trash" (p. 240) who arrived in "Bushville," in the coal-mining region of Pennsylvania, about 1815. Their main problem is not gross feeble-mindedness but deficiencies in control, ambition, and "higher reasoning ability," together with instability in "marriage relationship and in residence"—deficiencies summarized by the catch-all "lack of emotional control." The harsh "Dack" pseudonym evokes the sullen, aggressive nature that Finlayson attributes to the tribe.

Her descriptions indicate marked differences in the degree to which male and female Dacks suffered from the family affliction. If we take Finlayson's accounts at face value and operationalize "lack of emotional control" as a referent for delusions,[2] sudden anger, and quarrelsomeness, we find that only twenty Dack men, but forty-five Dack women, exhibited these traits. Finlayson herself does not take note of this difference, but it is instructive to try to explain it.

One source of the difference lies in gender-stereotyping, a process in which Finlayson unwittingly indulges. She is quicker to criticize female than male Dacks for "emotionally uncontrolled" behaviors such as shrewishness. Women have long been blamed for being shrill and pushy with their husbands; more blatant behavior, such as actual assault, is required to accuse men of irritability and bossiness. Finlayson uses this double standard and hence identifies more peevish Dack women than men.

A second—and related—source of the gender discrepancy in "lack of emotional control" is the author's tendency to hold Dack women responsible for spouse abuse. In cases of domestic violence—there are many in these pages—she almost invariably exonerates the husband. For instance, Nellie Dack often "drives George out of the house. . . . Although she accuses him of being a drunkard and of abusing and deserting her, she never fails to go to him or send for him after he has been away for several months" (p. 225). Nellie's willingness to reconcile becomes ground for suspecting the validity of her accusations. We are later told that George is "naturally a quite harmless man until angered by one of her outbursts" (p. 226). Similarly, Elizabeth Myers "deserted her first husband" (p. 222). That he abused her is apparently not reason to absolve her from the charge of desertion, or from her characterization as "complaining, disagreeable." Identifying with male Dacks, Finlayson censures their wives for self-assertion. In this as in other family studies, failure to conform to the patriarchal standard for marriage becomes evidence of genetic unworthiness (also see Hahn 1980).

Following Davenport, Finlayson concludes that quick temper must be "inherited as a Mendelian dominant, for the trait does not skip a generation" (p. 250). She attributes Dack degeneracy to two factors, both hereditary: "a lack of inhibitive control [the "trait" is thus used to explain itself] . . . and, secondly, lack of mental ability" (p. 250). Although nature can be trusted ("to

---

[2] Like bad temper, delusions were more typical of female than male Dacks. They included religious beliefs of which Finlayson could not approve: "Grace Brown . . . has recently become quite religious as the result of evangelistic services held in the neighborhood" (p. 228); "Maggie attended some Methodist revival meetings and the excitement sent her crazy" (p. 242).

a certain extent") to exterminate defectives, "man must complete the work which nature begins in limiting the procreation of the obviously unfit" (p. 251).

PREFACE

The family history that Mrs. Finlayson has recorded in the following pages is a good example of the results that accrue to a careful investigation made by a eugenics field worker—results that can be secured in no other way. These results are, in a word, a picture of the social reactions of each of a group of related individuals. Of such as have been placed in a state hospital we have often full descriptions made by psychiatrists of experience; but only a small proportion of those in this family whose social reactions are clearly inadequate have been under the observation of such experts. It is the psychiatrist who goes into the *field* and gets an account of the reactions of these people in their daily home life who completes the picture.

The field psychiatrist,—for such the best of the eugenical field workers, like Mrs. Finlayson, are—thus are opening up a new field of applied science. This applied science has an end of its own and methods of its own which differentiate it from others. It requires the securing of a description of the personal history of each important individual; it requires an account of environment—the stimulus offered to each individual in order that one may interpret the constitutional idiosyncrasies lying back of the reaction; it requires an adequate picture of the reactions of all who have passed the years of childhood. It is not concerned merely with *intelligence;* it is even more concerned with emotional control—with the affect life.

The methods of this new applied science are, on the whole, new. They comprise certain laboratory methods, like simple mental tests, and they make use of the judgments of intelligence afforded by school records. But they include certain new methods which, while not quantitative, are as adequate as the method of the criminal law—the method, namely, of competent disinterested witnesses confirmed by concordant independent testimony, and by the personal observation of the field worker himself—who has the judgment that comes from extensive comparative knowledge. In addition, the eugenics field worker is trained in the *analysis of the personality.* He considers physical, mental and temperamental traits. He also early acquires considerable clinical experience so that the more extreme reactions are already familiar to him and recognized when met with in the field.

To the criticism that the terms employed in describing social reactions are not quantitative it is to be said that this is unfortunately true. However, no adequate method of measuring social reactions has yet been devised. The terms applied to social reactions have a relative value, and usually such terms are applied to the extremes of the series. Thus, if the term "miser" is applied to one man and "spendthrift" to another the terms are, indeed, not quantitative. They imply that in the judgment of the field worker and of the fellowmen of the two persons there is a marked difference between them. It is to be noted that all persons do not fall into the categories "miser" or "spendthrift." The vast majority of people are neither though they differ greatly in their relation to spending. But when in the class to which he belongs and in the world in which he moves there is applied by two or more of his peers independently the descriptive adjective "miser" the probability is that in his relations as a spender he is more or less extreme for his class and in his world. And it is reasonable to look for some cause for his exceptional reaction to the lures that his world lays for his property. Thus the eugenics field worker collects the instances of more or less extremely abmodal reactions in the family, with the aim of supplying data for the discovery of the hereditary or constitutional factors in such aberrant reactions.

The critic of the eugenical field-work often maintains that the investigator is not competent because not medically trained. This criticism is made by physicians and is part of an assumption of superiority that is so wide spread among medical men and is so persistently emphasized by some of them that one is almost led to suspect that it is the result of an understanding in the profession, a bit of professional ethics. A priori considerations are usually less valuable than experience. The Eugenics Record Office has had rather extensive experience with medically trained and non-medically trained field workers. It so happens, probably by accident, that the one complete failure among our field workers was a graduate of an Eastern medical school of the highest standing and which lays much stress on psychiatry; and the two most obvious successes in capacity for analysis of personal traits and ability to secure the facts about social reactions were women of biological training but whose medical training was limited to such psychiatric clinics as most of our field workers soon get in the state hospitals and other institutions to which they are assigned. As for the superficial instruction in psychiatry given in most medical schools, it is prejudicial rather than otherwise, since it leads to the attempt to diagnose and to classify. However useful such classifications may be in the hospital their use by the field worker is unfortunate and, indeed, forbidden. Not because the field worker is not quite as capable of classifying the functional psychoses as the average medical graduate but because classification tends to satisfy the mind and stops further analysis. Indeed, it is the writer's personal conviction that psychiatry would progress faster were the use of the present categories of functional insanity abandoned.

The present study is of especial value since it illustrates again the fact that the aberrant behavior of each family group is stamped with its peculiar characteristics; because into each a unique combination of hereditary elements has entered. In the Dacks we have a group of hyperkinetics whose reactions to their environment,—a harsh environment, to be sure, which their reactions have tended to make such—are restlessness, quarrelsomeness, loquacity, abuse, pugnacity, intermittent outbursts of violent temper and sex offense. Drink tends to exaggerate these reactions; they are extraordinarily activated by religious and other emotional appeals. The Dacks show many typical examples of a general and a specific feeble inhibition. Through this warp runs the woof of laziness, of mental dullness, of tendency to intellectual deterioration, of a monkey-like instinct to steal and hide, of suspicion and jealousy, and of frequent resort to alcohol.

By outmarriages which bring in new traits the whole picture becomes greatly complicated. Some self-control is introduced and socially good strains arise; not a little hypokinesis comes in and this, combined with the excitability, yields the cases of typical manic-depressive reaction.

Such a population does not tend to form a good community. Without self-control themselves they can not educate any germs of inhibition that their children may have; a vicious circle is initiated and, unless society steps in and trains the trainable and segregates the uncontrollable, things will go from bad to worse until the natural processes of purification by high infant mortality and by sterility do their beneficent work.

This careful and extensive study of Mrs. Finlayson's is commended to students of social conditions for serious reading and analysis.

CHAS. B. DAVENPORT.

I. INTRODUCTION

SCATTERED ABOUT IN the western central part of Pennsylvania live the descendants of two Irish immigrants, William and Mary Dack.* Many of these individuals have been a decided menace to society, others not only a menace but an expense, while but few in the whole group

* All names of persons in this account are fictitious.

have been desirable citizens of even the most humble sort. The family does not belong to the low grade feeble-minded class, as does the Kallikak family, for instance. Very few if any of them have become state or even family charges because of gross feeble-mindedness. But a high percentage of insanity, criminality, lack of emotional control, sexual immorality and shiftlessness is found in the family. Why?

The aim of this paper is to present one phase of the answer, namely, the hereditary side. The writer frankly acknowledges that the physical and environmental aspects of the problem will be dealt with only in a general way, not because they are considered of small importance, but because the purpose of the present paper, like that of the investigation on which it is based, is merely to present as clear a picture as possible of three generations of one particular family.

No attempt was made, except in a few isolated instances, to apply any series of tests to the individuals under discussion. The emphasis in making the investigation was laid on social reactions; our aim was to obtain a history of the individual's conduct in his own home and in society; to analyze, where possible, his personality and especially to obtain information as to whether or not he had shown any evidences of nervous instability. For this reason the records of the children of the family are of secondary interest, for, although recognized peculiarities were noted, no routine intelligence tests were employed.

The sources of information for this study were largely personal. The family is essentially ignorant, and this fact made it impossible to obtain accurate dates, as few of them keep any records of the births or deaths occurring in the family. However, such dates are not indispensable, and it is far more important to know what sort of a disposition a man had than to ascertain whether he died at seventy-five or at seventy-six. Town records are also unknown in the section of Pennsylvania where these individuals live, so the writer had to depend entirely on information furnished by members of the family themselves, intelligent neighbors living in the same district, and physicians who have been acquainted with some of the individuals. The list of informants personally interviewed by the writer gives the names of thirteen physicians, sixteen persons not related to the family—some of whom were old residents who had been acquainted with the family for years and were able to give much valuable data—and fifty-six persons belonging to the family. More than fifty-six Dacks were interviewed personally by the writer; this is merely the number from whom some of the family history was obtained. Attempts were made to get information by letter concerning individuals who could not be reached personally, but the results obtained were negligible. In every instance the writer was very careful not to take the statement of one person alone unless that informant was known to be perfectly reliable. Many of the details given in this history were told to the writer again and again, and statements which could not be verified were discarded. Minor errors, of course, may possibly occur in the history, but an effort has been made to reduce them to the minimum, and the picture as a whole is accurate. Whenever an individual has been in a public institution, such as a jail or a hospital for the insane, the record from the institution has been obtained.

The family has been largely confined to Pennsylvania, but the members are scattered in many different towns. This fact rendered the situation quite different from that usually encountered, for most of the published reports have been of one degenerate family which has inhabited a particular town or locality for years. For this reason it is impossible to consider the environment of the family as a whole and to give full details regarding the educational facilities, the moral standards of the community, social life, etc. The environments are similar in so far as the majority of the family live in or near small mining towns. Very few of the family have had the opportunity of attending graded schools; in many of the districts where the family lives the school law is not enforced, and the schools are rather poor. Most of the homes in which the Dack family have been raised have been of bad moral tone; as children most of them became accustomed to quarreling, drinking, and dishonesty. On the other hand, the family has not suffered from social condemnation and, as they are scattered in a large number of towns, they are removed, in most instances, from the influence of other degenerate relatives.

An attempt was made, in a general way, to obtain information regarding the families into which the Dacks married. This could only be done in a rough way, for it would be practically impossible to obtain detailed information regarding all of these many families.

The reader will soon notice, in tracing the description of the family, the repetition of certain traits. He will possibly question whether the picture is a true one, or whether the writer, anxious to show the inheritance of specific traits, has been so bent on discovering them that the picture has been warped. In answer to such a criticism the writer would say that the investigation was done at odd intervals extending over a period of several months, that in some instances the different branches of the family were worked up entirely separately, and that the writer seldom remembered the details of one branch of the family when looking up the history of another. It was not until the work was brought together and an attempt made to summarize the descriptions of the different characters that the writer realized the prevalence of a certain few traits. Finally, the study was not made in an effort to substantiate any preconceived theories but to obtain a clear picture of a family network.

The Dack family, or at least many of its members, are considered by the communities in which they live as decidedly undesirable. One intelligent elderly lady smiled when the name was mentioned and said, "They have been one of the worst families around here." The original group, that is the two Dacks who came from Ireland and their children, were quite notorious; they are all dead now, however.

Some readers will probably ask the following question, "What part has syphilis played as an etiological factor in the cases of insanity and degeneracy cited?" Those greatly interested in this point will be disappointed at the small recognition the subject receives in this paper. It was impossible to obtain accurate data on this important subject, and it seems hardly worth while to obtain merely "suspicious histories," and record physical evidences of the disease, such as scaphoid scapula, which are not now recognized as conclusive proof of specific infection. The percentage of infection in this family is probably higher than for the population at large; but this seems rather part and parcel of their degeneracy—a result of their loose morals and sexual irregularities—than the *cause* of their immorality, mental weakness and lack of emotional control. One physician expressed to the writer his opinion that syphilis was the primary cause of the degeneracy in the one branch of the family with which he was acquainted. But it does not seem to the writer that syphilis could be regarded as the sole cause unless it could be proved that the two progenitors of the family had the disease and transmitted it to their offspring; even then, the fact would remain that these two parents were shiftless, dishonest, bad tempered, and lacking in mental ability. None of the twenty-five cases of insanity in the family have been of the type caused by syphilis; namely, general paralysis of the insane.

Under Part II is given an abstract of the family history. Only a very brief view of the first two branches of the family is given, as the descendants in both cases are widely scattered and satisfactory information concerning them could not be obtained. In most instances causes of death have been omitted; likewise children who died in infancy. The two original members of the family are described first and the names of their children given. Next is taken up each child in the order of birth, and then the descendants of that child. The names are, of course, fictitious, and places of residence have been omitted.

II. DESCRIPTION OF THE FAMILY

WILLIAM DACK (I 2) was born in Ireland and came to the United States about 1815. He settled near a little town in the northern part of the soft coal district of Pennsylvania, which we will designate Bushville, and raised his children in that vicinity. William died almost fifty years ago, but he is remembered by a few of the oldest settlers of the locality as a peculiar, silly old fellow who drank a good deal, stole sheep and household valuables from his neighbors, and did not seem to be very intelligent. He was married twice; his first wife died in Ireland and we know nothing of her. She bore him one child, John Dack (II 1), concerning whom a rather dramatic story is told. He had just finished his studies in preparation for the law when he got into a quarrel with a man who knocked him over the head. This blow, it is said, affected his mind and after that he wandered about from one relative to another and never worked. He talked about religious matters, and various delusions and took spells of sudden anger when he would be ugly and destructive. He was commonly known as "Crazy John," and he died in some institution near Philadelphia.

William's second wife (I 3) was Mary Murphy. They were married in Ireland and their oldest child was born in that country. Mary is said to have been quite like her daughter Isabelle in disposition and manner. She was an ignorant, quarrelsome woman who would talk abusively about a person one minute and be pleasant to him the next. She would occasionally become angry with her husband and leave him for several days at a time.

An old resident of Bushville, now deceased, once stated to a woman who was interviewed by the writer that William and Mary were first cousins. Another relative, a great-grandson of William Dack, told the writer that his grandfather had made the same statement to him. Other members of the family who were questioned denied any knowledge of the relationship. The two people who made the statement were both reliable informants, and there is a strong probability that some degree of relationship existed between William and Mary. This couple had nine children who reached maturity: Samuel, Rebecca, James, William, Jane, Isabelle, Mary, Curtis, and Maggie. We shall consider them and their families under separate headings.

Samuel Dack

II 2. We know little of Samuel Dack except that he married a disreputable woman whose unfaithfulness he gave as an excuse for subsequently deserting her. Six children were born; he then left home and did not return, and his relatives never knew what became of him, his children were scattered, and bonds between them and the rest of the Dacks broken. His oldest child, Sarah (III 2), was a discontented, quarrelsome woman. She would become angry at her husband and leave home for several weeks at a time. Previous to death she became demented. Little is known of the next two girls, both of whom lived in the west. The fourth girl, Kate (III 4), married and raised a family of eight children. She had one period of mental disturbance at the age of about thirty, and for several months she was very excited and restless. Her family is widely scattered; as far as could be ascertained they are normal.

JAMES DACK, III 1, Samuel's fifth child, is described as being "about as good as any of the Dacks." He did not show much ability in accumulating money, and lived on a rented farm all his life. We know nothing of his three sons. Ann, III 5, the sixth and youngest of Samuel's children, became mentally deranged at the age of twenty-one and for six months was "very crazy." After that she had periods when she would be talkative, irritable and scolding. It is impossible to determine from the history furnished by her relatives whether or not she had true normal intervals. The last five years of her life were spent at the Warren State Hospital. There she was at times quiet and orderly; once delusions of poisoning are recorded; and there were occasional periods when she was destructive, denudative, profane and untidy. She died at the age of sixty-three. Ann had eight children but only three of them reached maturity; Rachel, Harry, and Tom, all of whom are living. Rachel, IV I, aged forty-seven, is mentally unbalanced, but lives at home. Her relatives state that she began to have delusions of infidelity toward her husband and ideas of persecution by the neighbors, about three years ago. She has spells when she will laugh to herself; her conversation is incoherent and has a strong religious tone; and she becomes angry and threatening suddenly and without cause. The following is a sample of her conversation: "Did you ever have the Power? The Power and the bowels of the earth; it has come to me what it all means. You have to be a blockhead. Do you understand what I mean?" "No, but I wish you would tell me." "Can you talk through your hat?" She has a family of six children, the oldest of whom is only twenty-seven. Ann's two brothers, Harry and Tom, IV 2, are both farmers of limited intelligence, but both are honest and neither has shown any symptom of mental disturbance.

Rebecca Dack

REBECCA DACK, II 4, was a foolish, simple-minded scold; one of her own relatives described her as a woman "of little sense but much temper." Like her mother, she would quarrel with her husband and then desert him and her small children for days at a time. Rebecca lived to the advanced age of ninety-four, although for the last twenty years of her life she was demented and had to be cared for by her family. Rebecca married August Myers, a man superior to her mentally. He came from a hard-working, ignorant backwoods German family, and accumulated a fair amount of money by lumbering and farming. Rebecca Dack and August Myers had eight children who reached maturity.

HENRY MYERS, III 7, the first born, resembled his mother as far as intelligence was concerned. He supported himself by doing farmwork, but accumulated no property. He was a poor manager, excitable, occasionally intoxicated, good-natured, easy-going, and a man who laughed frequently, particularly at his own remarks. He married a quiet, passive, easily dispirited woman who was more intelligent than he. They had nine children who reached maturity. Three sons were patients at the Warren State Hospital. The first was Robert Myers, IV 3, the onset of whose mental trouble occurred at twenty-three. One year later he was sent to the Warren State Hospital and, after a residence of seven and one half years, was transferred to a chronic asylum, where he is still living. The history of the onset and subsequent conduct shows that the case is probably one of dementia praecox. He became indifferent, turned against his relatives, thought that the Odd Fellows were persecuting him and that his father accused him of a murder. At the Warren State Hospital he was dull, unoccupied, indifferent to surroundings, surly and at times threatening and ugly. Harry Myers, IV 4, the next younger son, was admitted to the Warren State Hospital at the age of thirty and died there about five years later of tuberculosis. The meager history would point to a diagnosis of dementia praecox. He is described as naturally bashful and seclusive. Sometime previous to being sent to this institution he imagined that people were talking about him. At the Hospital he would wander about in an aimless, indifferent manner, and at times was excited and ugly; his conversation was quite incoherent and his habits were untidy, and he showed a progressive dementia. John Myers, IV 5, the youngest, showed the first symptoms of insanity at twenty-four; one year later he was sent to the Warren State Hospital, where he died of tuberculosis after a residence of eleven years. The first notes describe him as surly, irritable, unoccupied, careless in habits, deluded and taciturn. He showed a progressive dementia and during the last few years of his life was mute and filthy. The most probable diagnosis of the case is dementia praecox. The remaining six children in this family moved to the Pacific coast some years ago and little is known of them. The four boys were all woodsmen.

WILLIAM MYERS, III 9, second child of Rebecca Dack Myers, lived rather an orderly uneventful life as a farmer and made a fair living. He married a woman of average intelligence and became the father of fourteen children. Two of these fourteen are undoubtedly below par mentally, although able to support themselves; the others are of mediocre ability but have shown no anti-social tendencies nor marked evidences of degeneracy.

JANET MYERS, III 10, died when rather young. She was twice married; she had two sons by her first marriage and one by the second. One of the older sons served a term in an Ohio penitentiary for bigamy. The other two boys have lived in the west; details concerning them are lacking.

ROBERT MYERS, III 12, is living at the age of seventy-four. He has always been quarrelsome; when young got into frequent fights and has always been very fond of getting into litigations with his neighbors. He misused his wife, has been chronically alcoholic and sexually immoral. His wife is highly spoken of and also Robert's family of fifteen children, who, with one exception, are all living. The boys have not taken any positions of special merit but are making honest livings as farmers, machinists, etc. Several of his daughters taught school previous to marriage. One daughter, Emma Myers, married her first cousin, Wilson McGinness, and one of her four children is an imbecile requiring institutional care. One of Robert's sons is the father of an idiot girl. These are the only two cases of degeneracy among Robert's descendants.

JOHN MYERS, III 13, a farmer, is a hale, hearty man of sixty-nine years; he was formerly considered a quick-tempered man but now is rather quiet and easy-going. He, like his brother William, has lived an uneventful life; he is a man of little education but with enough native ability to accumulate some money. He has seven children; two were very dull at school but have been able to support themselves; the other five were of average ability. One alcoholic son has a boy who is an epileptic.

ELLA MYERS, III 14, lived to the age of fifty; she married and had two children, both of whom died when young. During the last year of her life she was probably mentally unbalanced.

ANN MYERS, III 15, as far as we can learn, was fairly bright when young, but was mentally deranged for about five years before her death, which occurred at the age of fifty-three. She became absurdly jealous, and purchased a large telescope in order to watch more closely the actions of her husband when outside the house. She became indifferent to her duties, would wander away from home and at times was irritable and ugly. Ann married a thrifty, fairly intelligent and ambitious man and all of her eight children have obtained high school educations and so far have shown no peculiar nor undesirable characteristics.

ELIZABETH MYERS, III 16, is a patient at the Warren State Hospital. She was petted and spoiled by her father and abused by her two husbands. Elizabeth was dull at school; she has always been lazy, complaining, disagreeable, sexually immoral and a trouble maker in whatever community she lived. By her first marriage she had five children; one is living, while four died at the age of about thirty. Two of these four met accidental deaths, a third was shot supposedly by a disappointed lover and a fourth died of tuberculosis. Elizabeth deserted her first husband and children and some years later married her own cousin, Willis McGinness. By him she had a daughter, now twenty years old, who is a housemaid. This girl does not have a particularly good reputation but seems to be of average intelligence.

James Dack

JAMES DACK, II 6, was commonly known as "Rotten Jimmy"; the epithet was given because of the diseased condition of his legs, which were covered with chronic ulcers, although the term is said to have been equally applicable to his moral nature. He was a thief and general good-for-nothing, but neither shrewd nor cunning. His conversation quickly revealed his childlike mind. Once at a funeral he exclaimed: "My, what a fine funeral! If I die do you suppose so many people would come to see me?" When the minister assured Jimmy that such would be the case his face beamed with pleasure and he said longingly: "My, but I would like to be there to see it!" Jimmy had three wives but only two children; both of these died of tuberculosis. His son died at the age of twenty-five just after being released from the penitentiary, where he had served a three years' sentence for larceny; neither he nor the daughter, who died at twenty-two, left children.

William Dack

WILLIAM DACK, Jr., was a mild, pleasant man, rather lazy and of a weak nature. The fact that he led a respectable life is considered to be largely due to his wife, who was a strong-minded, high-principled woman. They never had any children.

Jane Dack

JANE DACK, II 9, who lived to the age of eighty-four, was an illiterate unintelligent woman whose family was notorious in her section of the country. She was a poor housekeeper; her home was always dirty and littered. Essentially lacking in good judgment and will power, she was a woman who would both indulge her children unwisely and go into flashes of temper when vexed by them. She was not of an aggressive nature, but when provoked would burst forth in a storm of abusive language. She was not in sympathy with the criminal tendencies of her family, yet had no influence in restraining them. Jane was pitied by her neighbors, who once endeavored to assist her to run away from her husband who mistreated her shamefully. Jane, however, stood in such fear of what he might do to her that she backed out at the last minute and stayed at home.

Jane married her first cousin, Patrick Dack. Old Pat was a queer combination of native shrewdness, book learning, uncontrollable temper and moral obtuseness. People who knew him state that his conversation and manners suggested that he was the black sheep of a cultivated family. He was fairly well read and so familiar with the Bible that he could out-do anyone in a theological argument. During the last years of his life the directors of the poor provided for his maintenance; even then he was so keen and sharp mentally that they avoided direct dealings with him because he seemed to delight in getting the best of them in calculations or arguments. He felt himself distinctly above his family; once he remarked to a neighbor that his children had degenerated, "and, as for my wife, I have tried to teach her, but she can't learn." In younger days he drank quite heavily, and all his life he would become intoxicated occasionally. His principal faults were stealing and an uncontrolled temper. His thefts he would admit in a cool, matter-of-fact way. His temper led him into continual quarrels with his family; these occasionally ended with court proceedings. Many of his children were of a similar nature, and the home is described as a hornet's nest—a place which everyone avoided. Often the family could be heard screaming and cursing at each other a long way off. These two first cousins, Jane and Patrick Dack, had a large and interesting family: John, Robert, Richard, Sally, Carrie, Nellie, Michael, Noah, Effie, Alice and Charles. Their respective fortunes will be taken up in the following paragraphs.

RICHARD DACK, III 19, enlisted in the army at the time of the Civil War and died of typhoid fever while in camp. He was twenty-two years old.

JOHN DACK, III 20, had an attack of fever at the age of twenty; following that he became dull and indifferent and his memory deteriorated. The Civil War broke out about this time, and he enlisted, declaring he was going to be a captain. One day on guard duty he got the idea the rebels were after him, so he threw down his gun and started to run. The government records show that he was then sent to an insane asylum and died about a month later, aged twenty-four.

ROBERT DACK, III 21, the next brother, was known principally as a drinker and fighter. As a boy he was a petty thief, but he showed a little more ambition than his brothers Noah and James for he became a miner and later a woodsman. He was a man of powerful physique, and had quite a local reputation for his success in combats. When drinking he was especially ugly and quarrelsome; he died of heart trouble at the age of forty-two and left no children.

SALLY DACK, III 22, aged sixty-eight, lives in a dirty home next to the railroad track. A physician who has known the family described her and her family as all "*non compos mentis.*" Sally is an ignorant and high-tempered woman who is honest in her business dealings and thrifty in a certain respect. She owns and rents a small house in the neighborhood where she lives, and is undoubtedly very proud of the fact as she mentions it frequently. She enjoys talking, especially about her family affairs, and her memory is quite good. Her husband, she says, was not a good man to start with, but she, by dint of beating him when he was drunk or inclined to be ugly, and chasing him to work when he was lazy, has improved his character. She has not hesitated to brandish fire arms in order to scare this erring partner of hers into good behavior. A great deal of her conversation deals with affairs of marital infidelity, terminated by murder, and she seems morbidly fond of relating sexual matters. She is able to read but cannot write. Sally's husband was born in Ireland; he has been a heavy drinker, and has had "the snakes" several times. She explained nonchalantly that "he's gettin' too old to drink much now; his health's not over good and he's all crippled up with the rheumatiz. But I make him hobble across those tracks jist the same. There ain't no sense in a man settin' around the house." Sally has had six children; Edward, the oldest, has moved frequently and has tried many different occupations; at present he is writing insurance policies, he says, although his thin, seedy, dilapidated appearance is more suggestive of a rag picker, and his wife is obliged to work out by the day. He is without doubt lacking in average intelligence; furthermore he is generally considered untrustworthy. Jane's second child died in infancy; the third, Maggie, is a feeble-minded girl who lives at home. She has had one or two illegitimate pregnancies, which had to be terminated by abortion because of renal disturbance. She is excitable and talkative. While the writer was at her house she lugged out a huge, enlarged picture of herself, saying with great pride, "Ain't I a fine lookin' girl there? Oh! I tell you I was handsome when I was young. I'm smart too." Jane's fourth child, Clarence, has neither steady work nor habitation. He becomes intoxicated as soon as he has any money; in this condition he sometimes becomes noisy and destructive and at other times wants to kill himself. Occasionally when drunk he is arrested. The next son, George, was wild as a boy, drank heavily and died at the age of twenty-six. Jane's youngest child died in early childhood.

CARRIE DACK, III 23, died of tuberculosis at the age of thirty-two. She became mentally deranged at the age of twenty-five and was sent to a hospital for the insane; upon admission "she talked incoherently, and was excited, mostly on religious subjects." After a ten months' residence she was discharged as "restored" (although her husband made the statement that she did not seem entirely normal mentally) but grew worse before her death. She married a fairly intelligent but easy-going farmer and had four children; the two oldest girls, neither of very high grade intelligence, are able to keep house fairly well, have married, and show no marked neurotic tendencies; the third child, a boy, died at eight years, of spinal meningitis; the fourth, Tessie, IV 10, now a woman of thirty-seven, has been a patient at the Warren State Hospital for over seven years. Two months previous to admission to the Hospital she tried to commit suicide by setting her clothes on fire; she thought her friends were against her and that they practiced hypnotism on her. This last idea she still clings to; she says that she did many peculiar things which she would not have done had she not been influenced by others. She had a horror of everything black; she wanted to wear white shoes and stockings and destroyed all black clothing. She was quiet and orderly when admitted to the Hospital, but hypochondriacal. She has shown little change during her residence; she is essentially a well-behaved patient who occupies herself doing a little sewing but complains a great deal. She is easily offended, self-centered and seclusive. She takes sudden dislikes to people and is often irritable and petulant.

Her history and general reaction are not suggestive of an imbecile. She gave satisfaction at various places where she did housework, although her sister states she was always seclusive, conceited and hypochondriacal. Carrie's youngest child died a month after birth.

NELLIE DACK, III 25, aged sixty-five, is a well-known character in the vicinity of R———, where she lives. Her small home is usually clean, and she herself neatly dressed. She was married at the age of fifteen to George Brown, a farmer, and since then they have parted countless times. The term parting, however, is too mild a term to describe the occasions, for Nellie usually forcibly drives George out of the house. During the few months that the writer was in touch with the family he left home "never to return," but, as usual, came back again. Although she accuses him of being a drunkard and of abusing and deserting her, she never fails to go to him or send for him after he has been away for several months. Nellie is jocularly referred to as "crazy" because of her treacherous and ugly temper. One day a boy started to her house on some errand; he happened to mention to the woman for whom he was working that he was going out to Brown's. She laughed and told him he had better be pretty careful or he might be chased out of the house with a log of wood. Nellie's little granddaughter related that one day when at her grandmother's home the latter took out a pair of shoes from the closet. Several buttons were missing; she immediately turned to the child and, accusing her of stealing the buttons, began to threaten her in all manner of evil language. The child, greatly frightened, ran off and has never returned to her grandmother's home. Any little thing which vexes Nellie will throw her into a rage. Sometimes she will scold and curse and threaten for a week at a time. Although she will throw any convenient article at her unlucky relatives and has used a gun on several occasions, she has never seriously injured anyone. Her home is similar to her father's and the physician acquainted with the family stated that he had never heard elsewhere such vulgar and profane language as in that home. Nellie has always been a "good woman" in the language of her people, although she enjoys running down the characters of others and shows a morbid fondness for sexual details in her conversations. She is ignorant, superstitious, and illiterate; she is greedy to obtain money but does not seem to have ability in keeping it. With a stranger she is apt to be seclusive and reticent. Some years ago she and her husband were arrested for being "a nuisance." Her husband, naturally a quite harmless man until angered by one of her outbursts, has the sympathies of all relatives and acquaintances. He draws a pension and has a little farm; his worst fault is occasionally becoming slightly intoxicated; and the greatest mistake of his life was his selection of a mate. Nellie has had fifteen pregnancies; two of them resulted in miscarriages, three children died in infancy and the other ten are living, the oldest being forty-seven and the youngest twenty-four. Not one of these ten children amounts to anything; none have even good grammar school educations, and all are bad tempered; the girls, beside showing tempers like their mother, have nearly all added to this defect the blot of sexual immorality. The physician already mentioned summarized the family as follows: "The boys have been wild and rough and the girls loose morally."

Thomas Brown, the first born, was a petty thief, a heavy drinker, and constant fighter until about ten years ago, since which time he has quieted down somewhat, largely because of failing health. He is a small wiry man with a high opinion of his own ability and of his knowledge of medical matters. When intoxicated he is particularly aggressive and quarrelsome, and his tale of his adventures is more thrilling than any "Diamond Dick" novel. The name he has given himself, "The Little Iron

Man from Hell," seems quite fitting for such a melodramatic hero. Mining has been his principal occupation. He married late in life and is the father of four small children, one of whom is unquestionably defective.

Hattie Brown, the second in the family, is a quick-tempered woman who is married but has no children. A physician who treated her three or four years ago regarded her as hysterical; the one under whose care she is at present does not consider her normal mentally, and states she is very queer and melancholy. At puberty she was subject to frequent fainting spells.

Elizabeth Brown, four years younger than Hattie, is married but without children; she has a bad reputation in her own and surrounding towns and those who know her say she has a bad temper. She is separated from her husband, with whom she has never lived peaceably. She states that they have not lived together more than ten years all told although they have been married for eighteen. She can be very suave and cordial to strangers and assumes an air of familiarity and confidence in describing some of her paramours. Her nervous instability is shown by a history of frequent fainting spells which are brought on by the sight of blood, sudden fright, etc.

Cora Brown, when young, was subject to what her mother called "mad hysterics" and has always been ugly tempered. She is a poor housekeeper and ignorant and in conversation she will wander from one detail to another, entirely forgetting the point she started to answer. Previous to marriage she had illegitimately a daughter who now, at the age of twenty years, leads an immoral life. Since Cora's marriage her reputation has been good. Her husband is a laborer and they have had seven children. The oldest child died, the next one is now eleven years of age. Both she and the next younger girl have failed to make average progress in school.

Lilly Brown, an excitable, high-tempered woman, noted for having a bad tongue, died at the age of thirty-five of tuberculosis. She neglected her house and failed to send her children to school. The oldest of the six children, a girl, is nineteen years old; the youngest, a boy, is just six. The family has kept together since the mother's death about a year ago. Although the father earns good wages they live in dirty, squalid surroundings and are clothed in rags. One girl, aged fourteen, has attended school only two winters and then went irregularly. None of them measure up to more than eight and one-half years by the Binet-Simon scale. It is a question whether or not lack of schooling, lack of healthy companionship and lack of home training can be held responsible alone for the ignorance and slowness shown in answering test questions and the indifference to the unusually bad surroundings in which they live. The fact that they failed in answering some questions not dependent on school knowledge—such as failing to see any absurdity in such a statement as "A young woman cut into eighteen pieces, was found yesterday; people think that she killed herself,"—as well as their complete failure in keeping house would seem to indicate that we find in them some element of congenital defect.

Mason Brown, like his oldest brother, is a rough character who is aggressive in starting a fight and is a heavy drinker. Occasionally he is locked up over night for this latter offense. He has the regular Brown temper and is generally considered a worthless character. He married a thrifty woman of some native intelligence, and those of their six children who are old enough to go to school have been making fair progress. According to the family physician one of these children shows evidences of inherited syphilis.

Jennie Brown, of bad temper and questionable reputation, has recently parted from her husband who had a pool room in New York City and has gone to live with her sister Elizabeth. She has had no children.

Grace Brown, a woman of mediocre intelligence who has recently become quite religious as the result of evangelistic services held in the neighborhood, is the eighth of this family. She and her husband both have been bad characters; she has a reputation for immorality. A physician who has attended her states that she has syphilis. She has one child of three years who, according to a physician, shows evidences of inherited syphilis. Previous to the birth of this child she had five miscarriages.

Adelle Brown, who is married and lives in the country, is the mother of four young children. She seems to be about the most respectable and intelligent member of the family, although even she is not of a very high order of intelligence and like the rest of the family loses her temper quickly. Max Brown, the youngest, is rather lazy, shows poor judgment in the use of money and becomes intoxicated every few weeks. At present he is working as a laborer in a factory.

MICHAEL DACK, III 27, a man now sixty-three years old, has done little or nothing toward his own support all his life. When young, he was regarded as the worst of the Dacks; everyone was afraid of him because of his ugly temper and he would steal anything he could lay his hands on. The older he grew the lazier and more disagreeable he became; at the age of thirty-three he was sentenced to the penitentiary for three years, for having broken into a box car. After his father's death his poor old mother lived in terror of him; she waited on him hand and foot, and would often trudge to the store several miles distant to buy tobacco for him. About fifteen years ago he began to show some symptoms of mental derangement and these continued for three or four years. He imagined that people were after him;

often he would refuse to leave the house and also insisted on carrying firearms to protect himself against these imaginary persecutors. Once he returned to his brother's house a short time after he had left it to go home; he said that there were so many lights on the road that he couldn't get past them. At the time of the death of his mother he became quite violent, insisted that the property should be turned over to him, and attempted to drive his sister and her family out of the house one night. For many years Mike's mother had carried loose cash in the front of her dress; Mike took this from her when she died and lived on the small sum for a year or two. Twice during the period when he was mentally deranged he was arrested, once for felonious shooting, the other time for carrying concealed weapons. He was locked in jail for thirty days for the latter offense. About two years after his mother's death, Mike went to the County Home and spent the winter; the cause of pauperism given on the records is "lack of ambition." Several years later he returned to that institution but stayed only a week, as the new manager would not let him carry firearms nor manage the place, which activities he felt were necessary for his happiness. Now he is living alone in a little shack in the woods; he rarely goes to town, keeps to himself, and does no work. His relatives all keep watch of their hen coops and small valuables when he visits them. He now shows no active symptoms of insanity. He can carry on a conversation about simple affairs, his memory is fairly good, but he has no knowledge of either local or general current events. When the writer saw him in January, 1915, he asked if the war was still going on; he said he thought it was probably over by that time.

NOAH DACK, III 28, is a lazy good-for-nothing who has never done much work and at times has been supported by the township. Although he would sometimes be ugly and abusive in his own family he has never troubled the neighbors and his thefts, if he engaged in any, were of a minor nature. For some years he lived with a notorious character named Maggie Rust; after she had had three illegitimate children and they had been twice arrested for fornication and bastardy the constable forced them to marry as there was a law in the township making it responsible for the support of illegitimate children born there. One child was born after the marriage and a few years later Noah left Maggie. He has lived with one or two other women since then, but has had no more children. Two of the four children died young; a girl, now twenty-four, has been practically a prostitute; a boy, aged sixteen, slow and lazy, reached only the second reader and now does nothing but stay at his mother's home.

EFFIE DACK, III 29, who never married, died at the age of thirty-one of tuberculosis and heart trouble. She was excitable and fainted on small provocation—when slightly scared, or when she heard any bad news. She had an illegitimate child which died shortly after birth. In disposition she is said to have been fairly pleasant and not as high tempered as the rest of the family.

ALICE DACK, III 30, had a violent temper and quarreled a great deal with her family. Once she had her father and her brother Mike arrested for assault and battery; she was put in jail at the same time, however, being arrested by them on a similar charge. She was a girl of bad reputation previous to her marriage. She died while giving birth to her first child, the cause assigned being nosebleed. The child was not delivered.

CHARLES DACK, III 31, the youngest of this notorious family, died in the penitentiary, age twenty-two years. Concerning him we hear the old story of an unusually bad temper, coupled with thieving tendencies. He was associated with his brother Mike in the box car theft and sentenced at the same time.

Isabelle Dack

ISABELLE DACK, II 10, was a silly, superstitious woman who had the reputation of being a shrew and yet who lacked the brains often found in that type of woman. When in an ugly humor she would curse and rail about everyone, but at other times, she was pleasant and good-hearted. When angry with her husband she would go to her neighbors' houses and complain about "the wretch," as she called him, and her favorite conclusion was: "The devil is going to get him." Her husband, Sol McGinness, was, as a matter of fact, a worthless, lazy, thieving drunkard; when intoxicated he was particularly ugly and would strike his wife or one of his children with anything he could lay his hands on. He belonged to the "Dack gang" which pillaged the neighborhood. Isabelle had by him eleven children, the two oldest, twins, died at the time of birth; then came Henry, Dillie, Flossie, Simon, Rachel, Thomas, Nancy, Kate and Mary McGinness. The members of this fraternity have been scattered; their history, as far as obtainable, is contained in the following paragraphs.

HENRY McGINNESS, III 32, the oldest, was a reliable farm laborer, successful at rough work but not possessed of good enough judgment to run a farm of his own successfully. Occasionally he became intoxicated and once, when driving in that condition, ran over and killed a young boy. He lived in the woods for a long time after that and the affair was never brought to court. He was a rough, profane man who mistreated his wife shamefully and was practically the cause of her death. He was honest, however, and not lazy. His wife, who was regarded as a normal woman, bore him five children. The oldest son, Harry, is illiterate, lazy, dishonest;

becomes intoxicated whenever he has enough money to buy liquor; and is of substandard intelligence. He is married and is the father of four young children; he abuses his wife and there has been much trouble between them. Henry's next two sons, both miners, live in a distant part of the state; the older, Jack, is reported to be industrious and well behaved; the other, Sam, becomes intoxicated two or three times a year. In that condition he is very quarrelsome but at other times is well behaved. The fourth child, Fannie, aged 27, is the mother of six children. She is ignorant and has little native intelligence; her conduct is good but her ability as a housekeeper is poor. Her younger brother ran off to California at the age of about twenty with a woman many years his senior. The youngest member of this fraternity, Katie, does housework, but is inefficient and has a poor moral reputation.

Dillie McGinness, III 33, aged seventy, has led a narrow, self-centered life and has purposely kept apart from her relatives. Her facial expression reveals her character strikingly; her features are suggestive of an animal, her eyes are small and bead-like and her wrinkled face is entirely lacking in humanness. She seems to enjoy shutting herself off from the world; she takes an unfriendly, bitter attitude toward nearly everyone, and several times she exclaimed gruffly when speaking of her relatives, "I don't bother them and I don't want them to bother me." Although she has lived very near street cars and railroads, she has never ridden on either, and has not been in a store for the last seven years. She has been a thrifty hard-working woman of limited intelligence; her hard life has soured and hardened a naturally peculiar disposition. Her husband, who died recently, was always a heavy drinker. She has had ten children: two died in childhood; a third at nineteen years, of tuberculosis, and three daughters and four sons are living. None had good educations, and one or two of the boys cannot even write. Two are employed as farmers, one is a miner, the fourth is a team driver. None has been an excessive drinker and all work steadily. The only daughter seen by the writer is, at forty-two, a facsimile—if that word can be used in speaking of human beings—of her mother. Gruff, scolding, seeming to delight in appearing half angry, she goes through life. When visited her house and porch shone from recent scrubbings and she seems to take a sort of savage pleasure in hard work. She is the mother of eight living children, one of whom is an imbecile; four died in infancy, and a son met an accidental death at eighteen. Dillie's other two daughters' histories contain nothing of special interest; one of them is the mother of an illegitimate boy who seems rather below the average in intelligence.

FLOSSIE MCGINNESS died suddenly at seventeen years, the supposed cause being heart failure.

SIMON MCGINNESS, III 34, met death by hanging at the age of nineteen. The coroner reported the cause as suicide, but the family state that no mental peculiarities which might account for such an act were noticed, and they have always considered the death due to an accident.

RACHEL MCGINNESS, III 35, aged sixty-four, married a drunkard and by him has had a family of nine children. Rachel is a tall straight woman with a quantity of iron-gray hair and with glassy blue eyes. There is a hard, bitter look about the deeply set mouth which droops at the corners. She is proud, haughty, of little education and narrow interests. She is snobbish toward some of her cousins whom she feels beneath her, and spoke disdainfully of "those Dacks" as though they were no connection whatever of hers. She practically disowns an insane sister who is in the County Home, and recently when a cousin stated that she had seen this sister at that institution Rachel replied "That's impossible, for she is all right and has married again." Her house is a model of cleanliness and order, and the fact that they do not own the small cottage is obviously due to her husband's alcoholic habits rather than any lack of thrift on her part. According to her children and other relatives she is an irritable woman who has a quick, unreasonable temper. Rachel has a good reputation and is considered by everyone as respectable; her five daughters, however, have the reputation in their home town of being loose morally; the youngest one, who alone is unmarried, is of undoubted bad character. A son, single, aged forty-three, has never amounted to anything and even his own family admit that he is a drunken tramp. He made poor progress at school and is probably congenitally defective. Another son, rather more capable and steady, died at twenty-three; the youngest son, aged twenty-five, is living, is apparently thrifty and a good laborer, and contributes to his mother's support. Only one of Rachel's children died in infancy.

THOMAS MCGINNESS, III 36, aged fifty-seven years, is a successful farmer and stone mason. As a boy and young man his reputation was not good; he was unreliable, would try to cheat in financial deals, and was associated with the Dack gang of thieves. He apparently mended his ways before he got into serious difficulty. Several expressed the opinion that the sentence of old Curtis Dack and his son to the penitentiary (which happened when Thomas was twenty years old) had a salutary effect on Tom's career. Another factor which must not be overlooked is the character of his wife; both in muscular strength and mental keenness she seems above the average. In physical appearance and facial expression Tom has a striking resemblance to his sister, Rachel; he has the same glassy blue eyes, the same deep-set mouth. His face seems to express no feeling and his frequent smiles, which seem entirely devoid of kindliness and geniality, give one an uneasy, uncanny feeling, probably because it seems to be a mockery that such a face should smile. In conversation he immediately showed himself to be untruthful and unreliable, for he pretended to know nothing about the mental condition of his insane sister Nancy, and instead of answering a question put to him would ramble on from one story to another, going into entirely irrelevant details and often failing entirely to make his point. He has two children, both grown up sons; one is quiet, steady and temperate and has been a night watchman in a factory for twelve years; the other has business ability, but has never stuck to anything for more than a year or two at a time and drinks heavily.

NANCY MCGINNESS, III 37, aged fifty-five years, at present is an inmate of one of the Pennsylvania County Homes. The history of the onset of her mental trouble is obscure, as her children from whom the history was obtained were quite young at the time. At the age of twenty-two, after the birth of her third child, she left home and did the same after the fourth one arrived. Then she began to have periods of anger which would last for half a day or more at a time. One of her son's earliest recollections is dodging articles which she would throw at him. She neglected her house and children, was abusive and ugly, and would give "tongue lashings" to everyone. The family suspected her of being the cause of the death of one of her children who was burned. After the death of her husband she tried to live with her children, but none of them could get along with her. She became filthy and dirty in habits and was very noisy at times. She was sent to the Warren State Hospital in 1901, where she remained for nine months and then was transferred to the County Home where she has been ever since. At her best she is talkative and pleasant but unoccupied; she knows where she is, but cannot give the date nor her own age; and her conversation is nearly all of a desultory type concerning old acquaintances. She has periods when she is very noisy and destructive to both clothing and furniture; they occur at irregular intervals and last only a few days or weeks. She imagines that there is a great deal of robbery and abuse going on at the County Home, and whenever anything is broken or destroyed she will ascribe the act to one of these enemies who she thinks are around the house. Her husband was a hard-working man who showed no marked mental peculiarities; he died at middle age. Nancy has five children living, all of whom are sober, industrious and of average intelligence. One son is a common laborer, another a miner and a third a clerk in a large general store. The oldest child is thirty-six, the youngest twenty-four; so far none have shown symptoms of mental trouble.

Kate McGinness, III 38, aged fifty-one years, lives in a town of several thousand inhabitants. A woman who went to school with her remembered her as dull and slow at books. Her memory is unusually poor; the causes of the defect seem to be a lack of observation and a dull inert mind. She referred questions concerning the order of birth of her brothers and sisters and even her own age to her young daughter who happened to be in the room. When answering the request for the names of her brothers and sisters she omitted the name of the sister who is in the County Home; later when questioned about it said that she had forgotten to mention her. Simon, the brother who committed suicide, died of dysentery, she said, when he was quite small. Like the other members of her family she has an orderly streak in her nature and her home is clean and quite comfortably furnished, although the family is not at all rich. Her seven children, ranging in age from thirty-one to seventeen, have shown nothing unusual; none of them is exceptionally intelligent, neither is any obviously defective. Two girls work in a factory, one is in high school and another married. Two of the boys, both young, drink quite heavily. Kate's husband, a fairly intelligent man, used to be quite a heavy drinker but some years ago became more moderate. He has always made good wages as a tile and brick layer.

Mary McGinness died at forty-four years, of tuberculosis. We know little of her or her five children save that her oldest daughter is neurotic.

Maria Dack

Maria Dack, II 12, lived to the advanced age of ninety-five. She was an intelligent, fairly well educated woman with an excellent memory but sharp tongue. She did not marry until rather late in life, then selected as her husband a fairly rich man many years her senior. There were no children and his death occurred in a few years. Shortly after that she was married again, also to a well-to-do man. By this union there were two children; the oldest was drowned in childhood, the other, Richard Selden, has always lived apart from the Dacks but they have heard that he is a successful manager of some wholesale business in a distant city.

Curtis Dack

Curtis Dack, II 16, one of the best known of this family, spent most of his life in the vicinity of Bushville. At one time he owned two farms, but he lost practically all of his property through poor management and alcoholic excesses. He was noted rather for the misuse of intelligence than its absence; he was fairly shrewd and quick witted, although one old neighbor lamented that "he was smart mostly to steal and lie." He was fairly quick tempered, although never to the extent of some of the other members of the Dack family. When slightly intoxicated he was decidedly ugly and quarrelsome and feared by many, as physically he was a very powerful man. He stole cattle and sheep for years and at the age of forty-eight was put in the penitentiary for three years for this offense. About the same time he had an illegitimate child by a woman of the neighborhood, and got into financial difficulties endeavoring to pay the costs. Curtis returned to the vicinity of Bushville after being released from the penitentiary, but soon deserted his family, left Pennsylvania, and was not heard from for many years. Shortly before his death he sent word to a daughter that he was in West Virginia. He had married again there and had two children. He died in W. Va., at the age of eighty-three. Curtis's wife, Liza, II 17, is still living; she is eighty-six years old, feeble physically and quite childish. She has been quite as notorious as her husband. She was a coarse masculine type of woman who was frequently seen working in the fields or unloading heavy sacks of meal. She came from an ignorant family showing evidences of neurotic taint and several cases of suicide. Practically all of the older inhabitants within a radius of fifteen miles of Bushville have heard of "Old Liz" at least by reputation. She was no mean power in the Dack gang, for she reprimanded the cowards, doled out whiskey to the successful ones, and helped secrete stolen booty. Lastly, she had an ugly temper and when aroused would scold and go into a tirade of profane and abusive language. Curt and Liza had seven children who grew to maturity.

MINNIE DACK, III 43, the first born, was of a snobbish, jealous disposition. Her mind is described as having been "naturally a little weak"; she was shallow, silly and narrow in her interests. She possibly had some mental trouble following an attack of typhoid fever at twenty years. At the age of about thirty-four she again showed symptoms of mental disturbance, became noisy, ugly, talkative and destructive. At the age of thirty-eight she was sent to the Warren State Hospital. After a nine months' residence she went home in a quiet, apparently normal condition. About three years later, in 1896, she again became restless, talkative and destructive and was again sent to the Warren State Hospital where she has remained ever since. Hers is probably a case of manic depressive insanity of circular type. The manic depressive tendency was probably inherited from her mother's family; the evidence is not conclusive, but the history of the mother's family makes such a hypothesis tenable. Her normal intervals have grown steadily shorter and less frequent, although she still has periods when she will answer simple questions relevantly, assist with scrubbing and ward work, and be tidy in her habits. Her memory, however, is quite poor and she shows considerable dementia. When excited she will be very destructive, ugly, elated, hyperactive, talkative and decorative [sic]. When depressed she will lie on the floor in her room for weeks and refuse to speak to anyone. Minnie married the only worthless son of an intelligent and prosperous family in the vicinity of Bushville. He made good pay as a miner but was frequently intoxicated, recognized as a thief, was unfaithful to his wife and finally deserted his children a short time after Minnie was taken to the Hospital the second time, and he has not been heard from since. Minnie had by him nine children; the two oldest both died when young of diphtheria; the third, Leah, IV 11, is now a patient at the Warren State Hospital. As a girl she was lazy, would have pouting spells and obtained but little education. The onset of mental trouble occurred at the age of about twenty. She began to talk a great deal about a certain man who she imagined was going to marry her; she would sit around unoccupied, at times refused to eat and occasionally became angry and ugly without cause. After being at the Warren State Hospital for about a year she was sent home very much improved, but returned a year later; this time she had rather suddenly shown a tendency to sing, laugh, use profane language, and expose her person; she tried to run away, imagined that she could see the devil and absent individuals, thought people were pursuing her, and would constantly repeat some one word or series of words. She had an illegitimate pregnancy just previous to coming to the Hospital but she succeeded in inducing an abortion. She has now been at the Warren State Hospital for thirteen years. Generally she is disturbed, excited, impulsive, denudative and destructive. Occasionally she will have periods when she is quiet and orderly and will do some work. Dementia praecox is considered to be the most probable diagnosis of the case, as she is always confused, irritable and markedly deteriorated. Minnie's fourth child, McKinley, IV 12, was considered a fairly intelligent boy, but at the age of nineteen he stole a keg of powder which accidentally blew up when he tried to open it, killing him instantly. The fifth child, Alex, IV 13, age thirty-four, has been a miner; he never stays in any one place very long, and recently lost his job because of mental peculiarities. He is naturally lazy, easy-going and the sort of drinker who becomes intoxicated on pay days. For the last two or three years he has been showing symptoms of mental disease. At times he will not want to talk to anyone, but will sit around unoccupied, occasionally laugh to himself, but become angry if anyone speaks to him. He has been known to take his bucket and go to work regularly each day for a week, yet do nothing but sit on a log when he got to the mine. He talks a great deal about wealth which he imagines his father used to have, and also about the estate of an uncle. When visiting a cousin he got up in the middle of the night and washed out his clothes and hung them up; then he carefully took them down and immediately repeated the operation of washing them. Next to Alex comes Jennie, IV 14, who also is in the Warren State Hospital. As a girl at school she was dull and lazy and would not apply herself; would sneak and lie and was always ready to pick a fight. Now at the age of thirty she measures up to nine and one-half years by the Binet-Simon scale. She has successive periods of depression, excitement and normal condition. The periods of excitement seldom last more than a month or two. When excited she is hyperactive, elated, noisy, untidy in appearance, and sings and laughs; when depressed she is unoccupied, seclusive, picks her hair and is retarded in answering questions. During these periods she has occasionally attempted suicide. Shortly after admission to this institution she gave birth to an illegitimate child, which was placed in an orphan's home and later adopted. The onset of Jennie's mental trouble occurred at sixteen; she was at the Warren State Hospital five years, went home, but was returned a year later and has been there ever since.

Next to Jennie comes Jack, IV 15, age twenty-seven years. Naturally he is lazy, shiftless, and quick tempered. For the last year or two he has been considered mentally unsound; he gets many queer religious ideas and talks a great deal about the invention of a perpetual motion machine which the Lord, he says, will aid him in doing. He does little real work.

Ella, IV 16, the eighth child, age twenty-five, is also insane. As a young girl she was shy, obedient and seclusive. At the age of twenty-four she gradually became silly and imaginative. She thinks a certain man is going to marry her and that her brothers are both married. She spent a whole day searching the church yard for a stone which she says has her name written on it and she has written to various people, accusing them of stealing this stone. In trying to tell the writer of her sister Dora's disappointment in love she said, "He didn't understand toward her; of course they all do, in that way. It seemed as though his heart didn't order up that he should go to her."

Effie, IV 17, the youngest of Minnie's children, and the only one living who is not considered insane, is just twenty-one years old. She was adopted by a family near Bushville, and never has associated much with her own people. The woman who brought her up is coarse and ignorant, and Effie's opportunities were no better but possibly no worse than she would have received at home. She is a quiet, listless, ambitionless girl who is careless in her personal appearance and does little house work;

her history, conversation and general attitude show her to be of substandard intelligence. She is married and has one child, a girl a year old.

ALLEN DACK, III 45, died from the effects of a gunshot wound received at the age of thirty-three. He was a woodsman by occupation, and a thief as well; a whiskey drinker, occasionally becoming intoxicated and subject to angry spells. He went to the penitentiary at the same time his father did; after serving a three-year sentence he returned to his home and resumed his former thieving habits. He was shot one night while getting out of the window of a house he had just looted. He had three children who grew to maturity; a daughter died at twenty-five; his son is living but we have no reliable data concerning him; the youngest child, now a woman of thirty-one, is weak physically and decidedly neurotic.

REBECCA DACK, III 46, or "Becky," age fifty-six, has never married; she lives with her aged mother on the old farm in an unpainted rickety house. Becky is quite a character; she loves to talk, has a fairly good memory and rather keen wit and she comprehends certain simple ideas quite readily. When it came to giving information about her relatives she was decidedly unreliable; according to her account, one would think there never was such an honest, healthy and intelligent family as the Dacks. One of her favorite phrases after recounting the virtues of an uncle or brother was "Yes, and that's the kind of a man he was," uttered in a rhythmical tone and with the accent on *that's*. The mild, childlike, high-pitched voice seems quite out of proportion with Becky's huge physical frame, for she weighs about three hundred. Her outlook on life and her manner of expressing herself are both childlike. In speaking of her niece, Leah, who is insane, she said, "She had the asmy and her pipes got rotten and that's what made her crazy." One of her aunts died of dropsy and the husband of this woman had the same disease; after Becky had given the cause of her uncle's death she exclaimed: "And don't it beat all—them a havin' the same disease!" In the neighborhood of her home she is considered excitable, high-tempered and of low-grade intelligence. She will have what her nephew calls "crazy spells" when she will curse and threaten and swear. As far as known she has never shown any thieving tendencies, and her reputation is good.

DELIA DACK, III 47, age fifty-four, resembles her sister Becky in physical build, mental caliber and vocal intonation. She has a flat face, coarse features and large nostrils. For many years she has suffered from diabetes. Her memory for family history seems unusually good and her information was found to be reliable. She talks too volubly, going into many wearisome details in giving even a short story, but she observes closely and does not attempt to shield the shortcomings of her relatives. She shows a morbid fondness to relate sexual details. It seems hard to realize when hearing this woman chatter on in a mild, high-pitched voice that she ever becomes thoroughly angry. And yet her history emphasizes this point; if vexed or if her suspicions are aroused she will scold and threaten and quarrel for several days at a time. She has attacked her husband on several occasions and has threatened to scald him, and also has frequently threatened to strike her daughter-in-law when angry at her. She does not "pick a quarrel" but is often unreasonable in suspecting people. Once, for example, having mislaid twenty dollars, she immediately accused her daughter-in-law, an undoubtedly honest woman, of having stolen it and scolded and threatened her angrily. She shows poor judgment in spending money and will buy anything that catches her fancy, but soon tires of her purchases. She spends money for articles of food that she happens to like, much as a child would. Several times when she has moved she has left bills behind which she has never paid. She has left her husband several times and even gone to live with other men. Her general reputation in the town where she has lived for ten years is bad; she is regarded as a low, ignorant, immoral woman. Her husband is a lazy, dishonest, good-for-nothing man. They have had six children; one met with an accidental death in childhood, another died in infancy, the other four are living. Two of them failed to obtain even enough schooling to enable them to read and write. The oldest, Harry, age thirty-three, is a heavy drinker, occasionally is put in jail for thirty days and can get no steady work because of his irregular habits. He is illiterate, of a slow, easy-going disposition, of substandard intelligence, but not quarrelsome; he is regarded about town as untrustworthy, although he has not been arrested for stealing, as far as the writer knows. The second child, Clara, is a nervous, excitable woman and has had "nervous prostration." Her moral reputation is good. She is the mother of five small children. Ray, the third child, is an easy-going, ignorant fellow who likes to tell improbable stories. He is a miner by occupation. His youngest brother, Homer, is barely able to read and write. He earns a laborer's pay of two dollars a day, and his habits are fairly temperate. He was in jail for a short time on one occasion for stealing some junk, and another time for riding freights.

EMMA DACK, III 48, age fifty-three, has moved from one town to another, and now is in Ohio. Her husband was Tom Biddle. No one speaks well of her; she is lacking in intelligence, is ugly, unreasonable and immoral. The following incident was related to the writer as illustrative of her character: "I went to her house one evening to see one of her daughters. Mrs. Biddle herself was out, but later in the evening came home. She went up to her husband and asked him why he was not at work. He replied that he did not work in the evening; but she apparently was bent on trouble and scolded and threatened him and finally ended up by hurling a dish at him." She seemed to vent her ill temper particularly on her husband and for weeks at a time would swear, curse and quarrel whenever he came near her. A relative stated that she "acted crazy" when she got mad. Once when in a rage she attempted to kill her husband with a butcher knife. Frequently she will part from her husband for months at a time and live with other men. She has heart trouble, and her eyesight is failing rapidly. Emma's husband, who met an accidental death on the railroad a few years ago, was an ugly-tempered man and a heavy drinker. Sometimes when on a spree he would not be heard from for several months. Between sprees he would work steadily. By him Emma had ten children who, as a family, are rough, unintelligent and bad-tempered. Two women who know the entire family each said, "You can't get along with any of them."

Helen Biddle, the oldest, aged thirty-four, is considered to be one of the best tempered and most intelligent in the family; she, however, in the words of a physician "just barely escapes being low white trash." Her two marriages have both been of necessity. She lives in a mining village and keeps boarders. She quarrels a great deal with her husband, who beats her periodically. She has had four children. Her oldest girl married an Italian at the age of fifteen; just previously she had taken poison, thinking she was pregnant, and this fear was the reason for the marriage. The second child died in infancy; the other two children are both young. Jerry, Emma's second child, is a mean, ugly, disagreeable man; he is a steady heavy drinker but is seldom seen intoxicated. Recently he deserted his wife and children for several months and lived with another woman in the same town where his wife was staying. His next younger sister, Edna, is nervous, faints easily, and, like her mother, is practically insane when angry. Her reputation has been bad both before and after marriage (she has been married three times) and she now has the reputation of a prostitute. She has one child, Elton. The fourth of the family is a butcher and lives a fairly respectable life. He married a capable girl and has two children. He can figure enough to attend to business but never writes a letter nor reads the newspapers. He is gruff and outspoken, at times drinks to excess, but will be temperate when "under a pledge." Fred, age twenty-six, the fifth child, can read and write, is temperate, and seems to have a fairly good history, although not much is known of him or the next brother, Jim, age twenty-four, who is a carpenter. Alice, one year younger than Jim, is nervous and excitable; is married and has one child. Gertie, the eighth child, twenty-one, works in a factory; the boy just younger than she died in infancy. Harold, the youngest of the family, has succeeded in reaching only the second or third grade in school at the age of fourteen.

MELISSA DACK, III 49, died in Colorado at the age of thirty-four. A woman who worked at the same hotel where Melissa was employed when a young girl said she used to "take tantrums" when she would bang dishes and furniture around but never strike anyone. She had two illegitimate children while she lived near Bushville; she then went west with a third man to whom she was not married. Her two children were raised by her sister Becky. The oldest, Fannie, obtained a fairly good education, taught school for a time and then married. The other child, Leslie, is not very bright, drinks a good deal and is a petty thief.

CATHARINE DACK, III 50, generally known as Kit, is forty-four years old. Naturally endowed with an uncontrollable temper, loose in her morals, and now mentally unbalanced, she is notorious among the Dacks. Her husband has been a miner and they have moved frequently; consequently she is well known in several places. Her marriage was one of necessity, and since marriage she has frequently deserted her husband to live with other men, some of whom have been foreigners. She is almost illiterate but has a good deal of practical ability and, before her mind became impaired, was considered an unusually good housekeeper and cook. It is difficult to determine just where her natural disposition ceases and where her mental trouble begins in considering her life history. As long as anyone can remember she has been subject to violent outbursts of temper when she has not only threatened but attacked her husband. They have parted countless times, but he always returns to her. They were separated when the writer last heard of them and he was living with the married daughter. In the last ten years the periods of excitement have occurred generally at the time of the menstrual period, and last for several days. She will either wander away from home then, or else attack someone, usually her husband. He is said to be battered and bruised from one end to the other as the result of her attacks. Several times proceedings have been taken to place her in an institution but these have never materialized. She has been seen dragging her oldest girl about by the hair. Once, in order to get away from her, her husband climbed a tree; she then chopped the tree down. One night while they were out driving she stuck a hat pin into him. Her last attack, some few months before the writer saw her, was with a butcher knife. At the time she stabbed her husband in the forehead, but gave him only a flesh wound. Three or four years ago, although recognized then by some as being mentally unbalanced, she kept boarders and one of them spoke most highly to the writer of her skill as a cook. Since that time, however, she has shown a steady deterioration. She will sit about the house unoccupied, will not mingle with her neighbors, and has "swearing spells." She imagines people call her indecent names and cast slurs at her; sometimes she will suddenly turn to one of her children and say, "What did you say that about me for?" She is fairly neat about her personal appearance, although she pays no attention to her home. Her immediate reply to a question is generally relevant, but then she goes on in an incoherent, meaningless style. The following is a specimen of her conversation: "Oh no, my sister Emma's girls were never crazy. It was the way their father served them. You know the way of a person handling $1,000. That is their way and not my way. He was a wicked man, and it's his wickedness that brought their crimes." "All that ailed my sister Emma was overfineness. She was overfine; her fineness was something grand. She was just like silk and it didn't suit her to the coal digger's hut. She had brightness but her brightness didn't carry her over."

Kit's husband Joe is a generally well-liked man; his principal fault is drinking, but domestic troubles are considered to be partly responsible for that. Kit's two oldest children died in infancy, the third, Blanche, aged twenty-one, is married and has one child. Her reputation previous to marriage was not good and her marriage was one of necessity. Her physician considers her a neurotic woman with hysterical tendencies. She is a good housekeeper, however. Kit's fourth child also died in infancy, but the fifth and youngest, Reed, aged sixteen, is working in the mines. He reached the fourth or fifth grade in school and has never gotten into any particular trouble, although intimate observers say that he has his mother's temper.

Maggie Dack

MAGGIE DACK, II 18, the youngest of the original Dack family, died at the age of eighty of cancer. Maggie lost her mind when quite a young woman, probably at the age of about twenty-five. According to the story which has been handed down through several generations, Maggie attended some Methodist revival meetings and the excitement sent her crazy. At first she wandered around the country a good deal, and would stay in vacant houses over night. Her son remembers as a little boy being taken to a big stone in the field by his mother; there she knelt down to pray. She imagined that people talked about her, and in reaction to this idea would come to the door and swear and scold at men working in the fields, or at anyone who happened to be passing the house. On cloudy days she would imagine that she could see her children in the sky. She was very jealous of her husband and frequently accused him of infidelity. She would often talk to herself. She did not associate with her neighbors. As far as can be ascertained her mental disease was continuous and she had no normal intervals. She seemed able to keep her house neat and clean however; everyone mentioned her ability in this direction. Her husband, Henry McGinness, II 19, was a cousin of her sister Isabelle's husband. He was a shoemaker, a far more industrious and temperate man than his cousin Sol, but of a miserly nature and, when angry, cruel and abusive toward his family. Maggie had by him eight children whose histories will next be considered.

WILLIS McGINNESS, III 51, the oldest, is probably still living somewhere in the west, although his relatives have lost track of him. A former employer said of him, "He had brains enough of a sort, but he was a perfect brute." He frequently beat his first wife, almost choked her on at least two occasions, and one time forced her to flee to a neighbor's house to spend the night because of his attempts to kill her. Willis tried to excuse these actions by saying that he was temporarily crazy and had no memory of his actions. In his work he was shiftless. He is considered to have been indirectly the cause of the death of his first wife. His second marriage was to his own cousin, Elizabeth Myers. He abused her likewise, did not support her, and she left him after a few years of married life. He had three children by his first wife, but only one grew to maturity. She lives in the west and nothing is known of her.

MOLLIE McGINNESS, III 52, the second of Maggie's children, died at forty-two years, of heart trouble. She was a jealous, unreasonable woman who lived an unhappy life. She was quick-tempered, and when angry was cruel in the treatment of her children. Her husband came from a fairly good family; he was of an ugly, surly disposition, drank to some extent but was seldom intoxicated. By him Mollie had eleven children besides a number of miscarriages. Susan, the oldest of Mollie's children, aged forty-eight, is a sensible, thrifty woman of average intelligence; she is a trained nurse, but now is occupied as a housewife. She has two boys; both are doing fairly well at school, but the older is of a nervous excitable temperament. Maxwell is an oilwell contractor in Indiana. He has been away from his relatives for twenty years and they know little of him. He used to be rather a heavy drinker and occasionally would become intoxicated, but did not lose work because of drinking. Percy is a laborer in a foundry and has a good history. The fourth child in Mollie's family, Anna, is a high strung, excitable woman who married an eccentric, dishonest man by whom she has had three children. The oldest, aged twenty-four, did not get along in school and stutters, but he is now employed in a grocery and is doing fairly well. Alfred, aged seventeen, is probably an epileptic; he has had no seizures in the past few years, but had a good many at the age of about six. He has an uncontrollable temper. Anna's youngest child, John, seems healthy and normal but he stutters a little. Little is known concerning the next two of Mollie's children, Albert and Percy McGinness, both of whom are in the oil business in the southwestern part of the United States. Maria, the seventh of the family, is a trained nurse; she is of an independent nature and of a calm, cool disposition. She is separated from her husband, a physician and drug fiend. By him she had two children: the oldest, a boy of twelve, is feebleminded; the other child seems normal, according to relatives. Alma and Lillian, the two youngest of Mollie's family, are trained nurses. Alma, a mild, pleasant girl in disposition, has serious heart trouble. Lillian is quick-tempered and has recently married a good-for-nothing man who does not support her.

ALBERT McGINNESS, III 53, next younger than Mollie, was a farmer in Kansas but died at fifty of typhoid fever, leaving a family of four boys. The child next younger than he died in infancy.

The next of "crazy Maggie's" children was WILSON, III 54. He married his own cousin, Emma Myers, III 55, but she left him because of his abusive treatment. We have already stated in the description of her that the oldest of their four children is feeble-minded and in an institution for defective children. Wilson is little more than a hobo; he wanders from one place to another, drinks whenever he can obtain any money, and exerts a bad influence over any he comes into contact with.

SOLOMON McGINNESS, III 56, a miner, aged fifty-five, was a heavy drinker until about fifteen years ago, since which time his wife says she has succeeded in keeping him from more than very occasional excesses. One can easily imagine that this tall, powerful woman with a determined jaw is not a person to be considered lightly. When he was younger Solomon would sometimes be drunk for a week at a time, and once or twice he deserted his wife for short periods. In disposition he is disagreeable, obstinate, quick-tempered. The family physician described him tersely as mentally and physically below the normal. His wife is a thrifty, fairly intelligent woman but at one time she was addicted to the use of drugs. According to her story she contracted the habit through the use of a physician's prescription for the drug one time when she was ill. She and Solomon have had eleven children. Alton, the oldest, aged thirty-two, is an illiterate miner. He has an ugly temper; "he is just like all his father's people," his mother said. He usually becomes intoxicated on pay days. He has recently deserted his coarse, unintelligent wife and five children for the second time. The next son, Austin, is more reliable but also illiterate and likewise an excessive drinker occasionally. He is a miner by occupation. He is married and has three children. The third son, Chester, had a very meager education; he is fairly temperate in habits but not thrifty and is of rather a thriftless [sic] nature. He is married and has two children. The fourth of Wilson's children, a girl, is loose morally. She deserted her first husband, went to live with another man, and even her own family do not know where she is now. Next to her is another girl, Rosie, who keeps a boarding house in a large city under an assumed name. No definite statement concerning her conduct was obtainable but some of her relatives think that her moral integrity is questionable. The sixth child, Viola, aged twenty-one, is a loud, vulgar, profane, quarrelsome woman with a bad reputation. She, according to her mother, is married and lives with the husband's people. Wilson's next child died shortly after birth; the four youngest children, ranging in age from fifteen down to seven years, have shown no marked symptoms of defect according to their histories.

ARTHUR McGINNESS, III 57, aged forty-seven, at present earns $75 a month working on an oil lease. For a long time he supported himself by gambling. He is a steady, heavy drinker, of a domineering, obstinate, and quick-tempered disposition. He is married but has no children.

DORA McGINNESS, III 58, has married a man who makes good wages and lives a "respectable" life. She is shallow mentally and seems a rather weak, colorless woman. She has three children, ranging in age from twenty-four to nine years; none of them show anything unusual.

CHAUNCEY McGINNESS, III 59, aged forty-seven, is a shiftless good-for-nothing man who spends for drink the money he occasionally earns painting a house. He has a weak, degenerate face and is not considered trustworthy. He has been married three times; he was divorced from his first wife, his second wife died, while the third, a notorious woman, lived with him only a few weeks. He has no children.

III. DISCUSSION OF DATA

In the complete Dack history, of which the preceding pages are an abstract, are found seven hundred and fifty-four individuals. This number includes all miscarriages, children who died in infancy, and individuals who have married into the Dack family. Some of this number have lived in distant parts of the country and no reliable information concerning them could be obtained; many died in infancy or early childhood, while others, although living, are too young to have shown what their characteristics will be. Taking out such cases, as well as individuals who have merely married into the family, we find that there are one hundred and fifty-three persons who have attained an age of at least twenty, and concerning whom reliable information was obtained. An attempt was made, first, to classify them according to their social worth. Forty of the number have shown no anti-social traits, have not been a burden to society and, although they may be of a low order of intelligence, have never exhibited any marked absence of emotional control. A number of these individuals, however, are still rather young and may develop undesirable traits later, but so far society seems no worse for their presence. In the second class we placed those who have been of little use from an economic standpoint and who have shown various evidences of degeneracy, such as shiftlessness, illiteracy, lack of average judgment in the conduct of affairs, sexual irregularity, heavy drinking, etc. This class embraced seventy-two individuals. That this type furnishes the material for many of our social problems is evident. The third group, made up of forty-one individuals, contains all those who have obviously been a burden to society; those who have been insane, in penitentiaries, a source of annoyance and loss because of their thieving propensities, or who have not been able to care for themselves because of lack of mental ability. Twenty of this number have been in public institutions for varying periods of time; some of the remaining twenty-one have received short jail sentences for a month or less.

No schedule blanks were used in obtaining the history of this family. The traits chronicled in most instances were those which the informants related voluntarily. Such a system has its advantages and disadvantages; it obviates forced and often erroneous statements but it also leads to the omission of certain traits. To illustrate: if a man was particularly shiftless and a heavy drinker the person describing him might be so impressed with these two prominent traits that he might overlook the fact that the man was also dishonest. An attempt has been made, however, to compute the number of times certain traits have been mentioned in describing these one hundred and fifty-three individuals. As we have endeavored to show, the statement that ten were mentioned as dishonest does not mean that the remaining one hundred and forty-three were honest, but that ten of them are *described* as being dishonest.

In making an analysis of the various peculiarities found in the family, we find twenty-five cases of insanity, only two of which were senile psychoses; twenty individuals are described as being lazy or shiftless; thirty-nine are below the average of intelligence; thirty-four are described as ugly, quarrelsome and bad-tempered. This last trait is found in various degrees; some individuals show so much irritability and violence that they are regarded as practically insane, while others merely become provoked easily and give vent to their feelings in a torrent of abusive language. A litigious tendency has been rather marked in the family, and we find the names of the family occurring frequently on the court records of the county in which they have lived. In many of these instances the matter was dropped and no sentence given. Fifteen other individuals are described as merely quick tempered. Thirty are mentioned as being alcoholic, this term being used to describe both those who become intoxicated occasionally yet whose indulgences do not interfere with their work and those who are chronic drunkards. In seven instances there was a history of thieving without jail sentence; in six others there was incarceration for breaking the law, the offense in each instance except one being larceny; eleven other individuals have a history of dishonesty, making, in all, a total of twenty-four dishonest individuals with thieving tendencies. It is rather difficult to obtain accurate data relative to sex offense, and under our present social standards little attention is paid to its occurrence among men unless the fault is very pronounced. We find mention made of sexual irregularity in twenty-seven individuals, practically all females. In some instances merely illicit relationship previous to marriage is recorded, while others are cases of prostitutes.

One trait which the reader has probably already noted is the tendency shown by the members of the family to desert the consort frequently for a short period of time. This tendency is mentioned in eighteen instances. One woman in the family has kept up for years this practice of separating from her husband and later coming back to him. Nine individuals are described as neurotic or excitable, and six others as eccentric.

In the summary which has just been made, all individuals under twenty have been excluded. Many of the family who are below that age have already shown themselves to be defective, however; one child is an idiot, four others are recognized imbeciles, one of whom is in an institution, two are epileptics, several young girls immoral, seven markedly neurotic, and a large number show evidences of some degree of mental deficiency in the unusually poor progress which they have made at school.

In considering which branches of the family are the most defective, the descendants of Jane and Curtis are immediately singled out. The reason why we find more degeneracy among Jane's descendants than in the rest of the family is found, probably, in the fact that she married her cousin. The reason in the case of Curtis is not quite so apparent. He married, it is true, a defective woman from defective stock, but his sister Isabelle contracted an equally bad marriage with rather better results. It is in the families of Jane and Curtis that we find the most pronounced cases of lack of emotional control. In both cases this trait was inherited from both sides of the family. Thus we find Jane Dack, of a moderately high temper, married to her first cousin, Patrick Dack, who was notorious for his ugly outbursts. Jane's brother, Curtis Dack, had a moderate temper unless under the influence of alcohol; lack of emotional control was a prominent trait in his family, however, and he married a woman from a neurotic family, who showed this trait in a pronounced form. Practically all of the offspring from these two unions show a lack of emotional control and have high tempers. The fact that three of Jane's offspring were insane is interesting as it points out another of the outstanding traits of the family—nervous instability. This cousin marriage seems to bring to light in rather a ghastly fashion the worst of the family traits.

Rebecca Dack married a thrifty German and among her children and grandchildren we can trace, to a certain extent, the blending of the two families. The slow, plodding German nature seems to have counteracted the quick Irish temper of the Dacks, for comparatively few instances of marked aggressive temper are found among her children, and the largest number of steady, capable citizens are found among her offspring. It is difficult to determine just why three cases of insanity are found in the family of one of her sons, especially as no cases are found among the other grandchildren; we can offer possible explanations, but the real etiological factors are obscure.

Isabelle's children might best be described as eccentric; they have a good deal of practical ability, but are lacking in other directions. Maggie's family shows a lack of average mental ability and a tendency to cruelty. This last named trait is also found in Maggie's husband.

This family history illustrates the fact that is being more and more widely recognized, namely, that feeble-mindedness is not a unit trait, but a complex of many traits. The defectives of this family, with few exceptions, are border-line cases who have some of the traits essential to normal development, yet lack others. One informant would, without hesitation, say that a certain individual was feeble-minded, the next would say that the same individual was normal, *but*—because of lack of education and proper environment—lazy, ignorant, and worthless. It was interesting to the writer to hear the comments of the different physicians concerning various members of the family who were about on a par intellectually. One physician would say, "Why, you couldn't say that A. and his brother are not normal. Of course they belong to that shiftless, good-for-nothing class that never pay bills, but you couldn't call them really constitutionally defective." The next physician would say: "There isn't one of the family who is really normal; not a one is bright or amounts to anything."

The results obtained from making Binet tests of a group of four children belonging to one of these families were instructive. Although the environment in which these four children lived was poorer than the average Dack home, the children, the oldest of whom was eighteen, do not appear on first acquaintance as obviously defective, nor do they seem less intelligent than the average of the Dacks. Not one of these children, however, obtained more than an eight and a half year rating by the Binet scale. The two members from another branch of the family who are at the Warren State Hospital rate nine and one half and eleven years, respectively; the woman who measures eleven years is, on the whole, more intelligent than most of her relatives.

Almost every individual in the family is endowed with enough practical ability to make a living. But as a family they are lacking in powers of self-control, in ambition, and in higher reasoning ability. Their lack of self-control, shown by violent outbursts of temper, has already been considered. Closely related to this is a lack of stability shown especially in the matter of marriage relationship and in residence. There is a high percentage of divorce and desertion in this family. In some instances it is only a temporary affair; the wife will lose her temper, leave home, be gone for a few weeks and then return. In other instances formal divorce proceedings are taken, and in other cases a promiscuity not covered by any legal veneer is practiced. Secondly, most of the members of the family change their residence frequently. The occupation of most of the males in the family is mining, and this fact is partially responsible for their nomadic tendency. But we find those who are not miners living in one locality to-day, and to-morrow they are departed.

Mention has already been made of the amount of illiteracy found in the family. Although all except four of the people described have been born and raised in Pennsylvania, a great many of them, even men of twenty-five, are illiterate. The majority of them have received so meager an education that they can hardly write and only a few ever attended a high school. There are few in the whole family who are intelligent enough to do anything more than rough laboring work. These few exceptions occur almost entirely among Rebecca's offspring and in one branch of Maggie's family. There seems to be a dead level of mediocrity above which the Dacks do not rise; in the younger generations this condition is being changed in some instances by the infusion of better blood.

IV. CONCLUSIONS

Although it is not possible to discover all the laws of human heredity by the analysis of one family, it is possible to make a few observations in each case, and learn a few practical lessons. Two factors seem to lie at the bottom of the degeneracy shown by this family: a lack of inhibitive control, or a nervous instability, and secondly, lack of mental ability. The evidence presented seems to corroborate Dr. Davenport's theory that a quick temper is inherited as a Mendelian dominant, for the trait does not skip a generation. So many degrees of emotional outbursts are recorded, however, that it is impossible to put the results into statistical form. A careful study of the different branches of the family reveals the fact that the intensity of the trait in the offspring and the number of the offspring who show it are directly dependent on the intensity of the trait in the parents and whether the trait is inherited from one or both parents. Four characteristics are common to nearly all the cases of insanity presented; early onset, deterioration, excited periods and an absence of normal intervals of any great length. The cases where the symptom complex approaches nearest to manic depressive insanity show, with one exception, marked deterioration; the cases that fall into the dementia praecox group show a tendency to periodic outbreaks of violent excitement. In nearly all the cases the onset of the mental trouble has occurred before the age of thirty.

The family, of course, has been an economic loss to society. Ten of them have been or are patients at the Warren State Hospital; their total length of residence is seventy-four years and two months. Figuring the cost to the state and county of these patients, we find that, until August 31, 1915, these patients cost the taxpayers of the state $16,354, allowing for the regular per capita cost. An attempt was made to estimate roughly the expense to the state of the individuals who have been in other institutions— county homes, other hospitals for the insane, penitentiaries, etc. Allowing $200 per year per person, this would make about $12,000, which would make a total of $28,354 spent in a period of forty years. Looking at the matter from an economic standpoint only, this figure would not be so alarming if the members of the family who had not been in institutions were productive and a source of wealth to society. Some few of them have been, but not the majority. Furthermore, many of them who have not been in institutions have been a cause of economic loss because of their dishonesty and thefts. No attempt has been made to estimate the cost of occasional jail sentences or the money that has been paid in poor relief to the family. These two items would not, however, assume any very large proportions.

The family has also been a decided detriment to society from the moral standpoint, and this loss, which cannot be estimated in dollars and cents, is more important than the economic loss. Finally, the economic and moral costs already entailed are only the beginning of a liability that will continue for many years. At the Warren State Hospital alone there are three Dacks, all about thirty-five years old and in good health; in all probability the three will be state charges for the rest of their lives. Among the younger members of the family can be found quite a few who seemed destined to become state charges, and there are at least five cases of insanity which will probably need institutional care in the near future.

To a certain extent, of course, degeneracy is self-limiting. Consider, for example, the young women on this chart who are sexually immoral. Few of them have large families; many of them are childless. That insanity which has its onset early in life often prevents, or at least limits, procreation. Only one of the three sons of Henry Myers, all of whom were patients at this institution, had offspring, and he but one child. Minnie Dack, now a patient at this institution, had six children who reached maturity; among the first five is found only one descendant, and there seems but small likelihood that there ever will be more, as all are insane and the three outside of institutions are not likely to contract marriages. The sixth and youngest of Minnie's children is married and has a child; if she never develops mental trouble and is free to rear a large family they may possibly become a burden to society. This natural limitation, as stated at the beginning of the paragraph, is only partially effective, and it would seem that man must complete the work which nature begins in limiting the procreation of the obviously unfit.

The analysis of this family emphasizes the fact which has been previously demonstrated, that the marriage of cousins of defective stock produces a large proportion of defective offspring. The marriage of first cousins is now prohibited in the state of Pennsylvania, but in the majority of the States of the Union such a marriage may be lawfully contracted, regardless, of course, of how defective the family from which the cousins come.

Finally, highly defective strains ought to be investigated and registered, if any wise measures are ever to be taken to prevent the propagation of the unfit. Careful collection of data now may be the basis of practical and effective work in the future. Eugenics will never be a panacea in the solution of all the questions of crime, poverty, and insanity, but bad heredity is one of the causes of these social pollutions and therefore any rational scheme for social betterment must take this important fact into consideration. We may not be ready to take any drastic steps at the present time, but we can at least survey the field, and collect carefully the pedigrees of our defective families.

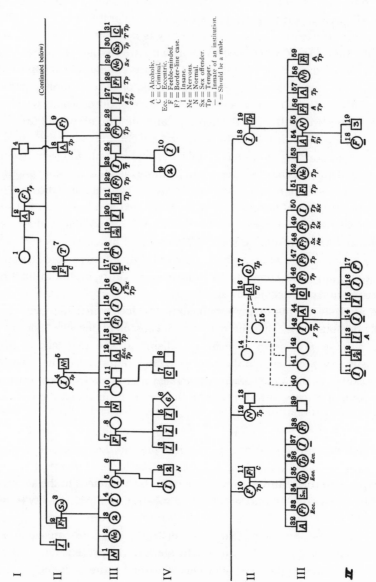

Chart of the Dack Family.

A = Alcoholic.
C = Criminal.
Ecc. = Eccentric.
F = Feeble-minded.
F? = Border-line case.
I = Insane.
Ne = Nervous.
N = Normal.
Sx = Sex offender.
Tp = Temper.
— = Inmate of an institution.
* = Should be a male.

10

MINA A. SESSIONS

The Feeble-Minded in a
Rural County of Ohio*

Preface

This study initially focuses on not a family but an impoverished coal-mining county in the hills of southeastern Ohio. Because its aim is "to discover the extent and social significance of feeble-mindedness in that particular part of the state" (p. 255), the study begins with a survey. Later, however, it shifts attention to the defective clans of the region. Here, using the genealogical techniques more typical of family studies, it introduces the Happy Hickories.

Methodologically, *The Feeble-Minded in a Rural County* shows the influence of the Royal Commission established in 1904 to formulate policy for dealing with mental defectives in Great Britain (Tredgold 1916). Like the Royal Commission, Sessions undertakes a survey to determine the extent, distribution, and effects of feeble-mindedness in a particular geographical area. Moreover, she draws upon the Royal Commission's definitions, distinguishing three types among the retarded: idiots, imbeciles, and (at the top) the feeble-minded ("morons"). Sessions's criteria for identifying members of the last category dictate the results of her study. Expanding the Royal Commission's already loose definition, she decides to include as feeble-minded all who are unable to support themselves in a competitive environment (pp. 256–57). Thus she subsequently is able to classify as feeble-minded those who pay low rent, squatters who pay no rent at all, miners who work under "direction," and the unemployed.

The report is organized methodically, if undramatically. After outlining her research procedures, Sessions enumerates the feeble-minded in county institutions (the Infirmary and the Children's Home) and those "at large" (in public schools and the general population). She devotes the second half of her report to descriptions of "defective and dependent families in the county"—mainly the Hickories but also the D., N., S. and X., Y., and Z. clans. Sessions concludes with a call for eugenic segregation of the feeble-minded —and more surveys.

Given her definition of feeble-mindedness as inability to support oneself in a demanding environment, and her view of coal-mining as undemanding, Sessions's findings come as no great surprise. First she discovers that large proportions of the inmates of the two county institutions are mentally defective; here she argues that many should be transferred to the state Institution for the Feeble-minded, from which they could not be "turned back into the community" (p. 265). The survey of public schools reveals that rates of

---

* Originally Bulletin Number Six (Publication no. 12), Bureau of Juvenile Research, Ohio Board of Administration, February 1918.

feeble-mindedness are higher in rural than in urban schools and especially high in two remote districts characterized by dire poverty. (In one, nearly half of the families with school children were on relief.)

Turning to other feeble-minded "at large," Sessions reports a countywide total of 494, three out of every five of whom are male. She does not attempt to explain the sex discrepancy, but it too may be an artifact of her definition of feeble-mindedness: expectations for competitive self-support were probably lower for women than for men. Again she finds feeble-mindedness more common in rural than urban districts and most common of all in remote mining regions hard hit by lay-offs and strikes.

One of these isolated townships, cut off in almost Himalayan fashion by "inaccessible ridges," is the breeding ground of the Hickories. A clan of sixty-two family units, the Hickories "descended from a common ancestor who came from a French port in the days preceding the American Revolution" (p. 288–89). Seven children of this man and an Indian squaw moved to Ohio about 1800. Sessions concentrates on one of these children, feeble-minded Happy, "most worthless of the brothers," tracing his 401 descendants. (The figure in fact includes progeny of his siblings.) Hickories live by foraging off land that belongs to others, begging, and basketmaking. They are not criminals because "the general mentality . . . is too low to permit any crime except petty thieving" (p. 291). Rather, the "chief characteristic of the family is their utter dependency": they constantly try to cadge relief from the county. The second familial disability "is their habit of wandering . . . from one Hickory house to another," the third "the promiscuity of their relationships. . . . They herd together, . . . little better than animals" (p. 291–92). Although "they seldom know what relation they are to each other," Sessions is able to report that "many of the matings are consanguineous" (p. 293). Most distressing of all is the Hickory mentality: 22.1 percent of Happy's descendants have been feeble-minded, and another "7.7 percent are suspected of having been so" (p. 293).

A graduate of the ERO's 1913 summer session, Mina A. Sessions replaced her classmate Mary S. Kostir as field worker for the Ohio Bureau of Juvenile Research, where she too collaborated with Dr. Thomas H. Haines. In 1918 she moved from Columbus to Chicago to become special agent for the Federal Children's Bureau and work on a juvenile court study ("Alumni Roster" 1919:25). *The Feeble-Minded in a Rural County* seems to have been her only publication.[1]

MAIN POINTS OF THE SURVEY

1. The county chosen for the Survey is in the hilly section at the southeastern part of the state, bordering the Ohio river.
2. On February 15, 1916, there were 253 persons in the various state institutions from the county studied. Of this number under state con-

---

[1] Contacts with several archives and searches of biographical dictionaries have produced no other personal information.

trol, 16% were known to be feeble-minded but less than 8% were inmates of the Institution for the Feeble-Minded.

3. It was estimated that 47% of the Infirmary population was dependent because of feeble-mindedness. Only 35% was dependent because of infirmity due to old age or illness.
4. There was proportionately five times as much feeble-mindedness among the dependent children in the Children's Home as among the public school children of the county.
5. Two district schools were found in each of which more than 40% of the children were feeble-minded.
6. The proportion of males to females among the feeble-minded was as 3 to 2.
7. The majority of the feeble-minded were descended from pioneer stock.
8. The percentage of feeble-minded at large in the rural districts was double the percentage in the urban districts.
9. Nearly half of the feeble-minded at large were being partially supported by the public.
10. Seventy-eight feeble-minded persons, or 13.5% of the total feeble-minded population of the county, belonged to one family strain which has been called the Hickory family.
11. Four other families contributed 48 feeble-minded persons or 8.3% of the total feeble-minded population of the county.
12. Approximately 1% of the total population of the county was found to be feeble-minded. It is believed that this percentage would not apply to the whole state. Other surveys should be made of other representative parts of Ohio.

A. GENERAL DESCRIPTION OF THE COUNTY

IT WAS DETERMINED to make a survey of a rural county in Ohio to discover the extent and social significance of feeble-mindedness in that particular part of the state. The county chosen as the subject of the survey is situated in what is known as the hill section bordering the Ohio River, and on July 1st, 1916, had an estimated population of 54,389. There are but two cities in the county, each of which has a population of between six and seven thousand. Along the bottom lands of the streams there is good farm land, but because of its rough surface the larger part of the county is not suitable for agricultural purposes. Coal mining is the principal industry of the county.

B. METHOD OF INVESTIGATION

The survey was begun March 1st, 1916, and carried on under the direction of Dr. Thomas H. Haines. The field work was completed on December 20th, 1916. Information was sought in each township, first of all from the public schools, and then from the physicians and township trustees. The county institutions were visited, and county and city officials, the one district nurse, the one social worker, and many private citizens were interviewed. When cases of feeble-mindedness were reported or discovered in the schools, their homes were visited and information obtained concerning their personal and heredity histories. This procedure frequently led to the discovery of other feeble-minded persons who were in turn followed to their homes.

In general no formal psychological tests were given, but the suspected cases were judged on a sociological basis, with possession of ability or inability to maintain existence accepted as the essential difference between the normal and feeble-minded person. The definitions of the English Royal Commission of 1904 were adopted as the standard. (Tredgold's *Mental Deficiency*. First edition.)

> Idiots are persons so deeply defective in mind from birth or from an early age that they are unable to guard themselves from common physical dangers, such as in the case of young children, would prevent their parents from leaving them alone.
>
> Imbeciles are persons who are capable of guarding themselves against common physical dangers, but who are incapable of earning their own living by reason of mental defect existing from birth or an early age.
>
> The feeble-minded (in the United States known as morons) are persons who may be capable of earning a living under favorable circumstances, but are incapable from mental defect existing from birth or from an early age (a) of competing on equal terms with their normal fellows or (b) of managing themselves and their affairs with ordinary prudence.

The idiots were easily distinguished and set off in a class by themselves, but it was more difficult to distinguish between the two higher grades of feeble-mindedness and between the moron and normal person. It was recognized that the environment into which a subject is born must be taken into consideration. There were many individuals who could not be considered defective in this rural county who would have been so had they been removed to a more complicated environment because they would not have been able to adjust themselves to the demands of the new life and would not have been able to maintain themselves. Also it was recognized that there are certain types of labor on farms, section gangs, or about the mines which do not require even an average grade of mentality. It is necessary in the life of a community that some one fill these places, and if the persons who were doing this were adequately self-supporting, they were not called feeble-minded. Therefore, those individuals were called imbeciles who were so scantily endowed with mentality that it was impossible for them to maintain themselves independently under any circumstances in the environment best suited to them, and those were called morons who possessed certain sorts of ability but in such unequal proportion that they could manage their affairs and earn their own livings only under direction and that in an environment which made the simplest demands on them. Those who were inadequate for any other reason than lack of intelligence were not considered feeble-minded.

C. FEEBLE-MINDED FROM THE COUNTY IN THE STATE INSTITUTIONS

On February fifteenth, 1916, there were 253 persons in the various state institutions from the county studied. They were distributed as shown in Table I and are classified according to their intelligence so far as we are able to classify them.

Table I. Inmates of State Institutions from the County Studied

Institution.	Intelligence.				Total.
	Feeble-Minded.	Possibly Feeble-Minded.	Not Feeble-Minded.	Unknown.	
Institution for Feeble-Minded	20	——	——	——	20
Girls' Industrial Home	8	4	5	——	17
Boys' Industrial School	8	1	11	10	30
Ohio State Reformatory	1	1	2	12	16
Ohio Penitentiary	——	2	4	9	15
Ohio Hospital for Epileptics	——	——	——	17	17
State School for the Blind	——	——	1	——	1
State School for the Deaf	——	——	——	9	9
State Hospital for Insane	4	——	124	——	128
Total	41	8	147	57	253

The girls in the Girls' Industrial Home, the one child in the State School for the Blind, and a part of the boys in the Boys' Industrial School had been given mental examinations, so the classification in those cases was made on the basis of those tests. Of the 128 people from this county in a State Hospital for the Insane, four had been diagnosed by the physicians as feeble-minded. When representatives of this county in the other institutions were classified as feeble-minded or possibly so, the classification was made on the basis of descriptions by reliable persons.

Of the 253 inmates of state institutions from this county, 41 or 16.2% were known to be feeble-minded, and 8 others or 3.1% were either borderline or suspected cases. Of the 41 known cases, only 20, or less than half, were in the Institution for Feeble-minded. This was not because they were not recognized as fit cases for that institution, but because there was no room to care for them.

D. FEEBLE-MINDED IN THE COUNTY INSTITUTIONS

I. The County Infirmary

On the first of March, 1916, there were 67 inmates in the County Infirmary, of whom 46 were men and 21 were women. Each inmate was interviewed, his social history obtained and the cause of his presence in the institution ascertained. Formal psychological tests of intelligence were given in a few cases by Dr. Thomas H. Haines.

1. *Nativity of Inmates* Of the 67 inmates, 53, or 79%, were born in Ohio, and 6, or 8%, were born in other states, making a total of 59, or 88%, native born. The other 8, or 11%, were foreign born. Four inmates were born in the County Infirmary and had been in some institution all of their lives.

2. *Mental and Physical Condition of Inmates* It was found that probably 32 individuals, or 47% of the whole population, were in the Infirmary because their mentality was so low that they were unable to maintain themselves independently in the community at large. Eleven individuals, or 16.4%, were there because they had so broken down their physical and mental health by the excessive use of alcohol that they were no longer able to make their own way in the world at large. It is probable that at least some of these alcoholics could also have been classed as feeble-minded since their inability to keep from becoming alcoholics may have been due

Table II. Classification of Inmates of County Infirmary According to Mental and Physical Condition

	Men.	Women.	Total.	Percent of Total.
Feeble-minded	21	11	32	47.7
Alcoholics	10	1	11	16.4
Senile Dementia	5	1	6	8.9
Old and Infirm	5	5	10	14.9
Blind	3	1	4	5.9
Paralyzed or Crippled	2	2	4	5.9
Total	46	21	67	99.7

to mental defect. Only 24 individuals, or 35.8%, were dependent because of some infirmity due to old age or illness.

Of the thirty-two feeble-minded in the Infirmary, two were low grade idiots unable to do the slightest thing for themselves. Ten others, seven men and three women, were of such low mentality that they could perform only the most simple tasks and could under no circumstances earn their own livings. The remaining twenty, twelve men and eight women, were able to do manual labor if some one remained near to direct the work. These were the ones who found it easy to maintain themselves outside under the most favorable circumstances but sought shelter in the Infirmary as soon as some unfavorable condition arose. The superintendent said that the work he got out of these inmates was costly because some one had to be hired to supervise them and the quality of their work was very poor. There was only one of the forty-six men whom he could trust with a team. This man was paid five dollars a month for his services during the summer months.

3. *Age Groups. Special Discussion of the Younger Inmates* We were most interested in the younger members of this infirmary population since they were the ones who had potentialities for living lives useful or detrimental to their communities. Fifteen members or 22% were found to be under forty years of age. Of these a boy of fifteen, imbecilic and deformed, was kept there rather than in the Children's Home because his mother was also an inmate. A boy of seventeen was a helpless idiot. A boy of twenty-one, high grade feeble-minded, was there because he had been accidentally shot through his own carelessness. He had been found living in an old tool house with his parents and a younger brother, all defectives. This boy has since left the Infirmary

Table III. Age Distribution of Infirmary Population

Age.	Men.	Women.	Total.
15–20 years	2	1	3
21–30 years	2	1	3
31–40 years	5	4	9
41–50 years	3	2	5
51–60 years	13	3	16
61–70 years	8	5	13
71–80 years	10	3	13
81–90 years	3	2	5
Total	46	21	67

and is now living a nomadic, make-shift life. It is probable that the Infirmary will again be his home before many years. A fourth young man, twenty-two years old, was of average mentality but had alcoholic and vagrant habits and was criminally inclined. The preceding winter he had made his home in one of the city's sprinkling wagons stored for the season. He has since left the Infirmary. Of the five in the thirty-one to forty year group, one was a hopeless cripple from locomotor ataxia, the second was becoming blind as a result of syphilitic infection, and the third was becoming totally blind from cataracts. The other two were so feeble-minded that all attempts to earn their livings independently had failed, so they spent most of their time in the County Infirmary, but were free to go and come at will. Of these nine young men, seven will probably be dependent all the rest of their lives. One of the other two is now at large but should be permanently segregated because of his low mentality. Five of the nine were without doubt feeble-minded.

We will now consider the women under forty years of age in the Infirmary. The youngest was a girl of nineteen, a low grade moron of bad sexual habits, who continually made trouble because of her attempts to approach the male inmates. (See history of a group of children in the Children's Home.) A girl of twenty-one was in the Infirmary because she had been living as a common prostitute, became infected with syphilis and the authorities did not know what else to do with her. She was an attractive girl, very active, but with the mentality of a child of ten years. (See history of the D. Family.) A woman of thirty-one had been in the Children's Home till nine years old and in the Girls' Industrial Home till sixteen. When eighteen years old, she was sent to the Infirmary where she had been ever since; but in the two-year interval of freedom she gave birth to an illegitimate child which died in infancy. She had the mentality of a nine-year-old child. A woman, thirty-three years of age, had been transferred from another infirmary. She was a high grade moron and crippled physically. A woman of thirty-nine years was said to have once been of good mentality, but because of drink and exposure had broken down her nervous system so that she was unable to take care of herself in the outside world. A woman, thirty-one years old, was of decidedly low mentality, probably an imbecile, with vicious habits. She had been in and out of the Infirmary at least five different times. On two occasions she was pregnant at the time of her admission and a third record reads, "Admitted with child." She has two children living, one the fifteen-year-old imbecilic boy described above, and the other an eighteen-year-old girl of somewhat higher mentality but still in the defective class who was found to be developing the sexual characteristics of her mother. (See history of the S. Family.) Five of these six women were feeble-minded and there was not one of them who would not be a decided menace to the community in which she was allowed her freedom; yet there was nothing beyond the influence of the superintendent and matron to prevent them from leaving the Infirmary at any time they wished.

4. Inmates Formerly in the Institution for Feeble-Minded It was found that three inmates of the Infirmary had been transferred from the Institution for the Feeble-minded. One of these was a low grade imbecile kept with several of the lowest grade patients in a small house removed from the others. He could tell nothing about himself, so all that is known about him was taken from the Infirmary records. He was born in 1859 in the Infirmary where his mother, unmarried, had sought refuge, "destitute and pregnant." When he was three years old, his mother took him, left the Infirmary, and so far as known was not heard of again. The records do not give the complete story, but in 1888 this boy was sent from the County Infirmary to the Institution for the Feeble-minded, and in 1895 was sent back. The remainder of his life can be spent only in some institution where he can receive a child's care.

Even less was known of the family of the second of these three. He was transferred from the Institution for the Feeble-minded to the Infirmary while still a boy and at the time of the survey had been living in the Infirmary about twenty years. He was in the habit of going at intervals to live with some woman of about his own calibre in the neighborhood and trying to support himself and her, but after a few months always came back. Once he got as far as Cincinnati, but was sent back by the authorities when he asked for aid. He was a good worker under direction, but spent all of the money he earned for candy and trinkets.

The third former inmate of the Institution for the Feeble-minded was a woman, forty-nine years old, whom we shall call Sally, also born in the Infirmary of an immoral and probably feeble-minded mother. Sally's mother, Anne, was first admitted to the Infirmary when seventeen years old and stayed for seven years. She left the Infirmary in July and returned in September of the same year, pregnant. She gave birth to twin girls, one of whom was Sally, and left them in the Infirmary while she went out again into the community. She soon had another child by a colored man which was later brought to the Infirmary and after several years transferred to the Institution for Feeble-Minded. This child remained there fifteen years and was then sent back to the County Infirmary, but she soon left the Infirmary, had an illegitimate daughter, and moved to another part of the state. Anne finally married and had a living daughter and a still-born child. It is not known what became of this daughter, but Anne died shortly after the birth of her last child. One of the twins left in the Infirmary died there when three years old. Sally, the other, was transferred to the Institution for Feeble-Minded when fourteen years old but was sent back again when twenty-nine years of age. The segregation in the Infirmary was not as complete as in the State Institution and after a time she gave birth to a mulatto child. He is now fifteen years old and has been an inmate of the County Children's Home since infancy. He is of borderline mentality and has a sneaking, deceitful nature. One can not help thinking what would have been saved the County and State if Sally's mother had been effectively segregated.

5. *Family Groups in the Infirmary* An important phase of an Infirmary population is the presence of family groups. In this particular County Infirmary there were several, and in looking over the old records it was found that those family names occurred all too frequently. There were three pairs of cousins, two sisters, a man and wife; but the most interesting were two groups of four. The first, which we will call the N. Family, consisted of a feeble-minded man, his son, a victim of locomotor ataxia, an imbecile nephew and a feeble-minded niece. Some time was given to looking up the family history of this group and it was found that in three generations, sixteen members of the family had at some time made their home in the County Infirmary. Of these sixteen, at least nine were feeble-minded. The superintendent said that he did not think there had ever been a time in the history of the institution when some member of this family was not an inmate. A complete description is given of the N. Family in the section on defective and dependent families.

The second group of four consisted of a feeble-minded girl, her cousin, this cousin's son, and her step-great grandmother. All four of this group were feeble-minded and all three women had been notoriously immoral. The two younger were girls of the street and the older woman, for a time, had kept a house of prostitution, but her mentality was so low that she could not successfully manage the business and so was ending her days in the Infirmary. Twelve members of the family had been in the County Infirmary.

6. *Summary*

1. A large proportion of the population of this County Infirmary, (47%), was dependent because of feeble-mindedness and not because of old age or infirmity.

2. Fifteen inmates or 22% of the Infirmary population were under forty years of age. Ten of these were feeble-minded and unable to earn

satisfactory livings or conform to moral standards when outside of the institution. Yet the superintendent had no authority to prevent them from leaving the Infirmary at any time they wished.

3. Several inmates had made a practice of leaving the Infirmary at intervals, only to return after a few weeks. One feeble-minded woman had been admitted five times. On two of these occasions she was pregnant. Both of her children were feeble-minded and one was a deformed imbecile who will be dependent on the public all his life.

4. Two of the most important family groups in the Infirmary, members of which had been inmates through several generations, were found to belong to feeble-minded strains.

II. The Children's Home

1. Feeble-Minded in the Home During the winter of 1915–16, 93 children in the Children's Home were given formal intelligence tests by Mr. Charles E. Skinner who very kindly placed all of his material in the hands of the investigator.

Dr. Thomas H. Haines visited the same Children's Home on December 18th and 19th, 1916, and made mental examinations of 25 of the 101 children then in the home. The 25 children were chosen by the matron as possibly feeble-minded. Of these ten, or 9.9% of the total population of the Home, were found to be feeble-minded. When one compares this with the proportion of public school children in the county found to be feeble-minded, it appears that there was five times as much feeble-mindedness among the dependent children of this county as among the children in the public schools.

Attempts were made to secure family histories for the feeble-minded children in the Home, but in most cases this was unsuccessful because of the death or disappearance of parents. In a surprising number of cases, one or both were still living; but many of them, free from the responsibility of caring for their children, were living more or less unsettled lives and so were difficult to locate. What information was obtained from the superintendent of the Home, township trustees, and distant relatives seemed to point towards the fact that, although some were there because their parents were dead, most of them had been sent to the Home because of alcoholism, sexual immorality, or some instability of character on the part of one or both parents.

2. Family History of One Group of Children in the Home The most interesting group of children in the Home for whom a complete history was obtainable was one consisting of two sisters, a brother and a niece. The sisters tested feeble-minded but the brother was of low normal intelligence. The niece, only four years old, was decidedly backward in development. She was the illegitimate child of the oldest girl in the fraternity of seven. This girl, 20 years old, is now an inmate of a State Hospital where her case has been diagnosed as dementia praecox. She was transferred to the Hospital from the Infirmary where she had been taken in November, 1915, with her second illegitimate baby, then only a few days old. The child was blind as a result of gonorrheal infection and died at six weeks. It is asserted that the girl's father was also the father of this child. The second in the fraternity was a 19-year-old girl in the County Infirmary, undoubtedly feeble-minded and so immoral sexually that she had to be watched constantly. The third and fourth in the fraternity, girls of seventeen and fourteen, were inmates of the Girls' Industrial Home where they were sent for immorality. The older of these was an imbecile with the mentality of a six-year-old child but the younger possessed low normal intelligence. Both were given intelligence tests on their admission to the Girls' Industrial Home. The other three children in the fraternity were the three in the Children's Home.

The mother of this fraternity died in 1914 in childbirth. She was slovenly and inclined to hysterical attacks. Definite information bearing on her mentality could not be obtained, but it was evidently much below the average in her family, for her people were in general respected citizens of good intelligence. She had two alcoholic brothers, an insane half-sister and two cousins, one insane and one epileptic.

The father of the fraternity was a man almost forty-five years old. He never got out of the primary grades in school and by the time he was eighteen years old was a hard drinker of whiskey, used tobacco to excess, and was known to have immoral sexual habits. He was considered mentally defective by many people, but others insisted that he was a good farm hand and worked well in a section gang. However, he had never been able to support his family adequately. When interviewed he showed a decided tremor of the hands, and at intervals the perspiration would start out on his forehead. He was unable to marshal his ideas in good order, gave detached pieces of information, and was more apt to answer some previous question than the one just put to him.

He had had a brother who was said to have been like him. This brother was the father of the seventeen-year-old idiot in the County Infirmary. A sister had a daughter who seemed intelligent but was a deaf mute. The mother of the two brothers and sister was sexually immoral as a young woman, but was not defective mentally.

The unusual thing about this family was that every one of the seven in the fraternity was being cared for by the public and although four of the seven were feeble-minded, not one of the four was in an appropriate institution. And unless room could be found for them at the Institution for Feeble-minded, three of them would be turned back into the community at the expiration of certain age limits.*

The problem of the feeble-minded child in the Children's Home is a serious one which in the past has been badly neglected. Feeble-minded children have been placed in families, unwittingly as a usual thing, but nevertheless negligently, or else they have been discharged as having reached the age limit. On a later page will be found an account of some feeble-minded adults who were placed out from county homes as children and the harm they have wrought in their communities. An effort has recently been made, however, to determine all feeble-minded in this Children's Home by means of psychological tests, and to have them removed to the Institution for the Feeble-minded.

3. Summary

1. At least 9.9 percent of the population of the Children's Home in this county was feeble-minded.

2. Proportionately five times as much feeble-mindedness was found among the dependent children in the Children's Home of this county as there was among the public school children of the same county.

3. An attempt has been made to determine the feeble-minded children in this Children's Home and have them removed to the Institution for the Feeble-minded.

E. FEEBLE-MINDED AT LARGE IN THE COUNTY

I. In the Public Schools

1. *Method Employed in the School Room* In the rural districts of the county 247 teachers were interviewed in 166 school buildings, and in the two cities, 50 teachers were interviewed in 6 different buildings, making a total of 172 schools visited and 297 teachers interviewed, or practically every grade teacher in the county.

---

* The two feeble-minded sisters and their niece have recently been committed to the Institution for Feeble-minded from the Children's Home, but the sister with the six-year mentality at the Girls' Industrial Home was paroled. After a few months, the report came that she was causing trouble by her activities in the vicinity of the National Army Camp. She was returned to the Industrial Home, found to be pregnant, and is now in a hospital awaiting the birth of her baby.

The general method employed was the choosing from the school register names of children three years or more retarded in their work. Each one of these, together with others suggested by the teachers as particular problems, was individually considered. Inquiry was made concerning ability in the principal mental functions, such as motor co-ordination, perception, memory, judgment, and reasoning ability. Anatomical anomalies and facial expression were noted and the developmental history obtained whenever possible. Information was obtained concerning the child's activity on the play ground and behavior with his playmates, and it was determined whether he had some particular ability along a practical line which was not brought out by the influence of the school room. In short, all his reactions were considered with the question always in mind as to whether he had sufficient mental equipment to keep him up to the level of the demands of the community in which he would probably spend his life, and to make it possible for him to maintain an independent existence.

2. *Number of Feeble-Minded in the School Population. Distribution in Rural and Urban Districts* Judged on this basis, 164 children, or 1.8 percent of the total school population were found to be feeble-minded and 77 other cases, because of possible further development, were classified as borderline. Of these 164 cases, the larger proportion were found in the country schools. As shown in Table IV, 2.1 percent of the children in the rural schools were found to be of defective intelligence while only 0.8 percent were found feeble-minded in the city schools.

Table IV. Distribution of Feeble-Minded School Children in Rural and Urban Districts

District.	Number of Children Enrolled.	Feeble-minded.		Total.	Percent of Total Enrollment.	Borderline and Suspected Cases.
		High Grade.	Low Grade.			
Urban	2002	9	8	17	0.84%	8
Rural	6928	86	61	147	2.1 %	69
Total	8930	95	69	164	1.83%	77

An attempt has been made to divide these feeble-minded children into two classes, high and low grades, though it is recognized that any division made in the absence of formal tests is entirely arbitrary. Those classified as low grade are those who will probably never be able to take care of themselves in any sort of environment, while those classified as high grade are those who will be able to take care of themselves, after a fashion, when conditions are most favorable, but who nevertheless will always need some wiser hand to guide them.

3. Degree of Retardation of the Feeble-Minded in the Schools Table V shows the one hundred and sixty-four feeble-minded children arranged according to their ages and school grades. The sixteen-year-old boy in the sixth grade was in the grade because of his age and not because of his ability. He had been unable to absorb the subjects taught since he reached the fourth grade. When fourteen years and four months old he tested nine years old mentally by the Yerkes-Bridges Point Scale. The twelve-year-old boy in the fifth grade had not been able to learn to read and would forget what he learned from day to day. His teacher said that he should have been put back in the second grade. He had a speech defect, his manner was surly, and he would seldom talk except with those he knew very well. The thirteen-year-old girl in the same grade could do nothing in arithmetic and was dull in all other subjects. She had a perfectly blank expression and when left to herself would walk aimlessly about the room. She was recognized by her mother as defective. The fourteen-year-old boy could do nothing in subjects requiring reasoning ability and was very poor in memory work. He had in addition several anti-social habits already developed. Neither could the fifteen-year-old boy do the work of the grade. He liked to draw and passed in papers decorated with carefully drawn borders but the general quality of the work he did was poor. His uncle said that he was "no good to work" and his schoolmates refused to play with him because of his sluggishness and peculiar behavior. So that whereas the usual child who has advanced to the fifth grade or beyond must

Table V. Feeble-Minded in Public Schools by Grades and Ages Showing Amount of Retardation

Grades.	Ages.													Total.
	6 Yrs.	7 Yrs.	8 Yrs.	9 Yrs.	10 Yrs.	11 Yrs.	12 Yrs.	13 Yrs.	14 Yrs.	15 Yrs.	16 Yrs.	17 Yrs.	18 Yrs.	
1	1	4	11	10	8	10	5	3	3	1	1	—	—	57
2	—	—	—	5	7	10	11	6	7	4	1	—	1	52
3	—	—	—	1	—	1	7	8	10	2	2	—	1	32
4	—	—	—	—	—	2	2	4	4	5	1	—	—	18
5	—	—	—	—	—	—	1	1	1	1	—	—	—	4
6	—	—	—	—	—	—	—	—	—	—	1	—	—	1
Total	1	4	11	16	15	23	26	22	25	13	6	—	2	164

have enough mental ability to take care of himself in the world, these five children, although graded in the upper grades, had neither the ability to do the work of the grades nor would they ever be able to adequately take care of themselves.

In the same way, for the usual six or seven-year-old to be graded in the first grade is not out of place, but the six-year-old in Table V was feeble-minded by psychological test and the four seven-year-olds were decidedly defective. One of them did not walk until he was four years old and at seven years had a vocabulary of very few words. He was a mouth breather, although both his adenoids and tonsils had been removed. And it seemed impossible for him to concentrate on any one thing for more than a few seconds at a time. The remaining three all had serious speech defects and although in their second years in school, had made no progress. One of them did not understand when spoken to and could not even go in the direction he was told to go. Another one of these did not know how to play with other children but stood about on the play ground disinterestedly watching the others. The teacher said of the third pupil that although he had been in school two years he was not yet able to recognize the letter "a" when he saw it. So that we seem justified in calling these four seven-year-olds feeble-minded.

If it were possible to give descriptions of all of the children here classified as feeble-minded, no doubt would remain as to their mental defect. Not one of them should have been in classes with normal children, but rather in special classes or in an institution where they would be receiving suitable training and, as they grow older, be properly segregated.

4. *Special Study of Two District Schools* It early became evident that the feeble-minded children were not distributed evenly through the schools of the county. Certain districts had a much larger proportion than others. A special study was made of two district schools located in different townships where a large proportion of defectives was found. Each child in the two schools was given a psychological intelligence test by Miss Alida C. Bowler, Mental Examiner of the Bureau of Juvenile Research. A revised Binet-Simon Year Scale was used for the younger children and the Yerkes-Bridges Point Scale for the older ones.

In school district A there were thirteen children enrolled. Table VI gives in detail the grades, ages, and ratings of the thirteen children according to the tests given. The coefficient of mental ability (C. M. A.) is obtained in each case by dividing the score made by the child by the average score attained by children of that age in an ordinary school population. It is really the rating expressed in terms of percentage. The fourteen-year-old

Table VI. Children in School A by Grade, Age, and Mentality

	School Grade.	Chrono-logical Age Yrs. Mos.	Point Scale.		Year Scale.	C.M.A.	Diagnosis.	General Facts.
			Points.	Mental Age in Years.	Mental Age in Years.			
1 Girl	I	5– 7	——	——	?	?	Not feeble-minded	——
2 Girl	I	5	——	——	?	?	Borderline	Sister of Nos. 3 and 6 Cousin of No. 11
3 Girl	I	6–10	——	——	4.9	.72	Borderline	Sister of Nos. 2 and 6 Cousin of No. 11
4 Boy	I	9	——	——	6.4	.71	Feeble-minded	Brother of No. 7 Belongs to Hickory Family
5 Boy	II	8	——	——	7.2	.90	Not feeble-minded	——
6 Boy	II	12	——	——	7.5	.62	Feeble-minded	First cousin of No. 11
7 Boy	III	14– 7	48	8.5	——	.59	Feeble-minded	Brother of No. 4. Thieving habits. Belongs to Hickory Family
8 Girl	III	12– 2	45	8.3	——	.58	Feeble-minded	Confused at all but simplest questions. Has been in Children's Home
9 Boy	IV	10– 5	——	——	9.2	.88	Not feeble-minded	Has imbecilic half-sister
10 Boy	IV	9– 2	——	——	8.6	.93	Not feeble-minded	——
11 Boy	IV	13	46	8.3	——	.58	Feeble-minded	First cousin of Nos. 2, 3, and 6
12 Boy	IV	15– 2	49	8.5	——	.59	Feeble-minded	Epileptic. Older sister feeble-minded. Mother epileptic. Marriage of parents forced when father 17 years old
13 Boy	VII	14	Not	tested	——	——	Not feeble-minded	——

boy in the seventh grade was absent and so was not tested, but according to the testimony of his teacher was of normal intelligence. Definite mental ages could not be obtained for the two five-year-olds because of their shyness, but a diagnosis was made on the basis of their behavior and the performance of part of the tests.

District A was one of the earliest mining villages in the county, but the mine has been exhausted for several years and most of the inhabitants have moved where there is better opportunity for employment. Four of the nine families represented in this school were receiving township aid.

The results of the tests in district A are summarized as follows:

Feeble-minded	6	46%
Borderline	2	15%
Normal	5	38%
Total	13	99%

In district school B, thirty-one children were examined aged from six to sixteen years, none of whom had been able to get beyond the fourth grade in school. Several of these children did not know their own ages and because of the impossibility of conducting all of the tests without disturbance from other members of the school, exact mental ages could not be secured in all cases. The detailed grading of the thirty-one children is shown in Table VII and the summary of the results is as follows:

Feeble-minded	13	42%
Borderline	8	26%
Normal	10	32%
Total	31	100%

District B differs from district A in that it is a rural community with the homes set at a distance from each other, located in a remote valley between two high ridges. Many of the inhabitants own small tracts of land worth little for agricultural purposes, and work in the mines. The families in the valley have seldom mated with families in other communities, but as yet there have been no consanguineous marriages.

Nos. 9, 14, 17 and 22 in Table VII, all feeble-minded, were brothers and sisters. All four had speech defects and not one of them could tell his age or anything about himself. No. 22 had such poor motor co-ordination that she walked with difficulty. No. 14 had a small low head and prominent ears. Neither of these two children had made the slightest progress in school. No. 17 made the best appearance of the four, but none of them were profiting in any way by the ordinary school subjects which the

Table VII. Children in School B by Grade, Age, and Mentality

	School Grade.	Chrono-logical Age Yrs. Mos.	Point Scale.		Year Scale.	C.M.A.	Diagnosis.
			Points.	Mental Age in Years.	Mental Age in Years.		
1 Girl	I	7– 7	——	——	7.	.93	Not feeble-minded
2 Boy	I	6	——	——	5.2	.86	Not feeble-minded
3 Girl	I	6	——	——	6.	1.00	Not feeble-minded
4 Boy	I	6	——	——	5.2	.86	Not feeble-minded
5 Boy	I	6	——	——	4.	.66	Borderline
6 Boy	I	8	——	——	6.	.75	Borderline
7 Boy	I	9	——	——	7.6	.80	Borderline
8 Girl	I	8– 6	——	——	6.4	.75	Borderline
9 Boy	I	8	——	——	5.4	.67	Feeble-minded
10 Boy	I	6	——	——	4.	.66	Feeble-minded
11 Girl	I	9	——	——	6.+	.66	Feeble-minded
12 Girl	I	9+	——	——	6.	.66	Feeble-minded
13 Girl	I	11	——	——	7.	.63	Feeble-minded
14 Boy	I	14	——	——	6.	.42	Feeble-minded
15 Boy	II	11– 3	——	——	7.8	.69	Borderline
16 Boy	II	10	——	——	6.	.60	Feeble-minded
17 Girl	II	13	——	——	8.	.61	Feeble-minded
18 Boy	III	9–11	——	——	8.8	.88	Not feeble-minded
19 Boy	III	11–	——	——	9.	.81	Not feeble-minded
20 Girl	III	11– 4	——	——	7.8	.69	Borderline
21 Boy	III	13– 1	57	9.1	——	.71	Borderline
22 Girl	III	15?	21	5.8	——	.25	Feeble-minded
23 Boy	III	14– 3	44	8.2	——	.54	Feeble-minded
24 Boy	III	13	46	8.3	——	.58	Feeble-minded
25 Girl	IV	10– 2	——	——	9.2	.91	Not feeble-minded
26 Boy	IV	14– 2	64	10.7	——	.79	Not feeble-minded
27 Boy	IV	14– 1	63	10.	——	.77	Not feeble-minded
28 Boy	IV	13– 5	62	10.	——	.78	Not feeble-minded
29 Boy	IV	13– 5	59	9.5	——	.74	Borderline
30 Girl	IV	15– 9	44	8.2	——	.52	Feeble-minded
31 Boy	IV	15– 2	46	8.3	——	.56	Feeble-minded

teacher was attempting to teach them. They belonged to a fraternity of ten, one of whom died at six years. A younger child not yet in school had a serious speech defect. An older brother, eighteen years old, who according to his own father was not as bright as he should be, was in the Boys' Industrial School where he had been sent for driving his mother out of the house at the point of a gun while drunk. Another brother was married but was entirely unable to provide for himself, to say nothing of his wife. "He never could learn," and was a heavy drinker. An older sister who was said to be of fair intelligence had married a man from the same valley, and an older brother was working in another county. The father of this family was a periodic drinker who became dangerously insane when drunk. His mentality was low, he was very pompous and talkative, had a narrow forehead, sunken temples and the general appearance of an alcoholic. He was said to have been a good worker when sober. His wife belonged to one of the valley strains, was a high grade defective and had a speech defect.

Nos. 23, 24 and 30, all feeble-minded, and Nos. 5, 7, 8, and 20, all borderline cases, belong in the same fraternity. All of these children would steal little things in the school room such as pencils or lunch from the boxes of the other children, and the three oldest had uncontrollable tempers. No. 30 would become so angry that she would make herself physically sick. This girl also showed a strong sex instinct. There had been fifteen in the whole fraternity of whom fourteen, ranging in age from twenty-five to three years, were living. There seemed little doubt that the four older brothers and an older sister were all high grade feeble-minded. The boys were all drinkers and the girl had an illegitimate baby. Both parents were rough looking specimens, were drinkers and petty thieves. It was said of the father, "He gets in jail every time he goes to town." He worked irregularly in the mine but supported his family largely from his garden and what township aid he could secure. The mother was of a lower grade of mentality than he, though both may be classed as high grade defectives. Both were sullen and quarrelsome with uncontrollable tempers. They were bringing up their children to be thieves and drunkards and with no idea of restraining their own desires or regard for the rights of others. Their three room house was occupied by eighteen people. Neither parent was in any way related to the other families in the valley.

Nos. 12 and 16, both feeble-minded, were brother and sister. No. 16 could not speak plainly, stuttered, was very slow and could not keep his attention on any one thing for long. His sister did not appear so defective but accomplished practically nothing in school. Their father was passably intelligent, but their mother was feeble-minded and had been a bad character. She had an epileptic brother, and No. 21, classified as of borderline mentality, was her half-brother. Another half-brother in the same school, No. 18, proved to be of normal intelligence.

Nos. 11 and 13, feeble-minded sisters, No. 28, a borderline case, and No. 2 a normal boy were first cousins of the mother of Nos. 12 and 16 on their father's side. Their mother was of fair intelligence but their father was of defective mentality, alcoholic, and a thief. He would not be able to make a living if it were not for the help of his mother's pension. No. 13 had an unsteady gait and could not seem to hold anything in her hand. Her head twitched constantly and she would never play with the other children.

No. 10, a feeble-minded boy, belonged to another defective strain. He was not a bad looking child but could understand only the simplest questions. His father had an imbecile sister and his mother had a brother who was an epileptic idiot with a cleft palate. Both families were living in the valley. The men in his mother's family were all heavy drinkers and his grandfather was shot while on a drunken spree. His great-grandfather died insane and his great-grandmother, who was still living, belonged to a weak-minded strain which had lived on the ridge bordering the valley under discussion for many years. She had two low grade imbecile nephews about forty-five years old, a feeble-minded sister who had two imbecile children sixteen and twenty years old, and an idiot grand-child, living near her. This child, No. 10, had two cousins, Nos. 25 and 26, one on her father's side and the other on her mother's, in the same school, but both seemed to be of good mentality. The mother of one of these belonged to the same family as the father of Nos. 11, 13, 28 and 2.

No. 31, a high grade feeble-minded boy, was not related to any of the other families in the valley and had lived there but a short time when the tests were given. Nothing was learned of his family history except that his father was of German extraction. Neither were the four brothers, Nos. 4, 6, 15 and 27, two borderline cases and two normal, connected in any way with the families of the valley. The same is true of the four remaining children, all of whom tested normal.

There were twelve family names in this school of thirty-one children. The nine children just described, but one of whom was feeble-minded, belonged to five different families and may be set aside as in no way connected with the other groups. The remaining twenty-two children had seven family names, each one of which stood for a defective strain. And members of five of these families had married back and forth freely.

5. Summary

1. One and eight tenths percent (1.8%) of the school population of the county studied was feeble-minded.

2. In the rural districts of the county two and one tenth percent (2.1%), and in the cities eight tenths of one percent (0.8%) of the school population was feeble-minded.

3. Certain districts had larger proportions of defectives than others as shown by the special study of two district schools where over forty percent of the school population was found to be feeble-minded.

II. Feeble-Minded in the General Population

1. Number of Feeble-Minded at Large in the County There were found at large in the county 494 feeble-minded persons, including school children, or 9.0 feeble-minded persons to every thousand of the whole population. Three hundred and seven of these were seen by the field worker and in the cases of the remaining 187, reliable descriptions of behavior were obtained so that there was full justification of the diagnosis. Over two hundred homes were visited in the course of the investigation and many suspected cases interviewed which did not prove to be feeble-minded. Cards with a short social and heredity history of each of the 494 feeble-minded are on file at the office of the Bureau of Juvenile Research in addition to which there are 496 other cards with similar information on the inmates of the county institutions and such anti-social persons or probable cases of feeble-minded as were brought to the attention of the field worker. If a system is ever perfected by which the state can exercise control of the feeble-minded at large, or if the time comes when attention is paid to the heredity of applicants for marriage licenses, this index will be invaluable.

2. Sex and Age of the Feeble-Minded As shown in Table VIII, the total number of feeble-minded at large in the county was found to consist of 303 males and 191 females. The proportion of males to females is approximately as 3 to 2.

It will be seen that the age-groups 6 to 10 years and 11 to 15 years contain a larger number of defectives than any other groups. This is probably largely due to the fact that children of those ages, because of their presence in the public school, were surveyed more carefully than it was possible to survey the whole population. The number under six years is small for two reasons; that only the more serious forms of defect may be recognized in young children, and also that the cases of such young children are not so apt to be generally known. From the 11 to 15 years age-group on, there is a gradual decrease in the number in each group. This can be explained by the probability that defectives who have no one to care for them and have not found some position in life where their efforts to maintain themselves can be guided, have either died in the natural process of elimination of the unfit or else have been sent to institutions before reaching the more advanced ages. It is important to note that larger numbers are included in the childbearing ages between fifteen and forty-five years than in the ages beyond forty-five years.

Table VIII. The Feeble-Minded Arranged by Age and Sex

Age.	Males.	Females.	Total.
Under 6 years	6	5	11
6 to 10 years	60	30	90
11 to 15 years	73	47	120
16 to 20 years	29	21	50
21 to 25 years	28	17	45
26 to 30 years	17	15	32
31 to 35 years	15	13	28
36 to 40 years	19	10	29
41 to 45 years	18	8	26
46 to 50 years	12	6	18
51 to 55 years	9	8	17
56 to 60 years	7	3	10
61 to 65 years	3	4	7
66 to 70 years	2	1	3
71 to 75 years	3	2	5
76 to 80 years	1	1	2
81 to 85 years	1	—	1
Total	303	191	494

3. *Nativity and Race of the Feeble-Minded* In regard to the nativity of the 494 feeble-minded persons, 457 of them were born in Ohio and 371 of these, or 75% of the total number were born in the county in which they are now living. Only 17 were born in other states. In 18 cases no record of the place of birth was obtained. But two of the feeble-minded persons were foreign born, and both came to America as small children. Seven persons were the native-born children of foreign-born parents and eleven others had one parent foreign born. This makes a total of 18 who were native-born of foreign or mixed parentage or 3.6% of the whole number of defectives. According to the 1910 census 9.2% of the population of the county were of foreign or mixed parentage at that time. The same census gives 5.3% of the population of the county as foreign born, while only 2 of the 494 feeble-minded persons or 0.2% were foreign born. So that feeble-mindedness was much less common among the foreign born and those of foreign and mixed parentage than it was among the native population in this county.

Thirteen of the 494 persons were negroes. In 1910, 2.6% of the population of the county were negroes and thirteen is just 2.6% of 494. So that there was no bigger proportion of feeble-mindedness among the negroes in this county than among the whites.

The county was settled in the pioneer days first by families from New England and later from Pennsylvania and New York. The families of a large proportion of the defectives now in the county can be traced back to the pioneers from these states. The progenitor of one bad strain was brought to Ohio as a servant in the family of one of the pioneers.

Another group, not so large, came from West Virginia stock. Some of these families, however, stayed in West Virginia only a few years in the course of their transit from the eastern states to Ohio. Another group, smaller yet, had come into the county more recently from Kentucky to work in the mines. Therefore, neither the negro race nor recent immigration could be blamed for the large number of defectives in the county, but rather the deterioration of the native stock or else the perpetuation of the mental defects of the old stock.

4. *Consanguinity* In general there did not seem to be a large amount of consanguinity in the country except in the Hickory family of which a description is given on a later page. In 55, or 11% of the cases, there existed some consanguinity in the parents. In three cases the parents were father and daughter, in one case brother and sister, in five cases double first cousins, in twenty-six cases first cousins, in seven cases first cousins once removed, and in thirteen cases second cousins.

5. *Distribution of the Feeble-Minded* Table IX shows that the feeble-minded were just twice as numerous proportionately in the country as in the city districts. Competition is not so high in the country and defectives can live in shanties where they will not have to pay any rent or in some hut in the woods or back on the hills where there is little interference with their primitive mode of life. They gather wood from the hillsides or else use bone coal, discarded at the mines, for fuel. One such family burned the rail fences on the farm where they were "squatting," much to the anger of the owner. Food is also easier to procure in the country when one has no money to buy.

Table IX. Distribution of the Feeble-Minded in Rural and Urban Districts

Districts.	Estimated Population. U. S. Census July 1, 1916.	Feeble-Minded.				Percent of Total Population.
		Moron.	Imbecile.	Idiot.	Total.	
Rural	40,921	295	107	18	420	.010
Urban	13,468	52	19	3	74	.005
Total	54,389	347	126	21	494	.009

Table X. Distribution of Feeble-Minded in County by Townships

Townships.	Estimated Population. U. S. Census Bureau July 1, 1916.	Feeble-Minded.				Percent of Total Population.
		Moron.	Imbecile.	Idiot.	Total.	
1	1,042	5	2	—	7	.006
2	1,123	3	1	—	4	.003
3	12,850	48	14	1	63	.004
4	1,326	12	3	2	17	.012
5	1,189	9	4	—	13	.010
6	980	5	—	—	5	.005
7	4,835	43	11	1	55	.011
8	985	6	1	2	9	.009
9	1,128	6	3	—	9	.007
10	1,474	12	6	2	20	.013
11	9,876	105	45	7	157	.015
12	1,688	13	2	1	16	.009
13	3,138	18	8	1	27	.008
14	12,755	62	26	4	92	.007
Total	54,389	347	126	21	494	.009

Table X shows the distribution of the feeble-minded in the various townships of the county. Township 11, almost exclusively a mining community, had the biggest proportion of feeble-minded, 15 to every thousand. There are in the township two good sized villages and numerous small mining villages. It is the township where the geographical barriers are greatest and what is probably resultant, it is the home of the Hickory family, a prolific and highly inbred family of defectives. Forty-eight feeble-minded members of the Hickory family were found living in this one township.

Townships 4, 5, 7 and 10, all of which had a proportion of defectives higher than the average for the whole county, are all mining centers with the exception of No. 10. This township has two mining villages in the northern part, many poor farms and a few good ones through the central part, and very steep hills entirely unsuited for agriculture in the southern part. The proportion of defectives in township No. 10 was 13 to every 1000, nearly as large a proportion as in township 11. Township No. 4, which had the next highest proportion of feeble-minded, 12 to every 1000, has quite as steep hills as township 11. Township 7 also included members of several Hickory families. Township 14 is of the same geographical character and is a mining center as well, but the largest city in the county is situated there, so the proportion of defectives for the township as a whole was not as low as it might otherwise have been. Townships 7, 11 and 14 include the greater part of the mining industry of the county and the three together had a proportion of 11 feeble-minded to every 1000.

Township No. 2 which had the smallest proportion of defectives, 3 to every 1000, is a prosperous agricultural community where the best land in the county for farming purposes is situated. Townships 1, 6, 8 and 9 are the other good agricultural districts and none of them showed a proportion of feeble-minded higher than the general proportion for the whole county. When the feeble-minded found in the five purely agricultural townships are added together, the proportion is 6 to every 1000 of the population, a little more than half as many as were found in the mining districts. The explanation is probably that the mines are situated in that part of the county where the physical barriers are greatest, thus limiting selection of mates and so lessening the chances of eliminating the defects already existing in the families living in these districts; also that the feeble-minded find it easier to exist in the mining districts than in the agricultural, because there are large tracts of land belonging to the coal companies which they occupy sometimes for a small rent and very often for no rent at all; because they are allowed to work in the mines just when they feel so inclined; and also because a high grade feeble-minded man can work in the mine under the direction of his brother or father and earn more money than he can on a farm.

6. Classification of the Feeble-Minded According to Degree of Mentality
Tables IX and X have classified the feeble-minded according to their grade of mentality. Twenty-one of the 494 feeble-minded persons were idiots of whom the youngest was four years old and the oldest thirty-two. All were heavy burdens on their families because of their entire lack of ability to care for themselves. One, a boy of four years, was a hydrocephalic whose parents had tried to have him committed to the Institution for the Feeble-minded but were told that there was no room. This child's mother also had to care for her sister, a low grade imbecile, who had never been committed to an institution because of sentiment for their mother who requested that she never be sent away from home. Consequently two other apparently normal children in the family were receiving scant attention, as their mother's time was completely taken up with the care of the two defectives and cooking for several farm hands. The heredity history of this hydrocephalic idiot is interesting. His head was unusually large and he could not raise it from the pillow. He was also subject to convulsions. He had a normal twin, a girl, and a normal older sister. Both parents seemed

to have average intelligence. The father had an alcoholic, epileptic brother. The mother had the imbecile sister above spoken of, a brother who was a successful lawyer, and another brother of fair mentality who had married a colored woman. The mother's father had had a brother who died at thirteen years of "some sort of fits," and a hydrocephalic cousin who, they stated, lived to be fifty years old. The mother's mother had a feeble-minded cousin and a niece who was a moron and grossly immoral.

The only other one who was different from the ordinary idiot was a male, twenty years old, whose intelligence was so low that he could not take anything in his hand, could not raise his head, could not pronounce even the simplest syllable. His mentality was no higher than that of a new-born baby. His body was badly twisted and emaciated, and he was less than four feet long. The only movement of which he was capable was rolling his head and uttering a weak little cry. His father had been a full blooded negro and his mother was half white, a quarter Indian, and a quarter negro. It is very probable that this creature's condition is due to congenital syphilis, although the story that the mother had been terribly beaten and kicked by the father two months previous to the child's birth was given credence by one physician. The mother was receiving frequent township aid and thought she ought to receive a mother's pension. She did not know and had never been told of the existence of the Institution for the Feeble-Minded.

Two of the idiots were also epileptic and one of these had a cleft palate.

From the social standpoint the idiots are of little importance because they are too helpless and have too small minds to do any harm in the community.

In Tables IX and X those school children who are classified as low grade are included as imbeciles and those classified as high grade are put with the morons. There were found in the county 126 imbeciles, all entirely unable to earn their own livings because of their mental defect, and 347 morons who were able to exist under the most propitious circumstances but were unable to maintain themselves satisfactorily without guidance.

7. Anti-Social Traits of the Imbeciles and Morons The imbeciles and morons are those who endanger the social health of a community. There were 20 imbeciles and 152 morons who possessed traits already developed which made them undesirable members of the ordinary community. All of the others might be called potentially undesirable, for the feeble-minded as a class lack good judgment and are easily influenced. Seven imbeciles and 15 morons were also epileptic and for that reason alone unfit to be at large. Following are some individual cases of imbeciles and morons who exhibited anti-social tendencies, presented as they were originally reported. An attempt has been made at classification but it is evident that there is much overlapping.

Table XI. Imbeciles and Morons Showing Anti-Social Traits

	Imbeciles.			Morons.		
	Men.	Women.	Total.	Men.	Women.	Total.
Epileptics	3	4	7	10	5	15
Alcoholics	1	—	1	28	5	33
Sex Offenders	2	5	7	9	43	52
Criminals	1	—	1	33	2	35
Wanderers	—	1	1	5	4	9
Syphilitics	1	2	3	5	3	8
Total	8	12	20	90	62	152

ALCOHOLICS

Case 1—Male, 36 years old. Moron. Left school at 15 years. Then in second grade. Cannot write. Constant smile. Childlike responses. Works irregularly in mine. Hard drinker. In court for fighting and drunkenness. Steals and bootlegs. Dependent on township. Has wife and two children. Oldest child is feeble-minded.

Case 2—Female, 47 years old. Moron. Never went to school. Cannot read or write. Smokes and chews. Drinks, fights, and carouses. Begs on the streets. Has a terrible temper. Married. Has had seven children, one a low grade imbecile, two others feeble-minded, one child who looks bright, one dead, and two others away from home.

Case 3—Male, 40 years old. Moron. Went to school several years, but cannot read or write. Shifting eyes. Narrow head. Can work only under direct supervision of a boss and then is unsatisfactory. Hard drinker. "Tough." Recently shot in a drunken row with another man over his wife. Has had eight children. Three died in infancy, two are feeble-minded and another is borderline. Two others are away from home.

Case 4—Male, 46 years old. Imbecile. Small brain space. Protruding ears. Constant silly smile. Never went to school. Cannot read or write. Understands only simplest questions. Seldom tries to work. Drinks when given opportunity. A physician said of him, "He exists, not lives. He hasn't mind enough to live." Supported largely by the township. Is father of at least one child.

SEX OFFENDERS

Case 5—Female, 25 years old. Low grade imbecile. Asymmetrical face. Went to school two years. Cannot read or write. Cannot tell about her mother or fraternity. Cannot dress herself without help. Does not understand an ordinary conversation. Does not know enough to support herself in any way except by prostitution. Lived three years in an immoral house in another county. Lived in one several months in this county. Begs and solicits on the streets. Had an illegitimate child born dead. Married a feeble-minded man who left her. Now living on charity.

Case 6—Female, 18 years old. Low grade imbecile. Never allowed to go to school. Sways from side to side. Family was forced to move from another town because girl was so often seen on street with several disreputable men following her. Has a two-months old baby whom she has tried to kill.

Case 7—Female, 36 years old. Moron. Can read, but not write. Very talkative. Told all her most intimate affairs with greatest simplicity and childlike trust. Could not tell ages of her children. Once cleaned all shanties in a small mining village and took turns living with the various men while she did it. Has had six children, two born dead, two died in infancy, two now living, older feeble-minded, younger possibly so. Married twice.

Case 8—Female, 15 years old. Moron. In second grade at 13 years. At that time tested 8 years old mentally in test given by school superintendent. Dull, drowsy, awkward. Inflamed and discharging eyes. Bad sexual habits. Acquired syphilis. Parents of school children object to having her in the public school.

Case 9—Female, 20 years old. Imbecile. Defect thought to be due to scarlet fever. Can go to the store on errands. Mother had a man arrested for rape on her, but girl testified it was done with her consent, so man was discharged by court. Parents would send her to Institution for the Feeble-Minded if she would be admitted.

Case 10—Female, 30 years old. Moron. Cannot carry on a conversation. Works at scrubbing and cleaning. Is away from home for days at a time. Often spends the night beside the railroad tracks and says she has been with as many as sixteen men in one night. Says she has been married four times, but is divorced from each husband. Has had three children. Two died in infancy. One living is bright.

Case 11—Male, 33 years old. Imbecile. Cannot read or write. Stunted growth. Asymmetrical face. Does no work. Complains that he can find no one to marry him. Neighbors do not allow their wives and daughters on the roads near his shanty because he has attacked several women. No one has ever tried to put him in an institution.

CRIMINALS

Case 12—Male, 31 years old. Moron. Is generally spoken of as "a natural thief." Steals anything he finds whether he has any use for it or not. Has "ugly spells" and vicious sexual habits. Absolutely unreliable. Generally considered defective. Moves frequently. Married a feeble-minded girl and has two children.

Case 13—Male, 30 years old. Moron. Never got beyond the first grade in school. Always plagued by his schoolmates. Works in mine. Could not make a living for himself before he was married. Now has wife and three children. Lives mostly on township aid and private charity. Steals little things such as wood, eggs, vegetables, etc.

WANDERERS

Case 14—Female, 28 years old. Probably a moron. Wanders about Southern Ohio, living with various men in old shanties. Has been known to live in a cave. Appears in her father's home every few months. Said by all who know her to be a low grade feeble-minded person. Has had three children whose whereabouts are unknown.

Case 15—Male, 20 years old. Moron. Tramps through river counties, staying in "hobo camps." Appears periodically in his home town. Is used by the Chief of Police in tracing gangs and hidden loot. Will tell all he knows for a quarter. Is generally regarded as defective. Is known that he steals, but has never been convicted.

SYPHILITICS

Case 16—Female, 30 years old. Moron. Never been to school. Could not add four and thirty. Stunted growth. Sexually immoral. Dirty. Syphilitic abcess on back. Inflamed and discharging eyes. Has a 12-year-old daughter in Ohio Hospital for Epileptics.

Case 17—Male, 62 years old. Moron. Can read print, but not writing. Cannot write. Makes axe handles. A petty thief. Receives township aid. Says he has had scrofula since a young man, but this is probably syphilis. Has running sores on his legs. Is lame. Has had two sons, both feeble-minded and supported in Children's Home. One showed evidence of congenital syphilis.

8. Dependency of the Feeble-Minded The very nature of feeble-mindedness viewed from the sociological standpoint implies dependency. In some cases in the county the burden of supporting the feeble-minded person was borne by the family or some relative but in a large number of cases the public had to bear either all or a part of the responsibility. Two hundred and thirty-five or 47 per cent. of the 494 cases of feeble-minded found at large were being or had been partially supported by the public.

Table XII   Public Support of the Feeble-Minded

Had been resident in State institutions	11
Received pensions	7
Had been resident of County Infirmary	18
Had been resident in Children's Home	15
Had been in county jail or workhouse	11
Received county aid	2
Received township aid	140
Received private charity	16
Begged on the public streets	15
Total	235

Seven feeble-minded individuals in the county received pensions. Two were soldiers' and one soldier's widow's pensions. One was a mother's pension and three were "blind" pensions. The woman receiving a mother's pension had three children but was "not fit to take care of them" in the opinion of the township physician. She also received aid from the school board and the township trustees. Her oldest child was defective and the other two were decidedly backward in school.

The 11, 9 men and 2 women, who had been in the county jail or work-house were committed for drunkenness, petty thieving, or non-support, and in two cases for contributing to the delinquency of their children.

Of the eleven who had been in State Institutions, two were in the Institution for Feeble-Minded, two in the Ohio Hospital for Epileptics, four in the Boys' Industrial School, two in the Girls' Industrial Home, and one in the Ohio State Reformatory. Descriptions of some of these cases follow. They are presented as originally reported.

Case 18—Female, 23 years old. Probably an imbecile. Was taken from Institution for the Feeble-Minded by her people after fifteen months residence, "because she was not getting any better." Reached second grade in school. Likes to play with little children. "She cannot even wash dishes or sweep a floor." In fall of 1916 had an illegitimate baby by a feeble-minded epileptic living near their home. Child had a hare lip and died at two months. Family have now moved to get away from the feeble-minded epileptic.

Case 19—Male, 33 years old. Moron. Discharged from Institution for Feeble-Minded after seven years residence at request of mother. Is physically deformed and can do no harm in the community.

Case 20—Female, 33 years old. Moron. Reached fourth grade at fourteen years. In Girls' Industrial Home as a girl. On her discharge married a man thirty years older than she, alcoholic and reputed "not bright." They have lived in a constant state of drunkenness and carousing. "Men of all classes, niggers, tramps and all," visit their house for immoral purposes. A company of men and boys once took her to an upper room in a saloon where she danced, nude, before them all. Had a child soon after her marriage whose father was not her husband. The husband, however, proudly declares that he treats this child quite as well as he does his own. They had two children, one of whom they smothered while drunk. The conditions were reported to the Juvenile Court. The two boys were taken to the Children's Home and the parents sent to jail for a hundred days. The older boy was soon sent to the Boys' Industrial Home for incorrigibility. He would steal, was unmanageable, and would "look at you innocently and tell the most awful lies." He was in the second grade at eleven years and is probably a high grade moron. His younger brother was given a special mental test in the Children's Home and proved to be feeble-minded. In May, 1916, the older boy was paroled and sent back to his own home. When the field worker visited the home both the parents were so drunk that they had difficulty in sitting up long enough to answer the few questions which they were capable of understanding. There was no food in the house, nothing but whiskey, which was freely given to the boy. It is difficult to see what had been gained by the jail and reformatory sentences and why the boy was returned to his old environment where even a normal child could not possibly make good.

Case 21—Male, 20 years old. Imbecile. Reached second grade in school. Old teacher's register says, "Promoted because of age." Evidences of congenital syphilis. Father says he had hydrocephalus as a child, but was cured. Committed to the Boys' Industrial School for delinquency. Has since been discharged. Does no work. Hangs around village store and is made sport of by all the men and boys who frequent the place.

Case 22—Female, 55 years old. Rapidly deteriorating moron. Epileptic. Discharged from Ohio Hospital for Epileptics. All statements unreliable. Whining.

Tries to keep house for her two children, but is unable to do it satisfactorily. Is supported by township aid and small earnings of her seventeen-year-old son.

There were at least eighteen feeble-minded persons at large in the county who had been in the County Infirmary, and fifteen who had been in the County Children's Home. In practically every case, although at large, they were still living lives of complete or partial dependency. Four rather pitiful cases were found of feeble-minded adults who had been placed out from the Children's Home, and as they developed had proved to be feeble-minded, but the foster parents had become so attached to them that instead of sending them back to the Home, they assumed the burden of caring for them all their lives. A description of individual cases from the Infirmary and Children's Home follows:

Case 23—Female, 68 years old. Moron. Was taken from Children's Home as a child by a good family, who adopted her. Proved to be feeble-minded, sexually immoral and a "tough character." Was well protected by her foster parents and is now being cared for by their estate. Asymmetrical face, protruding tongue. Is becoming demented.

Case 24—Male, 21 years old. Moron. Taken from Children's Home at seven years of age. Reached fifth grade at sixteen years, but never did satisfactory work. Had the habit of stealing little things from early childhood. Cruel to animals. Cowardly. Would work for a few days for farmers, go off and spend his money for trifles, then come back to his foster home for refuge, or would send for money to come back on. Has never saved enough to buy his clothes. At the time of the visit was in County Jail awaiting trial for having stolen fifty dollars from his foster father. He left forty dollars untouched in the pocketbook. Has an unusually large head.

Case 25—Female, 42 years old. Moron. Has been in County Infirmary. When visited was living in a one room shack beside a country road with her son, also feeble-minded. Had been put out of a house as an undesirable tenant. "She keeps a bad house for the low-down trash of the community." Looks like a young girl. Is childishly curious about unimportant things. Has been arrested for drunkenness.

Case 26—Female, 45 years old. Moron. Has been in the Infirmary with her husband. Is notorious in the township as a loose character. Begs and expects charity. Openly confesses to four illegitimate children, two of whom died in infancy. Of the other two, one is feeble-minded. Has two little children by her husband. Is dirty and disgusting in appearance. Says herself she is "no good with her head."

Case 27—Male, 50 years old. Imbecile. Husband of case 26. Had been twice in the Infirmary. Once ran away from there because other inmates told him there were spooks in his room. Proudly stated that he went to school until he was twenty-one and that he had studied arithmetic and geography. Anaemic. Paid no attention to investigator until spoken to several times. Would answer something foreign to what was asked him. He and his family are supported by his wife's oldest son and township aid. Does no work.

Case 28—Female, 25 years old. Moron. In Children's Home as a child. Her oldest child, born when she was fifteen years old, feeble-minded. A second child, born in the County Infirmary, has been blind from birth. Is supported by her mother and township aid. Quarrelsome, begs, chews, smokes. One morning ran after a boy with a knife because he asked her for a chew of tobacco. Cannot read or write. Is generally reputed as "simple."

Case 29—Male, 27 years old. Imbecile. Twice in County Infirmary. Is probably syphilitic. Wanders about the township living in barns or shanties, eating fruit, berries and whatever he can easily pick up. He does whatever he is told. Boys play pranks with him, for instance, telling him to do certain things in church. Children are afraid of him. Attempt was once made to send him to the Insane Hospital, but was not accepted because not insane.

Case 30—Male, 58 years old. Moron. Placed out from a Children's Home in New York. Splendid physique. Over six feet tall. Very small head. Works as a section hand. Generally considered "not bright." Tried to give the impression of being religious. Is the father of two children by two step-daughters. One is a deformed imbecile in the County Infirmary. Had three stillborn children by first wife. Now married second time. Syphilitic.

If these cases and all of the others at large in the county who have ever been in a state or county institution had been recognized as feeble-minded at the time of their admission and dealt with as such, the county would have been saved a great deal in actual expense given out in township aid and in the unestimated expense of bad influence and contaminated morals.

Table XIII. A Comparison of Amount of Township Aid Dispensed and Number of Feeble-Minded

Townships.	Population.	Average Amt. of Township Aid for 5 Yrs. from June 30, 1911, to June 30, 1916.	Amount of Aid Per Person.	Percentage of Population Feeble-minded.
1	1,042	$ 33.66	$ .032	.006
2	1,123	33.42	.029	.003
3	12,850	396.05	.030	.004
4	1,326	161.46	.121	.012
5	1,189	66.36	.055	.010
6	980	23.44	.023	.005
7	4,835	494.51	.102	.011
8	985	15.95	.016	.009
9	1,128	11.00	.009	.007
10	1,474	130.32	.088	.013
11	9,876	1,230.69	.124	.015
12	1,688	50.76	.030	.009
13	3,138	141.93	.045	.008
14	12,755	1,419.12	.111	.007
Total	54,389	$4,208.67	$ .077	.009

Table XIII attempts to show that there is a relation existing between the number of feeble-minded found at large in each township and the amount

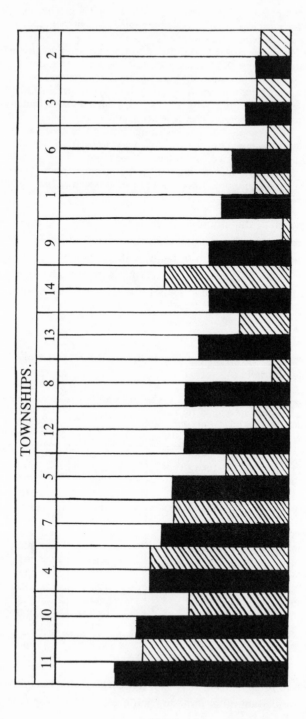

TOWNSHIPS.

Feeble-minded. (⅛ inch to each feeble-minded person per thousand of the population.)

Township Aid. (⅛ inch to each cent of township aid per person in the population.)

A Comparison of the Amount of Township Aid Dispensed and the Number of Feeble-Minded in Each Township. (See Table XIII) of township aid dispensed. Township 11, which had the largest proportion of feeble-minded, also gave the largest amount of township aid per person for a five-year period, an average of 12.4 cents per year to every person in the township. Township 10, which had the second largest proportion of feeble-minded, stood fifth in the amount of township aid given, but still had an average higher than that for the whole county. Township 4, which stood third in its proportion of defectives, stood second in amount of township aid. Township 7 stood fourth in both lists. Township 14, which stood third in the amount of aid given per person, was ninth in its proportion of feeble-minded. This apparent lack of relationship can be explained by the fact that the township employs a physician at $300.00 a year to care for the poor; and that one of the cities in the county is located in this township. Township 2 had the smallest proportion of defectives in the county and gave the third from the smallest amount of aid. Township 11 had 8.7 times the population of township 2, but gave 36.8 times as much aid, or 4.2 times as much to each member of the population. And township 11 had five times as many defectives in proportion to the population as township 2. Township 9 gave the smallest, and township 8 the second smallest amount of township aid. Both are prosperous agricultural communities and their feeble-minded were well cared for in their own homes.

There is one important factor which must be considered in this connection. During the years 1914–15 and 1915–16, most of the coal mines in the county were idle because of strikes and, later, difficulty in adjusting freight rates. Although the miners received benefits from the miners' union and were given work on the roads, many of them received township aid, especially during the second year of their idleness. But when one considers the mining townships individually, two of them spent less for township aid in either year of the depression than they had spent in the year just preceding when industrial conditions were good. In the cases of two townships there were incomplete reports. Two other townships, one of which is entirely and the other partially a mining community, spent less the second year of the depression than they did the first, and in one of these cases the amount spent the first year exceeded the amount spent the previous year by only $33.00, and in the other case by only $20.00. But in township 11, the amount of aid given the second year exceeded that given the first year by $1,089.00, and exceeded the amount given in a previous normal year by over $800.00. It was commonly remarked in this township that many of the defective families, especially the Hickory family, lived better during the second year of the industrial depression than they had ever lived before. The agricultural communities were not affected by the industrial condition and the amount given in the five years was fairly constant. So it seems fair to conclude that since the industrial depression did not have the same effect on the amount of township aid given in all of the mining communities, the difference must depend upon the character of the inhabitants of the township, and that in general those townships having a large proportion of feeble-minded have had to dispense a correspondingly large amount of township aid.

9. Summary

1. There were 494 feeble-minded persons found *at large* in this county, or 9 to every 1000 of the whole population.

2. The proportion of males to females was approximately as 3 to 2. The majority had not yet passed the child-bearing age.

3. The greater number of the feeble-minded were descended from pioneer stock.

4. Consanguinity cannot be blamed to any great degree for the number of feeble-minded in the county.

5. The feeble-minded were twice as frequent proportionately in the rural as in the urban districts. Geographical characteristics and industries of communities influenced the distribution of the feeble-minded.

6. The high grade feeble-minded were more numerous and more inclined to be anti-social in their habits.

7. A large proportion of the feeble-minded were dependent on the public. In general, communities having a large number of feeble-minded had to pay correspondingly large amounts of township aid.

F. DEFECTIVE AND DEPENDENT FAMILIES IN THE COUNTY

I. The Hickory Family

1. *General description* In considering the defective families of the county, one which we have called the Hickory Family takes pre-eminence because of the fecundity of its members, the anti-social nature of their habits and mode of living, their utter dependency and the large amount of inbreeding which promises to perpetuate the defective traits.

Sixty-two Hickory families were found living in the county of whom forty-eight were centered in one township. Thirty-four of these Hickory families were visited in twenty-eight different houses, all of whom were found to be related and descended from a common ancestor who came to the colonies from a French port in the days preceding the American Revolution. He settled in the back woods of Pennsylvania and married an Indian squaw. They had seven sons and a daughter. The oldest son was killed by the Indians and the other seven children emigrated to Ohio about the year 1800 and settled near each other. The descendants of five of these children were found living in the county studied. The oldest of the seven we have called Happy Hickory. He was considered the most worthless of the brothers, never worked except to make a few baskets, and felt no responsibility for his family. He was considered a shiftless no-account by his neighbors, and two older residents spoke of him as "not bright." There seems little doubt that he was feeble-minded. A chart has been made of his 401 descendants, on three hundred and nineteen of whom some information has been obtained. This chart includes many of the descendants of Happy's brothers and sister since there has been constant intermarrying, and practically all members of the family found in the county who were mentally defective.

The attitude of the community in general toward the Hickories is a peculiar one. They have been ostracized to a great extent and it is generally remarked that one would have to be pretty low down to mix with the Hickories. But on the other hand, the community seems to take it for granted that the Hickories shall steal their corn and chickens, live on their land, beg from their doors. They seldom bring any of them before the courts for their lawlessness. Even the school officials do not force the Hickory children into school as they say they cannot learn anything any way. Their fathers had to bear the burden of supporting this defective "tribe" and they expect their children to have to do the same. They seem calloused and entirely passive to the situation.

The township in which the larger part of the Hickory family was concentrated is No. 11, the one having the steepest hills and the most inaccessible ridges. The Hickory shanties are as a usual thing tucked away under the protection of a hill in some remote spot on land owned by the coal companies or on some corner of a man's farm where the land is worthless, but with very few exceptions in a place where no rent will have to be paid. Only two members of the family shown in the chart owned property. Where they have built their own homes, the more intelligent have built them of logs after the fashion of the pioneers; and those of lower intelligence of poles stuck together with mud aided with pieces of boxes, old shingles, strips of tin, or anything they can easily pick up, and these have sometimes been built directly on the ground with no floor. Only two of the homes visited could really be called clean. The majority were extremely dirty with tobacco juice all over the floor and an odor of filth in the air.

Their food consists of whatever can most easily be obtained. They eat berries gathered by the women and turtles and ground hogs as well as larger game shot by the men. In former days they caught fish, but since the mines have been opened there are no fish in the streams. They steal or beg what they can and when the supply runs short, work for enough money to buy some salt pork and corn meal. They must often go hungry, and it is sometimes a matter of wonder to their neighbors how they exist on so little.

There are distinguishing characteristics which every Hickory seems to bear and by which, after one has known a few, the others may be recognized. When seen on the road they walk in single file, plodding stolidly along, the men leading. Their figures are bowed, their bodies and clothes are dirty and odorous; the men are grisly, the women disheveled. Traces of tobacco juice may be seen about the mouths and teeth of both men and women, and the eyes of many of them have a gray clouded appearance said by several physicians to be due to trachoma.

The chief occupation of the Hickories is basket-making and the gathering of ginseng and yellow root. Some work as day laborers and a very few work in the mines. In general employers will not hire them because they "work one day and rest three," "loaf on the job," and are apt to stop in the middle of the day, demand their pay, and go down town to spend it for tobacco and whiskey, of which both men and women use an excessive amount. Some of them are not satisfied with whiskey, but buy pure alcohol and mix it with carbonated water or "pop."

The chief characteristic of the family is their utter dependency. The first inmates of the County Children's Home, when it was opened in 1878, were three Hickory children transferred from the County Infirmary. Officials say that there has never been a time in the history of the Children's Home when there have not been Hickory children as inmates. During the year 1916 there were nine children belonging to the family in the Home. The name appears twenty-four times on the books since 1878, but it is the belief of the field worker that the number is, in reality, greater, since the records at the Home have not been carefully kept. From the testimony of the Hickories themselves, it appears that 20 of the direct descendants of Happy as well as 12 other relatives who appear in collateral branches, making a total of 32 Hickories, have at some time been in the Children's Home.

The name first appeared on the Infirmary records in 1857, the year the Infirmary was opened, when Hank Hickory, Happy's oldest son, his wife and seven children applied for admission but were not allowed to stay by the directors. In the same year another Hickory was transferred from the County Jail where he had been confined a year as a pauper. He had formerly been in a State Hospital but had been discharged as incurable. The record reads, "Always partially an idiot in action but withal healthy, and can earn his living by proper attendance." He remained in the Infirmary until his death fourteen years later and was buried by the County. Twenty-three of the direct descendants of Happy Hickory and 4 relatives in collateral lines, making a total of 27 Hickories, have been in the County Infirmary. More recently township trustees have refused to send members there except in extreme cases, because they have been too willing to go. Two members of the family were in the County Infirmary on March 1, 1916.

The members of this family are seldom brought before the county courts, as they do not commit serious crimes. Since the general mentality of the Hickories is too low to permit any crime except petty thieving, and because of the lethargy of their neighbors, the cost of the family to the county in this respect is small.

But the township where the larger number live every year bears the greatest part of the burden of supporting the Hickory family. During the fiscal year June 30, 1915 to June 30, 1916, thirty-four Hickory families in Township No.11 were given township aid, some of them several times, the total amounting to two hundred thirty-four dollars and thirteen cents ($234.13) in orders on stores and doctors' fees. The township trustees say that they are continually pestered by members of the Hickory family applying for aid, but that the amount given in recent years is much less than it was formerly. Certain Hickories often try to get orders from two different trustees at the same time, holding one until the second is obtained and then presenting them both at the grocery store.

The second trait of this family which attracts attention is their habit of wandering. Most of them do not go outside of certain limits extending over three or four townships but within those limits go from one Hickory house to another, staying a short time in each place, or taking refuge in some tumble-down house, or even building a new shanty. The unmarried men and some of the girls seldom stay long in one place and the men with families move nearly as often. One family of five moved six times in as many months. They own so little property that there is little to hamper their moving at any time they wish. In no case did any Hickory own a cow. Three men had horses and one an old mule. Chickens and pigs were seen at only two Hickory homes.

The third most prominent characteristic of the family is the promiscuity of their relationships. The men and women live together whether they are married or not, and often consider themselves married when no ceremony has been performed. They herd together, especially in the winter, under the most crowded conditions, men, women, adolescents and children all in the same room, and they sleep three, four, and five in a bed. One home was visited where 13 people were sleeping in one room and the only sleeping accommodations visible were a double bed, a single bed and a crib. The field worker asked where they found room to put a young girl who had come to visit them, and the mother replied that she guessed they could find room for her in somebody's bed. One cannot wonder that the younger generation grow up with no conception of sexual morality and that there are so many cases of illegitimacy. Members of the family were perfectly free to talk of sexual matters, often to a revolting degree. There were four Hickory women in particular for whom the name of common prostitute is altogether too good. They were little better than animals. The moral influence these women were exerting on their own children, on the various relatives with whom they lived at intervals, and on the community where they gathered groups of degenerates about them, as well as the physical harm in the spreading of venereal disease, cannot be estimated. Even the school children in the section where these women lived knew their character and would call out taunting remarks to them on the road.

In 1915 a Hickory man was admitted to one of the State Hospitals and on his commitment papers the answer to the question, "Do any of the subject's relatives suffer from mental disease?" is, "All relatives are feeble-minded." This of course is an exaggeration but when one has a complete picture of the habits and manner of living of the Hickories, it need hardly be said that a large number of them are feeble-minded.

Table XIV. Summary of the Descendants of Happy Hickory and His Wife

Gener-ation.		F.	F.?	E.	A.	Sx.	C.	d. inf.	d. yg.	sb.	Not. F.	Under 10 Yrs.	Unk.
2	11 children	2	—	—	—	1	—	—	2	—	2	—	4
3	52 grand children	14	8	2	5	—	—	4	—	—	3	—	16
4	151 great grand children	48	5	—	4	2	2	21	9	7	21	—	32
5	183 gr. gr. grand children	24	18	—	—	2	2	33	9	2	8	55	30
6	4 gr. gr. gr. grn. children	1	—	—	—	—	—	—	—	—	—	3	—
	401 descendants	89	31	2	9	5	4	58	20	9	34	58	82

Table XIV shows the classification of the 401 descendants of Happy Hickory according to their defects. Eighty-nine of them are known to have been feeble-minded (F) and thirty-one others are suspected of having been so (F?). The two classified as epileptic (E) were not feeble-minded so far as known. Those classified as alcoholic (A), sex offenders (Sx), and criminalistic (C) are those possessing those traits who are not known to have been feeble-minded. Many of those who are classified as feeble-minded or possibly so, also possessed these traits. The number of those who died young (d. yg.) and in infancy (d. inf.) or were born dead (sb.) must in reality be much larger than shows here, as information on those points was hard to obtain except from the more intelligent and almost impossible to obtain for the older generations. Those classified as not feeble-minded (not F.) are those known to be not feeble-minded by personal observation or by description given, and free, so far as known, from alcoholic, immoral sexual, or criminalistic habits. Those classified as under ten years of age are those for whom diagnosis of mentality cannot be made at this time because of the possibility of further mental development. The unknown column (Unk.) includes those about whom no information was obtained because of the impossibility of getting accurate description, due in some cases to early death and in others to residence outside of the county.

It will be seen that 89 or 22.1% of the whole number of descendants of Happy Hickory in five generations are known to have been feeble-minded and that 31 or 7.7 percent are suspected of having been so. Of the total number of descendants 87 or 21.8 percent did not reach an age beyond 16 years, and 140 or 34.9 percent could not be classified because of lack of information or youth. That leaves 174 or 43.3% of the descendants of Happy Hickory who reached an age beyond 16 years and about whom definite information was obtained. Of the 174, 51.1% were known to be feeble-minded and another 17.8% were suspected of having been so.

There were found living in this rural county 78 feeble-minded Hickories, 43 men and 35 women, of whom 75 were direct descendants of Happy Hickory. Forty-eight of these, or 61%, were residents of township number 11, and 14, or 18%, were in the adjacent township, No. 7. The rest were scattered through four other townships in the county. There were also living in the county 20 others, thirteen men and 7 women, who are classified as probably feeble-minded.

As one reads the history one is impressed by the frequency with which tuberculosis is given as a cause of death. The lack of sanitation in their homes has a great deal to do with the prevalence of this disease. Physicians also told of epidemics of typhoid fever and diphtheria among the Hickories which it was impossible to check. In certain branches of the family trachoma is prevalent, and nothing is being done by physicians of the township to prevent the spread of this disease.

A glance at the chart makes it obvious that many of the matings are consanguineous. Of 89 marriages shown in the chart, 50, or 56%, are cousin marriages of varying degree, and 39, or 43%, are marriages between persons in no way related. This includes only those unions considered by the Hickories as legal marriages. The following is a table showing the degree of relationship in the 89 marriages.

1	Double first cousins
10	First cousins
10	First cousins once removed
21	Second cousins
5	Second cousins once removed
3	Third cousins
39	No relation
89	Marriages

Ohio law says that persons nearer of kin than second cousins may not marry. If this law could have been enforced, 21 of these marriages would not have been. The probate judge in the county where these people live has often refused them marriage licenses on the ground of their relationship as well as their defect. But it is an easy matter to go into another state if they happen to feel that it is necessary to have a marriage ceremony at all. Moreover, they seldom know what relation they are to each other when they are asked. The reasons for so many cousin marriages are probably twofold. The first reason is that in their own stock they find the most congenial companions, and the second is that they are largely forced to marry each other for the simple reason that no one else will marry them or have anything else to do with them. When they do marry outside of the family, they marry some member of a weak strain so that the progeny usually shows weakness of some sort; but the way is opened for greater variation and if the outmating continues will doubtless in time bring the stock back to normal. But while nature is carrying on this slow process, the county is having to pay the cost of maintaining them. And so long as members continue to marry back into their own strain, we can hope for nothing else than more defectives. Old residents say that the present generation of Hickories is physically inferior to the older generation. And the people of the community, in giving constant financial relief and shelter in county institutions, although they are being humane, are also defeating nature's attempt to eliminate the unfit.

A detailed history of Happy Hickory and his descendants follows with accompanying charts. It has been necessary to break up the original chart into 7 separate parts for the sake of greater simplicity. The reference numbers in the text refer to the individuals on the chart, the Roman numeral referring to the number of the chart and the Arabic numeral to the particular symbol.

It need hardly be said that all names used are fictitious.

2. Happy Hickory and His Descendants

Happy Hickory was born in southwest Pennsylvania about the year 1780 and emigrated to Ohio about the year 1800, where he took up forty acres of land bordering a creek. He was shiftless, and did not try to till his land, but spent his time hunting and fishing. He also served as a fifer in the war of 1812. When he sold the last piece of his land to meet a debt, his wife, who had no patience with his shiftless ways, left him. He lived about in shanties until he became old and blind and then went to live with one of his children, at whose house he died when past ninety years old. The only work he was ever known to do was to make baskets of hickory splits. Two old residents remembered him as "not bright." He was probably feeble-minded. His wife, also born in Pennsylvania, was more industrious than he and it was through her efforts that the family was provided for at all. Definite information concerning her mentality could not be obtained. She was remembered as a blind, childish old woman, feeling in the ashes for a coal to light her pipe. She died when about ninety-five years old. Neither she nor Happy could read or write and neither one knew his own age.

Happy and his wife had eleven children, who, with their descendants, follow in the order of their birth. They were: I—*Hank*, II—*Becky*, III—*Maria*, IV—*Sephronia*, V—*Jane*, VI—*Anne*, VII—*Martin*, VIII—*Susan*, IX—*Harriet*, X—*Sarah*, XI—*Robert*.

I—*Hank*, known as *"Old Hank"* (II 1). Described by an old neighbor as the most worthless one of Happy's children. Was entirely undependable, a liar and a petty thief. Was never known to work. Made baskets which he exchanged with farmers for produce. The story was told that he once made a half-bushel basket which was water-tight and carried it home full of whiskey. Was a hard drinker. A big man physically. Never wore a coat and even in winter went with his shirt unbuttoned. His chest was covered with long black hair. The records at the County Infirmary read, "Hank Hickory, his wife and seven children came to the County Infirmary, August 5th, 1857. Were not admitted by the directors. They left August 10th, 1857." Hank died old at the County Infirmary. His wife came from Pennsylvania. No description of her was obtained. Hank and his wife had nine children: 1—Hank, 2—Jim, 3—Joe, 4—Jane, 5—Jerry, 6—Nancy, 7—Harry, 8—Frank, 9—George.

1—Young Hank or "Sore-Eyed Hank" (II 3) was born about 1848. Cannot read or write. Cannot count his children. Could remember only five of them and told the field worker he had named eight. Is a drinker and a petty thief. Says he chews ten cents worth of tobacco a day. Never

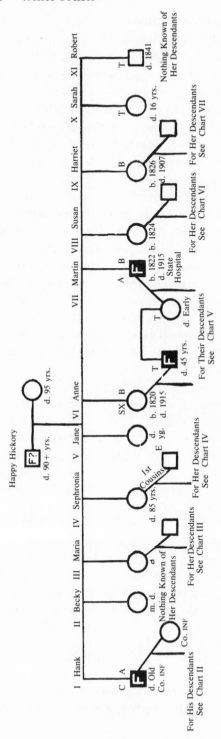

Chart I.

Key to the Charts: A square indicates a male, a circle a female. A straight line connecting a square and a circle designates a marriage. If the line is broken the union is illegal. A perpendicular line dropped from the marriage line leads to the children of that marriage. Each individual has an index number to the right of the symbol. When an individual has married some one already on the chart, that is, married a relative, the second index number is found in parenthesis. In such cases, the consort is omitted and the marriage indicated by a portion of the marriage line. The children of such marriages are found by referring to the second index number. The small solid black circle indicates a still birth. The other symbols and abbreviations are as follows: F—Feeble-minded, F?—Probably feeble-minded, A—Alcoholic, B—Blind, C—Criminal, E—Epileptic, I—Insane, S.—Syphilitic, Sx—Sex offender, T—Tubercular, W—Wandering or Roving, b—Born, d—Died, m—Married, d. yg.—Died young, d. inf.—Died in infancy, Co. Inf.—County Infirmary, Ch. H.—Children's Home, W. H.—Work House, Co. Jail—County Jail, B.I.S.—Boys' Industrial School, O.P.—Ohio Penitentiary.

works except to make a few baskets. Spends his time wandering about the country. Makes his relatives support him. Has had sore eyes since a young man and has been partially blind for the last twenty-five years. Gets a "blind pension" of five dollars per month. Has lived with his son's wife. Is a low grade feeble-minded person. Married Polly Hickory (II 4, also IV 10), his first cousin. She kept a dirty house and spent most of her time wandering around out of doors. Took no care of her children. Died at about fifty-five years of pneumonia. Was probably feeble-minded. Polly and Hank have seven children.

a—A daughter (II 20) died at nineteen of tuberculosis.

b—Laura (II 21) went to school three years but could not learn. Could not read or write. Died at forty-five of tuberculosis. Feeble-minded. She married for her first husband, her first cousin once removed (II 22, also V 18), an alcoholic. By him there were seven children of whom one (II 62) is definitely feeble-minded, and two others (II 65, 66) probably so. The remaining four died early. She married a stranger for her second husband and had one son (II 73) born in 1903. He has fair mentality. Her third husband was her first cousin once removed (II 24, also V 16), a brother of her first husband, an alcoholic and a wanderer. By him there were three children, one of whom died in infancy. The other two are in another county.

c—A son (II 25), born about 1868. Can read print. Cannot write. Works at day labor, but does a poor grade of work. Is not often hired. Wanders from place to place. Is crippled physically. Is the father of an illegitimate, feeble-minded son (II 77), born in 1904, at present an inmate of Children's Home. Uses an excessive amount of tobacco. Married his second cousin (II 27, also V 35), a feeble-minded woman, but "ran her off" after a few days. Is a low grade feeble-minded person.

d—A son (II 28) was killed by a train on a railroad crossing while bringing home wood. Probably feeble-minded.

e—Rachel (II 29), born about 1871. She has a very low forehead and is small in stature. Feeble-minded. Is dirty and wears her hair loose. Is notoriously immoral and widely known as a beggar. Could not name all of her children and treated the subject as of small consequence. Makes baskets. Sometimes works out by the day, but cannot tell whether she is fully paid or not. Receives frequent township aid. Has been in County Infirmary with three of her children. Had four illegitimate children (II, 78–81) by her second cousin (II 30, also IV 29), a

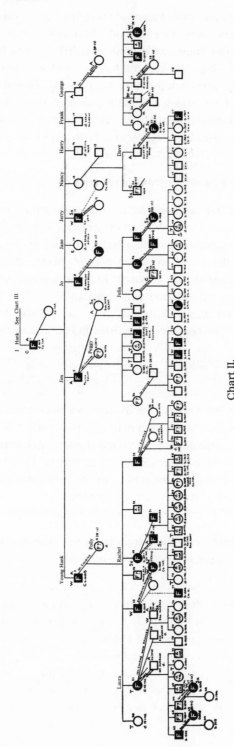

Chart II.

feeble-minded man. Two of these died in infancy. A third died at seventeen of tuberculosis, and the fourth ran away with a circus. She married a feeble-minded, deformed man (II 31), and has had seven children (II, 82–88), four of whom died in infancy and one at ten years of tuberculosis. Her daughter, born in 1907, bears the marks of congenital syphilis, and is probably feeble-minded. Her son, born in 1909, is a very dull child, probably feeble-minded. It is very likely that this woman has had other children than those named to the field worker.

f—A son (II 32) died in infancy.

g—A son (II 33), lazy, immoral, "not ambitious enough to steal." Receives township aid. Feeble-minded. Married for his first wife (II 34) his third cousin. She died of childbirth. He married his second cousin (II 35, also IV 36) for his second wife. She is of better intelligence than the average Hickory and reached the fourth grade in school. They have had four children; three boys and a girl (II 90–93). The boys all use tobacco and the two oldest are four years behind their grade in school. They are all too young to be definitely called feeble-minded.

2—Jim (II 5), second child of "Old Hank," owns a small piece of land and a team of horses. Is a day laborer, "works one day and misses three." Has always been partially supported by the township. Is a thief and a schemer. Has a speech defect. Drinks to excess. Cannot read or write. Has been twice arrested for not sending his children to school. Said to be only a little higher in mentality than his brother, Hank. Married for his first wife his first cousin (II 6, also IV 11) Peggy, a sister of Polly, wife of "Sore-Eyed Hank." She was dirty, a poor housekeeper and probably feeble-minded. They had five children:

a—A daughter (II 36). She keeps a fairly clean house. Was not interested in the field-worker's visit and left the house so no opportunity was afforded to speak with her. Does not look of good intelligence. She married her first cousin (II 37, also IV 35), a man of fair mentality, but lazy. They have six children, the oldest of whom (II 94), born in 1900, is a bright boy. The second, a girl, born 1902 (II 95), declares she is in the sixth grade at fourteen years, but looks and acts feeble-minded. The third child, a boy (II 96), born 1909, seems bright. The fourth child, a boy (II 97), died at five years. This child was never able to walk and did not develop mentally. The fifth child, a boy (II 98), born in

1912, cannot walk and makes only a few sounds, although four years old. Feeble-minded. The sixth child is a baby girl (II 99), born in 1916.

b—A daughter (II 38), born 1882. In Children's Home as a child. Now married. In another county.

c—A son (II 39), died at twenty-two years of tuberculosis.

d—A daughter (II 40), died at fourteen years of tuberculosis.

e—A son (II 41), was never able to talk, but could walk. Probably an idiot. Died in a State Institution at fourteen years.

Jim (II 5) married for his second wife a woman who was an inmate of the Infirmary. The story was told that she was pregnant by the Superintendent of the Infirmary and he paid Jim twenty-five dollars to marry her and take her away. The child, born in 1893, bears the Hickory name, was in the Children's Home as a child, and is now an inmate of the Ohio Hospital for Epileptics. The evidence concerning the paternity of the child was verified by the record at the Children's Home. The woman is an alcoholic and sex offender. No description of her mentality was obtained. She and Jim have had two children.

a—A son (II 42), born 1898, died 1916. He was poorly developed physically and was so feeble-minded that his defect was recognized by his own family.

b—A son (II 43), born 1901. No description of him was obtained.

3—Joe, third child of "Old Hank" (II 8), was unusually well developed physically, but had a speech defect and was a butt for jokes. Would only work for a day at a time when he was in immediate need of food. He was generally considered "not bright." Always suffered from "sore eyes." Was nearly blind the latter part of his life. Always lived in shanties on someone else's property. Died suddenly of apoplexy. He married his first cousin (II 9, also V 12). They were refused a marriage license in their home county because they were both feeble-minded. His wife is a dirty housekeeper and is not considered bright. They had three children:

a—Julia (II 44). No description of her mentality was obtained. She married her first cousin (II 45, also II 50*) and quarrels with him fre-

* Evidently a misprint in original text.—Ed.

quently. He is "not bright." Steals everything he finds loose and is sexually immoral. He has been run out of town for stealing chickens and is now serving a term in the workhouse for larceny. They have had four children who are now inmates of the County Children's Home. The oldest is extremely dull, and considered feeble-minded. The mentality of the other three was not ascertained.

b—A daughter (II 46) is so defective that she can not carry on a conversation. Married her second cousin (II 47, also V 64), a feeble-minded man who has never been known to do a day's work. They steal their food and receive township aid. They live in a pole shanty on the property of the coal company. They have had three children, one of whom died in infancy. The other two are six and four years old. (See Fig. VI.)

c—A son (II 48), is shiftless, unreliable, lives on charity and township aid. Works at irregular intervals for the coal company, but does not know whether he is paid the right amount of wages. The company keeps track of his grocery bills and the amount of wages due him. He went to school two years, but cannot read or write. He married his second cousin (II 49, also VII 25), who "hasn't any better sense than he has." She was born in 1888, went to school two years, but cannot read or write. She is sexually immoral and she and her husband quarrel frequently. They have had five children; one of whom died in infancy and another at ten years of tuberculosis (II 107, 108). The other three children (II 109–111) are under ten years of age.

4—Jane (II 10), fourth child of "Old Hank," was an epileptic and died while in an attack. Never married.

5—Jerry (II 11), fifth child of "Old Hank," is entirely undependable. Wanders from place to place. "Is here today and there tomorrow." His mentality is said to be on a par with that of his brother, Hank. He married, but left his wife and went with another woman. They were put in a county jail, he for sixty days and she for thirty, but since their release are living together again.

6—Nancy (II 14), sixth child of "old Hank." No description of her was obtained. She married and had two children.

a—A son (II 50), who married his first cousin, Julia (II 44). Description of them and their children is given under the history of Julia (II 44).

b—Dave (II 51). A good worker, but a hard drinker. Killed by a train while drunk. Married Jude Hickory (II 52, also V 35), his second cousin, a feeble-minded woman, notoriously immoral and a tramp. By her there were six children, all of whom have been in the County Children's Home. The three oldest have been placed out. The youngest (II 117), born 1907, is feeble-minded. One of the others is of borderline mentality, and the sixth child is of normal intelligence.

7—Harry (II 16), seventh child of "Old Hank," died in the Civil War.

8—Frank (II 17), the eighth child of "Old Hank," died early as the result of an accident.

9—George (II 18), the ninth child of "Old Hank," is a good worker, but never gets ahead because he is a hard drinker. Cannot read or write, but is said to have better mentality than any of his brothers. He married his first cousin once removed (II 19, also IV 25). She is a hard drinker, ignorant and a poor housekeeper. They have had seven children:

a—A daughter (II 53), is married.

b—A daughter (II 54), married her second cousin.

c—A son (II 56), works for a few days at a time and then spends the money he has earned getting drunk. Is living with his second cousin, a feeble-minded sex-offender. They are not married.

d—A son (II 57), died at thirty-two of sugar diabetes. He always had an unusually big appetite and could eat enough for three or four people. He married his second cousin once removed (II 58, also III 28), and had one son about whom nothing is known.

e—A son (II 59), born about 1894, is feeble-minded and has had epileptic attacks all of his life. A hard drinker. Cannot work.

f—A son (II 60), died in infancy.

g—A daughter (II 61, also II 67*), was born 1899. Is nothing more than a tramp. Wanders from one Hickory house to another, staying for a few days at a time in each place. Immoral. Cannot pronounce certain consonants. Chews and smokes. Has an illegitimate baby, born in 1916. The father of this child is her first cousin once removed. When the baby was about three months old they went outside the state and were married. Her husband is probably feeble-minded.

* Evidently a misprint in original text.—Ed.

II—*Becky* (See Chart I), second child of Happy, married and settled in another county. No description of her or her children was obtained.

III—*Maria* (III 1), third child of Happy, married and had four children, about three of whom nothing is known (III 3–5).

4—Pete (III 6), the fourth child, served in the Civil War and received a pension. Could not read or write. Was physically undersized. Farmers would not hire him because he needed such close supervision. His pension checks were always cashed by a grocer, who subtracted the amount due him for groceries and gave Pete the remainder. Pete was not able to figure out the amount of his bill and did not know how much was due him. He died in 1915. His first wife (III 7) was an ignorant woman who died of tuberculosis. His second wife (III 8, also IV 4) was a feeble-minded woman who is generally known because of her immoral behavior. There were no children by her. By the first wife there were seven children:

a—A son (III 9), spent his childhood in a County Infirmary. Now lives in another county.

b—A son (III 10). Unusually good physique. Is a fairly good, but unsteady, worker. Has received township aid. Of low mentality, but not feeble-minded. He married and has had six children; the oldest, a daughter (III 21), is immoral. His three sons are backward in school. One of these (III 24) is possibly feeble-minded. The other two are small.

c—A son (III 12), spent his childhood and early life in a County Infirmary. Was not considered bright by members of his own family. Died early. He married his second cousin (III 13, also VI 9), a feeble-minded woman, and had one son (III 27), probably born in 1905. This child has been in the County Infirmary with his mother, and is in the second grade in school at eleven years. Is feeble-minded.

d—A daughter (III 14), is married and lives outside of the county.

e—A son (III 15), is married and lives outside of the county.

f—Jake (III 16), is said to be of passable mentality, but is a chronic thief, shrewd at driving a bargain, cute and scheming. He married his second cousin (III 17, also IV 32), a woman with the reputation of being immoral. They have had nine children; the two oldest boys (III 28, 29) have been in the County Jail with their father for assault

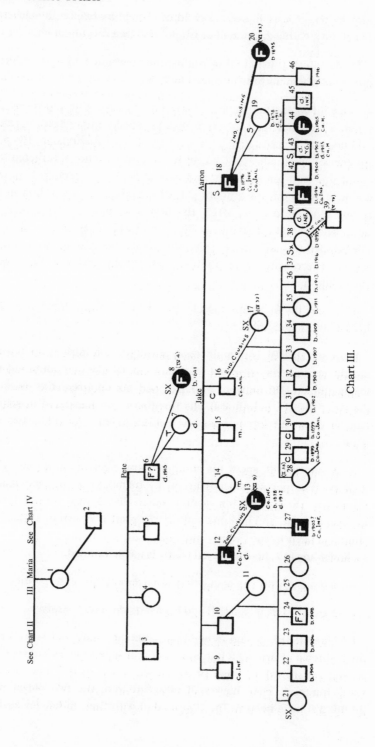

Chart III.

and battery. One of these sons has also been before the Juvenile Court for stealing a bicycle. No information was obtained in regard to their mentality.

g—Aaron (III 18) was born about 1876 and spent his childhood in a County Infirmary. Does not know his age and is so feeble-minded that he can tell little about himself. Cannot give the names of his family correctly. His eyes are sore and discharging. He is probably syphilitic, and is disgustingly dirty. Moves frequently. He, with his wife and two grown sons, lived during the winter of 1915–16 in a six by ten-foot shanty. He never works, but gets his living by begging and picking food from dumps and the refuse thrown out from houses. Has served a six months sentence in the County Jail for non-support. Married for his first wife (III 19), an illegitimate child of his step-mother. She was said to have been of fair mentality. She was born about 1878, spent her childhood in a Children's Home and died in 1911, probably of tuberculosis. They had seven children. The oldest (III 38), a girl, born 1892, is ignorant but keeps a clean house and seems to be of fair mentality. She is extremely immoral. Married her second cousin once removed, but has no children. The second child (III 40), died in infancy. The third child, a son (III 41), was born in 1896. Has never been to school. Spent one winter in the County Infirmary. Is feeble-minded. The fourth child (III 42), a boy, born 1900, seems to be of fair mentality. He has never gone to school. The fifth (III 43), a boy, born in 1902, died in 1915 in the Children's Home as a result of congenital syphilis. The sixth child (III 44), a girl, was born in 1905 and is now an inmate of the Children's Home. She is feeble-minded by intelligence test. The seventh child (III 45), a boy, died in infancy.

Aaron married for his second wife his second cousin (III 20, also VI 23), a girl younger than his oldest daughter, and said to be of as low mentality as he. They have one son, born 1916.

IV—*Sephronia* (IV 1), fourth child of Happy, was hard working and a clean housekeeper. Her mentality was probably good, and it was she who made a living for her children. She died at eighty-five years. She married her first cousin, Steve Hickory (IV 2). He was an epileptic from the time he was a young man and was never able to take care of his family. He made baskets and fished for a living. He was drowned during an epileptic attack. He and Sephronia had eight children:

1—Adam (IV 3), first child of Sephronia, was born about 1848. An old inhabitant described him as "the most defective of all the Hickories."

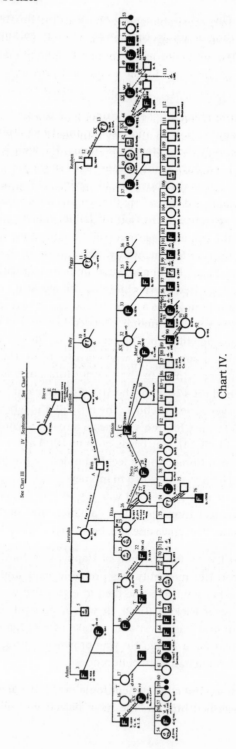

Chart IV.

He always lived in a miserable shack "back in the brush," and died in 1890 of tuberculosis. He married a woman (IV 4, also III 8) who is extremely dirty, a liar, and notoriously immoral. Although now seventy-five years old, she still lives the life of a common prostitute. She is a low grade feeble-minded person. She and Adam had five children:

a—A son (IV 14), born in 1880. Was four years in the Children's Home and spent a year in the Boy's Industrial School. Is not considered bright. Cannot hold a job because of inefficiency. Never pays his bills. Married his second cousin (IV 15, also VII 21), a feeble-minded girl, born in 1886. She has been in Police Court for drunkenness and prostitution. They have had seven children, the first of whom died at three years (IV 54). The cause of death was given as scrofula. The second child (IV 55) died at two and a half years. This child "was not right." The next two children (IV 56, 57) died at birth. The fifth child, a girl (IV 58), was born in 1914 and is a sickly looking baby. The last two children (IV 59, 60) were born dead.

b—A daughter (IV 16), is married and living in another county.

c—A daughter (IV 17) died at twenty-three years of tuberculosis. She married a feeble-minded man who works very little, begs most of his living, and gets help from the township. They have had three children, the oldest of whom could not be located. The second child, a girl (IV 62), is living with her paternal uncle and knows nothing of the whereabouts of her father. She is supposed to be about eleven years old, has been in school five years and is still in the first B grade. She already has bad sexual habits. The third child (IV 63), a boy, is supposed to be about ten years old. He is in the third grade, but his teachers say he is unable to carry the work of the grade.

d—A daughter (IV 19), is lazy, keeps such a dirty house that it is impossible to stay in it, and has no idea how to provide for her family. Is childish in appearance. Is feeble-minded without a doubt. She married her second cousin (IV 20, also V 34), a feeble-minded man who "has sense enough to dodge work, but that is all." He gets frequent township aid and at other times lives on the pension of his mother-in-law. He is dishonest and a cheat. They have five children. The oldest is a son (IV 64), thought to be about eleven years old. He is small for his age and is still in the first grade at school. He forgets what he learns from day to day. The second child (IV 65), a son, born 1910, has not been to school. Is an extremely dull looking child. The third and fifth children (IV 66, 68) died in infancy, and the fourth child, a girl (IV 67), was born in 1912.

e—A daughter (IV 21) died at thirty years of tuberculosis. She married her first cousin once removed, a feeble-minded man (IV 22, also VII 12) and had four children, two of whom died in infancy. Nothing is known of the other two.

2—A son (IV 5), second child of Sephronia, died in infancy.

3—A son (IV 6), third child of Sephronia, is working as a farm hand in another county.

4—A daughter, Jerusha (IV 7), fourth child of Sephronia, was probably of fair mentality. She married her second cousin, Ben (IV 8), born 1839, a man of good mentality, but lazy and a hard drinker. By him there were four children:

a—A daughter (IV 23) died in infancy.

b—A daughter (IV 24) died young.

c—A daughter (IV 25). Is an alcoholic. She married George Hickory (II 18), her first cousin once removed. For description of them and their children see description of George, youngest son of Old Hank.

d—Elza (IV 26) was born in 1867 and died in 1913 as the result of an injury in the mine. He is said to have been of good intelligence. He married for his first wife his first cousin once removed (IV 27, also V 30), who died early of tuberculosis. They had two children, a son (IV 73) of whom nothing is known, and a daughter (IV 74), who is probably feeble-minded. This daughter has a feeble-minded child (IV 76), eight years old, who can make no progress in school. Elza (IV 26) married for his second wife, his second cousin, Nora (IV 28, also V 86), an immoral woman of defective mentality. By her there were four children, the oldest of whom (IV 77), a girl of fourteen, is without doubt feeble-minded. It is possible that she is by another father. The other three children (IV 78–80) are under ten years of age.

5—A daughter, Angeline (IV 9), fifth child of Sephronia, was an intelligent woman. A physician said that he had often called on her to care for some sick person. She married her second cousin, Ben, the husband of her sister Jerusha (IV 8), as his second wife. By her there were five children:

a—Clinton (IV 29) is an inveterate thief, a hard drinker, lazy and lacking in judgment and common sense. He is generally considered defective in mentality. He lived with his second cousin, Rachel (II 29), without being married. They had four children, description of whom will be found under the history of Rachel.

Clinton married for his first wife, a woman of low mentality with a speech defect. They had five children (IV 82–86), one of whom (IV 86) died young of tuberculosis. No description was obtained of the others. Clinton married for his second wife his second cousin, Mary Hickory (IV 31, also VI 9), a feeble-minded woman who already had illegitimate children. By her there were three children (IV 87–89). Two of them died in infancy and the third child (IV 87) has been an inmate of the County Infirmary and the Children's Home. Clinton deserted this wife and her children and she was taken to the County Infirmary where she died. Clinton then went to live with Nora (IV 28, also V 86), the widow of his half-brother, Elza, and at the same time tried to make his father support her. They had a child (IV 81), born in 1916. When the child was about six months old they went outside of the state and were married.

b—A daughter (IV 32) is of fair mentality, but immoral. She had an illegitimate daughter and was pregnant a second time when she was married. She married her second cousin, Jake (III 16). For description of him and their children see the history of Jake.

c—A daughter (IV 33), born in 1876, "went to school until she was too old to go and can read and write some." She is dirty and feeble-minded. She married a low grade feeble-minded man (IV 34), illegitimate child of IV 4, who has a very small head. He cannot read or write. Receives township aid. He and his wife have had fifteen children, four of whom died in infancy. (See Fig. VIII.) The oldest son (IV 90) was born in 1894. He is feeble-minded. Wanders about the country earning a bit here and there with which to get drunk. He married his second cousin once removed (IV 91, also VI 22) and they have one child (IV 92), born in 1915. (See Fig. VII.) The second son (IV 93), a twin of the first, is very defective mentally. Cannot read or write. Seldom works and wanders all over the county. He is simple and child-like in manner, and dishonest. He is the father of the illegitimate child of his first cousin once removed (IV 44). The third child, a daughter (IV 94) was born in 1895. Reached the second grade in school at fourteen years. Is feeble-minded. Married her third cousin (II 62). The next two children died in infancy. The sixth child, a son (IV 97), born in 1899, was in the second grade when he left school at fourteen years. The seventh child, a son (IV 98), born in 1901, is in the fourth grade in school and is the brightest appearing child in the family. The eighth child died in infancy. The ninth child, a son (IV 100), born in 1903, is in the first grade at thirteen years. The tenth child died in infancy. The eleventh child (IV 102), a son, born in 1907, is in the first grade at nine years. The other four children (IV 103–106) have never gone to school, but are all dull in appearance.

d—A son (IV 35) is of fair intelligence but lazy. He married his first cousin (II 36), the oldest daughter of Jim Hickory. For description of their children, see history of Jim, second son of Old Hank.

e—A daughter (IV 36) is of fair intelligence. Married her second cousin, a feeble-minded man (II 33), the youngest son of Sore-Eyed Hank. See his description for history of their children.

6—Polly (IV 10), sixth child of Sephronia, was probably feeble-minded. Married her first cousin (II 3), Sore-Eyed Hank Hickory. For further description see his history.

7—Peggy (IV 11), seventh child of Sephronia, probably feeble-minded. Married her first cousin, Jim Hickory (II 5). For further description see his history.

8—Reuben (IV 12), eighth child of Sephronia, was born in 1860. Cannot read or write. Gets frequent township aid. Works only part of the time usually on a section gang. Is a hard drinker. In the last five years has developed epileptic attacks. Married his first cousin (IV 13). She has better intelligence than most of the Hickory family, but did not seem to possess normal feeling for her children and relished bringing stories of a sexual nature into her conversation. She has been very immoral. She and Reuben have had thirteen children.

a—(IV 37) born dead.

b—(IV 38) a daughter, born 1887. Went to school several years but cannot read or write. Keeps a very dirty house. Yells and curses at her children. Is a nuisance in the neighborhood. Is frank and childish in conversation. Married a man of low mentality who is, however, a good worker. They have had five children (IV 107–112); the oldest of whom died in infancy. The other four are all small.

c—A daughter (IV 40), died at two months.

d—A daughter (IV 41), died at fourteen months.

e—A son (IV 42), died at nine months.

f—A child (IV 43), born dead.

g—A daughter (IV 44), born 1892. Is cross-eyed. Went to school, but could not learn. Is now living with her second cousin (II 56), to whom she is not married. Is immoral. Has wandering habits and is feeble-minded. She has an illegitimate son (IV 112), born in 1915, by her first cousin once removed (IV 93), a feeble-minded man. At nineteen months this child was just beginning to cut his teeth and had made no attempt to walk.

h—A daughter (IV 47), born in 1898. Finished school at sixteen years and was then in the third grade. For two summers she has "bummed" her way over the country by means of freight trains in company with a man who is now serving a sentence in the Ohio Penitentiary for assault with intent to rape. She had one child by this man which died in infancy. She is feeble-minded.

i—A son (IV 49), born in 1902. Is fourteen years old and in the second grade. Feeble-minded.

j—A daughter (IV 50), born in 1904. Cannot talk plainly. Is cross-eyed. Has a swaying gait. Has never gone to school. Cannot take care of herself. A low grade imbecile.

k—A son (IV 51), born in 1907. Second year in the first grade. Feeble-minded.

l—A daughter (IV 52), born in 1911.

m—A still-born child (IV 53).

V—*Jane* (See Chart I), fifth child of Happy Hickory, died young.

VI—*Ann* (V 1), sixth child of Happy, born about 1820, was sexually immoral even after her marriage. Was blind for many years before her death. Died in March, 1915, at ninety-five years of age. She married a feeble-minded man (V 2), who died at forty-five years of tuberculosis. He could not read or write. Always walked in a stooped position and had sore eyes. No one ever hired him because he had no ability. He and Ann had seven children:

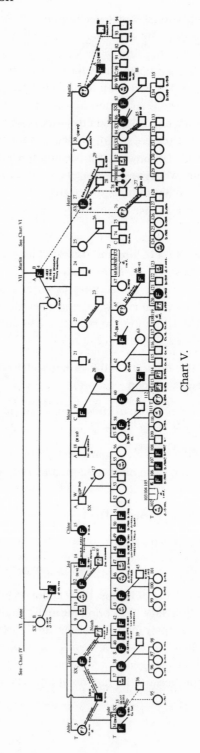

Chart V.

1—Abby (V 5). Old inhabitants declared she was "not bright." She died early of tuberculosis. She married her second cousin (V 6), Eben, a feeble-minded man, as his first wife. He was born in 1846, and is a never-failing source of amusement in the village where he lives. He has a very active imagination and, with a little encouragement, will tell the most amazing tales. The information he gave was wholly unreliable. He has never worked steadily until recently he was given a job as a street cleaner. Has frequent township aid. Someone once told him that Niagara Falls was burning, whereupon he became much excited and in the course of a few hours went into town to ask if the fire was out yet. He and his first wife had two children:

a—A son (V 34, also IV 20). No one considers him bright and he is the subject of jokes. Has tuberculosis. Married his second cousin (IV 19). For description of him and their children, see history of Sephronia's descendants.

b—Jude (V 35) was born about 1880, though she does not know her exact age. Is feeble-minded and notorious throughout the whole country for her immorality. Is loose-jointed, has projecting mouth and teeth and receding chin. When asked her last name, she replied that she had had so many husbands she did not know what it was now. She wanders about the country living with any man who will have her, under any conditions, and tries to get the young girls of her acquaintance to go with her. She and a feeble-minded cousin have "bummed" their way through several states by freight train and on foot. The authorities of the township where she lives once sent her to the infirmary in the hope of putting an end to her promiscuous life, but she soon ran away. When seen she is always smoking or chewing a big mouthful of tobacco. She married her second cousin (II 51), an alcoholic man, who was killed by a train. Her six children by him have been in the Children's Home. For further description, see the children of Nancy, the sixth child of Old Hank. She married for her second husband (II 35), a feeble-minded second cousin who soon "ran her off" because he declared she tried to poison him. Jude also had an illegitimate child (V 95) by a man of good standing in the community. This child is being cared for by his family and is said to be bright.

2—Lizzie (V 7), second child of Anne, was born in 1849. Has no reasoning ability. Could give no dates or ages. Told impossible things as facts. Talked in a whining tone. Tried to give the impression of being very religious. Is generally considered defective. Is very dirty and has "sore eyes." She married for her first husband, her second cousin, Noah (V 8), a brother of Eben. He was very ignorant and lazy. A story was told that one of the neighbors threatened to prosecute him if he did not feed his horse. "His horse was standing in the barn starving to death because he was too lazy to go down into the field and bring up fodder." Was said to be as defective as his brother Eben. He and Lizzie had three children:

a—A daughter (V 40), considered "not bright" by the Hickories. She died at twenty-eight years as a result of syphilitic infection. She was married but had no children.

b—A son (V 41), died at ten years. Was never able to talk and was probably an idiot. "He wasn't right no way."

c—A son (V 42), born in 1887. A low grade imbecile. Has animal-like appearance, a stooped position, mutters, and avoids strangers. Has periods of excitement when he thinks someone is chasing him. The county pays his step-father one dollar a week for his support. He does no work. At times becomes religious and wants to join the church.

Lizzie's first husband left her and went into another state, whereupon she went to live with Eben (V 6), her husband's brother and her dead sister's husband. When her husband returned they refused to allow him to enter the house. He was finally killed by a train on a crossing. Lizzie and Eben had two children. The first died in infancy. The second, a daughter (V 38), can read and write, but is dirty, shiftless, and considered below par mentally. She is married and has three little children.

3—Daughter (V 9), reads and writes. Is a neat housekeeper. Is much brighter than the average Hickory. She is married and has children, for whom descriptions were not obtained.

4 and 5—A boy and a girl (V 10, 11), died in infancy.

6—A daughter (V 12, also II 9), feeble-minded. She married for her first husband, Jo Hickory (II 8), her first cousin. For description of them and their children see the descendants of Old Hank. She married for her second husband another first cousin (V 13, also VII 3). They had no children.

7—Jed (V 14), born about 1861. He and his family have been supported by the township for years. He seldom works and gets drunk whenever it is possible. Has a speech defect. Is as simple as a child. Has never been outside of the township in which he lives. Says he owns five acres of land, but has no deed to the property and has never paid for it. Has trachoma. Is decidedly feeble-minded. Married his double first cousin, Chloe (V 15). The father of each is a brother to the mother of each. His wife was born about 1868. Is feeble-minded. Cannot read or write. Keeps a disgustingly dirty house. Picks berries and digs roots for their living. The whole family makes a practice of begging throughout the township. There are eight children:

a—A daughter (V 43), died in infancy.

b—A daughter (V 44), born about 1894. Can read a little. Cannot write. Is very dull in appearance and easily influenced. When sixteen years old she married an old soldier, said to be about eighty, thinking that after his death she would receive his pension. He died, leaving her with three little children. She found she could not get the pension, so has recently married her second husband, a feeble-minded man (IV 18), who had been living with her for several months. He is already the father of two defective children by a Hickory woman.

c—A daughter (V 46), died at sixteen years of measles.

d—A son (V 47), was found dead in bed when three months old. "Someone had rolled on him."

e—A son (V 48), born about 1898. A low grade imbecile. Went to school faithfully, but was still in the first grade at sixteen years. Has inflamed eyes. Does no work. Was afraid of the field worker and her camera.

f—A daughter (V 49), born about 1901. Has gone to school regularly, but has been unable to learn her letters and cannot learn to spell. She has "sore eyes" and fainting spells.

g—A son (V 50), born about 1904. Can make no progress in school. Eyelids are inflamed and the corners of his mouth are filled with sores. Has no eyelashes. Trachoma. Has been before the Juvenile Court on charge of incorrigibility.

h—A son (V 51), born about 1908. Has inflamed lids. Is still in the first grade in school. Feeble-minded.

VII—*Martin* (V 4), seventh child of Happy Hickory, was born about 1822. Could not read or write. Was quarrelsome and contrary. The most work he ever did was to cut poles for farmers. Was decidedly shiftless, and never owned any land. Had "sore eyes" for many years and was entirely blind for the last eight years of his life as a result of trachoma. Received a "blind pension." Always drank to excess when he had money to spend. He died in one of the State Hospitals of senile dementia in 1915. He married an ignorant woman (V 3), the sister of his sister Anne's husband, who died in middle age of tuberculosis. They had eleven children:

1—Chloe (V 15), born 1868. Feeble-minded. She married her double first cousin, Jed Hickory, and has been described under the children of Anne.

2—A son (V 16). A drinker and no-account. Does not live in one place very long. Has lived with several different women. He married first an epileptic woman and had five children, of whom nothing is known except that one died in infancy. He married for his second wife, Laura (II 21), his first cousin once removed. She was feeble-minded and died when about forty-five of tuberculosis. For description of her and their children see history of the descendants of Sore-Eyed Hank.

3—A son (V 18). An alcoholic who was killed by a train. He married the same woman, Laura (II 21), who was his brother's second wife, as her first husband. For description of their children see the history of the descendants of Sore-Eyed Hank.

4—Mose (V 19), the fourth child of Martin, is known as "Thieving Mose." "Steals everything he can lay his hands on." Never works and is constantly helped by the township. Has never served a jail sentence, but was once arrested for stealing corn. He has been run out of town for stealing chickens. Is entirely irresponsible, lies and cheats. He married a feeble-minded woman (V 20, sister of IV 4), who is described by one of the Hickories as "not as smart as the rest." She has always been immoral. She and Mose have had thirteen children, six of whom (V 68–73) died in infancy.

a—A daughter (V 57), born in 1869. Married a Hickory man. Nothing was learned about her.

b—A daughter (V 58), born about 1875. Does not know her own age. Says she cannot keep track of her children's ages. Went several years to school but cannot read or write. Has been subject to epileptic attacks but declares she has had none in the last two years. Is childishly curious. Followed the field worker to the houses of the neighbors. She married a man (V 59) who can read and write and works steadily in the mine, but never seems to be able to make enough money to support his family. They are always in need and expect the community to help them. He is thought to have some negro blood in his veins. They have had ten children; four of these died in infancy and another died at fifteen of tuberculosis. A son, born about 1900, left school at sixteen and was then graded in the fourth grade, but was not able to do the work of the grade. Is mean, vicious, and likes to fight. Has recently developed epilepsy. Another son, born about 1904, is in the third grade at twelve years. His teacher says that he does very poorly. A third son, born probably in 1905, is in the second grade at eleven years. It is his third year in the grade. The other two children are very young.

c—A daughter (V 60) is said to be even more defective than her sister just described. Married a feeble-minded man and is living outside the county. They have had three children, all reported to be feeble-minded. Their son (V 113) wanders from place to place and gets jobs here and there.

d—A daughter (V 62), born about 1883, died in 1914 of puerperal fever. She was married and had five children, one of whom died in infancy. The other four are in the Children's Home of another county.

e—A son (V 64) is described as "a chip off the old block," never works, and is said to be very defective in appearance. He married his second cousin (II 46), a low grade feeble-minded woman. For description of them and their children, see the history of the descendants of Old Hank Hickory.

f—A daughter (V 65) keeps a cleaner house than most of the Hickories and seems to have a little more common sense. Is a habitual beggar and expects the community to support her family. Is very ignorant. She married (V 66, also VII 12) her first cousin once removed. He was born in 1869. Is very dull in appearance, holds his mouth open, and has a projecting lower jaw. Is a hard drinker and has the reputation of being "tricky." Blind in one eye. Tries to get constant township aid on the excuse that he cannot see. He and his wife frequently go out begging together. He can neither read nor write and is feeble-minded. They have had four children, of whom one died in infancy. Their oldest son (V 120) is in the fifth grade at fifteen years. He is a sickly, dull looking child in appearance and is probably a high grade moron. Their daughter (V 121), born 1903, is in the third grade at thirteen years. She is slow, lazy, and unable to keep her attention on one thing long. She has absorbed very little in school and is without doubt defective. The fourth child, a son (V 122), was born in 1910 and has not yet gone to school.

g—A daughter (V 67), born in 1895. Lives at home and has never gone to school. No further description was obtained.

5—A son (V 21), fifth child of Martin, is married and living in another county.

6—A daughter (V 22) married her second cousin and lives in another county.

7—A son (V 24) is married and lives in another county.

8—A daughter (V 25) is married and living in another county. She has two sons, one of whom has been in the County Jail and recently left the State to avoid arrest for shooting a man.

9—Hetty (V 27), ninth child of Martin, born in 1860. Keeps her two room log house clean and is fairly industrious. Cannot read or write. Is childish and easily influenced. Before her marriage was sexually immoral.

Her oldest daughter (V 76) is said to be by her father, Martin. The truant officer, who has frequently had to visit the home of this daughter, said, "She don't act bright." She married her first cousin once removed (V 77, also VII 11), an alcoholic man, and they have had five children, of whom one died in infancy. No description was obtained of the other four.

Hetty had a second illegitimate child, a son (V 78). The father of this child was her second cousin, who was himself the illegitimate child of one of the Hickory women. His mentality was above the average of the Hickory family. This son works steadily at the brick plant and is a good citizen. He married his second cousin once removed (III 38), a woman shockingly immoral, but of fair mentality. They have no children.

Hetty married her second cousin once removed (V 29), who is the son of the father of her second illegitimate child. He is a very ignorant man, but probably of fair mentality. He was born in 1859. Can read a little, but not write. As a young man he was licentious and a thief, but is now proudly designated as a "preacher." He frequently holds services and is said to be able to preach a very good sermon. He works as a day laborer. In general he is considered honest, but last year while living on another man's place used all of his rail fences for fire wood. He and Hetty had eight children, of whom three were born dead and two died in infancy (V 79–83).

a—A daughter (V 84) married her first cousin once removed (V 85, also VII 6) and is living outside the county. He had left his first wife and six children and gone directly to live with her. She was pregnant for her second child by him before they were finally married. They have had in all five children, of whom nothing is known.

b—Nora (V 86, also IV 28) is a rough, coarse woman in appearance and has decidedly low mentality. She has always had immoral sexual habits. She married as her first husband Elza (IV 26), her second cousin. For description of them and their children see the history of the children of Sephronia. She married for her second husband, Clinton (IV 29), another second cousin, with whom she had been living for some time and by whom she had already had a child. He was a half-brother of her first husband. For further description see the history of the children of Sephronia.

c—A daughter (V 87) went to school, but never learned to read or write. Lives a wandering make-shift life and is disgustingly immoral. She married a shiftless man and has two little children.

10—A daughter (V 30), tenth child of Martin, died early of tuberculosis. She married Elza (IV 26), her first cousin once removed, as his first wife. For description of them and their children see the history of the children of Sephronia.

11—Mattie (V 31), eleventh child of Martin. One of the Hickories said of her, "She hasn't got any sense." Another described her as, "The meanest woman I ever knew." She is now living in another county with a mulatto, by whom she has two little children. She married for her legal husband her first cousin, Ralph Hickory (V 32, also VII 5), a feeble-minded alcoholic, and had four children:

a—A girl (V 89) died young.

b—A son (V 90), born in 1888. Never progressed in school. Has served several terms in the county jail and work house. One work house sentence was for "shooting his mother because she was running around with niggers." He, himself, married a mulatto, but is not living with her. He tramps all through Southern Ohio and lately has been "running with" Jude Hickory (V 35), his second cousin.

c—Nothing is known of the other two children (V 91, 92).

VIII—*Susan* (VI 1), eighth child of Happy Hickory, was born about 1824 and is the only one of the fraternity now living. Has been a hard worker and is generally respected. Receives a soldier's widow's pension and it is the general opinion that she would be better off if she did not have to support so many relatives. Has occasional township aid. Low mentality, but not feeble-minded. She married a worthless man of low intelligence as his second wife. He died in Libby Prison, leaving her with four children.

1—A daughter (VI 3) died in infancy.

2—A son (VI 4) died at thirty-five of typhoid fever. He could read and write, but never tried to get work. "He just worked around home."

3—A daughter (VI 5) born in 1858, has an uncontrollable temper and is subject to hysterical spells. Can read and write and has a fairly large vocabulary. Is dull of comprehension. Contrary and complaining. Is probably on the borderline of feeble-mindedness. She married her second cousin (VI 6), born in 1852, a lazy alcoholic, but of fairly good intelligence. They had six children:

a—Mary (VI 9) was born in 1878. She was generally considered feeble-minded. Her teeth never developed so that she was able to use them. She had an illegitimate daughter (VI 25), born 1900. This girl has never developed any teeth. Is sixteen years old and still in the first grade at school. Her teachers say that she cannot learn anything. Mary married as her first husband her second cousin (III 12), who had been brought up in a County Infirmary and was defective mentally. This husband and her one child by him are described under the descendants of Maria. Mary married for her second husband another second cousin, Clinton (IV 29), a feeble-minded man of criminal, immoral and alcoholic habits. Her three children by this man are described under the descendants of Sephronia. Mary's second husband left her while she was pregnant and she, with her three children, was sent to the County Infirmary. She died there in 1912, five weeks after the birth of her baby.

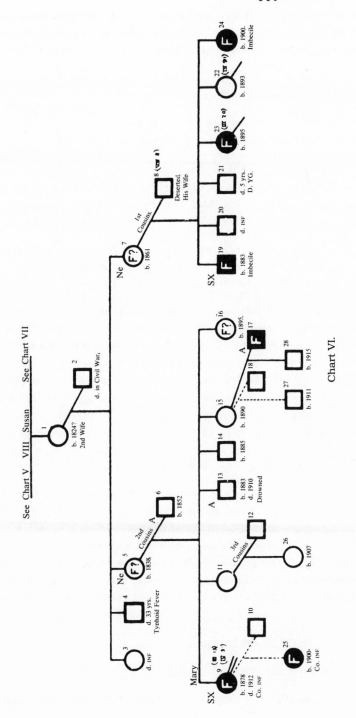

Chart VI.

b—A daughter (VI 11), said to be of good mentality. Married her third cousin, a hard worker and intelligent man. They have one child, born in 1907, who does well in school.

c—A son (VI 13) was born in 1883. Said to have been of fair intelligence. Was drowned while drunk.

d—A son (VI 14), born in 1885. Seems to be of fair mentality, but has never been known to work. Spends his time hunting.

e—A daughter (VI 15), born in 1890, is of good intelligence. She has an illegitimate boy, born in 1911, who is bright. She married a feeble-minded alcoholic as his third wife. He was already the father of at least two defective children. They have one child, born in 1915.

f—A daughter (VI 18), born in 1895. Could not learn in school. Described by her mother as "not as bright as the other children." Was away from home at the time of the field worker's visit.

4—A daughter (VI 7), born in 1861. Quick, nervous, uncontrollable temper, quarrelsome. Is hard working, but a dirty housekeeper. Writes a little, but cannot read. Cannot count money and has no idea of its value. At one time she took a roll of bills to a grocer and asked him to keep them for her. She had earned this money digging roots and taking in washings. He found that she had one hundred and forty dollars, but this seemed to mean no more to her than two or three dollars would to the ordinary person. She is probably on the borderline of feeble-mindedness. She married her first cousin (VI 8, also VII 8), who left her and went to live with another Hickory woman. They had six children:

a—A son (VI 19), born in 1883. Imbecile. Is considered defective by all the Hickories. Does no work and spends his time wandering through the woods. The inhabitants of the community are exercised because he is allowed to be at large, as they say it is not safe for a woman to go out alone when he is around. He has attacked several girls, but is not strong enough physically to overcome them. He complained to the field worker that he could not find a woman to marry him.

b—A son (VI 20) died in infancy.

c—A son (VI 21) died at five years.

d—A daughter (VI 22) can read and write. Is neat in appearance and seems more intelligent than the average Hickory. She married her second cousin once removed (IV 90), who is feeble-minded, alcoholic and dishonest. For description of his people and their children see the history of the descendants of Sephronia.

e—A daughter (VI 23), born in 1895. Said to be of about the same mentality as her oldest brother. Married Aaron, her second cousin (III 18). See history of the children of Maria.

f—A daughter (VI 24), born in 1900. Small and underdeveloped. Her mother thinks she is deformed and says that she behaves like a child six years old. She has never been able to get out of the first grade in school.

IX—*Harriet* (VII 1), ninth child of Happy Hickory, was born in 1826 and died in 1907 of pneumonia. She was blind for the last ten years of her life. An old resident described her, "As bright as any of them and a little brighter than some of them." She married a shiftless man (VII 2) as his second wife. The only work he ever did was to made axe-handles. He had seventeen children by his two wives. Nine of these children were by Harriet.

1—A son (VII 3). He is not considered bright, but does not drink and is law-abiding. His family gets along although he shows no judgment about spending money and his wife has no idea of economy. He earns a fair amount but they are always poor. He works as a laborer. Has been married twice. His second wife (V 12) was his first cousin. Nothing is known of his children.

2—Ralph (VII 5), born about 1870. A basket maker. Is usually supported by some of his relatives because he drinks up all the money he earns. Is rather pompous and likes to attract attention. Can read but not write. Employers will not hire him for day labor. Is a high grade feeble-minded person. Married his first cousin (V 31), who has since left him. For description of their children see the history of Mattie, the youngest child of Martin.

3—A daughter (VII 6) married and had four children, two of whom died early in life of tuberculosis. The family receive constant township aid.

4—A son (VII 8), now living in another county. Married his first cousin (VI 7) for his first wife. Left her and went to live with a first cousin

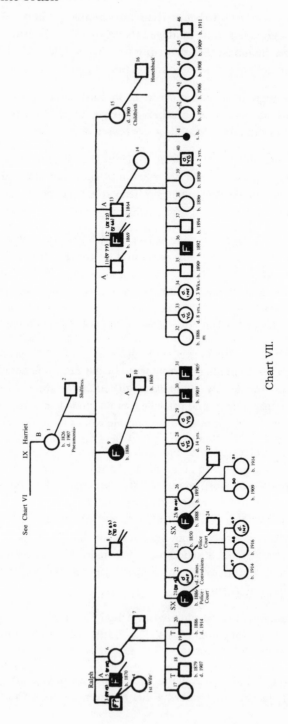

Chart VII.

once removed (V 84), whom he has since married. For further description of his children by these two marriages see the history of the descendants of Susan and Martin.

5—A daughter (VII 9), born in 1866. Eyelids are inflamed from trachoma. Never went to school. Cannot talk intelligently. Could not give the names of her brothers correctly. Feeble-minded. Married a man of passable intelligence (VII 2), who is an epileptic. He works steadily but does not get ahead because he has to support so many of his wife's relatives. He and his wife have had nine children.

a—A daughter (VII 21), born in 1886. Went to school two years, but could not learn. A sex offender before her marriage. In police court for slandering, cursing, and immorality. Married her second cousin (IV 14), a feeble-minded man. For list of their children see the history of the children of Sephronia.

b—A daughter (VII 22) died at two months in convulsions.

c—A daughter (VII 25), born in 1888. Went to school two years, but cannot read or write. Is immoral. Does not know how to manage her home. Quarrels frequently with her husband. Married her second cousin, a feeble-minded man (II 48). For description of him and their children see the history of the descendants of Old Hank.

d—A daughter (VII 23), born in 1890. Is considered the brightest child in the family. Went to school three years and reached the second grade. Was arrested with her sister for cursing, slandering, and immorality. Is married and has had three children, one of whom died in infancy.

e—A daughter (VII 26), born in 1893. Went to school two years but cannot write or read. Married a Hickory and has two small children. Living outside the county.

f—A daughter (VII 28) died at fourteen years. The cause given by the mother was, "eating too much sauerkraut."

g—A daughter (VII 29) died young.

h—A son (VII 30), born in 1901. Goes to school irregularly and is in the second grade at fifteen years. Teacher says he cannot do as well as first grade pupils. Cannot answer ordinary questions. Is pale and weak physically.

i—A son (VII 31), born in 1905. In the first grade at eleven years. Looks brighter than his brother, but makes no better progress.

6—A son (VII 11), is a fairly good worker in the mine. Is reckless and a "terrible drinker." Married his first cousin once removed (V 76). For description of her and her children see the history of the children of Martin.

7—A son (VII 12), born in 1869. A hard drinker and a habitual beggar. Receives frequent township aid and private aid. Does not work if he can help it. Married twice to first cousins once removed (IV 21 and V 65). For description of his children by these marriages see the histories of the children of Sephronia and Martin.

8—A son (VII 13), born in 1864. Cannot read or write, but is a steady worker. Owns a small piece of land. Is a regular drinker. He married (VII 14), a woman of good mentality who is industrious and can read and write. They have had fifteen children of whom eleven are now living. They all seem to be bright children with the exception of one, a son (VII 36), born in 1892. Although he went to school for several years, he cannot read or write. Works every day in the mine, but is considered defective. Has a peculiar gait and likes to do things to attract attention. Is a subject for jokes.

9—A daughter (VII 15) died in 1900 of childbirth, leaving three children. Nothing is known of this family except that her husband was a hunchback.

X—*Sarah* (See Chart I), tenth child of Happy Hickory, died at sixteen years of tuberculosis.

XI—*Robert* (See Chart I), eleventh child of Happy Hickory, died in 1861 of tuberculosis. An old inhabitant said of him, "He did not look sensible." He married and had ten children, of whom seven are now living in another county.

II. The D. Family

The D. family, although it does not approach the Hickory family in frequency of mental defect and extent of dependency, nevertheless was found to have contributed largely to the number of defectives and dependents in the county. It was interesting to find that defectives in six different families found in separated sections of the county traced back to the original D. stock. An officer who aided the field worker, when told of these relationships, was impressed by the fact that, as he put it, "All the families that cause us trouble around here are really one family."

The study was begun with a fraternity of six. A brief description of the family follows:

The Fraternity

1. Female, 33 years old. Not feeble-minded. Lewd. Lives life of a tramp and a prostitute. In court for drunkenness and prostitution. Married. No children. Probably an illegitimate child of her mother.

2. Female, 30 years old. Moron. Syphilitic. Described as Case 16. Married her second cousin. Daughter in Ohio Hospital for Epileptics.

3. Male, 28 years old. Moron. Perhaps epileptic. Alcoholic. Petty thief. Police court. Served a term in Ohio State Reformatory for larceny. Seldom works. Married. Two little children.

4. Male, 27 years old. Moron. Has been in workhouse for non-support. Petty thief. Seldom works. Married feeble-minded girl. Three little children.

5. Male, 20 years old. Moron. Petty thief. In Boys' Industrial School for truancy. In Ohio State Reformatory with cousin for forgery. Cousin made out the check and he tried to cash it. Both broke parole by breaking into a box car. Both now in Ohio State Reformatory.

6. Male, 18 years old. Not feeble-minded. Illegitimate child of mother. Only one of family who works steadily. His is the only legitimate support of the family.

Whole family is a nuisance to authorities because of constant thieving and demands for township aid. Are frequently threatened with Infirmary unless they go to work.

The Father and His Fraternity

Fifty-five years old. Moron. Blind since a young man. Has never worked. Cannot carry on a conversation. Stops in middle of a sentence and has to be prompted. Had a sister who died in Infirmary and a nephew is now an inmate there. Other of his fraternity are good citizens.

The Mother and Her Fraternity

1. Mother, fifty-four years old. Moron. In police court for petty thefts. Has been driven out of town because of lewdness. Is sly and scheming in a simple way. Unreliable. Blind in one eye. Dirty. Tall and gaunt. Syphilitic. Keeps a sickeningly dirty house.

2. Male. Probably borderline intelligence. Fairly good worker. Petty thief. Has two children, a son of low intelligence, a petty thief and alcoholic; and a daughter who has had several illegitimate children.

3. Male, sixty-two years old. Low grade moron. Lowest mentality in the fraternity. Makes axe handles. Receives constant township aid. Syphilitic. Described as Case 17. Had two children; younger an imbecile, in Children's Home, had congenital syphilis, now dead. Older, a moron, is living.

4. Male. Borderline mentality. Lazy. Sly. Scheming. Sexually immoral. Has lived with at least four different women. Two small children by fourth wife. By third wife were four children. Two died in infancy. Son, twenty-four years old, not feeble-minded. Now in Ohio State Reformatory with his cousin, No. 5 of original fraternity. Daughter, twenty years old, borderline mentality. In Girls' Industrial Home for immorality. Married her second cousin while out on parole. She is said to have had a syphilitic infection since eight years old. Husband also syphilitic. He has been in jail for drunkenness and fighting. His mentality unknown. One child, born in a box car, died in infancy from congenital syphilis.

5. Female. Mentality unknown. Alcoholic. Sexually immoral. Married.

The Mother's Father and His Fraternity

Mother's father was honest, but could not provide for his family. "Good for nothing." Became demented late in life. Died at eighty years. Four brothers were respectable. Two sisters died in County Infirmary, one early of tuberculosis, the other old.

The Mother's Mother and Her Fraternity

1. Mother's mother, born in 1819 in the county where she always lived. Feeble-minded. Was a popular superstition that she was a witch. Was avoided. "All she did was run around." Petty thief and a beggar. Sexually immoral. Was twice in the County Infirmary in old age. Died about 1904.

2. Male. Said to have been of fair intelligence. Died in County Infirmary. Had six children. Nothing known of three of these. Daughter is sexually immoral. Two sons are frequently in court for drunkenness and stealing. Generally considered worthless. So far as known is no feeble-mindedness in this branch of family, though are two suspected cases.

3. Male. Born 1806 in Pennsylvania. Mentality undetermined. Shiftless. Sexually immoral. Said to have been active in Methodist revi-

vals. Spent several winters in Infirmary. Three children by first wife. One died young. Second, a son, living in another county, said to spend much time in County Infirmary. Third, a daughter, was syphilitic and reported feeble-minded. She had a daughter, also syphilitic, in the County Infirmary and the Insane Hospital, and a feeble-minded grand-daughter is now in the County Infirmary. She is referred to in the section on the County Infirmary as the twenty-one year old girl who, while living as a prostitute, became infected with syphilis. One child by second wife. He, with this wife and child, was twice in the Infirmary. Wife died there. He left and was back the next winter with a third wife. Since his death she has been twice admitted to the Infirmary. Has now been an inmate since 1907.

4. Male. Born 1805. In County Infirmary when old. Old record says, "Previous habits worthless." Had eleven children. One daughter was epileptic and had an epileptic and feeble-minded son who died in the Infirmary at twenty-four years. A feeble-minded child was found in the public school who was descended from a second daughter. A third daughter was in the County Infirmary for the second time at twenty-six years. The record reads, "Simple and bad with syphilis." She afterwards married. A fourth daughter was in the Infirmary with her husband when they were old. They had an epileptic daughter, a son of borderline mentality, and an imbecile grandson. A fifth child, a son, is shiftless and of low mentality. Two of his nine children have been patients at the Ohio Hospital for Epileptics.

5. Female. No record of her descendants.

6. Female. No record of her descendants.

7. Female. Had four children. One was found living in the county. Now childish from old age. Physician says she has always been feeble-minded and sexually immoral. Has children by several men. Four daughters, all bad characters, two of them probably feeble-minded. One son, forty-five years old, feeble-minded and speech defect. Tends door in doctor's office for fifty cents a day. Two grandchildren, both illegitimate. Granddaughter is feeble-minded and immoral. Grandson, probably feeble-minded. Has gone off with a circus. A fifth daughter is intelligent. Only one in family who does not have a speech defect. Supports her mother, brother and niece by sewing.

Sixteen feeble-minded persons were found, two in the Ohio Hospital for Epileptics, one in the Ohio State Reformatory, one in the County Infirmary, and the other twelve at large in the county who were related by blood and descended from a common ancestor who came from Pennsylvania about the year 1800. Thirteen of his descendants have been in the County Infirmary together with six consorts, three have been in the Ohio Hospital for Epileptics, three in the Ohio State Reformatory, one in the Girls' Industrial Home, one in the Boys' Industrial School, and numerous others have been in police court and county jail. One branch of the family is characterized by the appearance of epilepsy, and there are also a large number of syphilitics throughout the whole strain.

III. The S. Family

John S. The father. Born in Southern Ohio, date unknown. Feeble-minded. Could not read, write or count. Could not distinguish pieces of money. His daughter said that he "did not seem to know how to manage." Lived in shanties on other people's farms and was several times an inmate of the Infirmary. Had a severe speech defect. Died at about fifty-four years of tuberculosis. First wife was feeble-minded. "She didn't know enough to take care of herself," and "She didn't have no sense at all," were things said of her by her own relatives. They had seven children. An old Infirmary record reads: "John S. and family received July 8, 1870. Ages not given, they all being idiotic." The family included his wife and four children. Their seven children were as follows:

1—The first child died young as a result of burns.

2—Daughter, born about 1860. Low grade imbecile. Epileptic. Was in the County Infirmary for ten years and has been in the State Institution for Feeble-Minded for the past thirty-seven years. Her mentality is that of a child between three and four years old.

3—Son. "Was not bright." "Took after his father." Was drowned at seven years at the Infirmary.

4—Daughter. Feeble-minded. Thinks she was born in 1865. Reached second grade in school. Remained in the Infirmary till she was a young woman. Went out, married a colored man and had eleven children by him. Has always been sexually immoral. Encourages her children to immorality. Neglects and mistreats them because they are colored, so she says. Goes out washing and cleaning. Will work all day for a few old clothes. Is not considered bright in the community. She married a Negro for her second husband, but he has since left her. Her children by her first husband follow:

a—Female, died at four years.

b—Male, born in 1885. A hard drinker and immoral. Left his wife and is now living with a young girl discharged from the Girls' Industrial Home.

c—Female. Married and living outside the county.

d—Male. Was killed by a train while drunk when thirty years old.

e—Female. Is married and living outside the state.

f—Female. Said to be brighter than her sibs. Working as a domestic. In court for fighting. Has an illegitimate daughter of good intelligence.

g—Female. Not bright. In court for theft several times. Sexually immoral. Has illegitimate son. Once tried to kill father of her child and then to commit suicide. Living in another county.

h—Male. Lives at home. Works in coal bank. A hard drinker. Low mentality.

i—Male. Lives at home. Works in coal bank. A hard drinker. Low mentality.

j—Female. At home. Sexually immoral. Had to leave school at fourteen years because pregnant. Has illegitimate son. Low intelligence.

k—Male. Born dead.

5—Son. Died at three years at County Infirmary. Idiot. Could never hold up his head.

6, 7—The sixth and seventh children were twins, born in the Infirmary in 1870. They died at birth.

John S.'s first wife died at the Infirmary at the time the twins were born. A record two months later in the same year reads: "John S. discharged for bad conduct." He had had bad relations with a woman who had come to the Infirmary to give birth to a child. This woman was married, but her husband had left her. She was of low mentality, sexually immoral, and later was known to have acquired syphilis. She and John left the Infirmary together, leaving their five children behind. They afterwards had eight children, who follow:

1, 2—The first two were born dead.

3—Male. Died at ten years of spinal meningitis. Speech defect.

4—Female. Died in infancy.

5—Female. Born about 1880. High grade feeble-minded. Works out by the day, cleaning and washing. Speech defect. Married but lives with her husband only at intervals. Quarrelsome. Very immoral. Her sister said, "But then, she only lives with one man at a time." Has had no children.

6—Female. Jane, born in 1883. Feeble-minded. Never went to school. Voluble. Poor memory and no common sense. Does not know the ages of her children. Says there is no use for any one to tell her because she won't remember them. Dirty housekeeper. Takes in washings. Receives private charity. Has been in jail several times for drunkenness and prostitution. Delights to talk about sexual matters. Has been very immoral. Had had four illegitimate children when married. Married a feeble-minded man with psychopathic tendency, a drinker of pure alcohol. Has had children by another man since her marriage. Her children follow:

a—The oldest, a boy, was born when she was sixteen years old. His father is supposed to be Jane's step-father, described as Case 30. Aunt said that child did not walk or talk until six years old. Is very backward in school. Has stolen money from cash box of corner grocery. Probably feeble-minded.

b—The second and fourth children died in infancy. Their fathers were not definitely known.

c—The third child, a boy, born in 1904. Backward in school but not defective.

d—Girl, born 1908. Cross-eyed and feeble-minded. Still in first grade in school. This child and the sixth who died in infancy were by her husband.

e—Girl, born 1910. Was by a blind alcoholic who lived neighbor to them. As yet shows no sign of mental defect.

7—Cynthia, born about 1885. Imbecile. Living in the County Infirmary. Can do simple tasks if someone watches her and directs her. Speech defect. Cannot read or write. Sexually immoral. She has been admitted to the Infirmary five times. The record reads as follows: "Admitted Jan. 16, 1899, destitute and pregnant." "Discharged Feb. 23,

1899." "Admitted March 19, 1901." "Discharged June 30, 1901." "Admitted Dec. 12, 1901, destitute and pregnant." "Discharged Sept. 6, 1903." "Admitted Aug. 30, 1907, with her child." "Discharged May 22, 1908." The date of the fifth admission does not appear on the books, but she is at present an inmate of the County Infirmary and has been for several years. Her oldest child, a daughter, was born in 1899 when Cynthia was fourteen. She reached the third grade in school at sixteen years. Is a moron and developing the sexual characteristics of her mother. She was in the County Infirmary as a child with her mother. Is now living with her Aunt Jane. The second child, a son, was born in the County Infirmary in 1901 and has lived there all his life with the exception of six weeks. He is a deformed imbecile and has not been sent to the Children's Home in order that he may be kept with his mother. His father was Cynthia's step-father, described as Case 30.

8—Female, died at twelve years of childbirth. Mentality unknown.

We are impressed with the fact that John S., recognized as feeble-minded and dependent upon the public for his maintenance, was allowed to choose a second wife from the Infirmary population, and leaving his four feeble-minded children in the Infirmary to be taken care of by the county, go out with her and bring eight other children into the world. But three of these eight survived and all three are both feeble-minded and viciously immoral. They are now bringing a third generation of defectives into the world. And all because a man with a child's mind was given the freedom and personal liberty which is the right of the normal-minded person, but which can never be wisely used by one of feeble intelligence.

IV. The N. Family

Peter N. came from West Virginia to the Ohio Country. Taught a back district school. Was a hard drinker. Died while on a drunken spree. Married a West Virginia woman who was "not very bright" and had a speech defect. She was possibly feeble-minded. They had twelve children, six boys and six girls.

1—Male, born 1829. Died 1911 in County Infirmary of apoplexy. Was twice admitted to the Infirmary and spent three years and eleven months of his life there. Basket maker. Occasionally worked in harvest field. Lazy, likable, good natured, heavy drinker, very religious, speech defect, partially dependent most of his life. Married a woman who had idiotic child in Institution for Feeble-Minded, and had five children:

a—The oldest son, born 1867. Steady worker. Hard drinker. Fair intelligence. Has feeble-minded child.

b—The second son. Hard drinker. Speech defect. Fairly good worker. Walked into the river when drunk and drowned. Never married.

c—The third son. Low mentality. Basket maker. Hard drinker. Never married. Died of tubercular abcesses.

d—The fourth son, born 1873. Generally considered feeble-minded. Speech defect, peculiar idioms. Works on farms, but cannot hold a job. Hard drinker. Has spent two years and nine months in the County Infirmary. Not married.

e—The fifth child, a girl born 1876. Died of cancer of the stomach. Could not read or write. Could not talk plainly. Lazy, dirty, immoral. Said on good authority to have been feeble-minded. Admitted to the County Infirmary January 29, 1896, "pregnant and destitute." Discharged May 7, 1896. Father of her child a worthless tramp. Child born 1896. Was sent to Girl's Industrial Home for immorality. Present whereabouts unknown.

2—Male, never married. Heavy drinker. Said to have been the brightest son in the family. Killed by a train while drunk.

3—Male, never married. Heavy drinker. Killed by a train while drunk.

4—Male, born 1843. Never married. Basket maker. Unusually heavy drinker. Said to have been much below par in intelligence. Was twice admitted to the County Infirmary. Spent five years there. Found dead in a creek. Had been on drunken spree.

6*—Male, born 1845. Went to school but was not able to learn to read and write. Made baskets and pick handles. Hard drinker. Speech defect. Small beady eyes. Expressionless face. Unable to carry on a conversation. Inmate of the County Infirmary. Has been there four years. Married a nervous hysterical woman and had eight children; four daughters are married. No description of them obtained.

a—One son, died young.

b—Second son, a heavy drinker. Shot in drunken fight.

* Fifth child skipped in original.—Ed.

c—Third son not married. Lives alone in a shanty with a couple of hounds. Makes pick handles. Is drunk most of the time. Generally recognized as feeble-minded. Is physically crippled.

d—Fourth son, born 1874. At present an inmate of County Infirmary. Has been there over four years. Helpless cripple, diagnosis, locomotor ataxia. Formerly a hard drinker. Better mentality than that of his father. Married and had four children; two were born dead, and two died at birth.

7—Female, considered much below average intelligence. Not considered immoral, but once ran away with her brother-in-law. Died at thirty-five of tuberculosis. Had four children, for two of whom no description was obtained.

a—A son was remembered by a former school-mate as a big boy in the primer class. Present whereabouts unknown.

b—A daughter was very backward in school. Was twice in the County Infirmary to give birth to children. Died in 1894 of childbirth. Her oldest daughter, born 1885 in County Infirmary, is now an inmate there. When a child was transferred to the Children's Home. When nine years was committed to the Girls' Industrial Home. At sixteen was paroled and went to live with her grandmother. At eighteen was sent back to the Infirmary, where she has been ever since. During her two years freedom gave birth to an illegitimate child which died in infancy. This girl makes a co-efficient of mental ability of .63 by the Yerkes-Bridges Point scale. She is feeble-minded. Her brother, born in the Infirmary, died in infancy. No description was obtained for another brother and sister.

8—Female, was probably of defective intelligence. A relative said, "Her house burned down and she paid no attention to it." Could read, but not write. Was dirty and immoral. Died about 1908 of old age. Married into a family of low intelligence and thieving habits. Had five children:

a—The oldest son not considered bright. Ran away with a circus at sixteen years.

b—A daughter died many years ago. Was married and had six children.

c—The third child, a son, born 1873. Is now an inmate of County Infirmary. Has been there four years. Worked at basket making, but could never make a living. Talks very little. Imbecile. Married and had two children who died.

d—The fourth child, a girl, had a speech defect. Said to be as feeble-minded as her brother in the infirmary. Now dead. Married her second cousin and had two children now in other states.

e—The fifth child, said to be "not very bright," settled in another county.

9—Female, hard worker and of good intelligence. Married an intelligent man and had nine children, one of whom died young and another at thirty years of tuberculosis. The others were all said to have been of normal intelligence.

10—Female, born in 1848. As a young woman spent a month in County Infirmary when ill with typhoid fever. Had good reputation, probably not below normal in intelligence. Married her first cousin and had five children:

a—A son died in the army.

b—A daughter married and is now dead.

c—Another daughter was never married and died at nineteen of childbirth.

d—A son not married. Died at twenty-four years of tuberculosis.

e—A daughter born 1874. Recognized as feeble-minded by her own relatives. Was twice in the County Infirmary. Spent in all ten months there. On second admission was "pregnant and destitute." Very repulsive in appearance, sore eyes and mouth, projecting teeth, dirty. The story was told that her husband left her because she "cooked a young pig with its eyes in." Had an illegitimate son, now in another state. Her daughter, born 1895, was for two months in the County Infirmary with her mother, as a child. Said to be of low mentality, but a clean housekeeper. Has married a member of a defective family. The third child was born in 1898 in the County Infirmary. The story is that when three years old her dress caught fire from a pipe that she was smoking. Her mother tried to put out the flames and both she and the child died as a result of the burns sustained.

11—Female. Dirty, lazy. Said to have been below average intelligence. "As near no-account as she could be." Died old. Married her first cousin and had five children:

a—The oldest daughter is of good intelligence.

b—The second daughter, born in 1861. Low grade imbecile. Microcephalic. Walks in stooped position, makes queer gestures and mumbles. Less than five feet tall. Is popularly believed to look like a muskrat. Defect thought to be due to maternal impression.

c—The third daughter. Much below average intelligence. Lazy. Extremely immoral sexually and alcoholic. Married her second cousin, who had a speech defect and was a hard drinker. They had ten children, for whom descriptions were not obtained.

d—The fourth child, a son, never married. Lives alone in a shanty. Works chopping wood or as a porter and bar-keeper in a country saloon. Hard drinker. His sister said of him, "People say he ain't bright."

e—The fifth child, a daughter, born in 1876. Recognized by her family as feeble-minded. Sexually immoral. Once in the Infirmary as a young woman and spent one winter there since her marriage. Married an alcoholic man, but they quarrel frequently and separate. They have had two children. A boy died at six years. A girl, born 1899, was sent to the Girls' Industrial Home for truancy when sixteen years old. At that time she had a mental age of 8.7 years by psychological test.

12—Female. Speech defect. Could not read or write. Died old. She, with her husband and son, were familiar figures on the country roads as they spent most of their time visiting their friends. She always carried some bread in the front of her dress. All three were said to be weak-minded. Her son is now living in another county. Was described as "anaemic and not bright enough to take care of himself." A physician said "He is almost a drooling idiot." He picks berries and digs greens for a living. He married into a defective strain and had eight children, all of whom died in infancy or died young.

Sixteen members of the N Family have been inmates of the County Infirmary in three generations, and the third generation is still young. Four were inmates of the infirmary when it was visited by the field worker. Eleven members of this family known to be feeble-minded were located of whom six were at large in the county and three in the Infirmary. There were several others who were probably feeble-minded but sufficient data are lacking for final diagnosis. The men of the family have been heavy drinkers, five of them having met sudden death while drunk. Many of the women have been sexually immoral. The family is best known for its dependent habits. Through the wife of Peter N. they are related to the Z Family, who are believed to have originally come from New Jersey, but remained several years in West Virginia before coming to Ohio. People with the Z name are numerous in the county and are generally shiftless, dishonest, and inclined to get into police court for drunkenness and petty offenses. Their mentality is generally of a low order but the larger number of them are self-supporting. Five feeble-minded persons were found in the county who were descended from Jo Z., a first cousin of the wife of Peter N. When these are added to the nine feeble-minded descendants of Peter N and his wife, it makes a total of fourteen feeble-minded persons found living in the county who belong to the N–Z strain.

V. Summary of Defective Strains

The 4 families which have been described in detail are the most important defective strains in the county. The Hickory family alone is responsible for 13.5% of the total feeble-minded population of the county. The following table shows the number of feeble-minded contributed by each of five family groups to the total number of feeble-minded in the county.

Table XV. Feeble-Minded in the County Belonging to Five Family Strains

	At Large.	In One of the County Institutions.	Total.
The Hickory Family	72	6	78
The N–Z Family	11	3	14
The D Family	12	1	13
The Y Family	9	2	11
The X Family	10	——	10
Five Families	114	12	126

There are many smaller family groups of feeble-minded included in the total. A summary of them is given below:

2 groups of 9 feeble-minded in a family = 18 feeble-minded
2 groups of 8 feeble-minded in a family = 16 feeble-minded
4 groups of 7 feeble-minded in a family = 28 feeble-minded
6 groups of 6 feeble-minded in a family = 36 feeble-minded
5 groups of 5 feeble-minded in a family = 25 feeble-minded
6 groups of 4 feeble-minded in a family = 24 feeble-minded
12 groups of 3 feeble-minded in a family = 36 feeble-minded
29 groups of 2 feeble-minded in a family = 58 feeble-minded

66 groups   241 feeble-minded

It is an established fact that feeble-mindedness is hereditary. Therefore, one need not be surprised that the feeble-minded in this county were found to group themselves in families. This fact makes the necessity of segregating the feeble-minded the more urgent as each one left at large in this generation may be the parent of numberless others in generations to come. One can not estimate the saving to the county if Happy Hickory had been segregated, but at least the community would have been saved its present burden of contributing to the support and submitting to the petty thieving and vicious immorality of seventy-five feeble-minded Hickories. The county would also have been saved the care of twenty-three Hickories in the County Infirmary, and twenty in the Children's Home. And in addition, neighboring counties would have been saved a similar burden by the segregation of Happy Hickory.

Another important fact brought out by the study was that members of these different defective strains tend to marry each other. The reason may or may not be clear but the result is evident, that when both parents carry a similar defect but do not show it, that defect is very likely to appear in their children, especially if the fraternity is large. Several instances might be pointed out where both parents of the defective child are seemingly normal, but have feeble-minded relatives. The only way of meeting this condition is to acquaint the public with the danger of a marriage between two people whose families show similar defects, and help them to realize that there are certain laws of heredity which govern feeble-mindedness.

G. TOTAL NUMBER OF FEEBLE-MINDED IN THE COUNTY

According to an estimate of the U.S. Census Bureau, this county had on July 1, 1916, 54,389 inhabitants. When the number of feeble-minded found at large in the county is added to the number in the state and county institutions, the total is 577 feeble-minded persons, or 1.06%, or 10.6 persons to every 1000 of the population of the county. The cases were distributed as follows:

	Males	Females	Total
In the Institution for Feeble-Minded	8	12	20
In other State Institutions	11	10	21
In the County Infirmary	21	11	32
In the Children's Home	6	4	10
In the population at large	303	191	494
Totals	349	228	577

Although 83, or 14.3% of the total number of feeble-minded were in various institutions, only 20, or 3.4% were properly segregated in an appropriate institution, the Institution for Feeble-Minded. Four were in an insane hospital where they will probably be confined the rest of their lives and very likely a small proportion of those in the Infirmary will always remain there, but the larger number were in institutions where the length of residence is limited and from which they will at some time be turned back into the community at large.

Approximately 1% of the total population of this county was found to be feeble-minded. In order to make an estimate of the number of feeble-minded in the state as a whole, it would be necessary to conduct surveys in other representative parts of Ohio. The percentage in this county is perhaps representative of the hilly section in the southeastern part of the state, though it is hardly possible that every county in that section should have a Hickory family. However, it may be said that when this county was chosen as the subject of the survey, the existence of the Hickory Family was not known. But whatever the percentage for the whole state, the fact that a few defective strains have contributed such a large proportion to the total number of feeble-minded in the county should impress upon one the fact of the inheritability of mental defects, and should make one consider means of checking the propagation of the feeble-minded. If Ohio is to meet this problem by segregation, provision at the Institution for Feeble-Minded must be made on a much more extended scale than is at present contemplated.

11

A. C. ROGERS AND
MAUD A. MERRILL

Dwellers in the Vale of Siddem*

Preface

Dwellers in the Vale of Siddem continues the trend of using ever-looser criteria to identify the mentally retarded. Rejecting the view of mental defect as a unit trait, the authors prefer to conceptualize intelligence as a continuum on which the cutoff point for retardation may be raised as civilization becomes more demanding. Like Sessions, they draw on the definition of the Royal Commission but expand it—in this case to include as "feeble-minded" people who are not mental but "moral defectives." These "are the 'feebly inhibited' of Davenport's ... classification" (pp. 344–45),

> the ne'er-do-wells, who lacking the initiative and stick-to-it-iveness of energy and ambition, drift from failure to failure, spending a winter in the poor house, moving from shack to hovel and succeeding only in the reproduction of ill-nurtured, ill-kempt gutter brats to carry on the family traditions of dirt, disease and degeneracy [p. 347].

Some—those who commit overtly criminal acts—are "defective delinquents" (p. 345). All are "the gravest sort of social menace" (p. 350).

That the family studies literature was inspired in part by professional self-interest is well illustrated by this example. Both authors worked at the Minnesota School for Feeble-Minded and Colony for Epileptics, Rogers as its superintendent, Merrill in its Department of Research. Their basic argument is that many Minnesotans—all who earn a metaphorical home in Siddem by doing "things they shouldn't do" (p. 347)—belong in their institution. Six from the actual vicinity of Hog Hollow are there already. This figure would be higher had not two been removed, "against the urgent protest of the superintendent, from the institution by a well-meaning relative"; they naturally got into trouble, one becoming a prostitute, the other wife to a drunkard (pp. 365–66). Officials of institutions for the feeble-minded are best equipped to handle defectives:

> Such communities as the Vale of Siddem bear eloquent testimony to the futility of trying to cope with such social inefficiency from the standpoint of the criminologist of holding the individual responsible for his misdeeds when he is fundamentally irresponsible, or from the point of view of the philanthropist improv-

---

* Originally published by Richard G. Badger, The Gorham Press, Boston, 1919.

ing his condition and helping him to help himself when he is fundamentally
incapable of self help [p. 347].

Institutionalization alone provides the eugenic segregation necessary to
staunch the flow of degeneracy.

Its first inhabitants migrated to the Vale from New York, "driven out for
fraudulently settling on Indian lands." Although originally several separate families, most today are "interwoven by marriage." Rogers and Merrill organize their discussion around various family groups: the Yaks
(641 individuals, 27 percent outright defectives and more "simply incapable"); the Coreys (products of By Corey and Tildy Yak, characterized by
feeble-mindedness and insanity); the Tams (offspring of Roxy Anne Corey
and Washington Tam, afflicted by illegitimacy, idiocy, and epilepsy); and
so on. The Vale also shelters serious criminals, as the chapters on "Little
Tommy" and "The Counterfeiters" are meant to demonstrate. These
criminals, however, have almost no genealogical links to the other
families.

Faster-paced than many family studies, *Dwellers in the Vale* is none-
theless weaker than others in substance and style. It shows signs of having been written hurriedly. For example, the authors (following Dugdale)
conclude with a chapter on "The Cost" but make no effort to tote up the
expense to the state of the 1,600 Hog Hollow residents they claim to have
charted. Even by family studies standards, they play fast and loose with
evidence. And this study is the most self-consciously "artful" in style.
These defects may reflect the circumstances under which it was produced: Rogers died not long after the work was begun, leaving his assistant to complete it; and she soon decided to move on to graduate school.

Arthur Curtis Rogers, trained as a physician at the State University of
Iowa, was superintendent of the Minnesota School for Feeble-Minded at
Faribault from 1885 until his death in 1917. Under him the school gained
national attention for both its rapid expansion and its research on mental defect. An active eugenicist, Rogers served twice as chair of the
committee on defectives of the National Conference of Charities and Correction and was for many years editor-in-chief of the *Journal of Psycho-
Asthenics*, an important vehicle for dissemination of information on the
care and control of the retarded.

The collaboration between Rogers and Merrill parallels that of family
study authors Henry Goddard and Elizabeth Kite, also an institutional
superintendent and his assistant. Maud Amanda Merrill was better educated than her New Jersey counterpart, however, and far more successful
professionally. Born in Minnesota in 1888, she graduated from Oberlin

College before joining Rogers's staff. In 1923 she received a Ph.D. in psychology from Stanford University, where she taught for many years, becoming a full professor in 1947. Merrill's publications dealt mainly with intelligence measurement and delinquency.

PREFACE

The story of the Dwellers in the Vale of Siddem is a study in feeble-mindedness in one of its various aspects. It was written in fulfillment of a plan of the authors to publish in story form the family history studies made at the Minnesota School for the Feeble-Minded with a view to portraying the conditions just as they have been found in the investigation of the homes of the institution children. It was Dr. Rogers' purpose to add his own commentaries and conclusions drawn from the wealth of his experience acquired during his thirty-three years of work with the feeble-minded.

The death of Dr. Rogers in January, 1917, when the work on the stories was but started, made it impossible to carry out the plan as at first outlined. It was his wish that I complete the work in accordance with the original plan. In its conception, the whole idea and purpose of the study are Dr. Rogers'. In partial fulfillment of that plan I am publishing the present story which is one of a series of studies of feeble-mindedness which will appear later.

The authors' grateful acknowledgments are due to Miss Saidee C. Devitt whose work in the collection of the data for the study made the work possible, also to Miss Marie T. Curial, fieldworker, and to Dr. F. Kuhlmann whose constant help and encouragement have been invaluable.

MAUD A. MERRILL

May, 1918.

INTRODUCTION

In 1911 were begun, at the Minnesota School for the Feeble-Minded and Colony for Epileptics, studies of the family histories of the inmates of the institution. The story of the "Dwellers in the Vale of Siddem" is a description of the conditions that were found in one section of the state where for several generations the descendants of a few families had lived and continued to intermarry. Starting with the case study of a child in the institution, all living relatives in the state are visited and interviewed, and such people who know the family, doctors, lawyers and officials, as are able to give information about them. These studies revealed an appalling amount of mental deficiency in particular districts of the state. Further investigations revealed the family connection of several children in the institution who were not known to be related. They were from a certain valley, where in one county we found such numbers of feeble-minded and degenerate people that we have selected that section for special investigation.

The data have been recorded as received from each member of the family who has been interviewed together with all additional information that could be gathered from people who knew the families. We have thus the testimony of a number of people in regard to each individual studied. These actual facts tell the story. In the making of the charts and where it has been necessary to express a judgment, we have classified a person as feeble-minded according to these criteria:

1. "One who is capable of earning a living under favorable circumstances, but is incapable, from mental defect existing from birth or from an early age, (a) of competing on equal terms with his normal fellows; or (b) of managing himself and his affairs with ordinary prudence."*

2. (In so far as practicable we have used the tests of intelligence to measure mentality.) "An otherwise feeble-minded person passing the social test"† (that is, possessing the ability to maintain existence independent of external support) and "A person with a mental retardation less than that of feeble-mindedness but failing in the social test."‡

We mean, then, by the mentally deficient or feeble-minded, those people whose mentality has never reached the normal level, whose development has been progressively retarded or whose approximately normal rate of development has been arrested at some point prior to the attainment of mental maturity. The evolution of the mental faculties seems to be complete about the age of puberty, sometime between the fifteenth and twentieth year. If the rate of development has been so much slower than the normal rate as to incapacitate the individual for normal functioning in his environment or if his normal rate of development has been arrested before mental maturity, we called the resulting condition feeble-mindedness.

And there are people, who though they seem to have all the intellectual faculties properly developed, yet lack self-control; they have no power of inhibition; they have no will power; and we have been designating them, for lack of a better term, "moral defectives." They are the "feebly inhib-

---

* Definition suggested by the Royal College of Physicians and adopted by the Royal Commission appointed by the English Government in 1904 to investigate the conditions of feeble-mindedness in the British Isles.

† "What Constitutes Feeble-mindedness." F. Kuhlmann, Jour. Psych.–As. XIX–4.

‡ Ibid.

ited" of Davenport's later classification. And among these dwellers in the Vale of Siddem are many whom one must classify as moral defectives.

Or "if the recognition of the condition" (feeble-mindedness) "has come as a result of some overt act of the individual, the latter would be known as a defective delinquent."

From the standpoint of eugenic consideration the existence of such communities as the Vale of Siddem makes our present attempts to care for the feeble-minded quite idle. The sources of the apparently inexhaustible supply of mental defectives remain unaffected. It is like trying to stamp out malaria or yellow fever in the neighborhood of a mosquito breeding swamp.

That feeble-mindedness is hereditary is no longer open to question. In 65 per cent. of our own cases it is directly traceable to hereditary causes. The percentage is probably even higher were all the data available. Goddard finds 65 per cent. of his cases directly traceable to heredity. Tredgold gives 64.5 per cent. traceable to neuropathic stock. Dr. Lapage found that 48.4 per cent. of feeble-minded children in the Manchester public schools had a neuropathic inheritance, and states that were all details available this percentage would undoubtedly be higher. Other ratios as high as 75 per cent. have been found in some investigations. There remains yet to be determined, however, the modus operandi of this inheritance. Several investigators, notably Davenport and Goddard, have concluded from their data that feeble-mindedness follows the course of the Mendelian law.

Mendel's law applies to what he called "unit characteristics." Unit characteristics are such single contrasting traits as, for instance, tallness or dwarfness in the pea, or in human beings such traits as hair and eye color. If the Mendelian formula can be applied to human inheritance and if we assume that feeble-mindedness is a recessive trait due to the absence of a determiner for normality in the germ plasm, then the following possible combinations would result:

Feeble-minded parents would have only feeble-minded children.

A normal parent and a feeble-minded parent would have only normal children all of whom would be capable of transmitting feeble-mindedness to their offspring.

In the case of a normal parent capable of transmitting feeble-mindedness and a feeble-minded parent, half of the children would be feeble-minded and half normal but capable of transmitting feeble-mindedness.

Normal parents capable of transmitting feeble-mindedness would have both feeble-minded and normal children in the ratio of one of the former to three of the latter. Two out of three of the normal children being capable of transmitting feeble-mindedness.

In the case of normal parents one of whom is capable of transmitting feeble-mindedness all of the children would be normal but half of them capable of transmitting feeble-mindedness.

Normal parents would have only normal children.

The small number of offspring in the human family, and the consequent limitation of the various possible combinations that might occur, makes it very difficult to apply this law of Mendel's, which is a law of averages, to the human family at all. And then, too, it seems improbable that so complicated a thing as general intelligence can be considered a unit character. Our definition of feeble-mindedness is a shifting one. A few years ago we did not recognize the high grade moron* as feeble-minded. And as Dr. Terman says,† "To regard feeble intelligence as always a disease, which, like smallpox, one either does or does not have, is a view which is contradicted by all we know about the distribution of mental traits. . . . It becomes merely a question of the amount of intelligence necessary to enable one to get along tolerably with his fellows and to keep somewhere in sight of them in the thousand and one kinds of competition in which success depends upon mental ability. . . . It is possible that the development of civilization, with its inevitable increase in the complexity of social and industrial life, will raise the standard of mental normality higher still."

In our efforts to determine the biological causes of that social inefficiency which we call variously degeneracy, criminality and mental deficiency, we have made it our own first task to discover the sources and habitat of these conditions. We are seeking the facts of race development that we may be able, if possible, to prevent some of this appalling waste of human energy. It is not the idiot or, to any great extent, the low grade imbecile, who is dangerous to society. In his own deplorable condition and its customarily accompanying stigmata, he is sufficiently anti-social to protect both himself and society from the results of that condition. But

---

* "Moron" is a term adopted by the Amer. Assoc. for the Study of the Feeble-minded in 1910. It was originally suggested by Dr. Goddard and is from the Greek meaning, literally, lacking in judgment and common sense. It denotes a grade of intelligence just less than normal. When expressed as a ratio between age and mental age, the moron grade of intelligence is that range between 50 and 75 per cent. From 25 to 50 per cent. constitutes the imbecile grade and from 0 to 25 per cent. the idiot grade. This percentage expresses mental development as a constant ratio between the development of the individual and the normal rate. For example if a twelve year child has a mental age of six years, he has attained only fifty per cent. of what an average twelve year old should have attained. The intelligence quotient, as this ratio is called, indicates what Dr. Kuhlmann has called the child's "capacity for development."

† Terman, L.M. The Standard Revision of the Binet-Simon Scale, Educ. Psych. Mon. No. 18.

from the high grade feeble-minded, the morons, are recruited the ne'er-do-wells, who lacking the initiative and stick-to-it-iveness of energy and ambition, drift from failure to failure, spending a winter in the poor house, moving from shack to hovel and succeeding only in the reproduction of ill-nurtured, ill-kempt gutter brats to carry on the family traditions of dirt, disease and degeneracy. Such communities as the Vale of Siddem bear eloquent testimony to the futility of trying to cope with such social inefficiency from the standpoint of the criminologist of holding the individual responsible for his misdeeds when he is fundamentally irresponsible, or from the point of view of the philanthropist improving his condition and helping him to help himself when he is fundamentally incapable of self help. A laissez faire policy simply allows the social sore to spread. And a quasi laissez faire policy wherein we allow the defective to commit crime and then interfere and imprison him, wherein we grant the defective the personal liberty to do as he pleases until he pleases to descend to a plane of living below the animal level and try to care for the few of his descendants who are so helpless that they can no longer exercise that personal liberty to do as they please—such a policy produces such communities as the Vale of Siddem.

DWELLERS IN THE VALE OF SIDDEM

"All the wicked people
In the Vale of Siddem
Thought of things they shouldn't do
And then they went and did 'em."

ONE DAY WHEN we were looking for the great uncles and aunts and cousins and forty-second cousins of a very small boy in our institution, we came quite unexpectedly upon the Vale of Siddem. The things the people in that valley could think of that they shouldn't do are equalled only by the things they couldn't think of that they should do. And this is because so many of them have minds that are so curiously twisted that we call them insane, or are so lacking in judgment and sense that we call them feeble-minded, or because they and their fathers before them, have for so long lived in degradation utterly heedless of moral values and of self help, that they seem to have lost the power to live decently, and we call them delinquents and degenerates. Among the worst of their "sins of commission" is marriage and inter-marriage and marriage again. And their children are legion, among whom the traditions of the family are not lost.

In the valley of the Mississippi, a river which is one of its tributaries flows through a land whose wild rugged beauty of wooded hills and rocky ravines makes it a place fit for the gods but which is inhabited instead by "grandchildren of the devil." Thickly wooded valleys harboring mysterious caves open into still other wooded valleys, sometimes the water course of a little stream tumbling riotously along to join the river. Or a little ravine may end abruptly, its rocky tree-grown sides well nigh inaccessible. The caves of the region have taken on a sinister aspect; the dark little ravines have grown forbidding; the shadowy forks leading from the river valley seem menacing; the region has acquired an unsavory fame in all the surrounding country.

And the dwellers in this Vale of Siddem are known to the surrounding country folk variously as "timber rats" and "bark eaters." The ravine is luridly known as "Dry Run," "Hog Hollow," or "Hell Hole," and the old settlers in the county will tell you how, in the early days, a group of squatters were driven out of New York State for fraudulently settling on Indian lands. These people started west, after a general fracas with the government officials when they threatened to blow up the court house in revenge for being driven off from the Indian land. The dwellers in the hollow are their descendants. The families have intermarried and their children and their children's children have for generations lived in little shacks and dugouts in the ravine.

Twenty years ago if a fugitive horse thief could reach this region and hide in some cave or wooded gulch of the valley, he was safe from pursuit. Even if the sheriff had the hardihood to follow him into the ravine "the man was dead who'd seen him." Some nuggets of gold were found near the river bed and more families moved into the valley. The gold was never found in paying quantities and a gaunt row of abandoned shacks known as "Smoky Row" marks the flurry. A murder was committed; horse thieves were traced to the mouth of the ravine and the earth swallowed them; counterfeit money was circulated; and finally one of the dwellers in the Vale was convicted. The hollow was the scene of continual feuds and quarrels. But if one of these folk had a quarrel with an outsider not a man, woman or child in the hollow could be found who knew anything about it. And for years no one interfered.

Of late years as the timber has been cleared, the conditions in the hollow have somewhat improved. A church was built, but that was torn down by the inhabitants after the religious fervor of their revival subsided. The children still carry open knives to school; every little while someone gets slashed in an argument and the doctor is called. Dances in the hollow are associated with drunken brawls and the social ideals of the community may be measured by their surroundings.

Among these people, we have found some of the ancestors of our institution children. The stories of several families interwoven by marriage, show with striking vividness that these folk seek their own kind and that whether they live in the secluded fastnesses of the ravine or move to the city or to the fertile farm lands of the state their condition varies but little and exceptions are notable. They are still persistent dwellers in the Vale of Siddem.

YAKS

In 1855 the Yaks, journeying West from New York, with the rest of the crowd who were driven off from the Indian lands, drifted at length to the ravine and most of their descendants have lived in the hollow or in the neighborhood ever since. There were eight of them originally; two of the brothers died under thirty years of age and left no progeny; the other six, three brothers and three sisters, have intermarried with the descendants of other squatters, all people of the ravine, until there exists a veritable network of interrelationships. The topographical isolation of these people has given rise to a curious social life. Many of them are defectives and more of them are simply incapable, and they are the descendants of others who in similar conditions have been likewise incapable. To quote Dr. Jordan, "In a world of work where clear vision and a clear conscience are necessary to life they find themselves without sense of justice, without a capacity of mind, without a desire for action." So close are the ramifications of these clans that, in spite of the continual quarrels, feuds and bickerings among themselves, there is a tribal solidarity that defies justice and the interference of the advocates of decency and order.

In the study of the Yaks 641 individuals are included. Of this number 53 feeble-minded, 24 insane, 10 epileptics, 44 grossly immoral and 39 habitual alcoholics include the direct descendants and consorts of the six Yaks, who originally settled in the ravine.

There were Tildy, Lige, Kate, Jo, Delia and Jim.* Tildy Yak married a Corey and left the ravine. A daughter of Tildy's married one of the Tams; in this family the prevalence of insanity and epilepsy is particularly striking. Of the 79 descendants of Tildy 10 were insane, 15 feeble-minded and 8 epileptic. The direct descendants of Jim numbered only 8, among whom is one insane person. Lige and Kate married into the Sadhun family of the ravine. Their descendants number 110 of whom 11 are feeble-minded

* It is understood, of course, that all names used throughout the story are purely fictitious.

and 2 are insane. This branch of the family remained in the hollow and added materially to its burden of misery. Their moral standards, their petty thievery, neglect of decency, carelessness and vindictiveness stamp them, even where they are not mentally deficient, as the gravest sort of social menace. Both Jo and Delia Yak married representatives of the Chad clan. Degeneracy is the outstanding characteristic of this group. Their 205 descendants include 14 feeble-minded, 6 convicted criminals and 17 who were flagrantly immoral.

In these people of the hollow is "humanity stript of its adventitious social trappings." Exposed by the candid hand of Gorky, these "ugly cancers of the social system" would not alone "shame the devil" but outrage the community. The complacent Americanism of us who regard with such patriotic superiority the evils of London slums and the pauperism and organized vice of an éféte [sic] old world civilization! The commonwealth of Minnesota, young and vigorous, harbors already such nests of social incompetents, degenerates, defectives and criminals as existed in the Jukes' ancestral mountain fastnesses. Mental deficiency is indigenous to the same soil that produces criminality, sex laxity, alcoholism and pauperism. Whatever the relation of cause and effect in the matter, the sociological evidence is indisputable.

COREYS

Descendants of Tildy

In the days when a horse thief could lose himself suddenly and completely in the hollow, the Coreys lived and prospered in its wooded defiles. Where By Corey came from originally no one knows, but his wife, Tildy Yak, came from New York State at the time the squatters were driven off from the Indian lands. By was a queer old fellow. Legend concedes him insane streaks and the gossips call them "Corey spells." To hang a cow bell round his neck and run up and down the street to annoy his neighbors when the spell was on him, to steal chickens and run them up and down the streets to hear them cackle—these were "Corey spells." By Corey and Tildy were a common sight on the street corner of the nearest village, each with a chicken secured by the leg with a string, and By would swing his about his head shouting "I'm crazy, crazy, crazy"— "And gosh darned if he wasn't right," affirmed old Caleb Sadhun, my informant. "We could a told that anyhow." The story goes that when he was drafted for the Civil War he played on the popular notion that he was crazy to avoid military service. Whenever his regiment was off duty he would take a string out of his pocket, tie it to the end of a stick and sit around wherever he happened to be diligently pretending to fish. The officers and doctor would come by, look at him and shake their heads. Finally he was told he had better go home. By lost no time; his curt comment to the soldiers, "Boys that was what I was fishing for"—attested a degree of cunning. After his return from "the war," By developed epilepsy. His last years were spent in a Soldiers' Home where he died at the age of eighty years of paralysis.

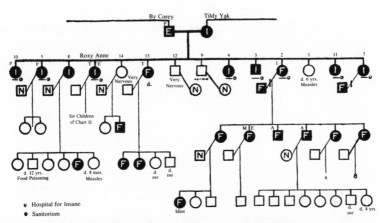

Chart I. Descendants of By Corey and Tildy Yak.

Explanation of Charts: The squares indicate males and the circles females. A horizontal or oblique line joining a square and a circle indicates a marriage if a solid line, and illicit sexual relations, if it is a broken line. A perpendicular line dropped from a line joining a square and a circle indicates descent. Small solid black circles indicate still births or miscarriages. A line under a symbol indicates institutional care. The hand indicates patient in the institution from which the study was made. The letter N in a square or circle indicates the person is known to be normal. F means feeble-minded; Sx. sexually immoral; A alcoholic; T tuberculous; D deaf; I insane (with a small s beside it senile dementia); C criminalistic; P paralyzed; M migrainous; S syphilitic; W wanderer; and d. inf. died in infancy. A short perpendicular line through a line indicating marriage signifies separation; two short perpendicular lines divorce.

The sons and daughters of By Corey were fourteen in number. Of these nine were insane, seven having been cared for in hospitals and asylums, and one was feeble-minded. None of these children has remained in the ravine. One of them married a feeble-minded man from the hollow and remained in the neighborhood until she was sent to an insane asylum. All but two of these children married. Of the consorts two were feeble-minded, four are known to have been normal, one of the others is presumably normal and the mental status of the rest is unknown. Of the thirty-four grandchildren one is insane, one epileptic, ten are feeble-minded, five died in infancy, two are known to be normal, and the mental status of the rest in unknown. Among the thirty-nine great grandchildren are two feeble-minded and eight who died in infancy.

The principal occupation represented in this group is farming; there is, however, one insurance manager, one photographer, one bookbinder and one teacher, who became insane. These people are scattered from Minnesota to California and their economic status varies from indigence to the moderate prosperity of the middle class tradesman. The poorest home was that of the insane woman who married her feeble-minded cousin from the hollow. She was cared for in an asylum and there were no children. The best home is that of the woman who married a normal business man of moderate means. This woman developed insanity. One of her children is feeble-minded, and one is a university graduate.

And these are the Coreys who came from "Hog Holler at the Crossroads."

TAMS

The oldest daughter of old By Corey, who lived at the Cross Roads in Hog Hollow, was Roxy Anne. Roxy Anne was ambitious; she attended school and assayed to teach. But her teaching and the sewing which she took up, and the marriage with Washington Tam, which later engaged her attention, were interrupted by her sojourns at the hospital for the insane, whither her spells of manic depressive insanity carried her. Roxy Anne

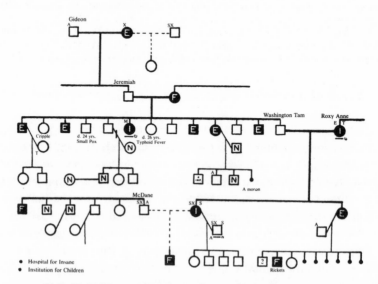

Chart II. Children of Washington Tam and Roxy Anne Corey.

developed epilepsy in middle life and her last years were spent in an asylum for the insane where the last phase of her trouble was a religious mania.

The oldest daughter of Roxy Anne and Washington Tam is an erratic votary of the muse of science and has studied the family, as she says, with a mind attuned to the "symphony, precision, and rhetorical analogy of psychology." Her garishly furnished mind harbors a motley throng of ideas. A paranoiac exultation of personality and a certain Malapropish use of polysyllabic words make the daughter's account of her family and connections grotesquely vivid in the light of her psychopathic heredity. Her father, Washington Tam, though a day laborer, it seems was an averted philosopher. A man "as tranquil as the deep sea, he was never excited except over vital issues"; he was a "square peg in a round hole." This daughter brought her illegitimate son, who began life as "an unusually brilliant and precocious child," to the school for the feeble-minded because at four years of age "a nervous hunger set in which caused him to lose his power of speech—aphasia." Her scientific study of him revealed to her "that things denied him made him resentful and apparently left a vacuum, filled with aimless occupations." We have found it so!

This psychological daughter was one of two children. When a young girl, "young and foolish" as she loftily explains, she had an illegitimate child by a man of good family whose parents objected to his marriage with the daughter of Roxy Anne. This child, an idiot, is the one she brought to the institution with a note-book full of psychological observations on his early precocity. McDane, the father of the child, was excessively alcoholic at the time of his conception. McDane and his feeble-minded brother were the unruly members of a well regulated family. The paternal McDanes belong in the class of "respectable married people with umbrellas" of Stevenson's category. McDane and sons appeared at the store on Monday as religiously as they went to church on Sunday. Father was mayor of the town, his armour of middle class respectability pierced only at one point, the notorious conduct of these two sons. But Roxy Anne's daughter married another man,—like the Kallikak woman, she didn't object to the marriage ceremony when it was attended to for her,—and by her husband she has four children. These children are not mentally defective and show as yet no mental abnormalities though all are extremely nervous. The oldest is only seven. The father of these children is very alcoholic and syphilitic.

The other daughter of Roxy Anne and Washington Tam is an epileptic, like her mother. Her husband is alcoholic. Of her five children the youngest has not developed normally.

Washington Tam was one of thirteen children of whom five were epileptic and one was insane. Only three of his brothers and sisters married and of the nine offspring, two are normal. One of these normal grandchildren of the Tams married a normal woman.

Old Jeremiah Tam, who was the father of Washington and his brotherhood, came to Minnesota from Ohio in the days when land was very cheap and was able to stock a farm, from which he succeeded in making a poor living for his wife and thirteen children. The wife was a woman who ruled her children by fear, caprice, and a birch rod. Both husband and children suffered under her insane temper. And the parents of Jeremiah, the grandparents of Washington Tam, were a notorious pair. Old Gideon was a great drunkard and his wife who had been crippled by a fall in her youth was an epileptic. She had had an illegitimate daughter before her marriage to Gideon. There were seven epileptics among the descendants of this pair.

DESCENDANTS OF LIGE YAK

To Lige Yak and his wife Leda were born six children. In the sunless gulch which was their home, a gaunt shack, one of the old "smoky row," still bears testimony to Lige's short lived interest in the "gold diggings" of 1855. Lige was never ambitious. His laziness was proverbial. A stranger drove up before the shack that passed for a general store and inquired of the solitary lounger for Lige Yak. "He-e don't live here no more," he drawled.

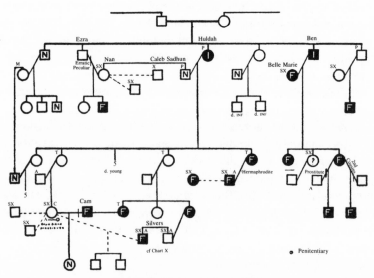

Chart III. Children of Lige Yak.

"Moved, has he?"

"Ya-as he's moved, he's dead."

Lige's son Ben still lives in the hollow. In the neighborhood, Ben is known as the "Old Bear," for he lives all alone in a little dingy shanty to go near which is the dare of the boldest passing school children, for the demented old man growls at them in much the fashion of his namesake. But old Ben is shrewd; he never commits himself about affairs in the ravine. He boasts of chicken stealing for a living but other things he cunningly forgets.

Before Belle Marie died it had been the custom of this deluded pair to engage their days in the pursuit of happiness by way of cards. While the one had lost his mind, the other had never had much of any to lose; Belle Marie was an "almost." And the two would sit day in and day out in their barren shack, shuffling the same grimy old deck and dealing the cards on an upturned dry goods box that served for table, till their numbed fingers and the gauntness of hunger at last aroused their dull consciousness to a sense of too insistent realities. Thus spurred they would get up shivering, go to a neighbor to beg or "borrow" enough flour to "make up a bit of something," drag in a little fire wood to mend their dying fire and then return to their interminable game. The children of old Ben and Belle Marie were three daughters. Ellie was an "almost" like her mother. She was twice married, deserted by her first husband and divorced by her second. To each she bore a feeble-minded son. Nell was brighter than her sister, but as the New Englander says, "not over an' above bright herself." She was deserted by her husband, a second cousin. Nell has thirteen descendants whose history has not been fully traced. The third daughter, Lillie, was a woman of the streets. She married, also, and has had four children.

Belle Marie had been the Widow Bun before her marriage to old Ben. Now Bun was a white man but Belle Marie's children were both white and black. When Belle Marie died she was buried with much pomp and ceremony dear to the heart of her bereaved family, and at the funeral her negro children rode in one carriage and her white children in another.

The second child of Lige Yak was a daughter who married a man of average intelligence and has no living children. This woman was very nervous but never became unbalanced.

Two sons of Lige, John and Jesse, married, both consorts being women from the ravine, and their homes were ordinarily decent but without the amenities of education.

Huldah, the fifth child of Lige, married Caleb Sadhun of a family which had been brought up with the traditions of the place and its customs. The

Sadhuns were among the earliest settlers in the hollow. But Caleb is a man of normal intelligence. A man without education, lacking the initiative to change his ancestral condition, he has yet an innate fineness of nature quite foreign to the native stock of the hollow. He is now an old man past eighty and he tells with the detached view of old age of the people of the hollow and their ways. A gentle, white haired, old man, he sits most of the day in his old arm chair at the sunny window of his little cottage on the outskirts of the ravine and will tell you, if you ask him, with rather keen insight and no malice about the folk of the hollow and of the early days. Huldah, his pitiable little wife, has been for years harmlessly insane. She will finger you with the curious eagerness of a child and will ramble on aimlessly following a thread of conversation of which she has caught a snatch as you talk with Caleb. And Caleb is altogether gentle with her and forbearing.

There were nine children of Caleb and Huldah. Four daughters lived to grow up and each married a man of the ravine. One of them was feeble-minded and never developed normally physically. Her husband, also, was feeble-minded and a miserable reprobate, alcoholic, sexually immoral and abusive. This daughter died shortly after her marriage. Another of Caleb's daughters had a daughter who was mentally normal but vicious. She was a thief, was alcoholic and a drug addict and a degenerate. This girl, married to a feeble-minded man of her mother's choosing, left her husband to live with another of the same kind. Then left the second for a third, and when partially under the influence of the drug to which she had become addicted, robbed him, was convicted and sentenced for six years. Paroled, she stole money from a sister of her original husband with whom she had encamped on leaving the penitentiary. She has now left the state. Another daughter of Caleb's has a daughter who married a member of the notorious Silver family. Their noisy quarrels and midnight brawls often result in knife wounds, for the ancestral Silvers were Indians accustomed so to settle their arguments. Then the long suffering doctor is called; some one meets him with a lantern and he is led back into the woods to the shack where he sews up the wounds and is again lighted back to the road. And still another of Caleb's daughters married one of the Hanks. The cousins of her children are mulattoes.

The other Sadhun-Yak marriage was that of Ezra Yak and Nan of the Sadhuns. Poor old Ezra's only companions are his horses and a feeble-minded cousin, Bill Sadhun, with whom he keeps house alone on his little farm. Bill, he salvaged from a dugout on the hillside beyond the stable lean-to built against the side of the ravine and covering the entrance to Bill's dugout. Ezra's horses are the more companionable and he is a great talker. His wife, Nan, "never did stay by" him much. "You jes' never knew when you had her." She liked to go off with other men but after a month or two would ask to be forgiven and allowed to come back, and Ezra was "glad to get her back as she took good care of the house and was a good cook—good as could be when you had her, but you jes' couldn't keep her." Ezra is a sort of a philosopher of the soil in his own queer way. These descendants of Lige Yak are the aristocrats of the family. Ezra's son and heir, according to his father's testimony, is not much of a student. He didn't go far in school, but never-the-less can "read fair, write pretty fair, and figger some!"

JIM YAK

Jim Yak married a woman of the hollow, one of the Barts. In the Bart family the prevalence of insanity is appalling! Jim's wife was one of five brothers and sisters, three of whom were insane. Of the fourteen descendants of these five Barts, seven are either feeble-minded or insane.

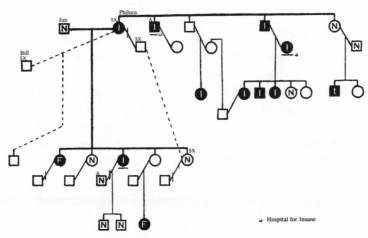

Chart IV. Jim Yak.

When the Civil War broke out Jim enlisted but never returned. His wife thereupon married and went down South to live with her new husband. But Bill, her brother-in-law, wanted her, so after the death of Bill's wife, he went down South to get Philura. Philura deserted her second husband as soon as she found out Bill wanted her and together they returned North to the ravine. This time Philura didn't trouble about the marriage ceremony as that would involve the formality of obtaining a divorce from husband number two. Philura, like two of her brothers, was mentally unbalanced at times. The insanity of the Barts took the form of harmless peculiarities or mild melancholia. For days sometimes, Philura would stay shut up in the house and would speak to no one.

Philura's children numbered six. Five of these children are Yaks, daughters of Jim, and the sixth is the son of Bill, the brother-in-law. The feeble-minded daughter, Lib, has been married but has had no children. The daughter who became insane married a normal man by whom she had two normal sons. The other three daughters were bright women. One married another of the Yaks, a second married a Chad, who is a descendant of Delia Yak and Jake Chad, and a third, finding the society of her stepfather more congenial than her mother had found it, left her own husband to live with her mother's deserted second husband.

The family solidarity of these people is truly remarkable. Such marked preference for their own people is seldom met with! The man "marries his deceased wife's sister" happily ignorant of Carlyle's jeremiads; the daughter consoles her mother's discarded second husband; and other daughters marry men of the same name or remotely connected.

DESCENDANTS OF KATE YAK

There were six children of Kate Yak and another of the Sadhuns of the hollow. Four died, only one of them leaving any descendants. A fifth, the feeble-minded companion of Ezra, the son of Lige, married a Corey who was the insane daughter of Tildy Yak and By Corey. There were no children. The sixth was Vina Sadhun who married a brother of the deserted second husband of Philura Yak.

The descendants of Kate have not been traced further.

CHADS—DESCENDANTS OF DELIA

The tribe of Chads, who are the descendants of Delia Yak and Jake Chad, are scattered from the hollow north as far as counties bordering on Canada and in their wake they have left a trail of criminals, paupers, and degenerates who will patronize our county jails, poor houses and houses of prostitution for several generations.

Jake himself was the Don Juan of the hollow, and a sordid tale it is, of this sorry old reprobate and his miserable adventures. The legend is that he had a wife in every town in which he had sojourned. And certain it is that his progeny is legion. He was married by process of law three times. Jake was by trade a plasterer, by choice a counterfeiter. Indeed before

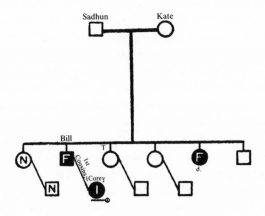

● Hospital for Insane

Chart V. Kate Yak.

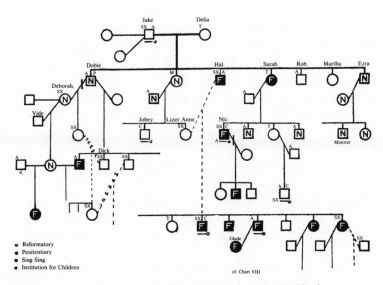

● Reformatory
● Penitentiary
● Sing Sing
● Institution for Children

cf. Chart VIII

Chart VI. Descendants of Delia Yak and Jake Chad.

coming to dwell in the ravine he had served a term in Sing Sing for counterfeiting. While a dweller in the hollow Jake became involved with the Jincades in other counterfeiting schemes and escaped apprehension for his misdeeds, it is said, by enlisting in the U.S. Army when rumor connected one of the Jincades with counterfeit money which had been passed in the neighborhood of the ravine and an arrest of the younger Jincade followed. But possibly Jake could not pass the physical examination (it was at the time of the Civil War) or possibly he was discharged for incompetency; in any event he put in an appearance again long before the close of the Civil War.

There were seven children, the offspring of Delia Yak and Jake Chad.

Hal, the son of Jake, was feeble-minded but Lizer Anne was a degenerate. Lizer Anne did not marry Hal, for Hal was her uncle, but she lived with him and bore him twelve children than whom a more miserable abjectly wretched set can scarcely be imagined. Five at least of them are feeble-minded. Three of these feeble-minded ones married and two have offspring. One, a gambler and thief, has been apprehended for his crime and sent to the reformatory. The prevalence of sexual laxity among them is a foregone conclusion. One can scarcely call them immoral. They are quite unmoral.

Of Rob and Martha, another son and daughter of Jake, little definite information has been available. Martha married and moved out west years ago and the family ties of these people are not strong enough to withstand the strain of distance and the lapse of years. Rob was killed some years ago in a drunken brawl, and the village folk say "his family turned out very bad" but of his children no trace remains in the neighborhood, though Chads of the same character and mental calibre appear in the investigations of other neighborhoods not far distant.

But the record of Doble, the son of Jake, out-Herods Herod in the sum of abject degeneracy among his descendants. Doble married Deborah who bore him one daughter. And Deborah's daughter lived with her half brother, Dick, who was one of Doble's eight children by a second wife. The illegitimate daughter of Deborah's daughter lived with her father's brother and bore him one child. Now Deborah was a woman of more intelligence than Doble. She left Doble and married Vide. But the daughter of Deborah and Vide married the feeble-minded son of Doble and his second wife!

Nic, a son of Sarah, who was a feeble-minded daughter of Jake, has been in state prison for burglarizing a post office with a gang from the hollow. This man who has offended against the state, against chastity, against decency and against reason, is just feeble-minded and his son is likewise feeble-minded. He has been imprisoned twice for robbery and once for indecent assault and is again at large to commit more crimes against society! Society would not so treat a boy of his mental capacity, exacting of him the penalty for the betrayal of responsibilities which he is unable to shoulder and then thrusting him out again to undertake the same responsibilities of living but with even worse preparation, as punishment has made him vindictive and revengeful.

A brother of Lizer Anne and grandson of Jake's who was always called "Jobey," presumably to mitigate the biblical solemnity of Job, spent seven years in state prison after he held up and almost murdered a sober homeward bound farmer at a lonely spot in the road. Jobey asked for a lift and was accommodated by the farmer who invited him to a seat beside him. But Jobey preferred the wagon box as he was going but a short distance and there was a convenient spade there on the grain sacks. By some lucky chance Jobey's blow from the rear didn't kill the farmer and Jobey was apprehended at his own home with the money, by means of the farmer's half delirious babbling of a man in a gray cap, and Jobey's gray cap was a familiar feature. Jobey passed in the neighborhood for a desperate character but the story doesn't say whether he was brought up on the lurid tales of the Jesse James gang; though the gang is said to have had a rendezvous in a cave in the hollow. A cave it was, which fairly cried out for a robber gang to infest it. Its chief entrance is in an open field where a lookout could descry a man as far as he could see him with never so much as a stone to cover his approach; its other secret entrance, and exit when trouble threatened is, nobody knows just where, in the wooded defiles of the ravine. The villagers point it out to you with a mingled sense of historic pride. But whether Jesse James haunted it or not it is no myth that the inhabitants of the ravine found it a very convenient means of effecting a quick disappearance when the sheriff became too curious.

Two of the Chads, a son and daughter of Ezra, the son of Jake, rose conspicuously above the family level by affiliating their interests with the church. The son became an adventist minister and the daughter married a man of the same persuasion. The other sons and daughters of Ezra were not vicious nor were they given over to bad practices of any sort, living for the most part in farming communities where they followed their occupations without conspicuous success or conspicuous failure.

DESCENDANTS OF JO YAK AND LOU CHAD

Jo Yak also married a Chad. Lou is variously described as "the meanest woman that ever breathed," "the devil's granddaughter" and other titles which bear eloquent testimony to her evidently ungentle character. Poor old Jo met his end by drowning while he was crossing the lake in a row boat in company with his wife, Lou. Lou was one of the many daughters of Old Jake. She was indeed her father's own daughter. Lou wanted another man and it is supposed she took this convenient way of disposing of husband number one.

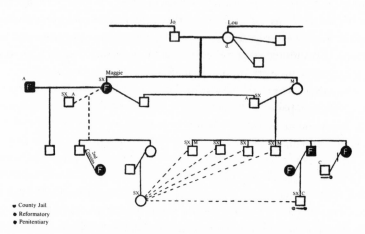

Chart VII. Descendants of Jo Yak and Lou Chad.

The two daughters of Jo and Lou have lived in the ravine and their children and their children's children. In them the vicious practices of the Chads are continued without alleviation. The elder, Maggie, is a feeble-minded woman of the moron type. Maggie has outlived two husbands and is now sojourning with her third, to whom her former husband sold her for a shotgun. Maggie's stupid granddaughter was the passive victim of the vicious practices of her five cousins, sons of Maggie's younger sister. These five sons live with their mother in a miserable little shack in the woods near the ravine. The mother and sons all occupy the same bed room, sleeping on filthy rags on the floor. Their dull cousin had come to help with the so-called "housework" of the shack. The son of one of the men paid the jail penalty for the vicious conduct of the five.

THE HOUSEHOLD OF THE GLADES

Making your precarious way down the steep sides of the ravine, expecting momentarily to meet destruction around the next turn in the road, you find yourself shortly in the very heart of the hollow. The few widely scattered shacks evince few signs of life. Occasionally a ragged child stands staring to watch you pass and sometimes a slattern woman watches you listlessly from the doorway of her home or some curious one shows a very lively interest in your course as you drive on along the river deeper into the heart of the ravine. At length you arrive at the crossroads. The right fork, which you follow, leads you into one of the thickly wooded gullies that join the hollow. Deeper and deeper you penetrate into its wooded fastnesses. There are no more huts, no ragged children or barking cur dogs. You reach a footpath through the woods. Here you must leave your team and pick your way along the little used path which leads you finally into a ravine beyond, which is so shut in by dense woods and hills as to be inaccessible except by the way you have come.

In this ravine, where the sun shines only four hours in the middle of the day, lived the Glades. Their home was a deserted log hut whose un-chinked crevices allowed the winter winds clear sweep, and bitter cold it was when a Minnesota blizzard howled down the gulch. Later they were found living in a dugout in the hillside, the entrance boarded loosely and the doorway hung with old carpet.

An infrequent winter visit of a neighbor revealed the children bare-foot in mid-winter clothed in a single calico garment. Summer solved for them the problem of clothes; the dress was kept for whatever school attendance was compelled and for the rest, they went naked. On the rare occasion

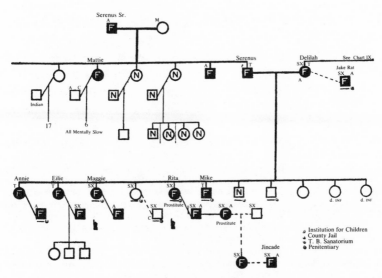

Chart VIII. The Glades.

when a stranger put in an appearance, the children, wild as hares, ran for cover. On one such occasion the place seemed quite deserted when presently a shock of sunburnt hair popped curiously from behind the door of the shed. The stranger was persuasive, and lured by sweet meats, shortly a small brown body appeared clad in a hastily donned gunny sack.

The parent Glades were a "do-less" pair. The father was as little inclined to provide for his offspring as the mother was to utilize what was provided. On one occasion the clothes, which had been furnished and made by some charitably inclined woman from the town in the vicinity, were found, rain soaked and muddy, back of the cabin where the mother had thrown them rather than wash them. Serenus Glade, the father, spent most of his active time "shanging." The people of the ravine pride themselves, and it is their only known source of pride, on their knowledge of herbs. This knowledge of herbs was presumably acquired from the Indians, with whom some of the dwellers in the hollow intermarried. "Shanging" in native parlance means gathering ginseng which they brew for remedies. But Serenus was not over-ambitious even about "shanging" as most of his time was taken up with smoking; seated on the overturned soap box by the back door of the cabin, it was his steadiest occupation. Any money that came into his hands, Serenus invested in alcoholic beverages for his health. There is a court record, in proof of the contention that he worked for a living, that he once helped a man husk corn for two days.

Delilah, the wife, is a daughter of the Cams of the ravine, a woman of excitable temper, loves her bottle, and when over excited and nervous is subject to mild epileptic attacks which the children call "throwing a fit when she gets mad."

The eleven children born of this union are all living except the two youngest who died before they had had time to become acclimated to the life of cold, starvation, and blows upon which the others seemed to thrive. With the exception of one all of these children have functioned as feeble-minded.*

The eldest daughter, Eilie, feeble-minded and tuberculous, married an

* This is one of the very few instances where we have found an apparently normal individual the offspring of feeble-minded parents. The boy in question gives every evidence of normal mental ability, his school record is excellent, his social reactions normal and his traits seem to be abnormal in no respect. Since the sexual morality of the mother is very much open to question the reputed father may not be the real father. The mother is now living in open adultery with a feeble-minded man and it is not improbable that the father of the normal boy was a normal man.

The other instance (occurring on Chart IX) is that of a normal man, the son of feeble-minded parents. In this case the individual in question is a man of fifty who owns a store and has made a decent living for his wife and ten children all of whom are of average mentality. The evidence for the feeble-mindedness of the parents of this man seems indisputable. The mother was, in this case also, however, notoriously immoral.

"herb doctor." Eilie and her husband are both morons and the "professional" character of the husband's occupation, selling herbs to the ingenuous natives of the hollow, lends an air of condescension to Eilie's social intercourse with her relatives of inferior social strata. There are three children not yet of school age—the "potentially feeble-minded" of Goddard.

Annie Glade married a typical scion of the Chad family. He has always been able to make a sort of living for himself and his feeble-minded wife working under direction as a farm hand. And, as he is a dull, rather faithful worker, he has never been a troublesome member of society except once when he tried to steal oats and was attacked by a woman with a pitchfork. There are no children.

Mike has, until recently, been working as a farm helper. Mike, also of weak mentality, did not marry. He, too, is tuberculous and is now in a county sanatorium.

Five younger children, when the home was broken up, were committed to an institution whence two of them were later transferred to the Minnesota institution for the feeble-minded. These two feeble-minded sisters, Rita and Maggie, both pretty girls of the moron type, were taken, against the urgent protest of the superintendent, from the institution by a well-meaning relative, sponsored by a minister who promised to be responsible for them. The extent of that responsibility may be judged from the results.

Rita is married. Her husband is Bill Hemp, the feeble-minded son of Hank Hemp and a feeble-minded woman. Hank was feeble-minded. He and the woman cared for nothing except something to eat and a place to loaf. Bill has a feeble-minded twin brother also married. Bill's former wife was a feeble-minded prostitute, who, while living with Bill, gave birth to a feeble-minded daughter who doesn't belong to Bill. This feeble-minded daughter is now living with the son of old Rob Jincade the counterfeiter of the ravine, a worthless degenerate wretch. Bill has a feeble-minded uncle whose wife died at the poor farm of the county a number of years ago. Danny, a son of this man's, works around for the farmers in the neighborhood of the ravine, his labor bought with the promise of "a nice woman for Danny." It is Danny's one ambition to get married but the women of the ravine won't have poor simple-minded Danny. This is Bill's family, citizen of Hog Hollow. When Bill married Rita he took her home to live with his former wife and Rita "got mad and left him." She is now a prostitute.

There is Maggie. For a while, she worked in cheap restaurants. Then she married, not however a citizen of the hollow, but a feeble-minded man like herself. On the night of her wedding there was a family celebration. The groom and his friends became so intoxicated that they were dumped unconscious on the only bed the establishment furnished and the bride and her relatives slept on the littered floor.

Another daughter of the household of Serenus and Delilah was the victim of her vicious adopted father. The man is serving a penitentiary sentence for the crime. The younger children with one exception are slow in school and show the characteristics of mental deficiency. One child of the eleven is normal in every way.

Serenus finally succumbed to tuberculosis and Delilah took up her abode with Jake Rat, the wife and one child of the not over-ambitious Jake having deserted him for non-support. Jake and Delilah live at the expense of the parents of Jake whose father draws a small pension and on which the whole family subsists. Jake's drunkenness and disorderly conduct landed him in jail for a sojourn of from ten to thirty days, four times within a twelve-month.

The Glades have been, for the four generations of which we have knowledge, people of the ravine. Among those who have remained in the vicinity of the hollow eight are feeble-minded. The fraternity of Serenus consisted of thirteen brothers and sisters and Serenus senior was feeble-minded. The maternal progenitor of Serenus Glade and his twelve brothers and sisters is intricately related to our ravine friends the Sadhuns, the Jincades and the Yaks. They are steeped in the traditions of the hollow. A brother and one sister of Serenus are known to have been feeble-minded, the brother lives alone in a miserable little shack in the hollow made of sheet iron and boards. This brother is an insatiable drinker. His poverty is his greatest blessing as he cannot always command the price of a drink. The feeble-minded sister, Mattie, married a shiftless brother of Jobey and Lizer Anne. Their children are all mentally slow. One sister, however, is a bright capable woman; her home is comfortably furnished and well kept; her husband is a successful farmer; and her children are normal attractive youngsters. Another sister married a full-blooded Indian and bore him seventeen children. One other of normal mentality married a man of the hollow also normal, a man who owns a small farm in the ravine. The son is rather erratic but a fairly industrious fellow, a carpenter by trade. The others are average people.

The Cams were the ancestors of our Glade household on the maternal side. Delilah, originally wife of Serenus and later consort of Jake Rat, mother of children for the most part feeble-minded, was one of nine children. Of these seven were feeble-minded, the offspring of an epileptic,

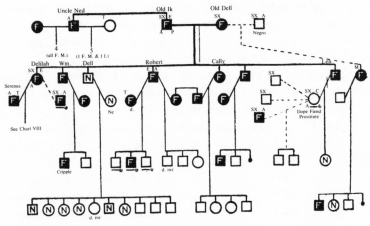

Chart IX. The Cams.

feeble-minded father and an immoral mother. These children are the following:

1. Cally Cam is a slovenly woman whose home bears witness to her total unfitness for the responsibilities of parenthood. When she married she moved away from the ravine, but her paternal home in the hollow was not dirtier or more carelessly kept than her own in a city removed by the width of the state from her old environment. The husband is not so incompetent as his feeble-minded wife but he is not a man of normal mental ability. The visits of the school nurse to this home reveal the futility of the feeble-minded mother in coping with her responsibilities. A six year old child with a severe cold was barefoot in mid-winter because his mother "can't make him wear shoes when he doesn't want to."

2. The children of Robert Cam and his feeble-minded wife were taken from them and placed in orphanages. Dick proved to be feeble-minded, one boy has been lost track of and a third was brought before the court for neglect and ill treatment. He was found to be covered with sores. His testimony was eloquent of the neglect of his stepmother. "My aunt Cally gave me a bath last fourth of July and dad gave me one when school began, and I guess I ain't had any since." The step-mother too is feeble-minded, and now there are two children born to her.

3. Dell Cam by a woman of average mentality had ten children who are mentally "up to par."

4. Another brother, William, just manages to eke out a miserable exis-

tence on a little farm in the ravine. His wife is feeble-minded of feeble-minded stock and he has an imbecile child who is crippled.

5. Lon and his fourteen year old wife used to live in the ravine, but poor feeble-minded Lon could not long satisfy the lurid fancy of his wife and she went to live with another gentleman friend of hers. After three years she moved again. Then she became a professional prostitute and later was arrested and convicted for burglary.

6. Beck, the last sister with whom our story deals, was a mulatto. Her father was "Nigger Ned" who used to hang around the ravine. Beck's husband is Al Harder, a worthless cruel brute. Her children show their negro heritage. The oldest boy is an imbecile with very vicious tendencies. He will steal whenever the opportunity offers, carries a revolver to school and threatens the teacher and will draw a knife like a flash in a quarrel. The little girl is a normal child and exhibits none of the vicious tendencies of her brother and the other boy is an average child.

The maternal grandparents of the household of the Glades continue the same dull tale. Old Ik, the father of Delilah, was feeble-minded and an epileptic. So, too, was old Dell, her mother. Old Dell had a passion for jewelry and whenever her husband's pension came she would invest it in tawdry laces and cheap jewelry. Ik had a brother, "Uncle Ned" everybody called him. Uncle Ned was a benevolent old soul whose idea of bliss was a pipe and a bottle and no work to do for eons and eons. Uncle Ned had tried two matrimonial ventures. Mary, the first wife, was a normal woman so far as we can learn. She died of tuberculosis after having given birth to five children. Then Uncle Ned took unto himself another wife, this time however his helpmate was a feeble-minded woman of his own stamp. The four children of his second wife were all feeble-minded. Of the five children of the first wife only one was feeble-minded and one insane. Ry, the eldest was a gambler. He was very ugly and neglected and abused his wife; later he became insane. His wife was a bright woman and his daughter became a school teacher. Len was a great drunkard, married a feeble-minded woman, the illegitimate child of nameless parents. Len deserted her for her fairer cousin who ran away from some other man to join Len. Two of the children were epileptics, also a grandchild. Two daughters of Uncle Ned had normal children and a feeble-minded daughter had two feeble-minded children. The three sons and one daughter of Maria Bride, Uncle Ned's second wife, are all feeble-minded and three of the six surviving grandchildren are likewise feeble-minded.

Is it to be wondered at that the household of the Glades are dwellers in the Vale of Siddem?

LITTLE TOMMY

Little Tommy is the son of Old Moose Silver, the half-breed, and is known to fame as the desperado of the hollow. In the very heart of the hollow on one side the river, on the other the sheer wall of the ravine, lives old Moose Silver in the little one room log cabin where Little Tommy and his seven brothers and sisters were born and raised, or rather allowed to come up.

Surrounded by his children who have built little shacks in or near the ravine, old Moose lives now as he has lived for fifty years drinking when he can get anything to drink—and whiskey always maddens the old man—stealing wood, grain and chickens from the more prosperous farms in the

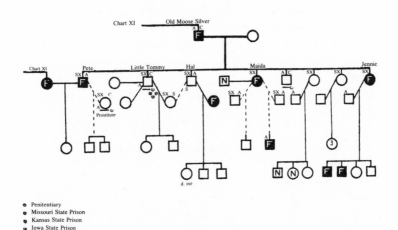

● Penitentiary
◉ Missouri State Prison
◕ Kansas State Prison
◔ Iowa State Prison

Chart X. Moose Silver.

neighborhood and enlivening the monotony of existence by disputes with his sons and daughters which frequently take the form of physical violence. Father, one son, the son's wife and a troop of ragged children journeyed into the village in their old ramshackle wagon one day and we arrived simultaneously at the door of the sheriff, Pete with a black eye and a pocket full of hair which had been extracted the night before in an argument with his brother and Pete's wife. Later I saw Pete's wife, a dejected sodden creature with a bedraggled child hanging on her skirts, waiting for old Moose and Pete who were fortifying themselves at the corner saloon.

Moose Silver is a picturesque old fellow, his grizzled hair straight and harsh; his large nose and high cheek bones bear testimony to his Indian origin. Moose never could stick at a job. He hired out to the farmers in the vicinity but was a firm believer in conserving his energies when the farmer's back was turned. He has always lived in abject poverty and when not intoxicated is rather stupid and sluggish. Moose combines the worst elements in both races, the cruelty and vindictiveness of the Indian with the vice and degeneracy of the white man. Moreover, he is mentally deficient. Years ago he had a violent quarrel with his brother-in-law. The day after the quarrel, the brother-in-law, forgetting all about their differences, went hunting with Moose. The brother-in-law never came back. When later the body of the brother-in-law was found with a bullet hole through the back and Moose was accused of shooting him, he stoutly affirmed it was an accident and pretended to go insane through grief. He was tried but was not convicted.

But none was so daring and none so clever as Little Tommy. He has served prison sentences in Iowa, Kansas, Missouri and Minnesota. Three times has he been convicted of larceny and once of bigamy. Of the eighteen years Little Tommy was out of the state, he served twelve years in some prison or other. Little Tommy is not more immoral than the rest but he did things on a more daring scale. Instead of chicken thieving, he indulged in horse stealing; instead of one wife at a time he had three; instead of county jail and work house sentences he served his terms in the penitentiary. With the sheriff on the watch for him and several indictments hanging over his head, Little Tommy frequently returns to the hollow and the utmost vigilance fails to trap him now. Night after night the sheriff has watched for him driving from a town lower down the river and after nightfall, hitching his horse in the woods, watched the mouth of the ravine for Little Tommy to slip down the river. He has sometimes been hiding for weeks in the caves of the hollow and then has mysteriously dropped out of existence. Once in the sheriff's absence, he made his escape from the county jail by throwing a lamp at the head of the sheriff's wife when she came to give him his supper and, choking her into insensibility, fled. They are all a little proud of Little Tommy and more than a little afraid of him.

Little Tommy has not been seen around the hollow for a number of years, and the people of the ravine say that he and Dut Jincade are bold, bad "hold-up men out west." They were, indeed, implicated in a train robbery in Montana but they somehow escaped conviction. The memory of Little Tommy's exploits is still rife in the minds of the people of the hollow.

With the exception of Jerry all of the rest of the sons and daughters of old Moose have remained in the ravine. Jerry went out west and has not been heard from for many years.

Hal Silver married a descendant of the Sadhuns, a feeble-minded woman. Their home is in the ravine. Hal drinks and carouses with the rest of the family. He and Pete and old Moose are the cronies of the Jincades and the Chads, though the Silvers are the most quarrelsome and frequently "fall out with" all their friends.

Jennie Silver, sister of Little Tommy, a woman of the moron type, and her quarrelsome spouse live in the vicinity of the hollow. Jennie is very lax in her morals and her husband is a drunkard. Jennie's husband's mother was a half-sister of Jennie's father.

Maida Silver married a normal man but not until she had already given birth to two children whose fathers were men of the hollow. One child, a feeble-minded boy, belonged to one of the younger Sadhuns, the other who is on the borderline between feeble-mindedness and normality belongs to a man intermarried with the family. Maida is a moron herself and one of her children, by her husband, is a boy whose vicious tendencies are already apparent and he is now only a school boy. The little girl of this union is a normal child.

The other two sisters "went wrong" when young but have since "married and settled down." The husbands are both men of the ravine. One family has remained in the vicinity of the ravine and has done fairly well. The farm is ordinarily prosperous, the children are in school and are doing average work. The other family has left the neighborhood.

Little Tommy's brother, Pete, lives about a stone's throw from the cabin of old Moose in a little tumbledown shack, poor shelter for cattle. Pete it was, who won the affections of the fifteen year old wife of Lon Cam. She left Pete with two children and then Pete married his feeble-minded cousin, Mamie Rat, daughter of Muskrat Charlie and niece of Jake Rat whose consort was Delilah of the Household of the Glades. Pete is feeble-minded.

The family of Pete's wife can almost equal Pete's in point of social inefficiency. In a fraternity of nine of whom Mamie's father was one, the three living brothers are all feeble-minded. Mamie's paternal grandmother was a twin sister of Moose Silver. And Mamie's father was Muskrat Charlie, her mother Lizzie Redky whose ancestors came to the hollow in the early days. Both parents were feeble-minded but the mother was the "better man" of the two. It was the custom of this family to live on a rented farm as long as the owner could tolerate them, and then move on to the next. At the time of our story they are tarrying awhile at a "farm" consisting of unimproved land,—land covered with stumps and undergrowth which Lizzie and the children are grubbing in the hope of raising a patch of corn. The stress of a regular occupation is too much for the unstable constitution of Muskrat Charlie and if he labors for two or three days, he has to stop and go "on a drunk" for a couple of days to "rest up." At one time

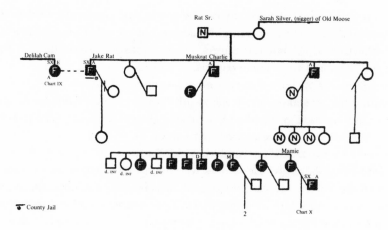

Chart XI. Jake Rat.

when money was unusually scarce he sold the cow and invested the proceeds in whiskey.

There were eleven children in this household, Mamie and ten brothers and sisters of whom three died shortly after birth and the rest are feebleminded. Two of the other girls are married and established in other households of that ilk.

Little Tommy and his family are the kind of citizens that the stock and the conditions of the Vale of Siddem produce. They combine all the vice and the only virtue—if a rather picturesque indigence can be called a virtue—of the ravine dwellers.

THE COUNTERFEITERS

About twenty years ago counterfeit money began to be circulated in the vicinity of the ravine. Suspicion at once fastened on the dwellers in the Vale of Siddem and, shortly, arrests followed. Three brothers were suspected. The Jincades, Rob, Dut and Lem, were a rough set, brawlers, hard drinkers and as untrustworthy as any in the hollow. Rumor connects them with almost every disorderly occurrence in the neighborhood.

Rob Jincade was a giant of a man and as quarrelsome as a cross grizzly. His voice rumbled along like the thunder which so often reverberated through the little winding valleys of the ravine. Technically he kept a general store in the hollow but the energies of Rob were not by any means confined to store-keeping, even though store-keeping in the hollow was not the easy-going country store variety with its crackerbox philosophers and its wood-stove politicians. Indeed any certified resident of the hollow knew that Rob's "back-room" was a short cut to the saloon just beyond in the village. Raw alcohol and corn whiskey, the popular beverages of the hollow, were kept for the convenience of his customers and friends. Once Rob and one of his "pals" "filled up" a sixteen year old boy with alcohol. Thinking the unconscious boy was dead, Rob and his cronies carried him out into a field and buried him under a hay stack. Fortunately they were seen by a farmer out looking for his cattle, the boy was pulled out and resuscitated but Rob escaped punishment.

Yet sometimes justice is swift in the hollow. Rob was caught stealing flour in the house of neighbor Chad. Rob was arrested and brought before the county court on the charge. But with fine contempt for our clumsy methods of meting out justice the accuser sent his wife, while his trial was in progress, to retaliate by stealing corn from Rob.

In Rob's old store were carried out the counterfeiting schemes of the Jincades. Neither Rob nor his brother was clever enough to escape detection, but somehow or other, whether through his colossal stupidity or through the fear that his brawling manners seemed to inspire, Rob always escaped and only Dut was convicted and served a term in the penitentiary for the crime. Rob lived and died in the ravine and Dut, after having served his penitentiary sentence, went farther west and has accumulated property.

There were eight of the Jincades originally, two sisters and six brothers. Since Rob's death almost a year ago, only two are left in the ravine. Lem manages to make a living at farming his little strip of ravine land. His wife, a Sadhun of the Sadhun tribe who originally settled the ravine, and four remaining offspring constitute the household of Lem. Lem himself is very alcoholic and his sons are like their father but the daughter is a bright capable girl. Lem is the most desirable member of the family. Emmy, the other Jincade remaining in the hollow, has always been regarded by the other members of her family as "rather simple" but it does not appear that she is feeble-minded. Emmy's husband is "the Squire." Two of Emmy's daughters have married and done well; one remained in the neighborhood of the hollow but moved out of the valley itself. Another daughter was driven out of the town to which she had moved after her marriage, for disorderly conduct, and has returned to her parents. The son's wife, another Sadhun woman, and daughter are prostitutes, and the son himself is a good for nothing fellow who cannot be trusted in any way.

It is regrettable that we have no means of knowing what sort of people the other members of the Jincade fraternity have become in their new environment.

Rob appears to have been a feeble-minded man. His large frame and blustering ways,—he had the strength of an ox,—were yoked with the judgment of an immature boy. He was twice married. The first wife was divorced and had dropped out of existence before the story began for us. No one has been found who could bear accurate testimony as to her mental status. There were two sons. One was an idiot and suffered from epilepsy. His limbs were paralyzed and he walked with his hands dragging the helpless body. He was an inmate of our institution. The other son is a degenerate wretch. Rob's second wife was a feeble-minded woman who had a feeble-minded son by a former husband when she married Rob. The second wife has a feeble-minded sister who is the mother of another child in our institution.

And there is Dut. He was a horse thief when he lived in the hollow. Rumor connects him with the murder of an old man of the hollow but no proof could be found sufficient to convict him. Yet his old neighbor, now that Dut has left the country, "knows he did it." Dut has a wife and several children and since he has completed his term in the penitentiary for the counterfeiting, he has left the state and become well-to-do. Dut, unlike his brother Rob, is a shrewd scoundrel, but for all that was not so fortunate in escaping the consequences of his misdeeds.

THE DOCTOR'S STORY

"The Hollow? Well I should think I did know those people. Bark eaters, we used to call them, and the timber rats!" The Doctor's professional air vanished as he dropped into his office chair and leaning back, grinned reminiscently.

"I was a kid just out of college then. Happened to go into practice in the village of N—— about five miles from the hollow, and used to go down there to sew up their cuts. Many a time I've been down there in the night. They used to have their rows and cut each other up. They'd meet me with a lantern and conduct me through the woods and when I was through escort me back to the roadway. But just let me tell you once I nearly got caught."

The Doctor had forgotten all about his long line of waiting patients and was again revelling in the boy's spirit of adventure.

"One night I was returning from a long drive to see a patient some miles beyond the ravine. It was very cold, the snow was drifted deep in the hollows but it was late and we had driven about forty miles that day and the road through the ravine made the journey back to the village several miles shorter than going around by the prairie. We decided to take it. My driver was cold and the horses tired out after their long day's trip. I slipped my revolver into one of the fur mittens that I wore.

"Everything was quiet in the hollow. The occasional shacks looked lifeless and only the trees and clumps of dead underbrush cast weird shadows across the snow in the moonlight. We had passed the Gold Diggings and Smoky Row when suddenly from a road joining the ravine we were hailed by a couple of men driving the inevitable jaded old horse and familiar tumble down box on runners which was the winter conveyance of the timber rat.

" 'That you Doc?' one of the men called. 'Woman awful sick up here at the forks, we were goin' in to get yuh.'

" 'It's Doc all right,' I assured them, 'but I'm not going up to the forks tonight for any sick woman. My horses are tired and I've driven forty miles today. Not on your life am I going to the forks tonight.'

"But the woman was 'suffering terrible' they insisted and maybe wouldn't live till morning. They would take me with their own horse and bring me clear into town so my horses needn't make the trip.

"Well—I went. Climbed into their old junk boat and started up the steep narrow gulch that leads to the forks. I didn't like the looks of things; the men were surly and kept muttering together in undertones. I took care to keep behind the fellows who were seated on a board laid crosswise on the box for a driver's seat. They had been drinking just enough to make them ugly.

"Afraid? Hum, not of those rats. I used to be something of an athlete in college and—well, I wasn't afraid."

And I could well believe he was not afraid. A man of about forty, he is now, cleancut and vigorous, with a closely knit frame, clear gray eyes and a firm mouth and chin. No, the Doctor was not a man to fear timber rats.

"They were not intending that I should go back to the village. They stopped at a narrow point in the trail but drove on again at my sharp command. Finally we reached the cabin. It was a God-forsaken spot where the gully forks, one branch ending in a sharp inaccessible wall, the other winding out toward the prairie. It was then about midnight. The cabin was a story and a half shack built partly into the hill and surrounded by gaunt trees.

"I entered. The shack was the scene of a brawling swearing crowd, about a dozen of them, I should say, drinking and gambling in the flare of two or three smoky lanterns hung from the grimy beams. The sick woman was in the loft above as her occasional moans directed. I scaled the ladder nailed against the side wall of the shack with one hand on my revolver and my back to the ladder. After tending the woman I descended in the same way. Then the fun began. They had no idea of taking me back. In fact, they assured me, they had only brought me out there to kill me. You see, I knew too much about them and besides they owed me a good many bad bills. Well, I backed into a corner and invited them to come on.

"Afraid of that crew? I should say not. They are abject cowards every one of them. There is a yellow streak in all of them. Some of the bunch I knew, Old Rob Jincade and one of the Sadhuns. Young Jim Silver was among them and Muskrat Charlie. They're all sneaks and don't dare attack a man except from the rear.

"Remember Jobey? He was one of the Chad tribe who robbed and almost killed a farmer as he was driving home after selling his grain. But Little Tommy—he was the son of old Moose Silver, the half-breed—was the only real desperado of the hollow. The rest are a lot of defectives and degenerates. Those people didn't know the meaning of morality. They lived with each other's wives and stole anything they could lay their hands on. Did you ever hear about that fellow, one of the Chads, I think, who traded his wife for a shot gun? He said, 'The other fellow would a got her anyhow,' and he was a shot gun ahead. I don't think you could find another section in the country to compare with that.

"Did I get home that night? You bet, I did. They hitched up their old raw bones and landed me safe in town before daylight!"

THE COST

It would be well nigh impossible to estimate how much these dwellers in the Vale of Siddem have cost the commonwealth in toll of human misery. Moral obliquity, pauperism and vice, and the deadening social burden of deficiency and dementia have been their chief contribution to the life of the times and to posterity.

Of the sixteen hundred individuals who have been charted as inhabitants of the hollow or their descendants in other parts of the state, sixteen per cent. have been mental variants, epileptic, insane, or feeble-minded. Moreover, these sixteen hundred individuals include only people of American ancestry. This is particularly striking as it indicates their family solidarity in a part of the state where the population is to a certain extent made up of foreign elements.

The ethical standards of this group are such that one can scarcely measure their behavior in terms of ordinary social values. One hundred and twenty-five have been classified as sexually immoral. This includes only prostitutes and those whose illicit relationships were flagrant. The fifteen classified as criminals have, for the most part, been guilty of some felony. Misdemeanors, for which the offender received only a jail sentence or which more often passed unnoticed, have not been included. The arrests of ravine inhabitants recorded in the court house of the county between 1895 and 1917 are for the following offenses:

Larceny, 35%	Arson, 6%
Rape, 33%	Forgery, 3%
Assault and battery, 20%	Drunkenness, 3%

It is a significant commentary on our social order that it is the offenses against property which are prosecuted though the actual occurrence of such crimes is less frequent than offenses against persons. Arson is a crime very infrequently committed, as is also forgery, the latter probably because of the inferior mental status of the group in general, but that only three per cent. of the arrests are for drunkenness indicates that the condition is so common as to escape drastic action. One hundred and thirty-four of the inhabitants are classified as habitual alcoholics and by "alcoholic" we mean not the occasional drinker but an individual who drinks habitually and to excess. This region has been represented in the institution by ten inmates; the number is now only six; three having been withdrawn from the institution and the fourth died. That means that in this one section out of 199 individuals known to be mentally defective only about five per cent. have been cared for in the institution for the feeble-minded or by any sort of supervision or guardianship!

That our present methods of treating this problem of mental deficiency are costly and ineffective is scarcely open to argument in view of the facts which our studies lay bare. The "liberty to act as they please without check or hindrance, in so far as they do not violate the criminal laws," is liberty only in name. The Mental Deficiency Act of 1913 adds, "The liberty of the subject does not consist in allowing persons who are not responsible nor accountable for their actions to commit crime, to drift into intemperance and immorality, to be cruelly treated or neglected or to injure the community by reason of their uncontrolled reproduction of their type, but rather by an organization that is humane and adaptable to mould their lives and conduct so as to secure for them the maximum of comfort and happiness conformable with social order"—[sic]

The classification of the dwellers in the Vale of Siddem is as follows:

Normal	156	Paralyzed	12
Feeble-minded	199	Migrainous	24
Epileptic	15	Nervous	96
Insane	34	Miscarriages	17
Sexually immoral	125	Died in infancy	87
Criminalistic	15	Died young	27
Alcoholic	134	Unclassified	892
Tuberculous	47		——
		Total	1619

The classifications frequently overlap; the same individual may be classified at the same time under several headings, as for instance feeble-minded, sexually immoral and alcoholic. Nor does it necessarily mean that we have no information about the individual if he is listed as unclassified. In many cases the symbol has been left open when the information about the individual has left us in doubt as to whether he should be classified as normal or feeble-minded. Often we are not satisfied to mark the individual feeble-minded and yet his reactions are such that he cannot be considered normal. In all such cases where there is any doubt about the classification the case has been considered doubtful and counted among the unclassified.

And what are we going to do about it? Certainly the first step must be to find out where the mental defectives are and who they are and whence they came. Until we know the extent and proportions of our problems, we are but working in the dark, trying to fill a bottomless pit shovel-full by shovel-full.

The dwellers in the Vale of Siddem have surely been "allowed to multiply themselves to an alarming extent and in their degradation and misery to be associated with the pauper, inebriate, criminal and immoral classes." They are themselves not only the chief source of feeble-mindedness in the next generation, but as Dr. Kuhlmann says "give rise to a dull low level of intelligence in normals to whom the defect is transmitted in minor degree." When we realize that such communities as the Vale of Siddem exist not only in the older eastern states but in Minnesota and the younger states; when we realize that our special schools and classes care for the feeble-minded only until they reach the most dangerous age for society and then turn them out without supervision; when we recognize the fact that many of the people whom our charity organizations carry from year to year are feeble-minded; when we realize that the institutions for the feeble-minded care for about 4.5 per cent. of the total number of feeble-minded*—then we begin to realize something of the magnitude of our problem.

* F. Kuhlmann. "Part Played by the State Institutions in the Care of the Feeble-Minded." *Jour. Psycho-Asthenics*, Vol. XXI, Nos. 1, 2, 1916.

REFERENCES

"Alumni Roster. Eugenics Course. Summer School, Cold Spring Harbor, Long Island." 1919. *Eugenical News* 4 (3):21–28.

Bannister, Robert C. 1979. *Social Darwinism: Science and Myth in Anglo-American Social Thought*. Philadelphia: Temple University Press.

Binet, Alfred, and Thomas Simon. 1916a. *The Binet-Simon Measuring Scale for Intelligence: What It Is; What It Does; How It Does It*. Trans. and with a brief biography of its authors by Elizabeth S. Kite. Philadelphia: Committee on Provision for the Feebleminded, Bulletin no. 1.

———. 1916b. *The Development of Intelligence in Children (The Binet-Simon Scale)*. Trans. by Elizabeth S. Kite. Baltimore: Williams & Wilkins.

———. 1916c. *The Intelligence of the Feeble-minded*. Trans. by Elizabeth S. Kite. Baltimore: Williams & Wilkins.

Blackmar, Frank W. 1897. "The Smoky Pilgrims." *American Journal of Sociology* 2 (January):485–500.

Bronner, Augusta F. 1914. "A Research on the Proportion of Mental Defectives among Delinquents." *Journal of Criminal Law and Criminology* 5 (September):561–68.

———. 1916. Review of *The Feebly-Inhibited: Nomadism or the Wandering Impulse* by Charles B. Davenport. *Journal of Criminal Law & Criminology* 7 (2):311–13.

Carlson, Elof Axel. 1980. "R. L. Dugdale and the Jukes Family: A Historical Injustice Corrected." *Bioscience* 30 (August):535–39.

Connelly, Mark Thomas. 1980. *The Response to Prostitution in the Progressive Era*. Chapel Hill: University of North Carolina Press.

Danielson, Florence H., and Charles B. Davenport. 1912. *The Hill Folk: Report on a Rural Community of Hereditary Defectives*. Eugenics Record Office— Memoir no. 1. Cold Spring Harbor, N.Y. (August).

Davenport, Charles B. 1911. *Heredity in Relation to Eugenics*. New York: Holt.

Davenport, Charles B., H. H. Laughlin, David F. Weeks, E. R. Johnstone, and Henry H. Goddard. 1911. *The Study of Human Heredity: Methods of Collecting, Charting and Analyzing Data*. Eugenics Record Office, Bulletin no. 2; Cold Spring Harbor, N.Y. (May).

Davenport, Gertrude Crotty. 1896. *The Primitive Streak and Notochordal Canal in Chelonia*. Boston: Ginn.

———. 1907. "Hereditary Crime." *American Journal of Sociology* 13 (3) (November):402–9.

de Beauvoir, Simone. 1974 [1952]. *The Second Sex*. New York: Vintage.

Doll, Edgar A. 1928. *The Problem of the Feeble-minded in New Jersey*. Trenton: Prepared for State Department of Institutions and Agencies by Research Department of the Training School at Vineland, N. J.

Dugdale, Richard L. 1875. "A Report of Special Visits to County Jails for 1874." In Prison Association of New York, *Thirteenth Annual Report*, New York Sen. Doc. no. 78:129–92.

———. 1877a. *"The Jukes": A Study in Crime, Pauperism, Disease and Heredity; also Further Studies of Criminals*, with an introduction by Elisha Harris, M.D. New York: Putnam's.

———. 1877b. "Hereditary Pauperism as Illustrated in the 'Juke' Family." Conference of Boards of Public Charities, *Proceedings 1877:* 81–95.

Estabrook, Arthur H. 1916. *The Jukes in 1915.* Washington: Carnegie Institution of Washington.

Estabrook, Arthur H., and Charles B. Davenport. 1912. *The Nam Family: A Study in Cacogenics.* Eugenics Record Office—Memoir no. 2. Cold Spring Harbor, N.Y. (August).

Estabrook, Arthur H., and Ivan E. McDougle. 1926. *Mongrel Virginians: The Win Tribe.* Baltimore: Williams & Wilkins.

Eugenics Record Office. 1913. *How to Make a Eugenical Family Study.* Eugenics Record Office, Bulletin no. 13. Cold Spring Harbor, N.Y.

Eysenck, Hans. 1973. *Crime and Personality.* St. Albans (Engl.): Paladin.

Farrall, Lyndsay A. 1979. "The History of Eugenics: A Bibliographical Review." *Annals of Science* 36:111–23.

"Field Trips and Clinics of the 1919 Training Class." 1919. *Eugenical News* 4 (9):73–74.

Finlayson, Anna Wendt. 1916. *The Dack Family: A Study in Hereditary Lack of Emotional Control.* Eugenics Record Office, Bulletin no. 15. Cold Spring Harbor, N.Y. (May).

Foucault, Michel. 1977. *Discipline and Punish: The Birth of the Prison.* New York: Pantheon.

Galton, Francis. 1914 [1869]. *Hereditary Genius.* London: Macmillan.

Goddard, Henry Herbert. 1923 [1912]. *The Kallikak Family: A Study in the Heredity of Feeble-mindedness.* New York: Macmillan.

Gould, Stephen Jay. 1981. *The Mismeasure of Man.* New York: Norton.

Gusfield, Joseph R. 1963. *Symbolic Crusade: Status Politics and the American Temperance Movement.* Urbana: University of Illinois Press.

Gutman, Herbert G. 1977. *Work, Culture and Society in Industrializing America.* New York: Vintage.

Hahn, Nicolas F. [Nicole Hahn Rafter]. 1978. *The Defective Delinquency Movement: A History of the Born Criminal in New York State, 1850–1966.* Ph.D. dissertation, State University of New York at Albany.

———. 1980 . "Too Dumb to Know Better: Cacogenic Family Studies and the Criminology of Women." *Criminology* 18 (1):3–25.

Haller, Mark H. 1963. *Eugenics: Hereditarian Attitudes in American Thought.* New Brunswick, N.Y.: Rutgers University Press.

Harding, Sandra. 1986. *The Science Question in Feminism.* Ithaca: Cornell.

Heron, David. 1914. "Mendelism and the Problem of Mental Defect: A Criticism of Recent American Work." *Questions of the Day and of the Fray* 7. London: Cambridge University Press.

Herrnstein, Richard J. 1973. *I.Q. in the Meritocracy.* Boston: Little, Brown—Atlantic Monthly.

Hirschi, Travis. 1983. "Crime and the Family." Chap. 4 in James Q. Wilson, ed., *Crime and Public Policy.* San Francisco: Institute for Contemporary Studies Press.

Hofstadter, Richard. 1955a. *The Age of Reform.* New York: Vintage.

———. 1955b. *Social Darwinism in American Thought,* rev. ed. Boston: Beacon.

Hofstadter, Richard, ed. 1963. *The Progressive Movement 1900–1915.* Englewood Cliffs, N.J.: Prentice-Hall.

Kamin, Leon J. 1974. *The Science and Politics of I.Q.* New York: Wiley.

Kaye, Howard L. 1986. *The Social Meaning of Modern Biology: From Social Darwinism to Sociobiology.* New Haven: Yale University Press.

Kevles, Daniel J. 1985. *In the Name of Eugenics: Genetics and the Uses of Human Heredity.* New York: Knopf.

Kite, Elizabeth S. 1912 a. "Method and Aim of Field Work at the Vineland Training School." *The Training School* 9 (6):81–87.

———. 1912b. "Two Brothers." *The Survey* 27 (22) (May 2):1861–64.

———. 1913. "The 'Pineys.' " *The Survey* 21 (1) (October 4):7–13, 38–40.

Kostir, Mary Storer. 1916. *The Family of Sam Sixty*. Ohio Board of Administration, Publication no. 8 (January).

Kuhn, Thomas S. 1970. *The Structure of Scientific Revolutions*, 2d. ed. Chicago: University of Chicago Press.

Lewontin, R. C., Steven Rose, and Leon J. Kamin. 1984. *Not In Our Genes: Biology, Ideology, and Human Nature*. New York: Pantheon.

Ludmerer, Kenneth M. 1972. *Genetics and American Society*. Baltimore: Johns Hopkins University Press.

McCulloch, Oscar C. 1888. "The Tribe of Ishmael: A Study in Social Degradation." Conference of Charities and Correction, *Proceedings 1888:* 154–59.

McCulloch, Ruth. 1911. "Plymouth Church—II." *Indiana Magazine of History* 7 (3) (September):89–99.

MacKenzie, Donald A. 1981. *Statistics in Britain, 1865–1930: The Social Construction of Scientific Knowledge*. Edinburgh: Edinburgh University Press.

McPhee, John. 1967. *The Pine Barrens*. New York: Farrar, Straus & Giroux.

Marx, Karl, and Friederich Engels. 1970. *The German Ideology*, ed. C. J. Arthur. New York: International.

n.a. 1892. [Memoir of Oscar C. McCulloch] Pp. vi–xxi in *The Open Door: Sermons and Prayers by Oscar C. McCulloch*. Indianapolis: Press of William B. Durford.

n.a. 1954. "In Memoriam: Elizabeth S. Kite." *The Training School Bulletin* (January):201–2.

Neff, Joseph S. 1910. *The Degenerate Children of Feeble-Minded Women*. Philadelphia: Department of Public Health and Charities.

Pastore, Nicholas. 1949. *The Nature-Nurture Controversy*. New York: Columbia University, King's Crown Press.

Pearson, Karl. 1914. "Mendelism and the Problem of Mental Defect." *Questions of the Day and of the Fray 9*. London: Cambridge University Press.

Phalen, Dale. 1969. *Samuel Fels of Philadelphia*. Philadelphia: Samuel S. Fels Fund.

Pickens, Donald K. 1968. *Eugenics and the Progressives*. Nashville: Vanderbilt University Press.

Pivar, David J. 1973. *Purity Crusade: Sexual Morality and Social Control, 1868–1900*. Westport, Conn.: Greenwood.

Platt, Anthony M. 1977. *The Child Savers: The Invention of Delinquency*, 2d ed. Chicago: University of Chicago Press.

Rogers, Arthur Curtis, and Maud A. Merrill. 1919. *Dwellers in the Vale of Siddem*. Boston: Richard G. Badger, Gorham Press.

Rosen, Ruth. 1982. *The Lost Sisterhood: Prostitution in America, 1900–1918*. Baltimore: Johns Hopkins University Press.

Rosenberg, Charles E. 1974. "The Bitter Fruit: Heredity, Disease, and Social Thought in Nineteenth-Century America." *Perspectives in American History* 8:189–235.

———. 1976. "Charles Benedict Davenport and the Irony of American Eugenics." Chap. 4 in Charles E. Rosenberg, *No Other Gods: On Science and American Social Thought*. Baltimore: Johns Hopkins University Press.

Sarason, Seymour B., and John Doris. 1969. *Psychological Problems in Mental Deficiency*, 4th ed. New York: Harper & Row.

Schlossman, Steven L. 1977. *Love and the American Delinquent*. Chicago: University of Chicago Press.

Sessions, Mina A. 1918. *The Feeble-Minded in a Rural County of Ohio*. Bulletin Number Six [Publication no. 12], Bureau of Juvenile Research, Ohio Board of Administration (February).

Shepard, Edward M. 1884. "The Work of a Social Teacher. Being a Memorial of Richard L. Dugdale." *Economic Tracts*, no. 12. New York: Society for Political Education.

Smith, Dorothy E. 1974. "Women's Perspective as a Radical Critique of Sociology." *Sociological Inquiry* 4 (1):7–13.

——. 1978. "A Peculiar Eclipsing: Women's Exclusion from Man's Culture." *Women's Studies International Quarterly* 1:281–95.

——. 1983. "No One Commits Suicide: Textual Analysis of Ideological Practices." *Human Studies* 6:309–59.

——. 1984. "The Ideological Practice of Sociology." *Catalyst* 8:39–54.

Sproat, John G. 1968. *"The Best Men": Liberal Reformers in the Gilded Age*. New York: Oxford University Press.

Stehr, Nico, and Volker Meja, eds. 1984. *Society and Knowledge: Contemporary Perspectives in the Sociology of Knowledge*. New Brunswick, N.J.: Transaction Books.

Stevens, H.C. 1915. "Eugenics and Feeblemindedness." *Journal of Criminal Law and Criminology* 6 (July):190–97.

Tredgold, A. F. 1916. *Mental Deficiency (Amentia)*, 2d ed. New York: William Wood & Co.

Tyor, Peter L., and Leland V. Bell. 1984. *Caring for the Retarded in America: A History*. Westport, Conn.: Greenwood.

Wallin, J. E. Wallace. 1916a. "Who is Feeble-Minded?" *Journal of Criminal Law and Criminology* 6 (January): 706–16.

——. 1916b. " 'Who is Feeble-Minded?' A Reply to Mr. Kohs." *Journal of Criminal Law and Criminology* 6 (May):57–78.

——. 1916c. "Rebuttal," *Journal of Criminal Law and Criminology* 7 (July):222–26.

Weibe, Robert H. 1967. *The Search for Order 1877–1920*. New York: Hill and Wang.

Wharton, Edith. 1970 [1920]. *The Age of Innocence*. New York: Scribners.

Wilson, E. O. 1975. *Sociobiology: The New Synthesis*. Cambridge, Mass.: Harvard University Press.

Wilson, James Q., and Richard J. Herrnstein. 1985. *Crime and Human Nature*. New York: Simon and Schuster.

Winship, A. E. 1900. *Jukes-Edwards: A Study in Education and Heredity*. Harrisburg, Pa.: R. L. Myers & Co.